HOW TO DRAW
PHOTOREALISTIC ANIMALS
with Colored Pencil

Learn to Draw **16** Lifelike Animals Like a Pro

irodoreal

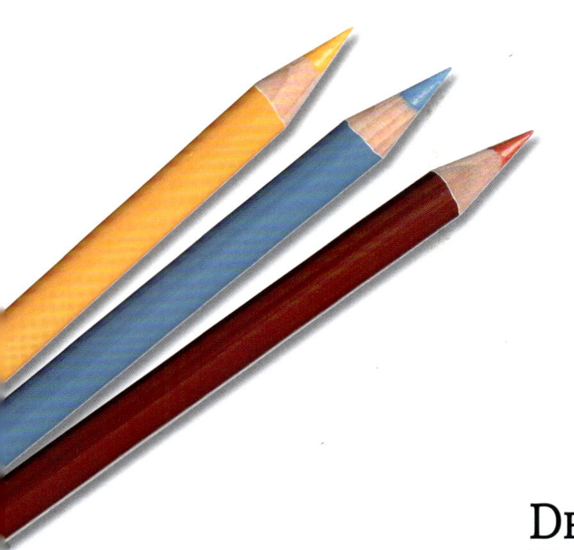

DESIGN ORIGINALS
an Imprint of Fox Chapel Publishing
www.d-originals.com

INTRODUCTION

Thank you very much for picking up this book. Irodoreal is a six-person colored-pencil drawing group formed by colored pencil artists who work mainly on social media. Since our formation, we have been spreading colored-pencil drawing and improving each other's skills through friendly rivalry.

Colored pencils are one of the most familiar art materials, and their overwhelming convenience has an irreplaceable appeal. They require no time for setup or cleanup, and coloring with them is easy.

Colored pencils are also an excellent art medium that can create a wide variety of expressions, depending on how they are used.

In our previous book, *Photorealistic Colored Pencil Drawing Workbook*, we explained how to draw simple and basic subjects such as food, landscapes, and small objects. In this book, however, we focus on what is arguably the most popular subject of all: animals. It covers a wide range of tips for drawing animals, including how to capture their distinctive features, such as clear, expressive eyes and fluffy fur.

This book features 16 colored pencil artworks of various animals, such as adorable pets, tiny insects, and sea creatures, presented in a format you can enjoy as coloring pages, just like in the previous book. You can color directly on the included line drawings or trace them onto your preferred paper for repeated practice.

Once you've mastered how to draw various animals, we hope you'll try creating your own original works, perhaps by drawing your beloved pet or favorite animal at home!

All of us at Irodoreal would be absolutely delighted if this book helps you enjoy your colored-pencil drawing even more.

irodoreal
(Representative: Bonbon)

CONTENTS

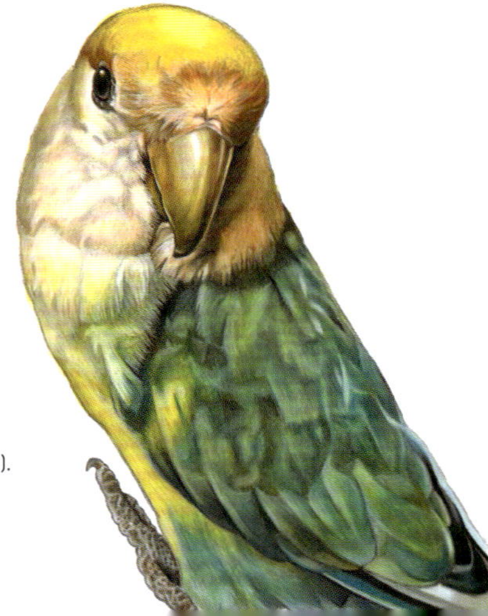

Peach-Faced Lovebird (p.30).

- The stars (⭐) in this book indicate the level of difficulty. The more stars there are, the more difficult the coloring is.
- You can cut out the outline drawings in the appendix at the end of this book and use them to draw the animal while looking at the instructions for it.
- You can reuse the outline drawings as many times as you like by transferring them onto your preferred drawing paper using transfer paper.
- Take care when using knives, such as design knives.

HOW TO USE TRANSFER PAPER

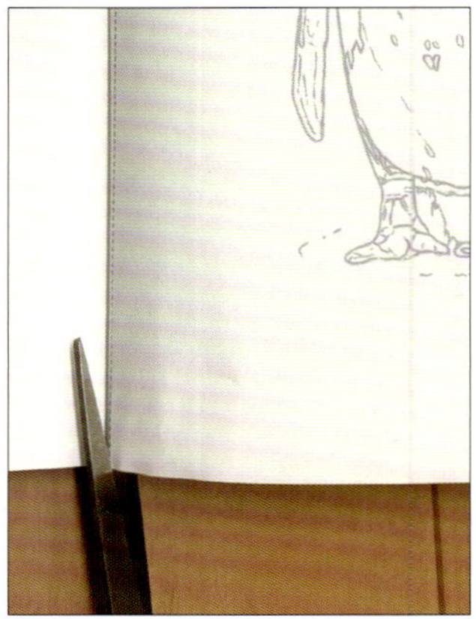

1 Cut out the outline drawing from the appendix along the dotted lines.

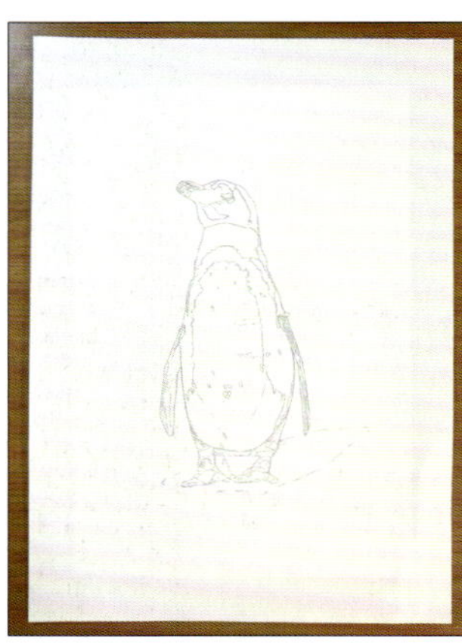

2 Place a thin sheet of paper over the outline drawing and trace it. If you have a printer, you can simply make a copy of the outline drawing instead.

3 Shade the back of the traced line drawing with a pencil.

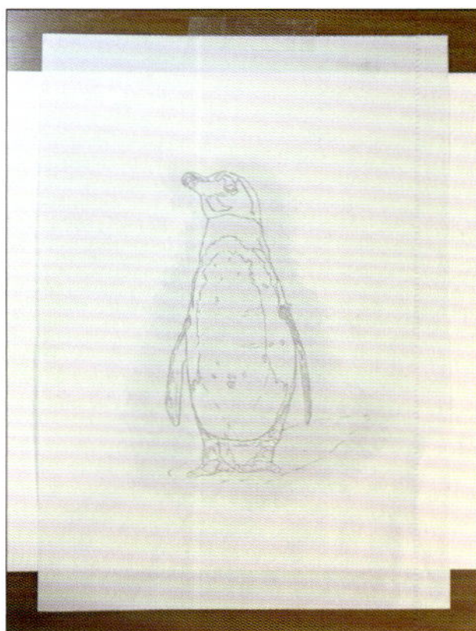

4 Place the traced line drawing onto Kent paper (or similar drawing paper). To prevent shifting, secure it with removable tape for ease.

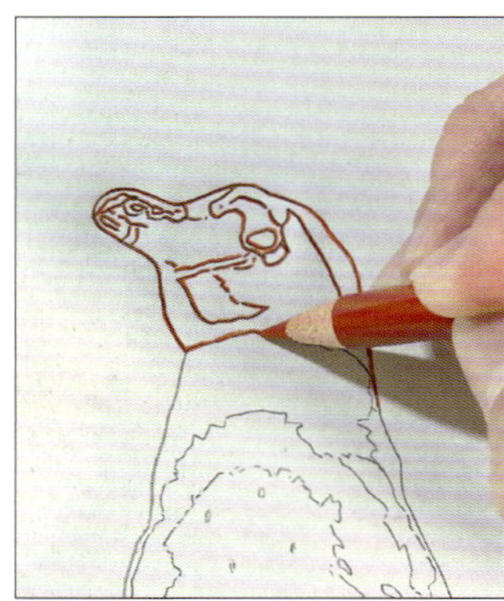

5 Trace over the lines of the copied drawing with a pencil to transfer it onto Kent paper (or similar drawing paper). Using a colored pencil makes it easier to see which lines you've already traced, preventing missed areas.

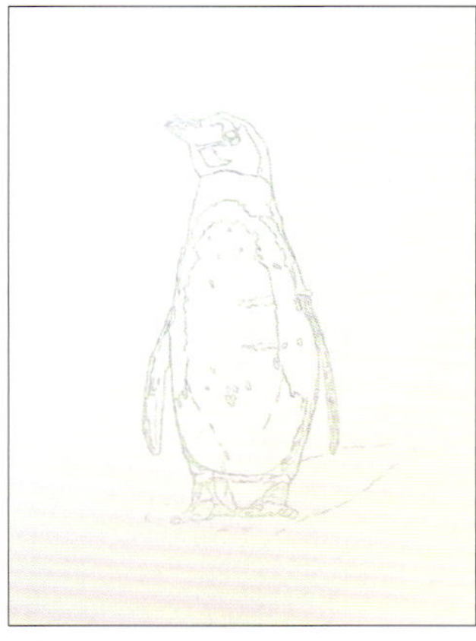

6 The transfer of the line drawing is complete. Enjoy coloring it!

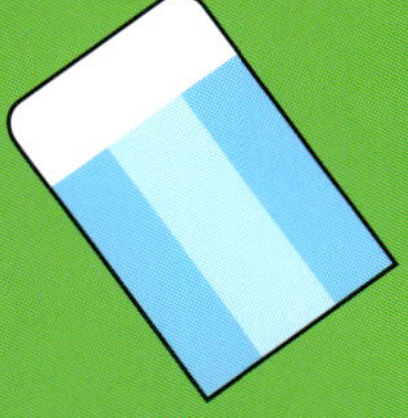
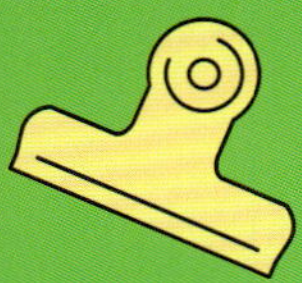

Basic Knowledge of Colored-Pencil Drawing and Tips for Drawing Animals

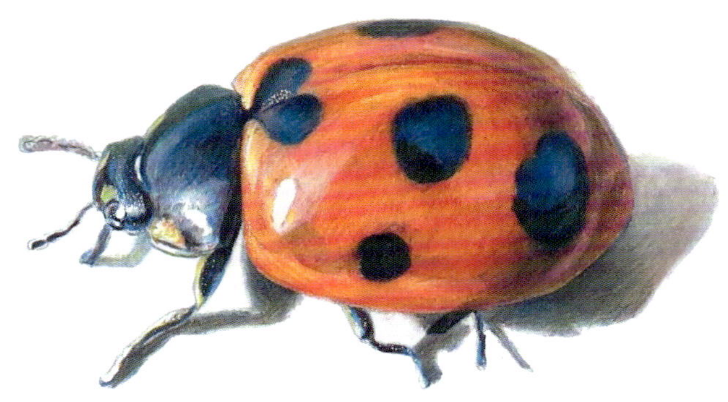

NECESSARY TOOLS AND USEFUL ITEMS

Tools & Items

Colored Pencils

Colored pencils are broadly divided into two types: oil based and water based. The feel when drawing, the hardness of the core, the range of colors, and the way they render on paper can vary depending on the manufacturer. Please use the colored pencils featured in the works in this book as a reference, and choose the ones that best suit you, or switch between types depending on what you want to draw.

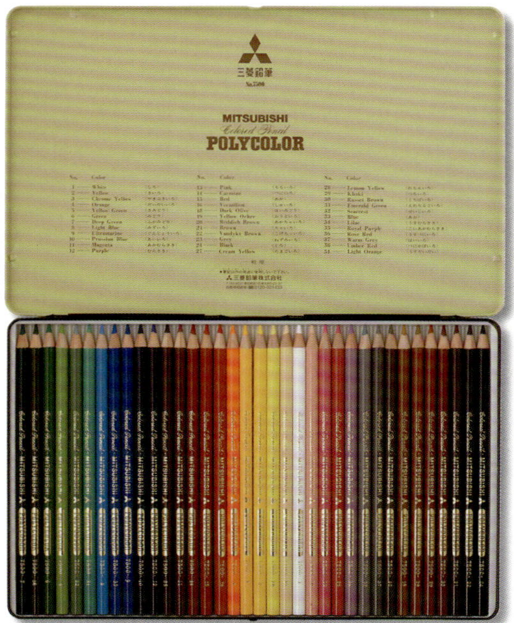

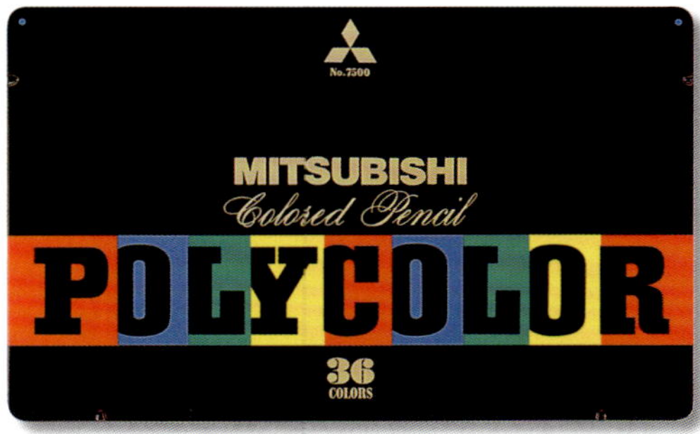

Polycolor 36 Color Set (Mitsubishi Pencil)

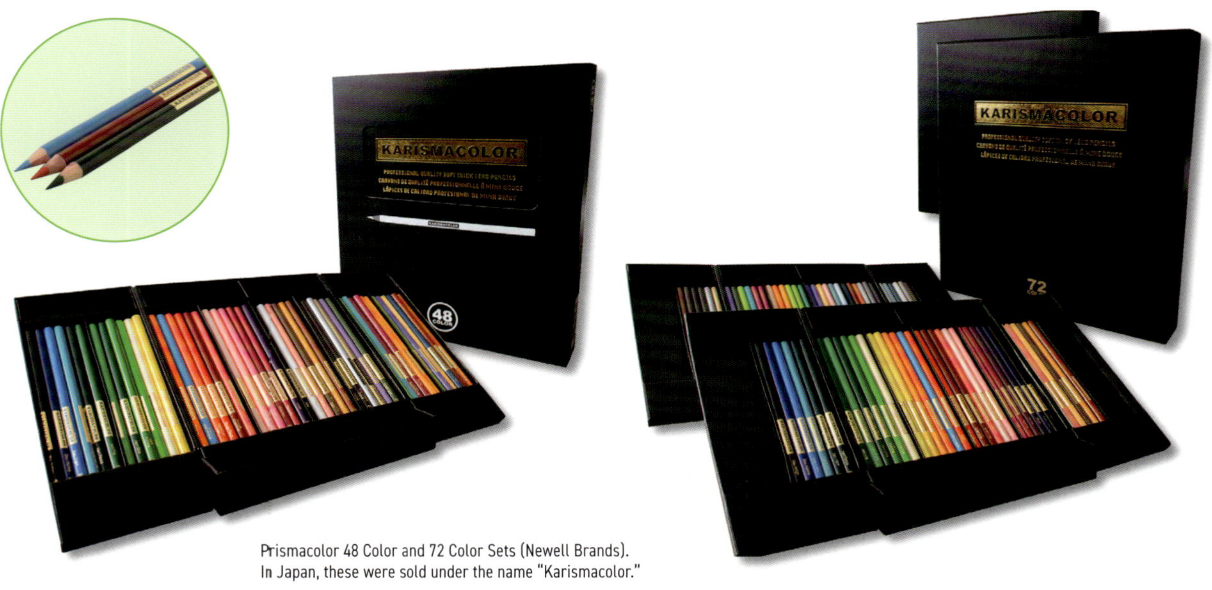

Prismacolor 48 Color and 72 Color Sets (Newell Brands).
In Japan, these were sold under the name "Karismacolor."

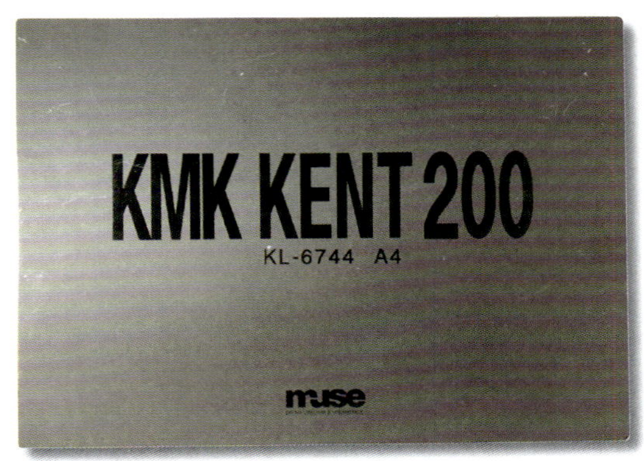

Paper

Just like colored pencils, there are many types of paper available. At first, it's a good idea to try out different kinds to see which you like. We used Kent paper to make many of the pieces in this book. It is easy to draw on and offers excellent color vibrancy, so we recommend using it or something similar.

Pencils and Mechanical Pencils

These are mainly used for sketching the outline drawing. You can use either a regular pencil or a mechanical pencil, whichever you find easier. The thickness of the lead is up to you, but thinner leads are better suited for detailed work. If you use softer, darker leads such as B or 2B, be careful as they can easily smudge and stain the paper.

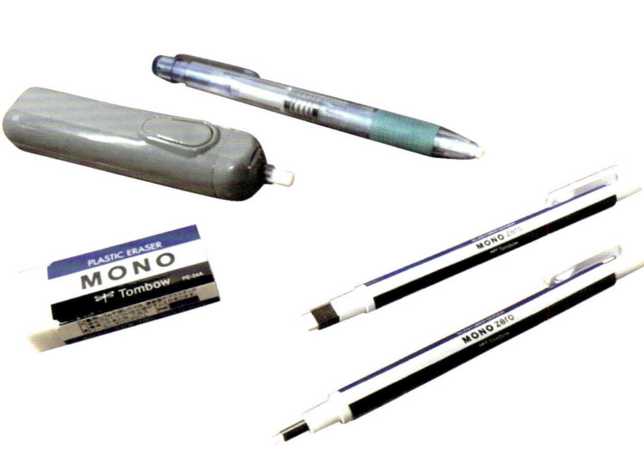

Erasers

In addition to standard plastic erasers, you can also use fine-tipped pen-style erasers or electric erasers. Unlike graphite pencils, colored pencils are difficult to erase completely, but an eraser is still an essential tool. Many types can even be found at bargain stores.

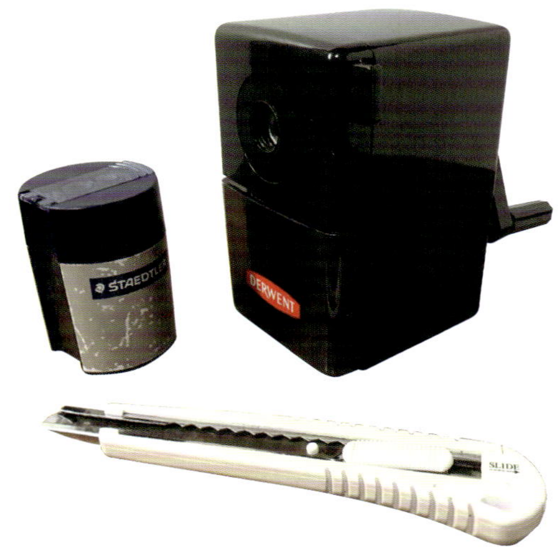

Pencil Sharpeners and Craft Knives

Pencil sharpeners come in a wide range of types, from desktop models to portable ones. Depending on the sharpener, the pencil tip (wood and core) can be sharpened to either a fine or a blunt point. Since the hardness of colored-pencil cores varies by manufacturer, choose a sharpener that suits the pencils you are using. You can also use a craft knife to carefully sharpen and shape the tip.

One very important tool for realistic colored-pencil drawing is the stylus. It is used like a pencil to create indentations on the paper. A dotting tool or tracer can also be used as a substitute. Since these tools come with various tip sizes, it's helpful to have several types on hand, depending on how wide you want the indentation to be. An empty ballpoint pen can also work, but be careful, as there's always a risk that the ink might suddenly start flowing again.

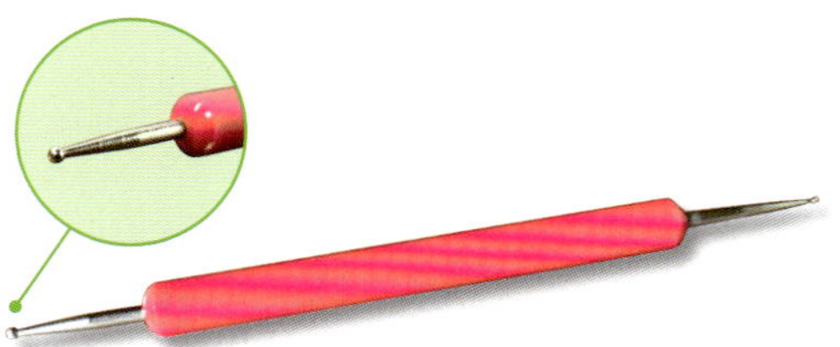

Dotting Tool

A dotting tool, commonly used in nail art, can be used in the same way as a stylus because of its rounded tip. These can even be found at discount stores.

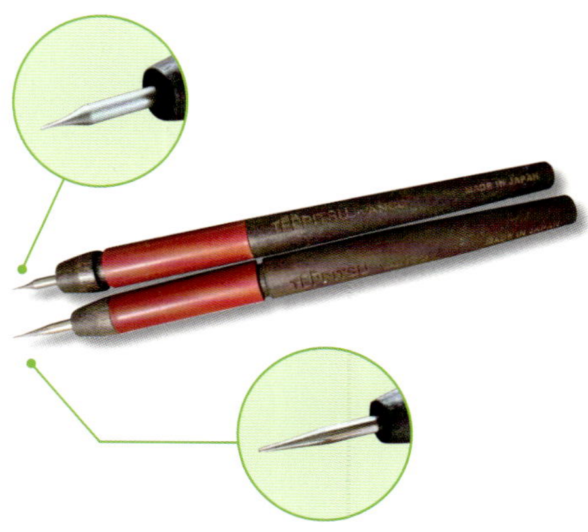

Styluses

A stylus is used like a pen to create small dots or lines as indentations on the paper. As colored pencils don't leave any color on indented areas, this technique is great for adding fine highlights or depicting animal fur textures.

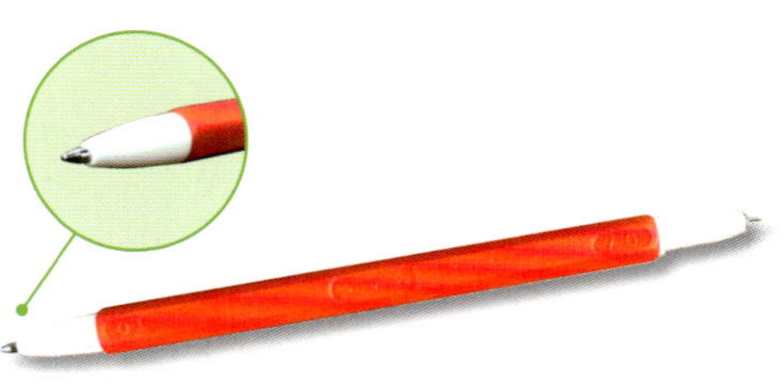

Tracer

A tracer is a tool commonly used in sewing and crafts for transferring patterns with transfer paper. Because its tip is rounded, it can be used in the same way as a stylus.

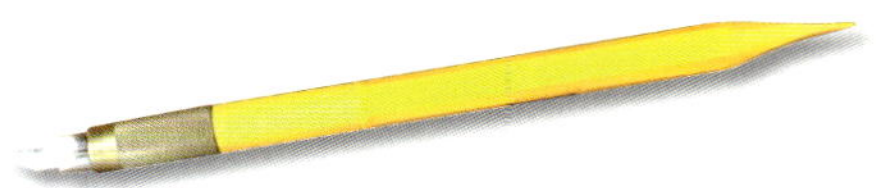

Design Knife

A design knife is a pen-style knife that is better suited for detailed work than a craft knife. It is used for scraping a colored surface to add highlights or create fur textures.

* Handle the blade with care.

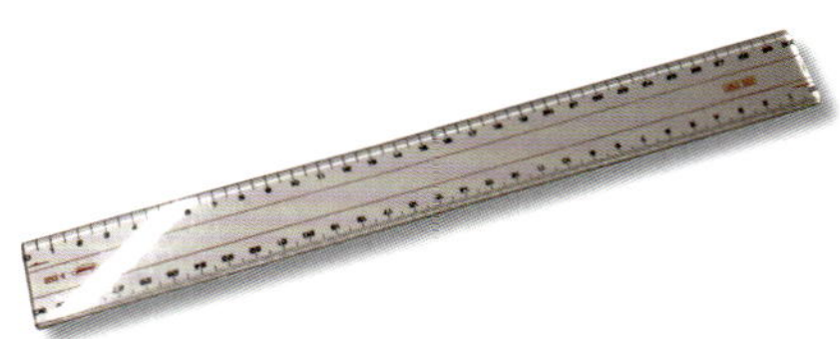

Ruler

Used for drawing grid lines when creating a sketch, or for drawing straight lines. Rulers come in various materials, such as plastic or metal. Just choose whichever feels most comfortable for you.

Hand Rest (to Prevent Smudging and Sweat Marks)

When drawing with colored pencils, your hand can sometimes leave sweat marks on the paper. A hand rest helps prevent this by placing it between your drawing hand and the paper. It also helps protect the paper from smudges and pencil dust. You can use a standard plastic sheet, a clear file folder, or even a tissue as a hand rest.

Basic Grips

Basic

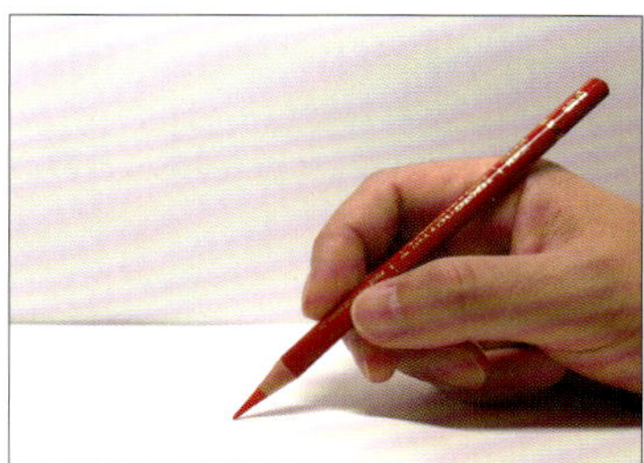

The common grip. As long as you can control the pressure and move the pencil easily, you can use any grip that suits you.

Horizontal

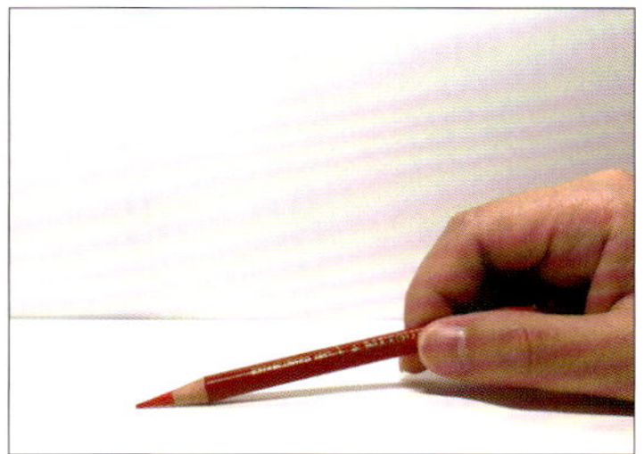

Hold the colored pencil high up the shaft, and lower your hand so that the pencil lies almost horizontal to the paper. Hold a colored pencil like this when you want to apply a light coat of color or a smooth coat on a large surface.

Upright

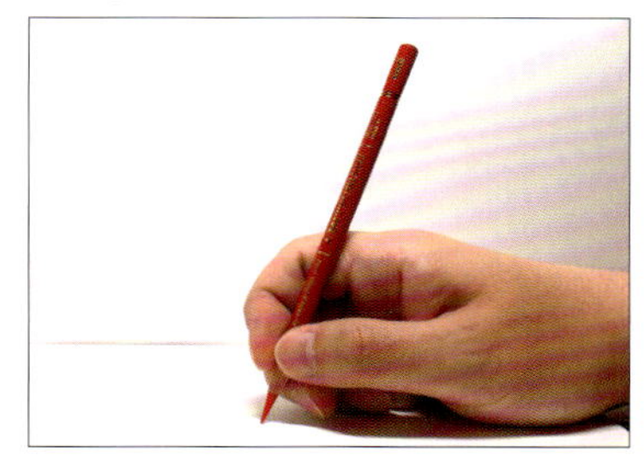

Hold the pen low down the shaft near the lead and tilt the pencil into an almost vertical position. This allows you to apply pressure, so it's suitable for strong and thick coloring.

Basic Coloring Methods

1. Apply vertically

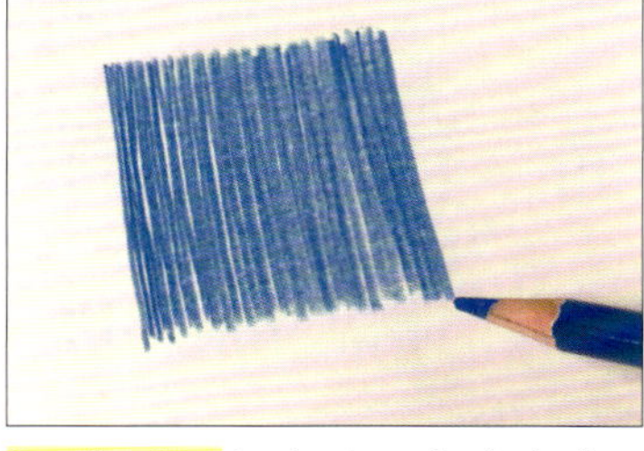

2. Apply horizontally

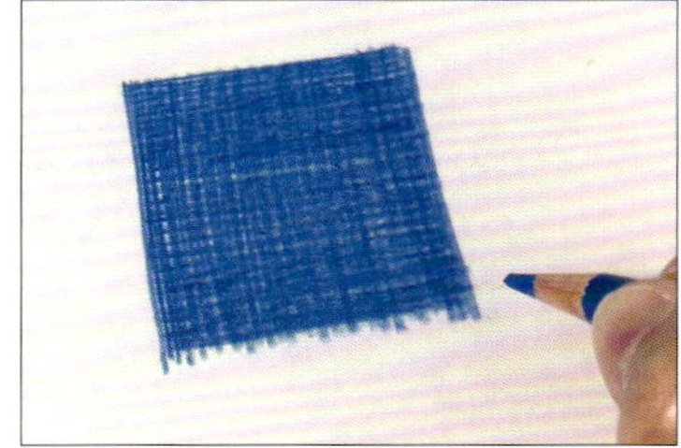

3. Apply diagonally

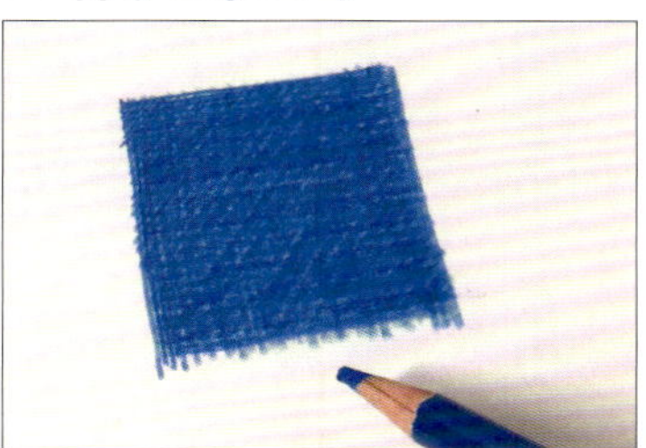

Crosshatching is a basic method of colored-pencil drawing. By applying the color vertically, horizontally, and diagonally (in this order) to the desired area, you can eliminate unevenness. The more you do this, the more even the color will be.

Color Shading

Light

Medium

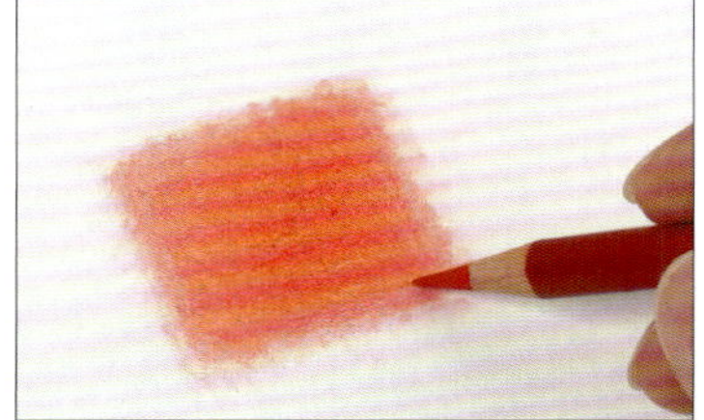

Dark

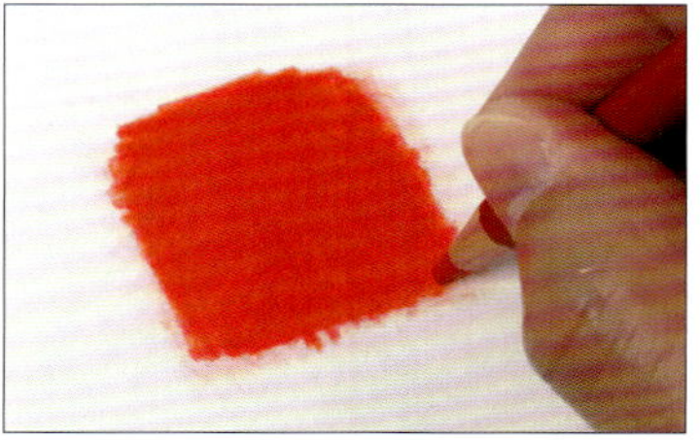

Color shading is created by applying multiple layers of the basic coloring method, which is crosshatching. If you want to apply colors lightly, use crosshatching with a light pressure for a smooth finish. If you want to apply colors more thickly, use crosshatching repeatedly and vigorously with firm pressure.

Tip 1 | How to Achieve Three-Dimensionality

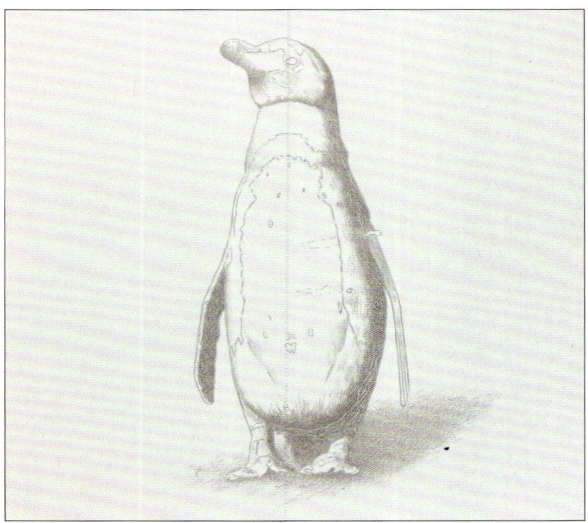

We will use the grisaille technique. Grisaille refers to a coloring method where shading is first created in monochrome, and then color is layered over it. This approach makes it easier to achieve a sense of three-dimensionality while preserving the depth of the shading.

Tip 2 | How to Create a Glossy Effect

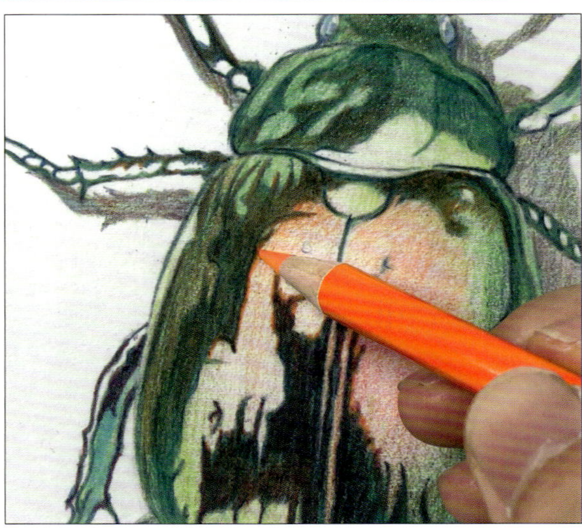

We create a glossy effect by using techniques such as burnishing to bring out surface shine, adding highlights with the white of the paper, a stylus, or white pencil, and enhancing edges with highly saturated colors or touches of reflected light.

Tip 3 | How to Draw Eyes

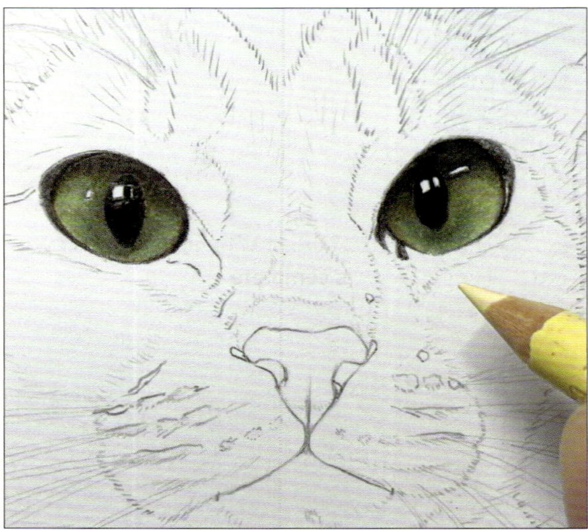

Eyes with transparency and three-dimensionality are one of the defining features of animals. The key points are shading, layering colors with varying intensity, and placing highlights in the areas where light is most concentrated.

Tip 4 | How to Draw Fur

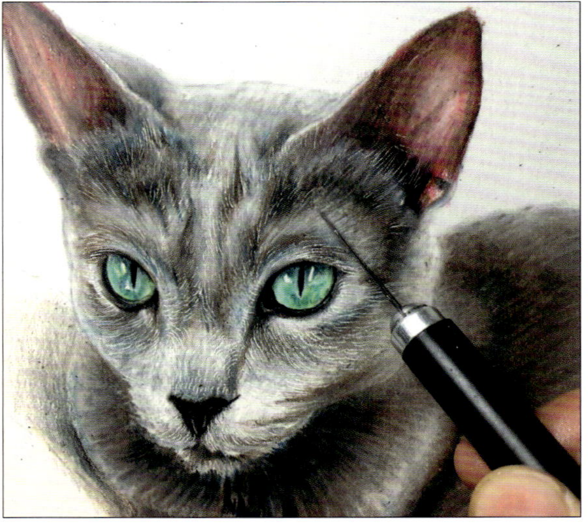

There are many stylus-based techniques for this, but this book also introduces methods such as layering light colors over dark ones and scraping the surface with a design knife on dark shades of the same color family.

Adding Three-Dimensionality for a More Realistic Look

The three attributes of color (hue, value, and saturation)

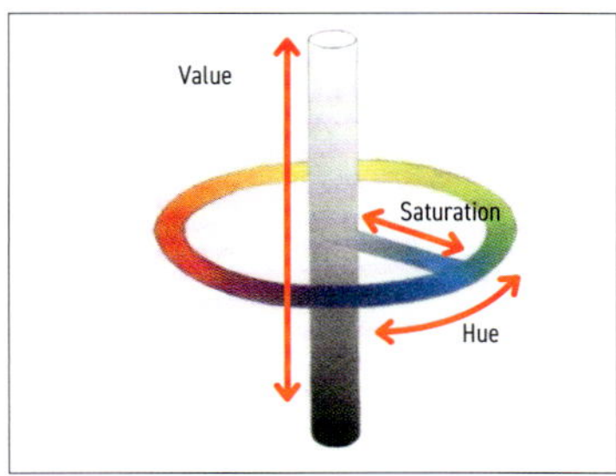

The relationship between light and shadow

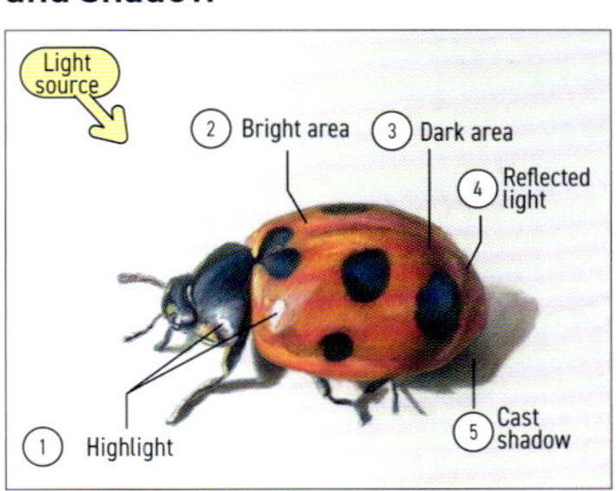

Black-and-white photograph

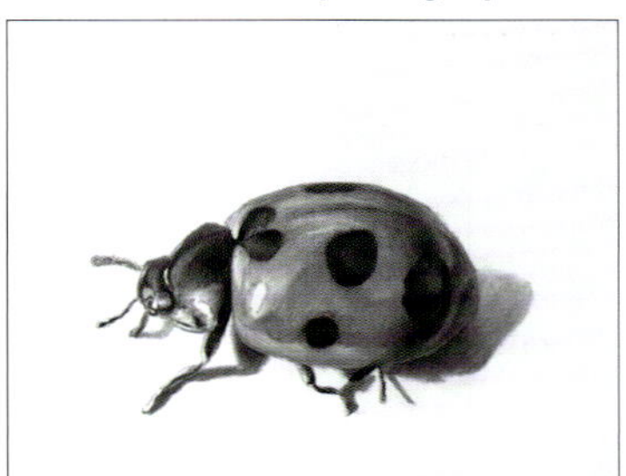

Colors have three attributes: hue, value, and saturation. Of these, value is particularly important when creating a sense of three-dimensionality. When light hits an object from a certain direction, five distinct areas are created: (1) The brightest area where the light hits most directly, (2) The general lit area, (3) The shadowed area where light is less likely to reach, (4) The bright area illuminated by reflected light from surrounding surfaces, and (5) The cast shadow created where the object blocks the light. By paying close attention to value, you can achieve realistic, three-dimensional results. In this book, we refer to the dark area (3) as "shade" and the cast shadow (5) as "shadow." If it's hard to distinguish these, try converting the image to black and white.

Shading the dark areas

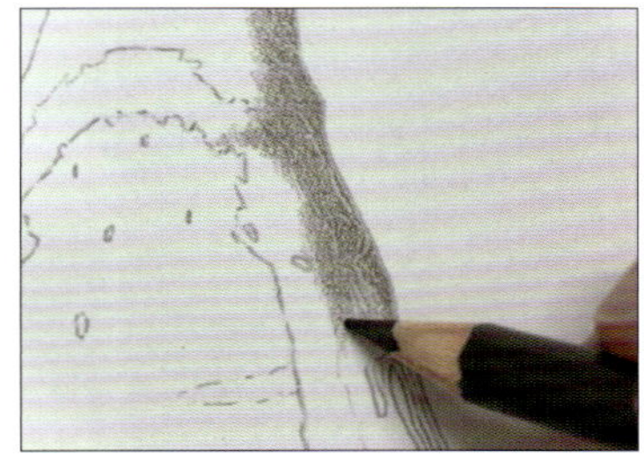

Filling in the cast shadow as well

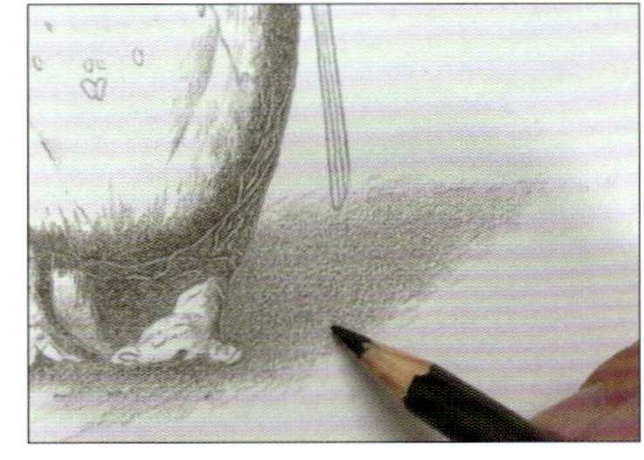

A rough separation of light and dark areas

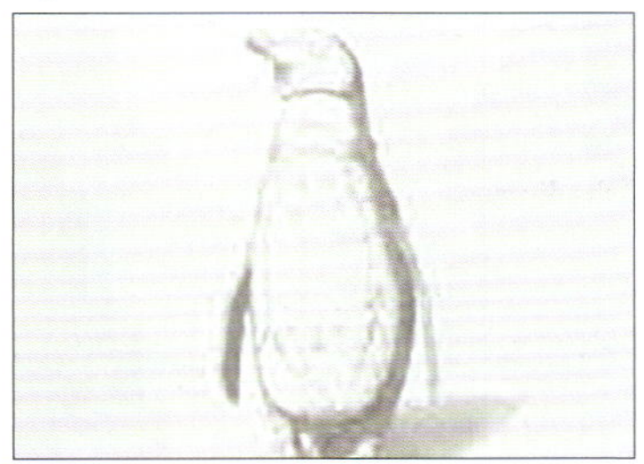

When you begin applying color, it's easy to forget about value. Here, we'll introduce the grisaille technique, which involves first shading in black and white and then layering color over it. The advantage of the grisaille technique is that it allows you to add color without losing the underlying shading. However, be careful, as the colors can become muddy if not applied properly. Start by shading in the dark areas (including the cast shadows) so that the light and dark areas are clearly separated. Avoid applying a heavy layer of light grey, as this makes it harder to build up color on top. Instead, lightly layer a darker grey.

Drawing in the details

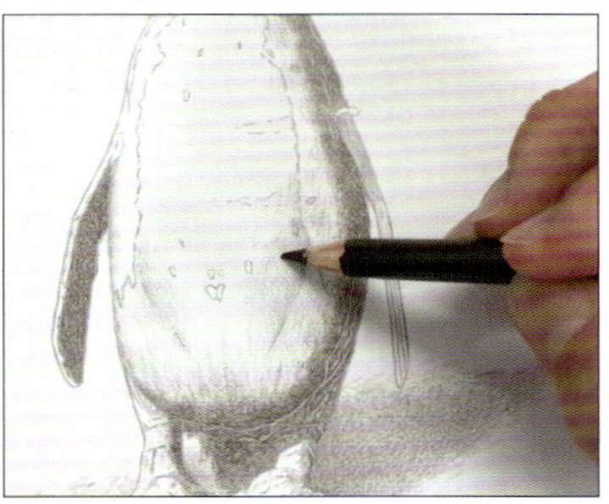

Adding gradation

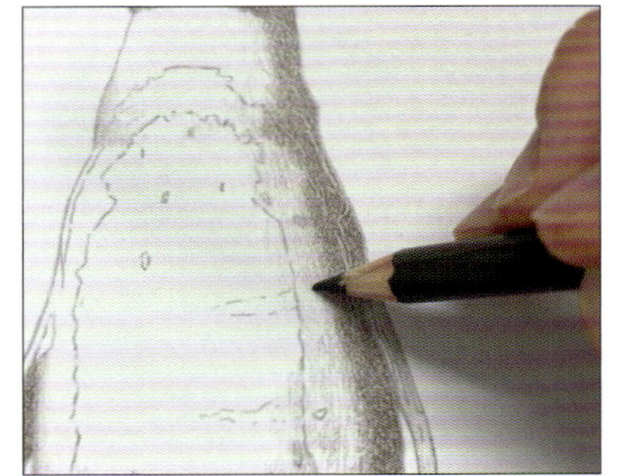

Addition of shade and shadow is complete

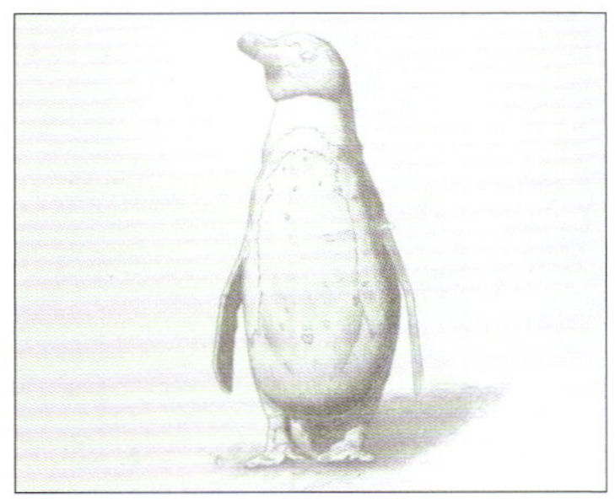

Once you've roughly separated the light and dark areas, add fine shade and shadow effects without disturbing that balance, and create smooth gradations from light to dark. After that, begin layering various colors over the top.

How to Create a Radiant Glossy Effect

Without burnishing

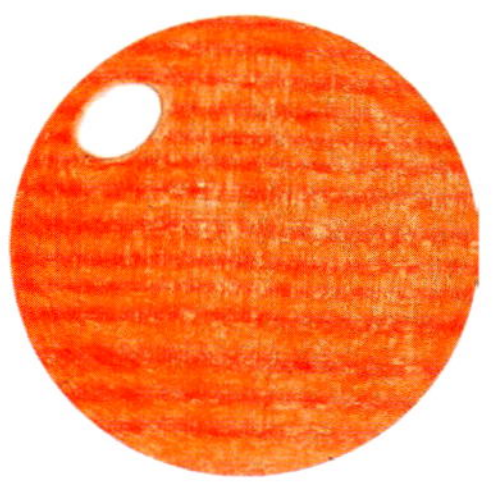
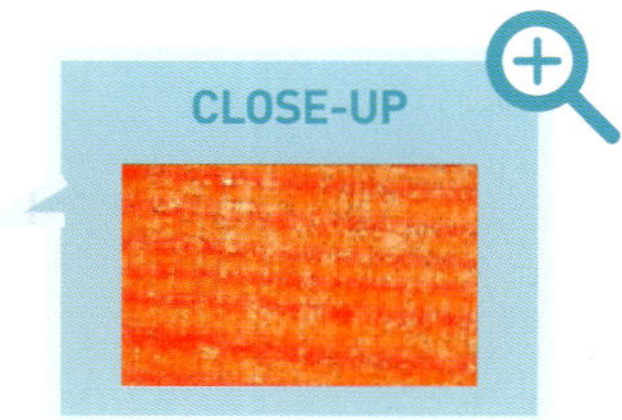

With burnishing

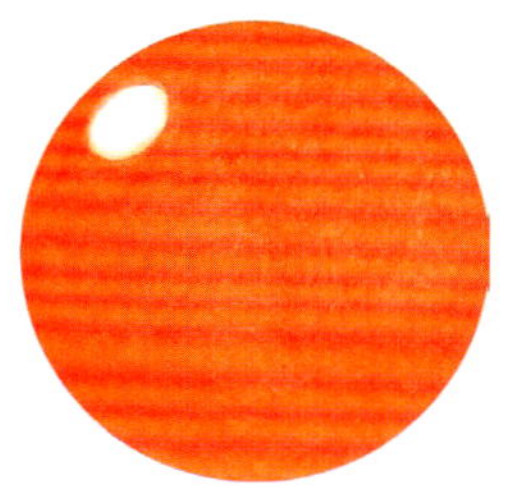
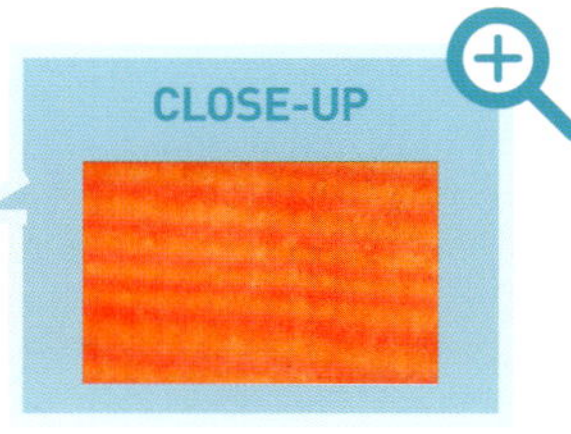

Burnishing is a technique for adding luster to a colored surface. For example, if you apply a thin coat of color to an area on the paper, the surface indentations in that area will appear when viewed up close. If you compare such an area to another area where the color has been thickly applied, you'll see a difference in the surface luster between the two areas. By applying layers of white or some other color to the coated area using colored pencils and blending them in, you can create a uniform luster and obtain a blur effect.

Indent the paper with a stylus to leave some parts uncolored

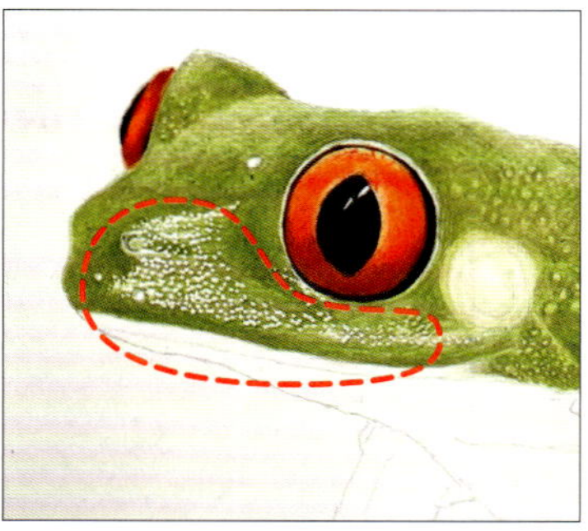

Don't color the white parts

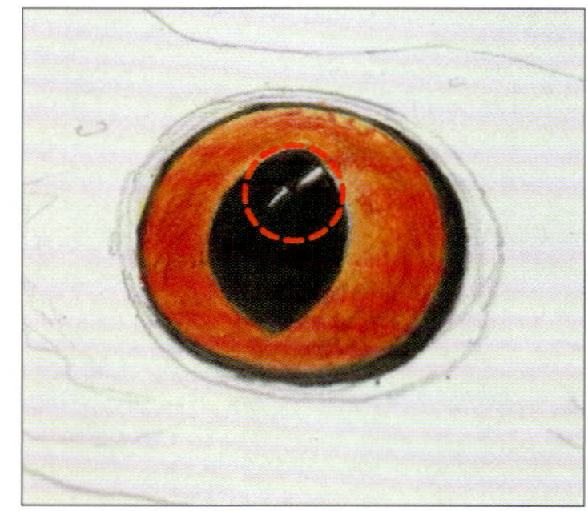

Use a white colored pencil

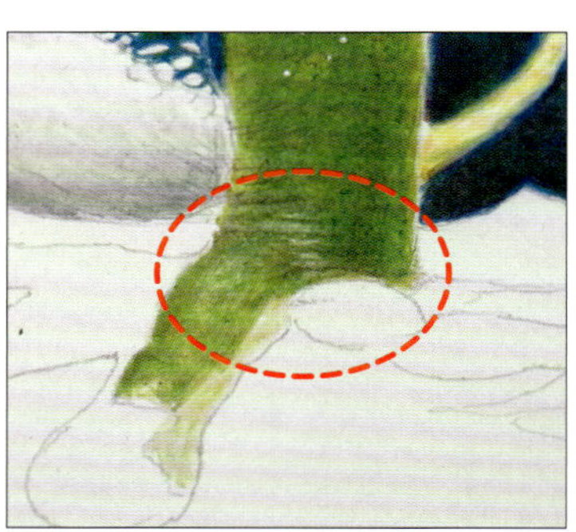

A highlight is the brightest part of an object. Adding highlights increases both three-dimensionality and realism. There are many ways to create highlights: not coloring certain areas of a white sheet of paper, using a stylus to make indentations that create fine highlights, or applying a white colored pencil.

Clearly separate the light and dark areas

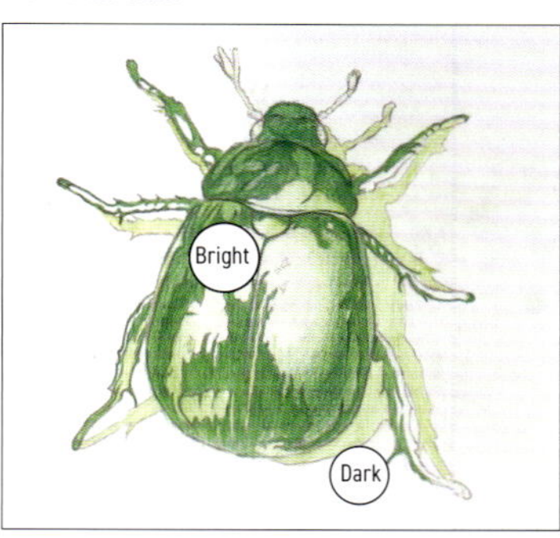

Apply highly saturated colors along the edges

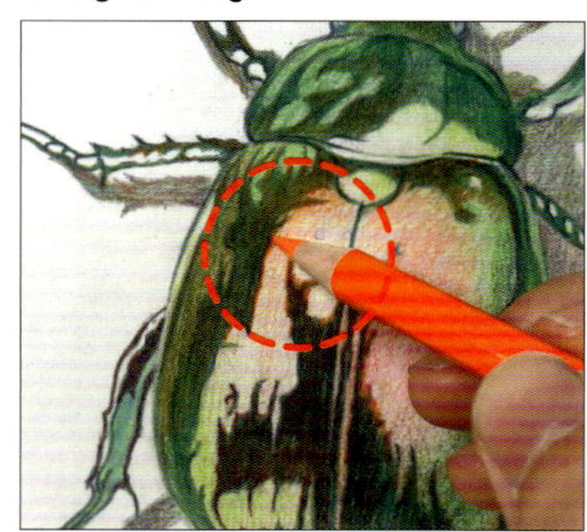

Add reflected light

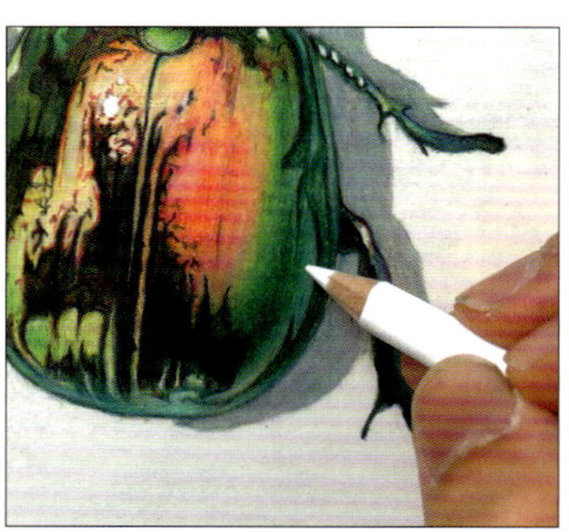

For creatures with a strong glossy effect, such as the scarab beetle (p.42), you can enhance their glossy effect by clearly separating the light and dark areas, adding highly saturated colors along the edges, and adding reflected light.

How to Combine Transparency, a Glossy Effect, and Three-Dimensionality in Eyes

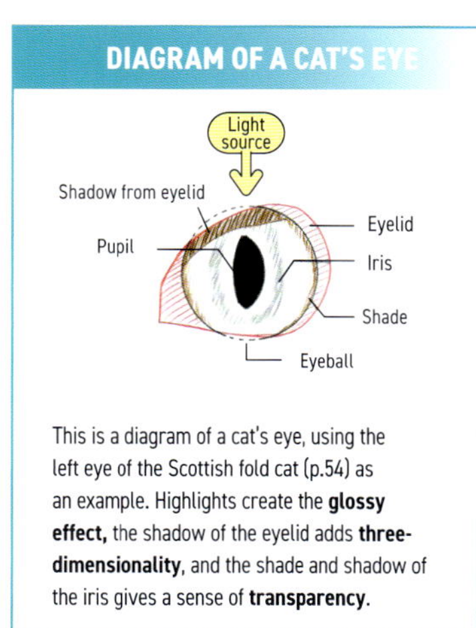

This is a diagram of a cat's eye, using the left eye of the Scottish fold cat (p.54) as an example. Highlights create the **glossy effect,** the shadow of the eyelid adds **three-dimensionality,** and the shade and shadow of the iris gives a sense of **transparency.**

Color of the iris ①   ### Color of the eyelid

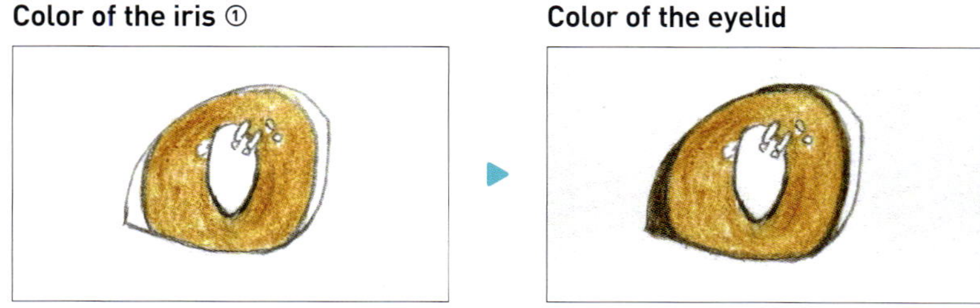

Start by applying a base layer of color to the iris, matching the color of the cat's eyes you want to draw. For this Scottish fold cat, which has brownish eyes, I used an ochre tone. Be careful not to color over the highlight at the top of the pupil, as it should remain uncolored until the end. Shade the inner corner of the eye and the outer edge with a darker brown tone.

Color of the iris②   ### Pupil   ### Shadow of the eyelid

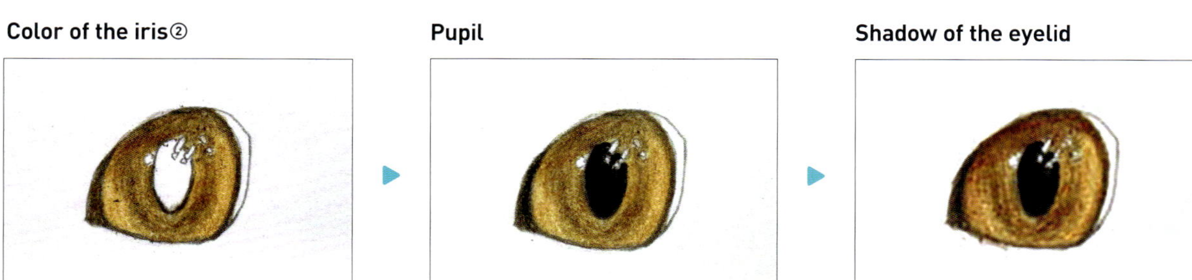

The outer edge of a cat's iris often appears brighter because light passes through its eye. You should therefore darken the area surrounding the pupil, as shown in this diagram. You can also slightly darken the areas where the eyelid casts a shadow. Capturing this effect will help convey the transparency of the eye.

　　After filling in the pupil solidly with black, add the shadow cast by the eyelid onto the iris. As the light source is above, the area closer to the eyelid will be darker. Be careful not to accidentally cover the highlight.

Eyelid (corner of the eye) ①   ### Eyelid (corner of the eye) ②

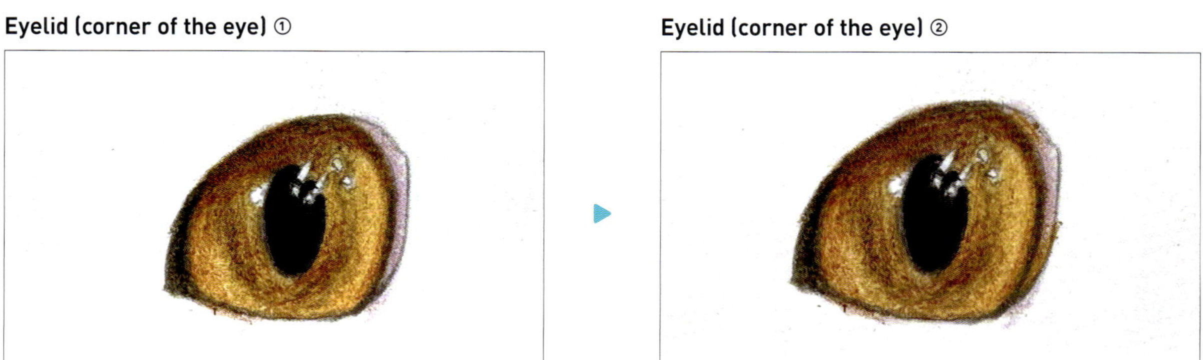

Finish detailing the eyelid. On the outer corner of the eye, the skin color under the fur is visible, so add a pinkish tone there. Then lightly layer the same color as the facial fur (in this case, ochre) over it to blend the colors.

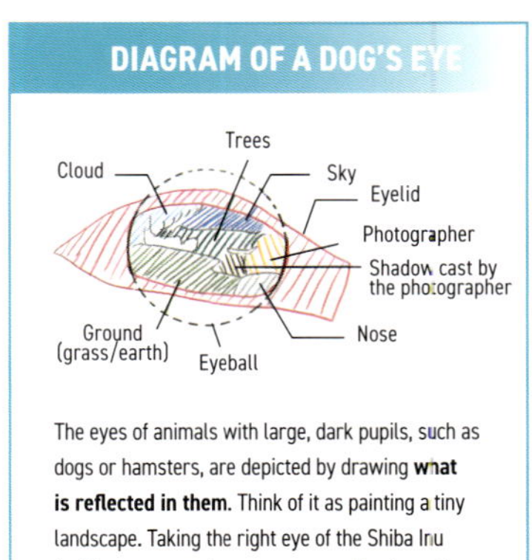

The eyes of animals with large, dark pupils, such as dogs or hamsters, are depicted by drawing **what is reflected in them**. Think of it as painting a tiny landscape. Taking the right eye of the Shiba Inu (p.80) as an example; you can see reflections of elements like a park scene or even the dog's own nose, as shown in the diagram. It isn't necessary to draw every detail, but incorporating these colors will help you capture the look of a **shiny black eye**.

Color of the eyelid

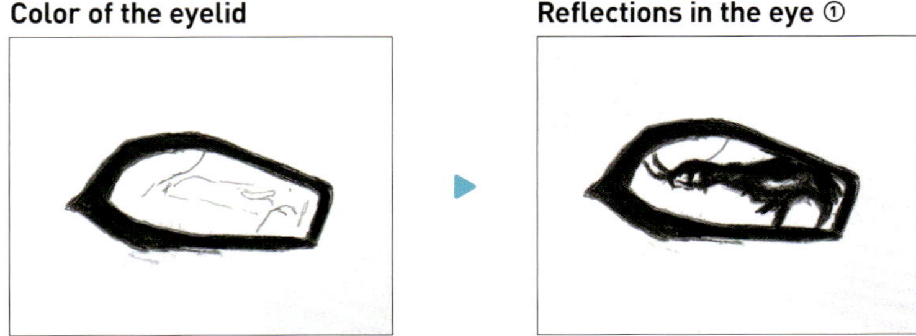

Reflections in the eye ①

First, color the eyelid that surrounds the eyeball. Since there is no fur along the edge of the eye and the black skin is visible, fill this area with black. Next, draw the reflections inside the pupil. For simplicity in this example, we will fill in the parts labeled **Trees** and **Photographer** in the diagram with black.

Reflections in the eye ②

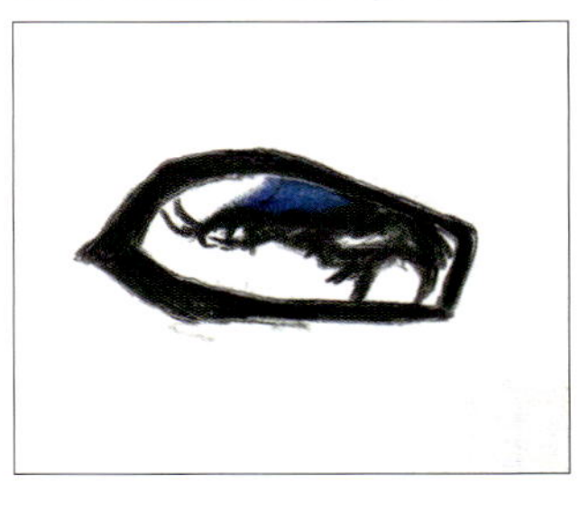

Reflections in the eye ③

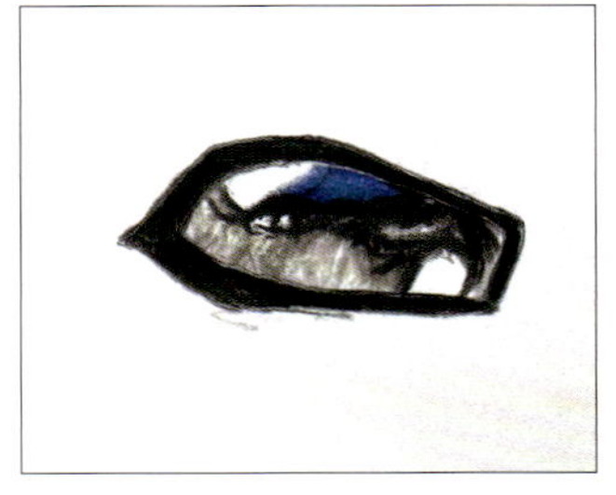

Reflections in the eye ④

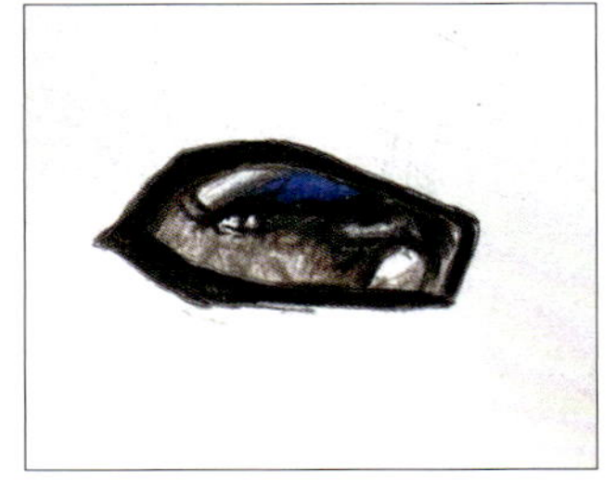

On the upper half, apply a blue tone to represent the sky, which is one of the most striking reflections. Because it's reflected in the black eye, shade it darker than the actual sky. Next, use beige or dark brown tones to color the ground in the lower half. Applying the color with slight irregularity will help suggest the texture of uneven ground.

If you reduce the amount of reflected detail in the pupil, the eye will appear lighter and more metallic; if you increase it, the eye will look heavier and more intense. For this example, we've kept the look somewhat bright.

Reflections in the eye (reference)

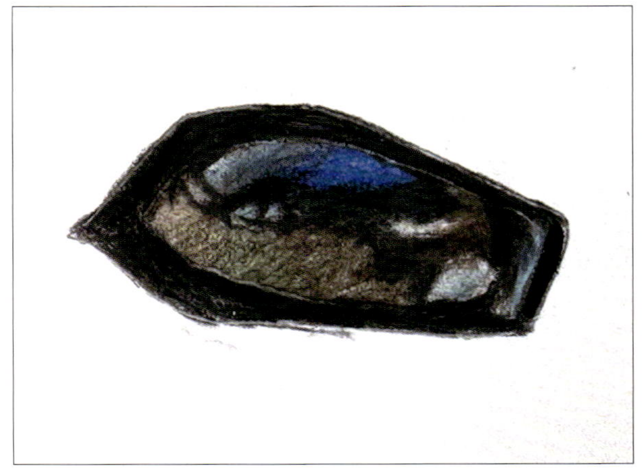

As a reference, here is an example with even more reflections added, such as patches of green for the grass on the ground and stronger blue tones for the sky. Compared to Reflections in the eye ④ , you can see that this results in a heavier, more intense look.

Keep in mind that painting the sky and ground in this way is just one example. When drawing black eyes, the key is to avoid filling them in with pure black alone. Instead, make an effort to add the colors of the reflections as well.

Four Different Ways of Drawing Fur

1. Draw everything with colored pencils

First, apply the base color of the fur with firm pressure over the entire area. Next, use a darker tone of the same color family to draw the shaded areas within the fur, following the natural direction of the strands. Instead of straight lines, add a slight curve to create a more natural look. Finally, use a lighter color to draw the highlights of the fur.

Apply the base color.

Add shaded areas within the fur with a darker tone of the same color family.

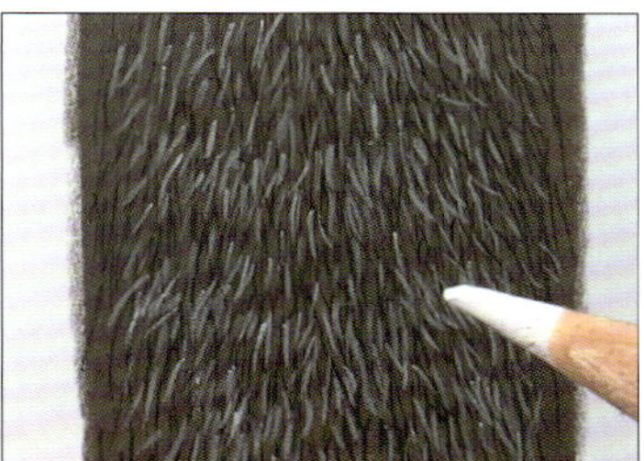

Draw the fur texture with a lighter color.

2. Scrape with a design knife *Take care when using a knife.

If you want the fur to look sharper, scraping with a design knife is effective. After applying the base color, follow the same steps as in Step 1 to shade. Hold the design knife at a slight angle and gently scrape only the colored surface of the pencil layer. Be careful not to damage the paper.

Apply the base color.

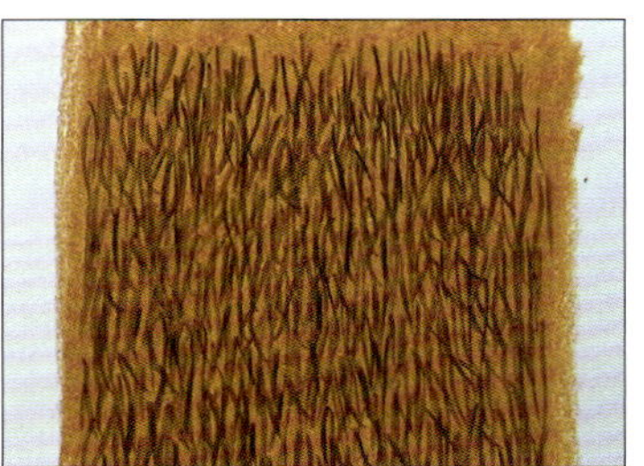

Add shaded areas within the fur with a darker tone of the same color family.

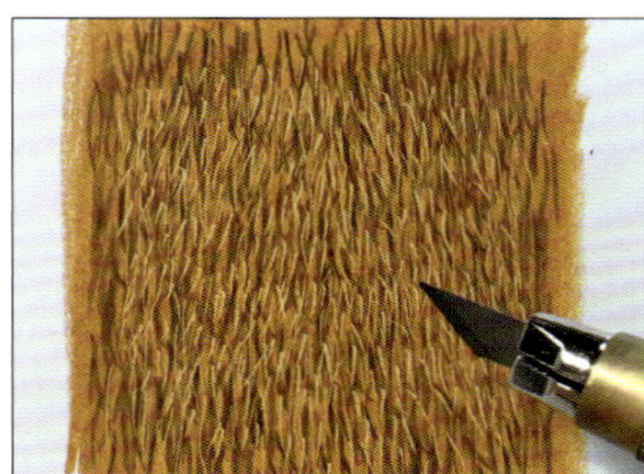

Scrape with a design knife.

3. Depict light fur with a stylus

This method makes use of the white of the paper. First, indent the paper with a stylus, then apply color on top. To prevent pigment from entering the grooves, begin coloring with the pencil held at a slight angle, which also makes the stylus lines easier to see. Adding a darker tone of the same color family on top will make the fur appear more three-dimensional.

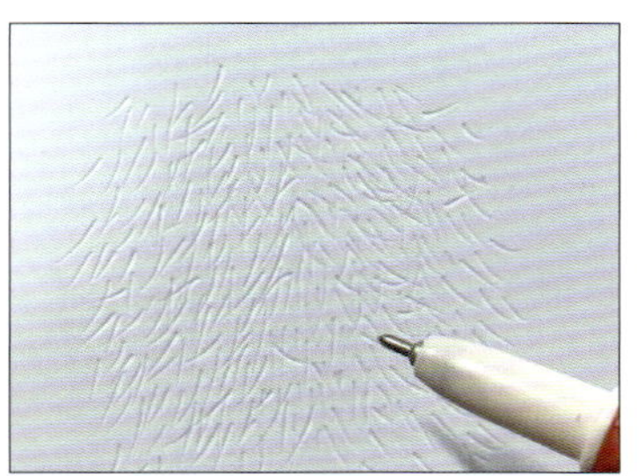

Carve the paper with a light, sweeping motion of the stylus.

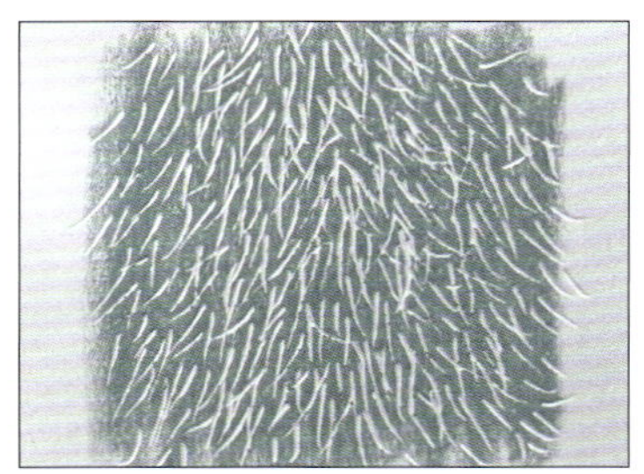

Apply the base color.

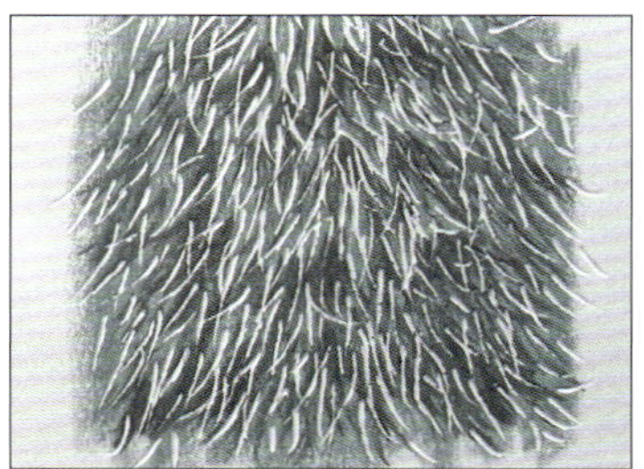

Add shaded areas within the fur with a darker tone of the same color family.

4. Depict colored fur with a stylus

When you want to add color to fur, apply the color before using the stylus. To prevent the stylus from scraping off the pigment, apply the color with moderately firm pressure.

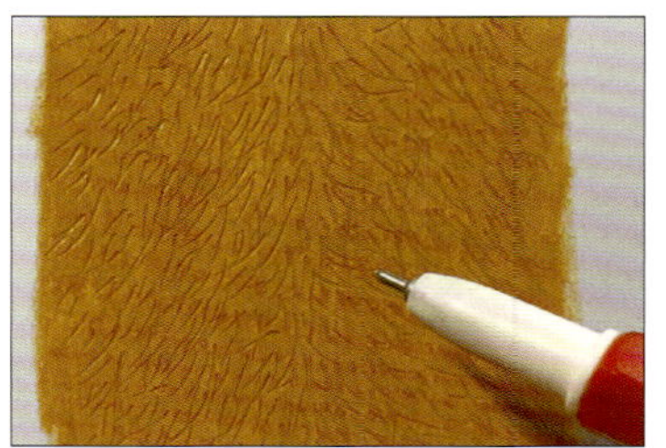

Carve the paper with the stylus after applying color.

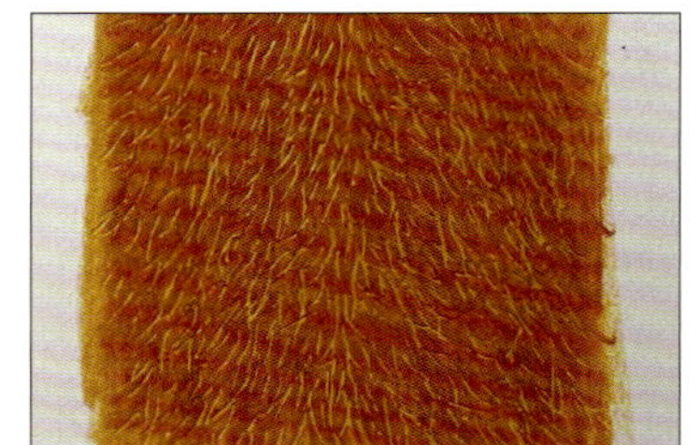

Apply the base color.

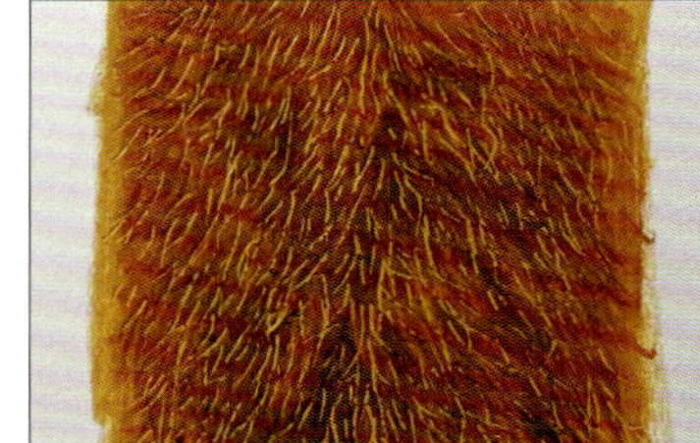

Shade the fur with a darker tone of the same color family.

Putting It All Together

Here, you'll use all four techniques (1–4) to depict fur. Carefully observe the subject, choose the most suitable methods, and try to create rich and varied fur textures.

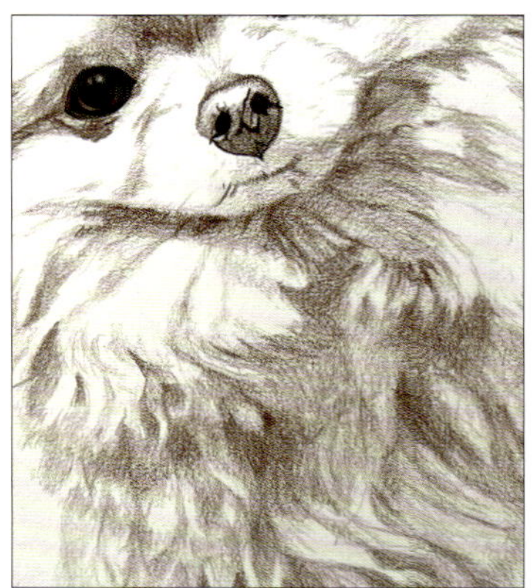

Add broad shading to the clumps of fur.

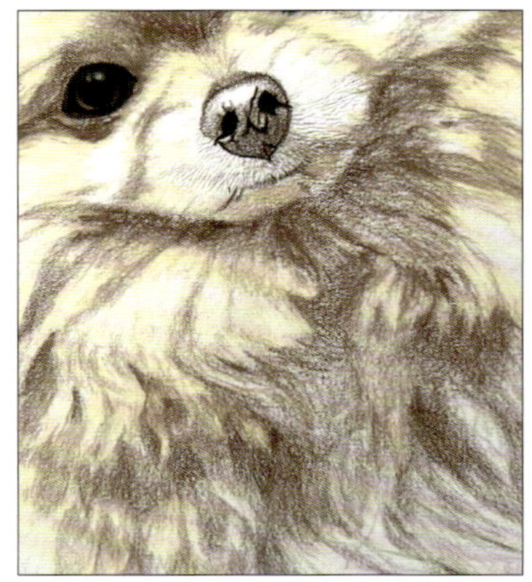

Apply a light color to all areas except where the fur will be white.

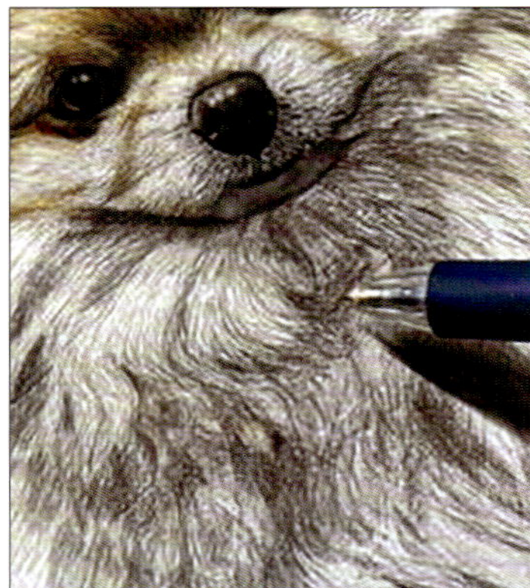

Carve the fur texture with a stylus.

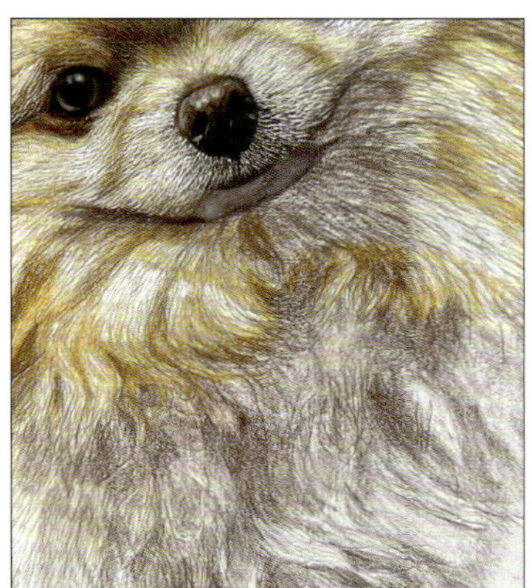

Use a darker color than the base to shade the fur texture.

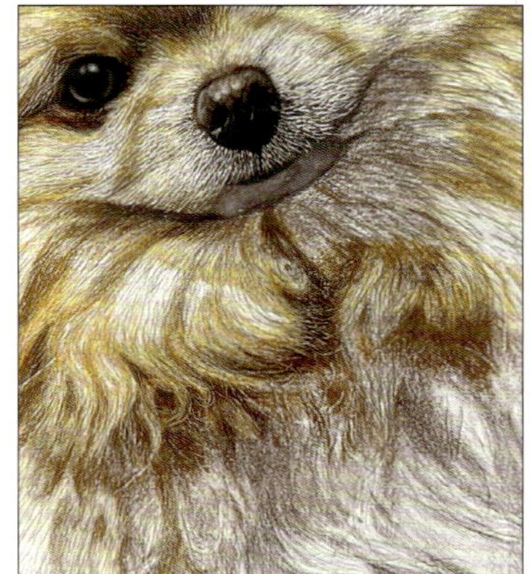

Shade the fur clumps with a dark color.

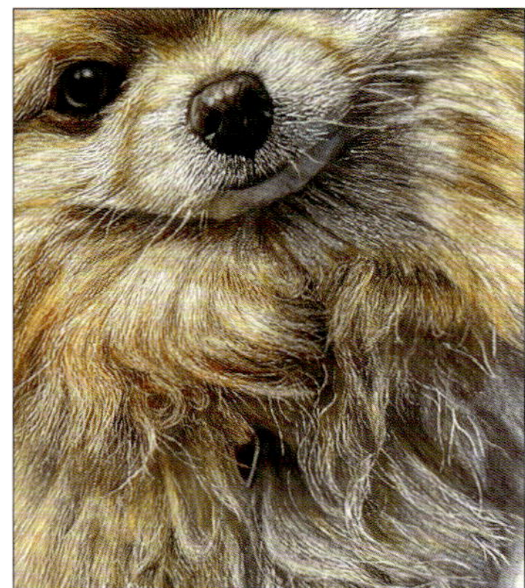

Scrape with a design knife to add fine hairs (especially effective in darker areas).

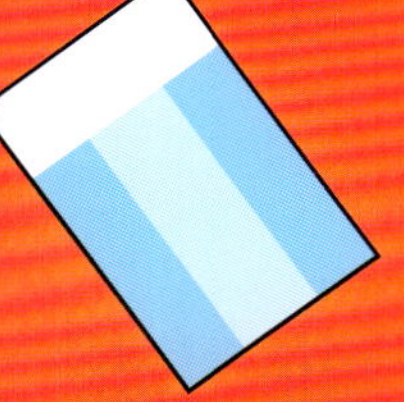
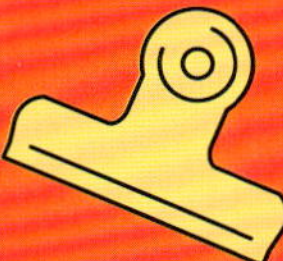

Drawing Animals with Colored Pencils

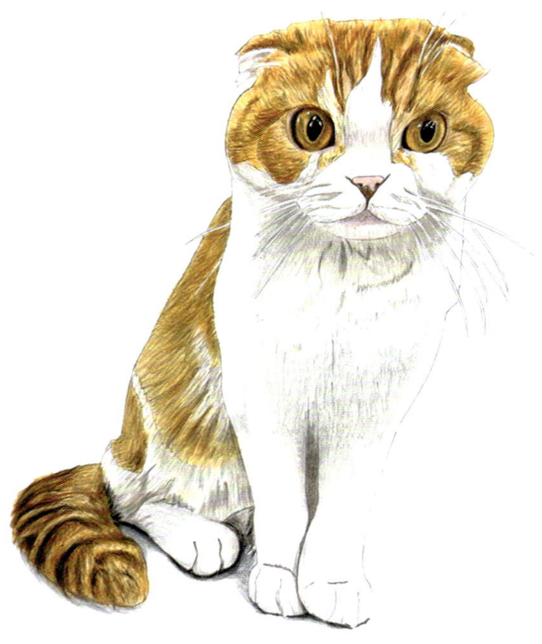

Draw a Ladybug

Colored pencils: Prismacolor
Paper: KMK Kent
Drawn by Rihito

Coloring Key Points

1. Be aware of the shades and shadows caused by the light source (p.11).

2. Be aware of the boundaries between light and dark and the reflected light in shades and shadows (p.12)

Colors Used

PC914 Cream	PC903 True Blue
PC901 Indigo Blue	PC919 Non-Photo Blue
PC924 Crimson Red	PC935 Black
PC921 Pale Vermilion	PC938 White
PC926 Carmine Red	PC916 Canary Yellow
PC929 Pink	PC913 Spring Green

Reference Photo

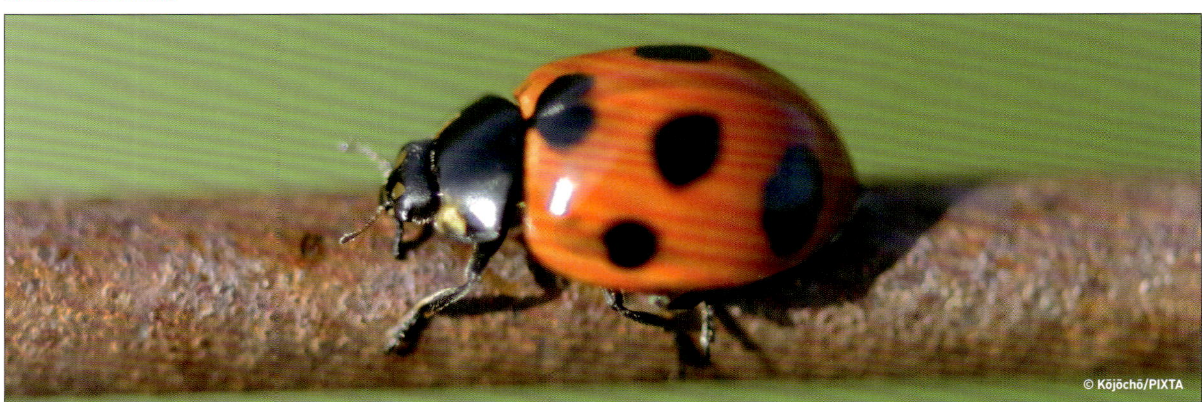

Preliminary Drawing

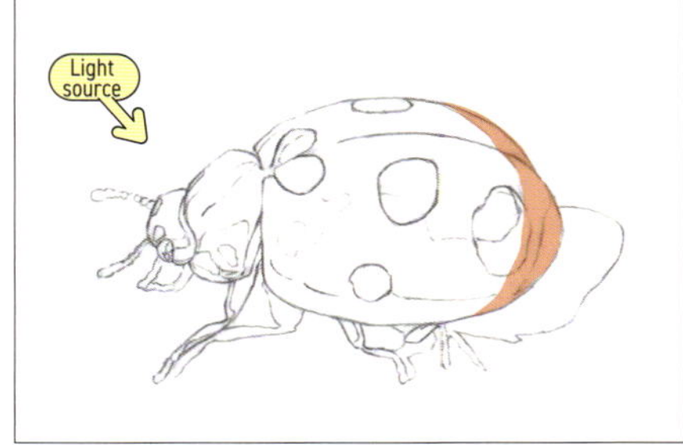

The theme of this work is awareness of a sense of three-dimensionality. Observe the shape of the ladybug and think about where the shade and shadow will fall when light hits it. Also consider how to exaggerate those areas to enhance the effect. As the surface has a glossy finish like a well-polished leather shoe, avoid leaving uneven strokes. Layer color carefully and repeatedly to reproduce subtle tonal differences rather than applying a single coat.

The light is coming from the left side of the page, so the shade and shadow will fall mostly on the red areas shown in the diagram. Be sure to make these red areas especially dark.

Begin the preliminary drawing by first establishing the overall balance. Pay close attention to the proportions, position, and orientation of the head and body as you outline the form. Once the balance is right, add the finer details. Erase any unnecessary lines, and your preliminary drawing is complete.

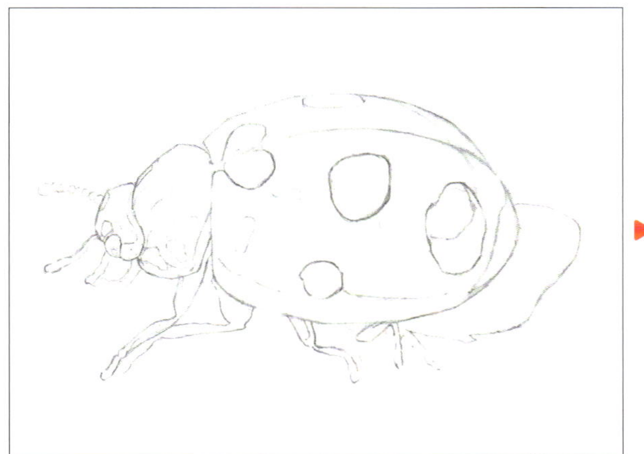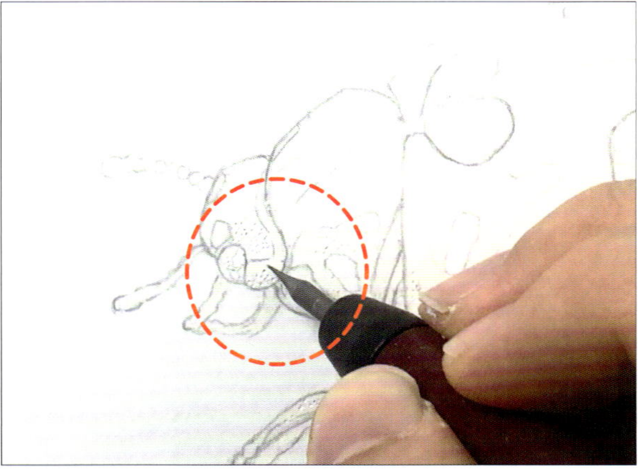

1 Fill in all areas except the highlights with a cream color. Hold the colored pencil at an angle and apply the color lightly and evenly to avoid streaks. Then, use a stylus to indent the head area.

☐ Cream

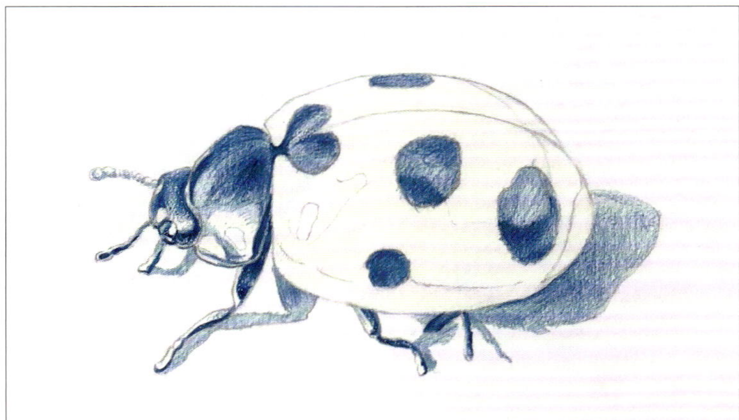

2 Add light and dark variations with indigo blue. Hold the colored pencil at an angle and apply the color lightly and smoothly.

▬ Indigo blue

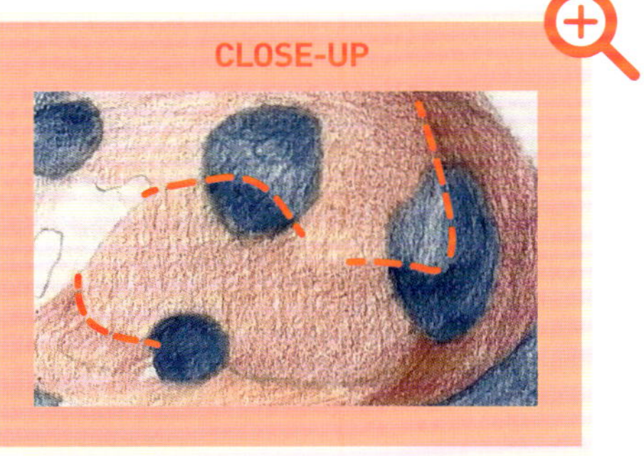

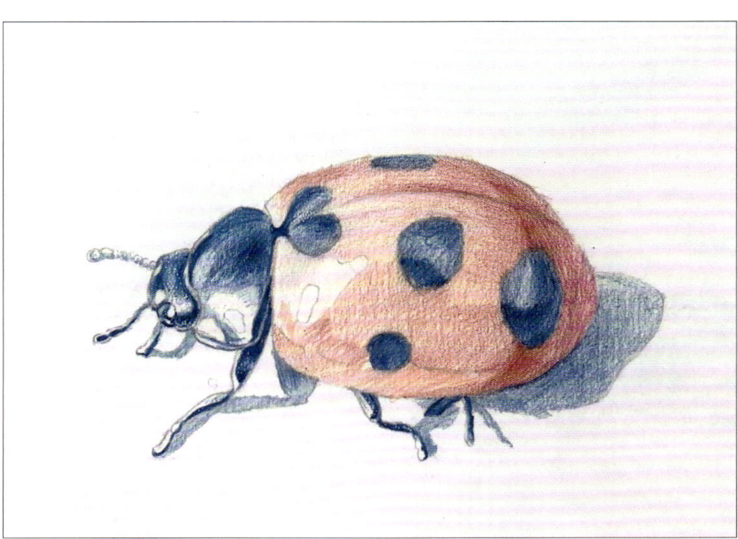

3 Add light and dark variations with crimson red. As mentioned in Coloring Key Points, apply the color a bit more firmly along the boundary between light and dark to create a stronger contrast.

▬ Crimson red

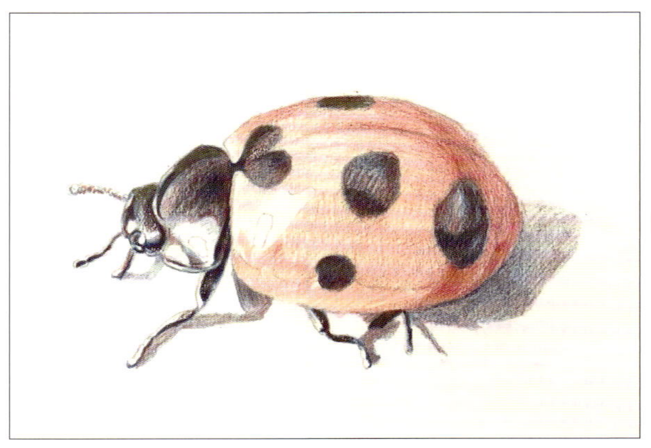 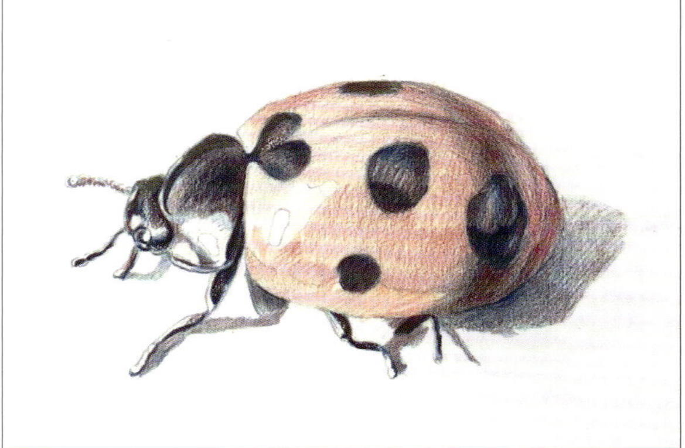

4 Layer crimson red over the indigo blue, then apply another layer of indigo blue to further strengthen the contrast.

■ Indigo blue ■ Crimson red

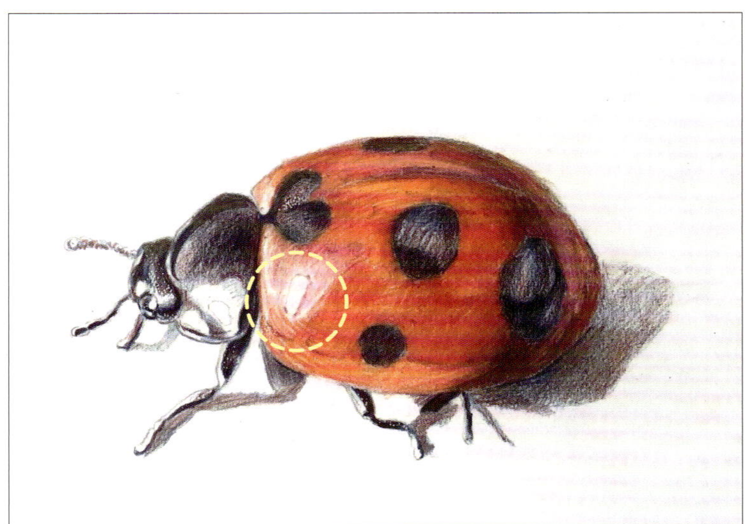

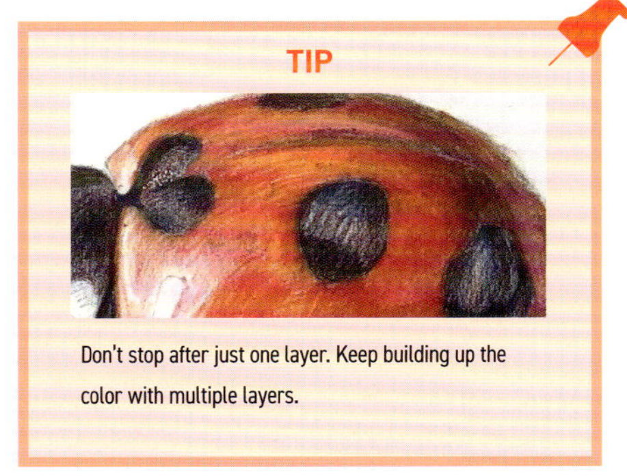

Don't stop after just one layer. Keep building up the color with multiple layers.

5 Create variations of light and dark by applying pale vermilion, carmine red, and crimson red with a little bit of pressure. Leave the areas around the marked highlights uncolored.

■ Pale vermilion
■ Carmine red ■ Crimson red

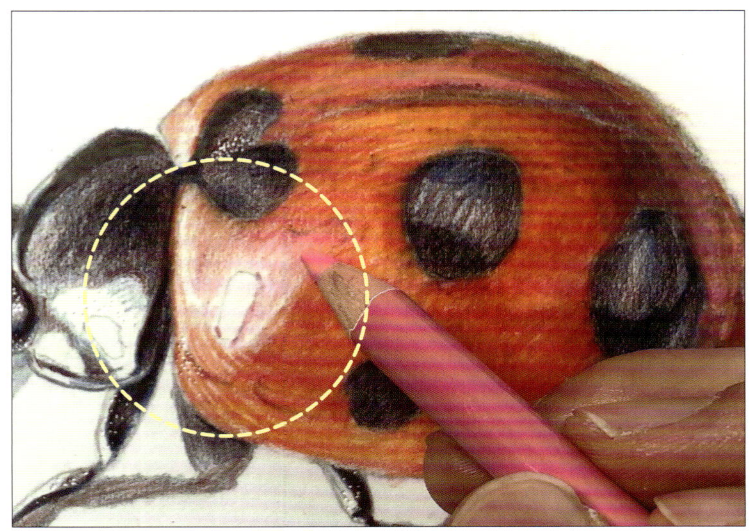

6 Lightly apply pink around the highlight areas that were left uncolored.

■ Pink

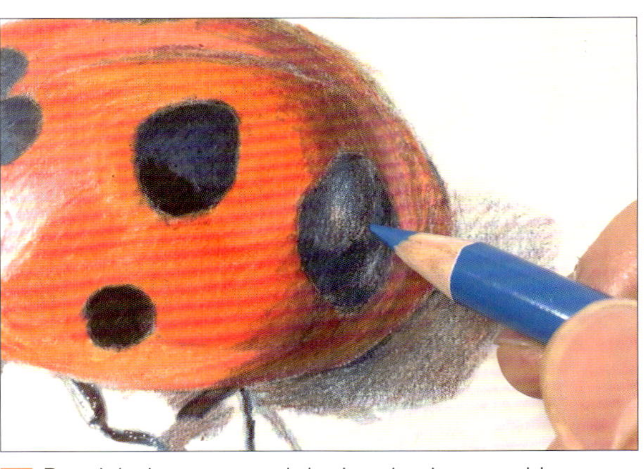

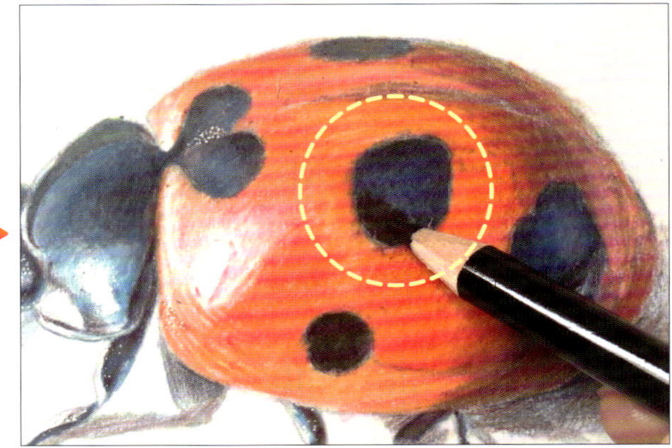

7 Burnish the spots and the head using true blue, non-photo blue, and black (p.12).

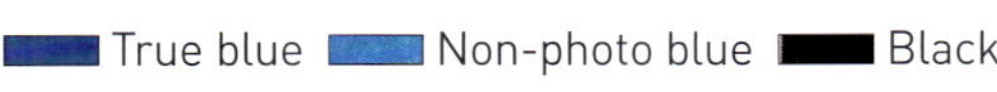

■ True blue ■ Non-photo blue ■ Black

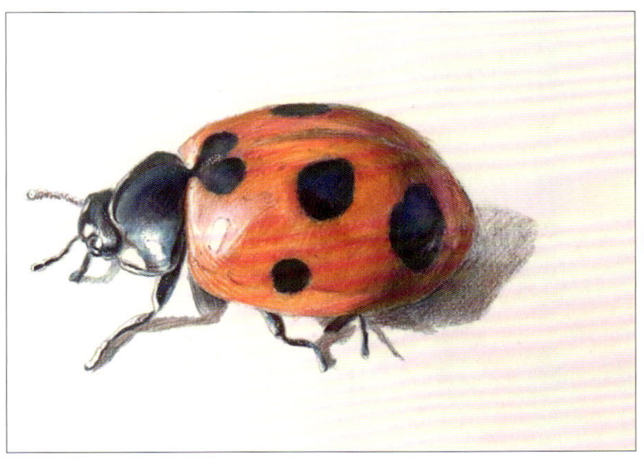

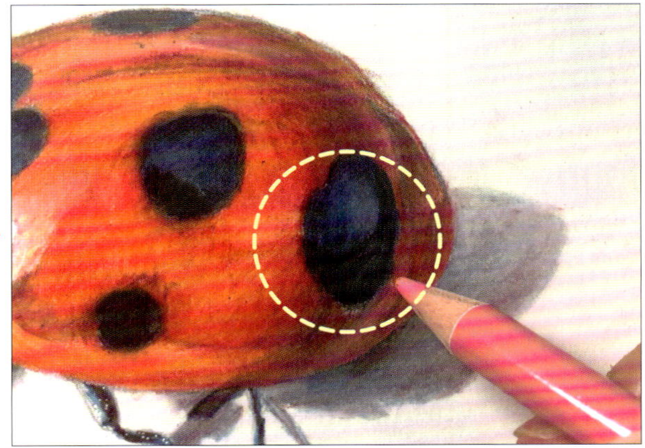

8 The image on the left shows the current overall state. From here, add the reflected light within the shade using pink and white. Burnish the cast shadow on the ground with white.

■ Pink □ White

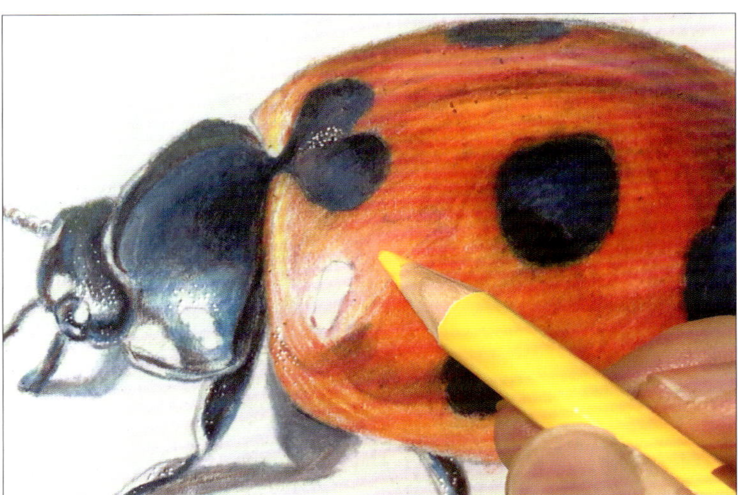

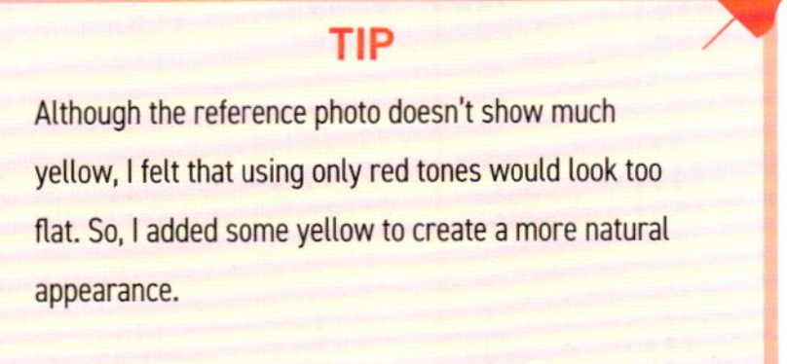

TIP

Although the reference photo doesn't show much yellow, I felt that using only red tones would look too flat. So, I added some yellow to create a more natural appearance.

9 Apply canary yellow around the highlights and in the brighter areas.

■ Canary yellow

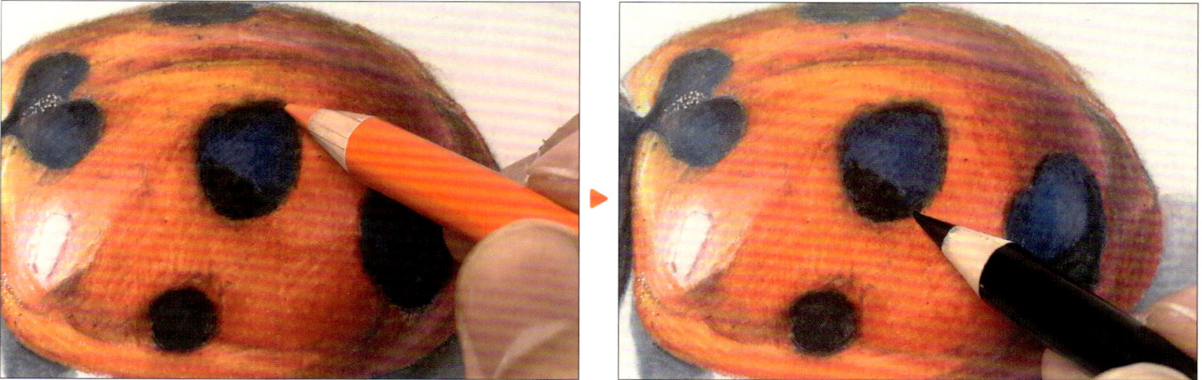

10 Soften the edges of the spots with carmine red. For the areas of these softened spots that are closer to the front of the image, sharpen the outlines using black or indigo blue.

■ Carmine red ■ Black ■ Indigo blue

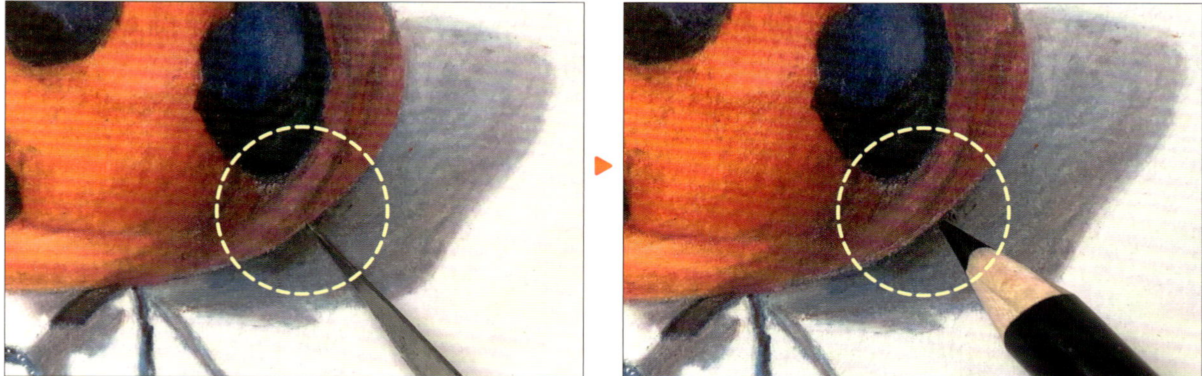

11 Scrape the boundary between the foreground outline and the shadow cast on the ground with a design knife. Then, lightly shade the cast shadow side with black to make the outline more distinct.

■ Black

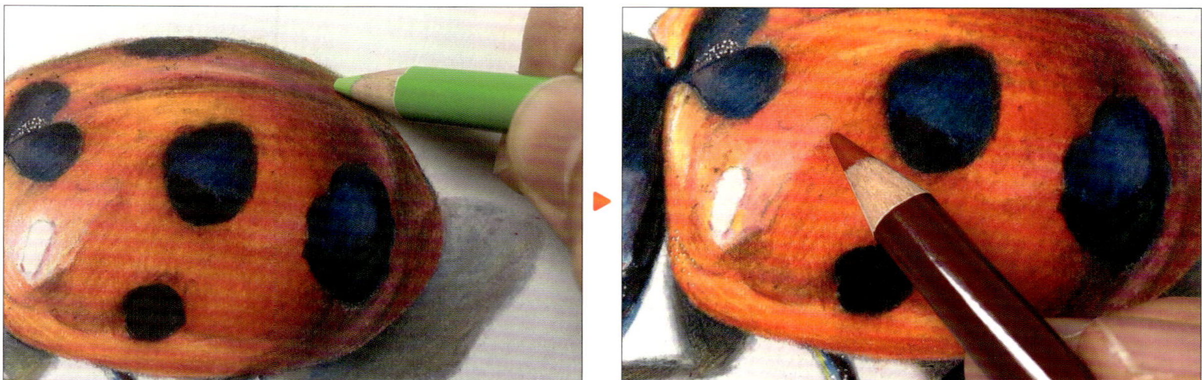

12 For the shaded areas, lightly apply spring green to the back of the ladybug's shell. Then, use crimson red to depict the reflections on the front of its shell. While doing this, step back from the paper to compare the overall balance of light and dark with the reference photo and adjust as needed.

■ Spring green ■ Crimson red

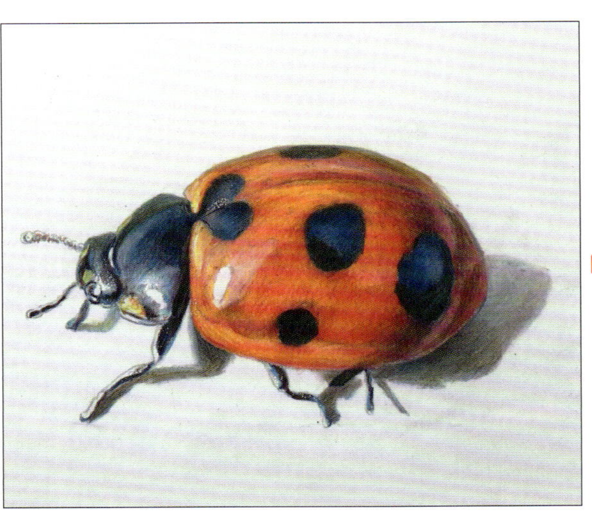
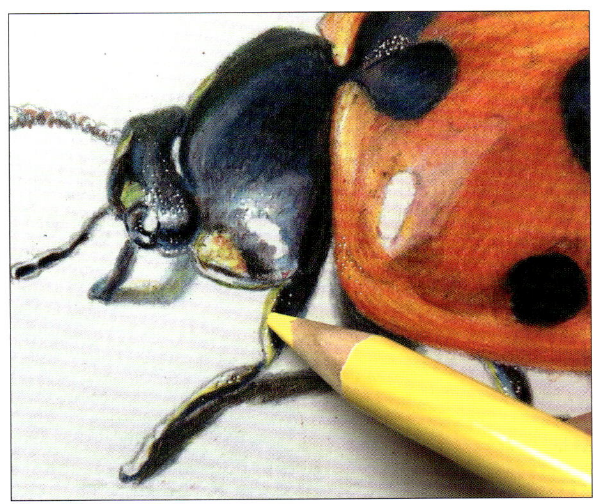

13 Color the yellow pattern near the head with canary yellow, and also apply canary yellow along the boundary of the highlights on the legs.

⬛ Canary yellow

COMPLETE

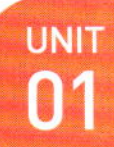

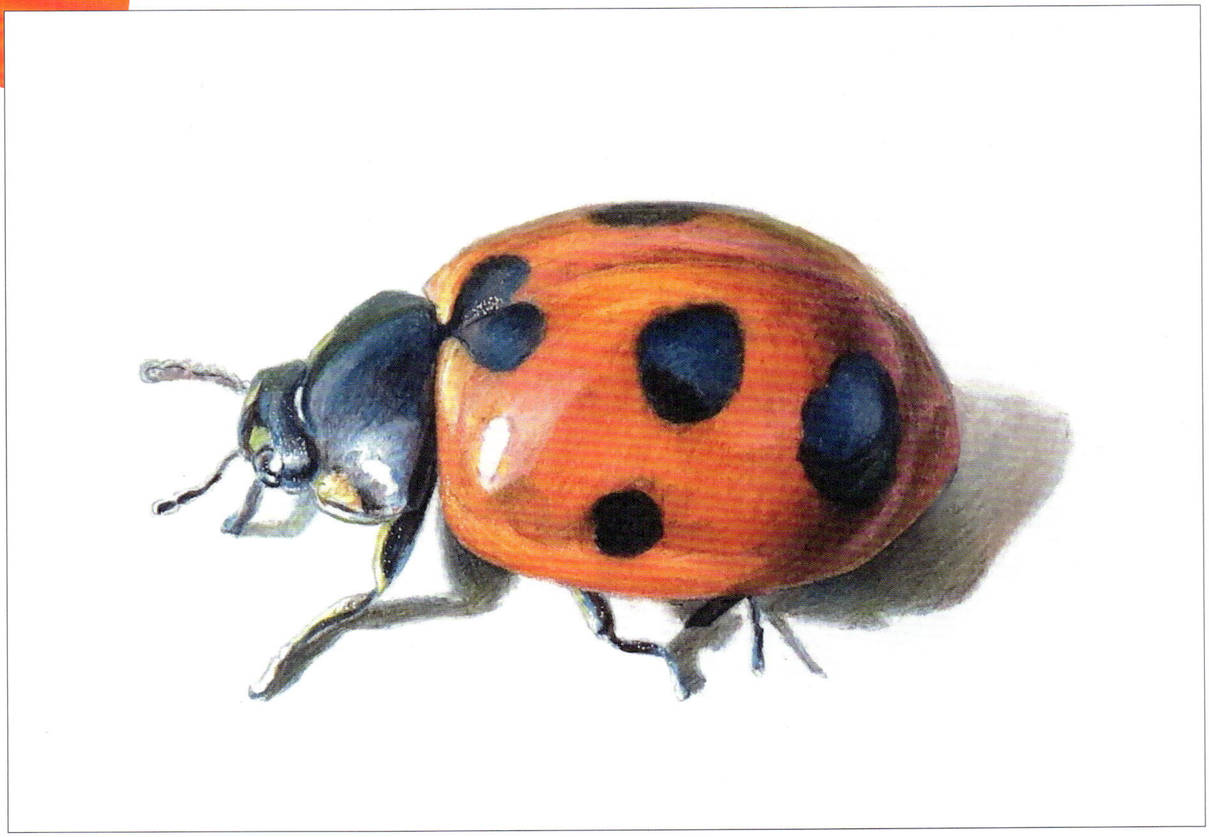

Draw a Tropical Fish

Colored pencils: Prismacolor
Paper: New TMK Poster Paper (A4)
Drawn by Ryosuke Mika

Coloring Key Points

1. Study the light source and the shape of the tropical fish to accurately capture the shaded areas.

Colors Used

PC916 Canary Yellow	PC930 Magenta
PC1003 Spanish Orange	PC1023 Cloud Blue
PC922 Poppy Red	PC946 Dark Brown
PC919 Non-Photo Blue	PC935 Black
PC902 Ultramarine	PC938 White

Preliminary Drawing

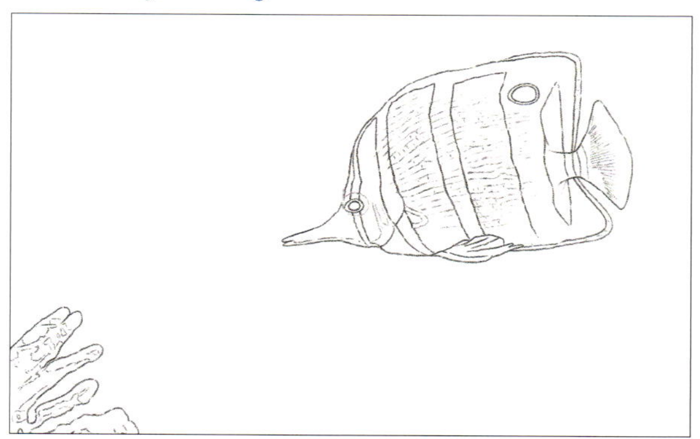

When sketching your preliminary drawing, remember that this piece will be finished with bright, vivid colors. If your sketch lines are too dark, they may stand out too much. Use light pressure and keep your lines faint.

Reference Photo

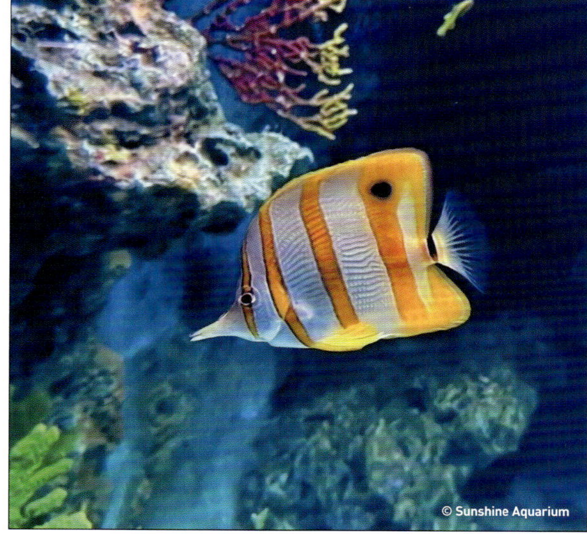

The theme this time is the use of vibrant colors and the depiction of three-dimensionality. By using bright, vivid colors, you can bring tropical fish to life. To create a sense of depth, be mindful of the light source and the shape of the fish as you add shade. Since the scene is underwater, the light generally comes from above. Although you can start by shading first and then layering color (grisaille), this approach can easily become muddy, so for this piece we will begin by applying vibrant colors.

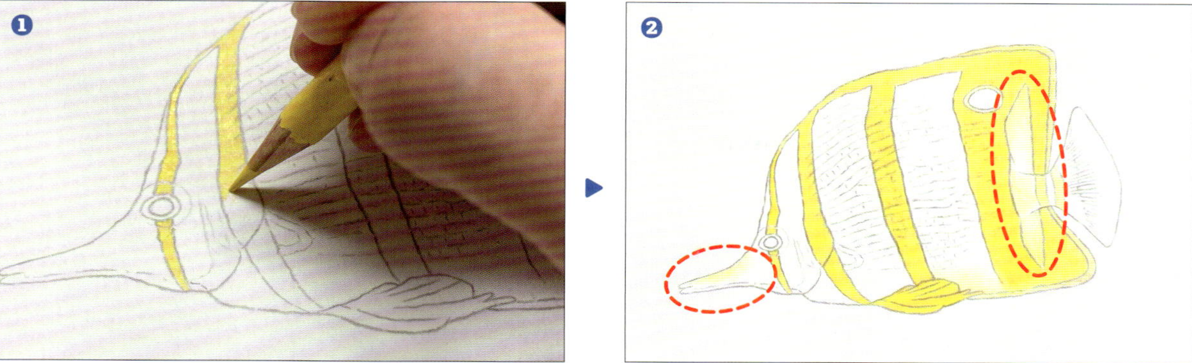

1 ❶ Fill in the yellow areas of the fish's body with a strong, solid layer of canary yellow. Hold the colored pencil fairly upright and apply firm pressure so the texture of the paper is almost completely covered. At this stage, there's no need to worry about shading. ❷ Add a bit of canary yellow to the areas marked with red circles as well.

🟨 Canary yellow

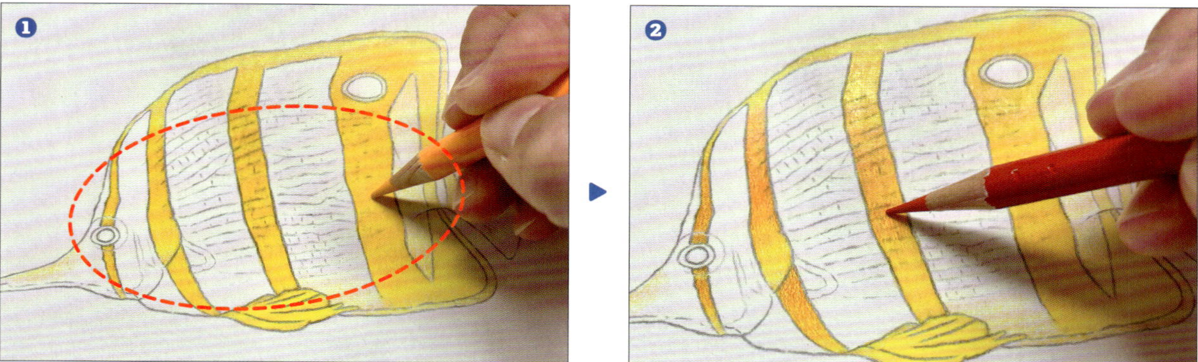

2 ❶ In the central areas of the sections colored in **Step 1**, deepen the tone by applying Spanish orange with firm pressure. ❷ Next, add touches of poppy red in selected areas. Be careful not to press too hard, as this can completely cover the canary yellow and Spanish orange layers, making the poppy red overpowering. Instead, hold the colored pencil at a slight angle and apply the poppy red gently for a softer effect.

🟧 Spanish orange   🟥 Poppy red

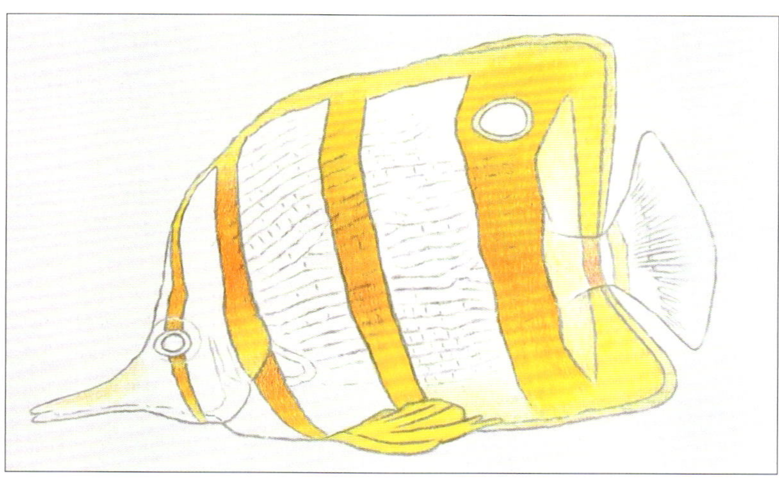

This is what the drawing looks like after applying the canary yellow, Spanish orange, and poppy red layers.

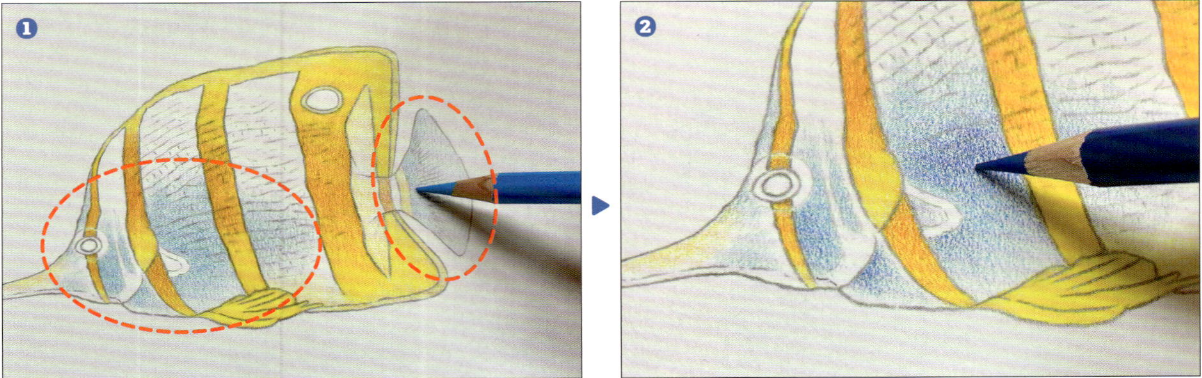

3 Now let's begin coloring the grey areas outside the canary yellow sections. Since various colors are mixed in, be sure to study the reference photo carefully. **❶** Lightly apply non-photo blue around the areas marked with red circles. **❷** Then, add touches of ultramarine in specific areas as needed.

[ ] Non-photo blue [ ] Ultramarine

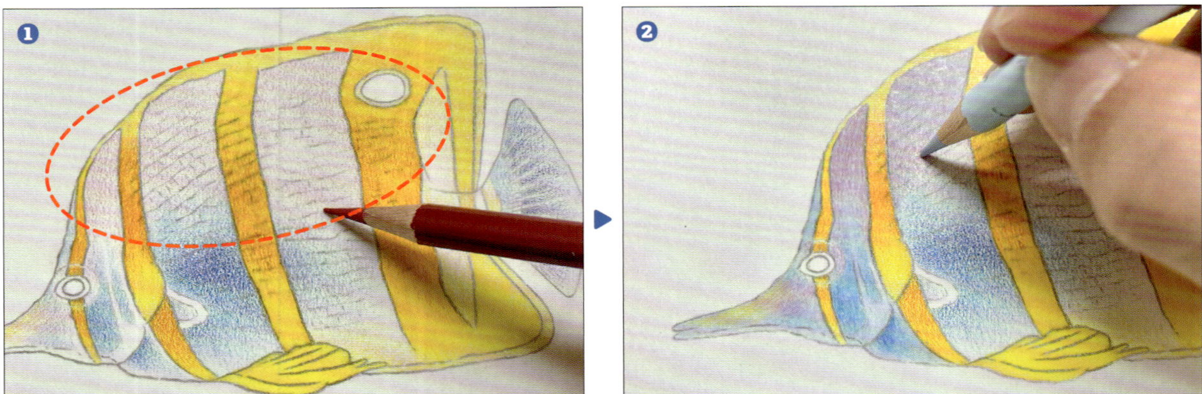

4 **❶** Lightly apply magenta inside the red oval. **❷** Then, layer cloud blue over the areas where you had applied non-photo blue, ultramarine, and magenta to blend the colors. In this step, hold the colored pencil more upright and apply firm pressure with confidence.

[ ] Magenta [ ] Cloud blue

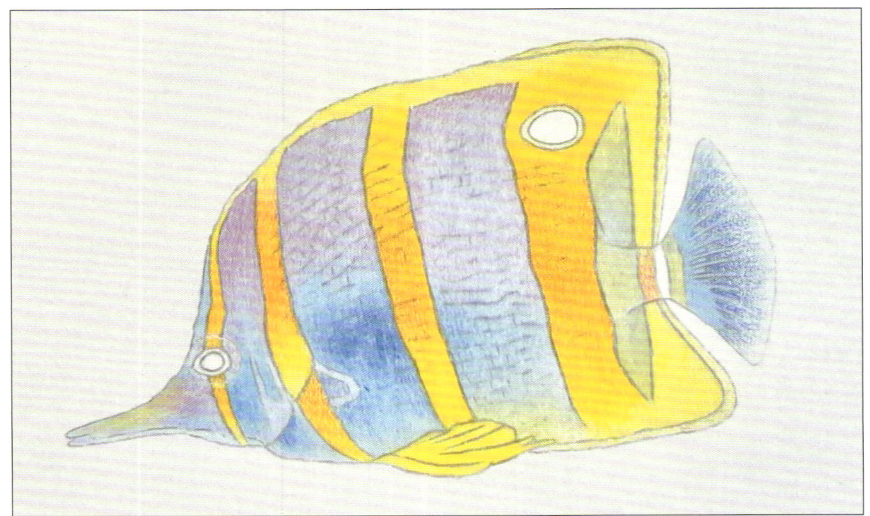

This is what the drawing looks like after applying the non-photo blue, ultramarine, magenta, and cloud blue.

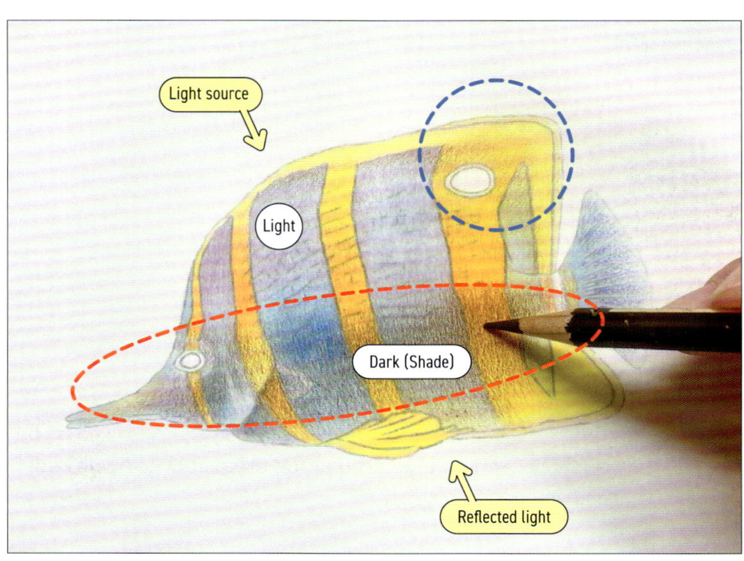

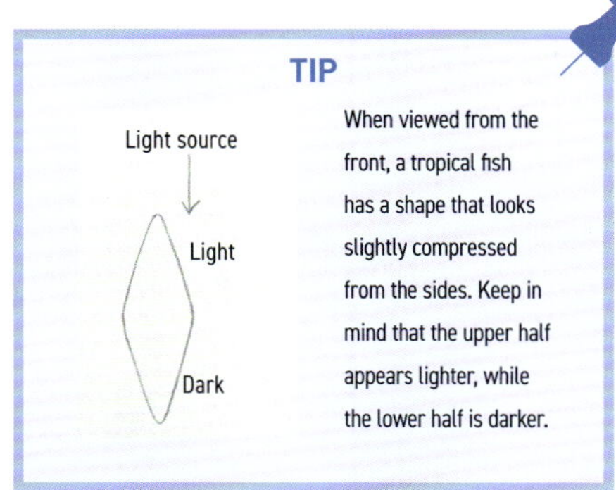

5 We'll now begin working on depicting three-dimensionality. Shade the lower half (the area marked with a red oval) using dark brown. Apply the color gently. However, keep the very bottom slightly lighter, as it's catching some reflected light. Also, don't forget the area around the blue circle in the upper right—there are some slightly darker parts there as well.

■■■■ Dark brown

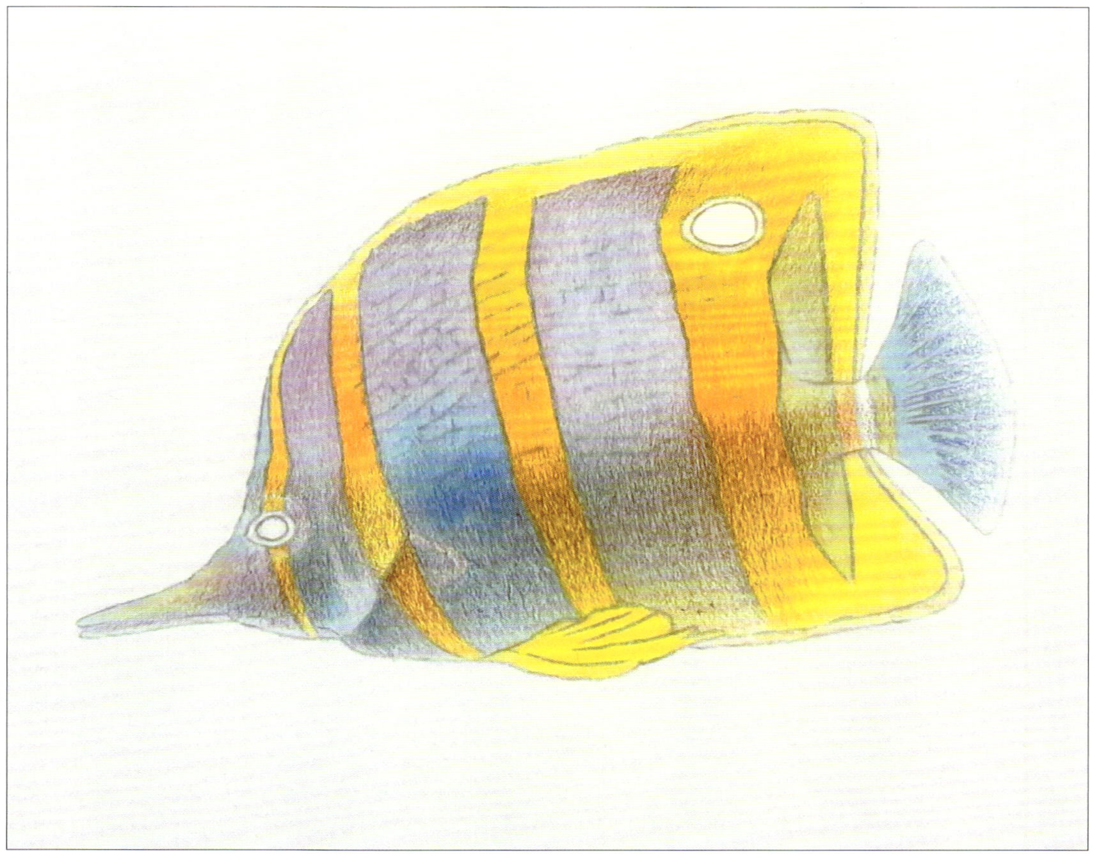

After the shade has been added.

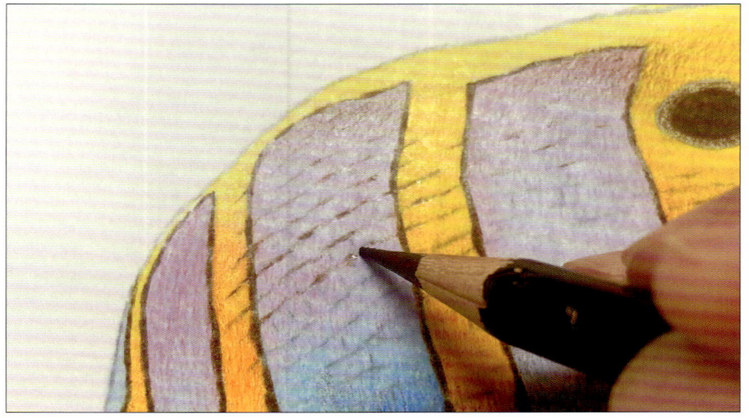

6 Now add the finer details. Use dark brown to draw the eyes, scales, and other small features. When drawing the scales, vary the pressure of your colored pencil, and avoid drawing every single one. Less is more.

■ Dark brown

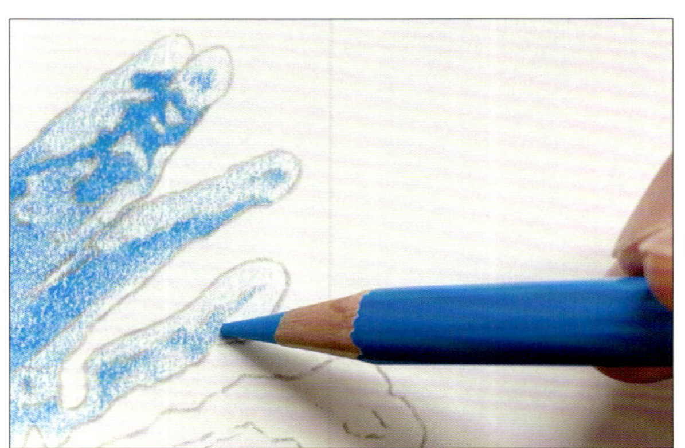

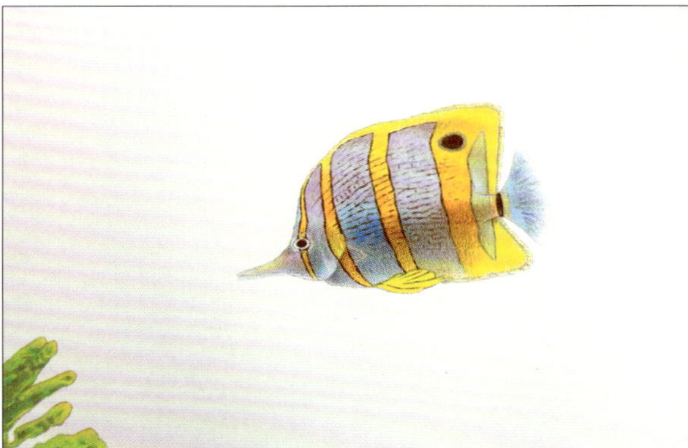

7 Now let's draw the seaweed. The green of the seaweed in the lower left of the image is expressed using a mix of non-photo blue and canary yellow. Simply using green can make it look flat and lacking in depth, so blending is very important. Start by applying non-photo blue, paying close attention to subtle variations in tone. Next, layer canary yellow over it. If the non-photo blue feels too faint, you can add more. For extra depth, try adding touches of magenta in certain areas to tighten the overall look.

■ Non-photo blue   ■ Canary yellow   ■ Magenta

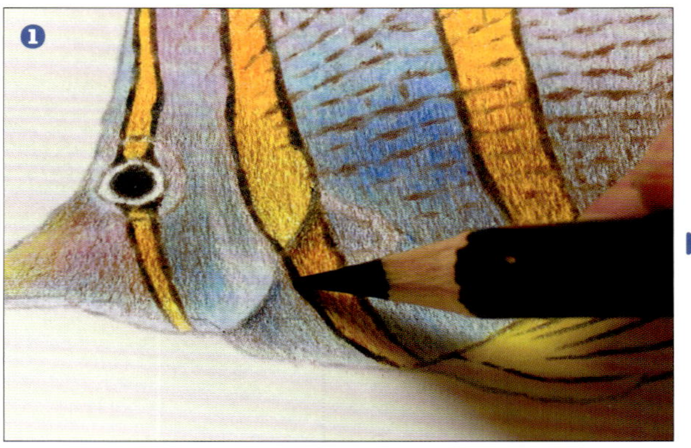

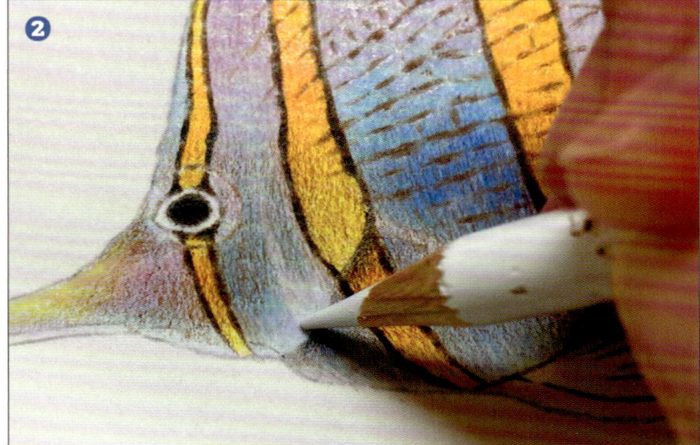

8 We're now moving on to the final touches. **1** First, add black in certain areas to tighten up the tropical fish. **2** For spots with a slight shine, use white to smooth out the paper's texture by pressing firmly as you apply it.

■ Black   □ White

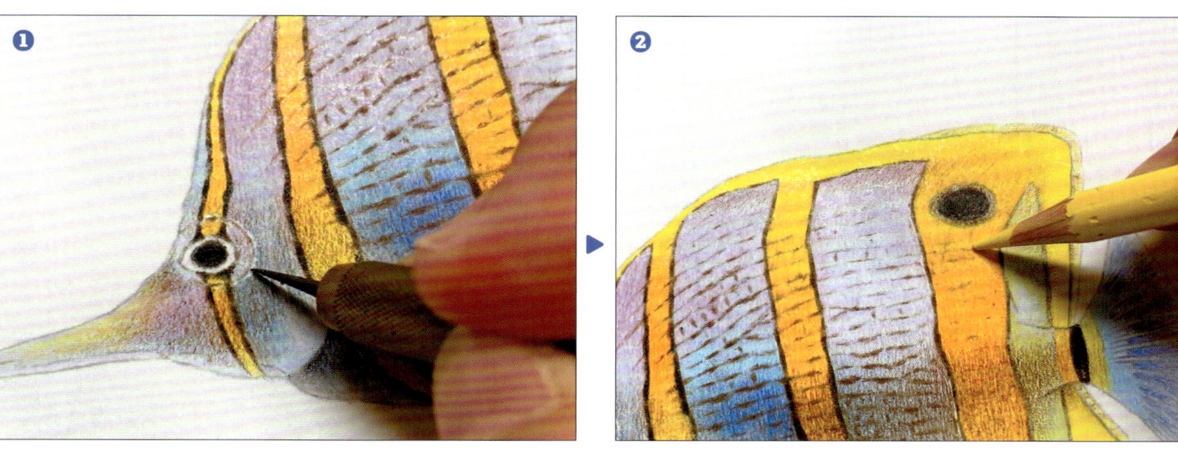

9 ❶ For fine highlights and details, use a design knife to gently scrape the surface. ❷ After that, carefully compare your work with the reference photo and add any colors you feel are missing.

COMPLETE

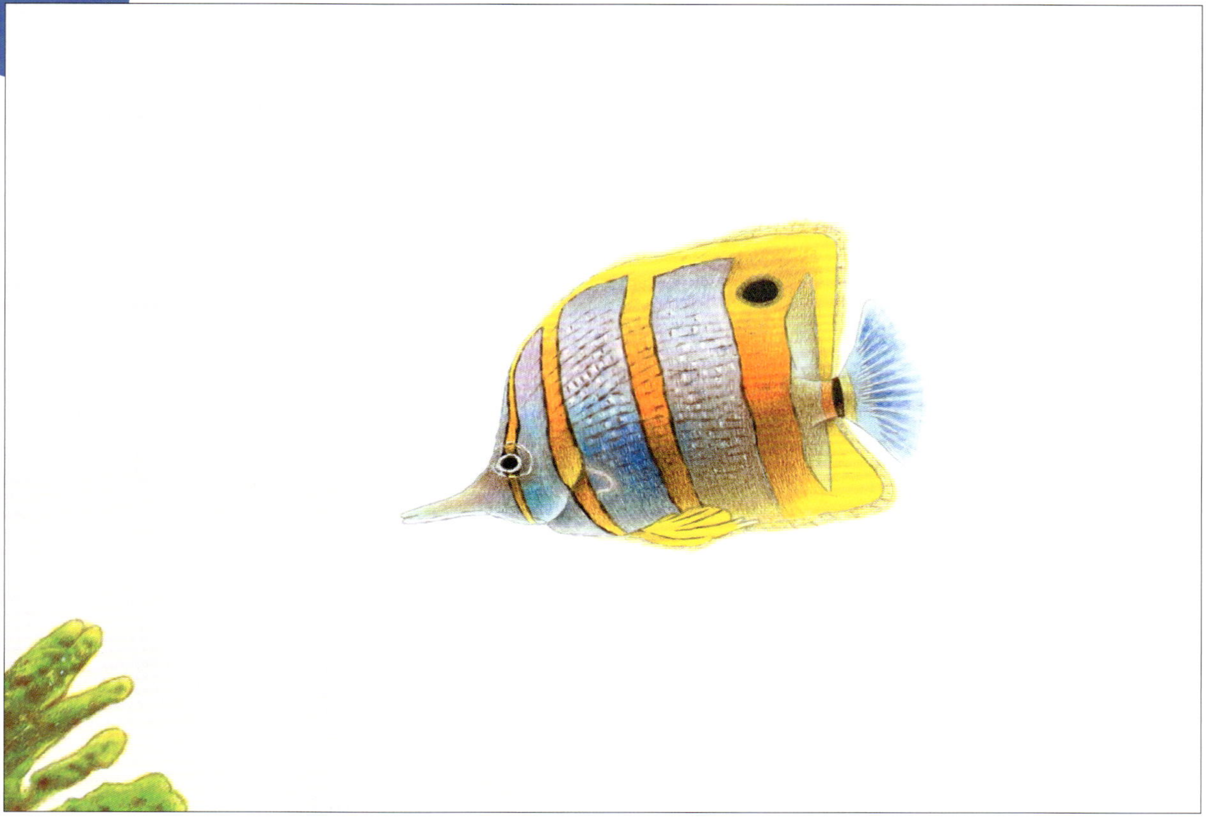

Draw a Peach-Faced Lovebird

Colored pencils: Prismacolor and Holbein
Paper: Daigen Thick Kent Paper
 **Drawn by Bonbon**

Coloring Key Points

1. Instead of drawing every feather on the entire body, selectively depict the feather texture in key areas for a more effective result (p.15).

2. Use grisaille to enhance the shade and shadow so the image doesn't appear flat, even under a weak light source (p.11).

Colors Used

▮ PC947 Dark Umber	▯ PC938 White
▮ PC916 Canary Yellow	▯ OP501 Soft White (Final layer)*
▮ PC903 True Blue	
▮ PC922 Poppy Red	▮ PC935 Black

*Holbein

Preliminary Drawing

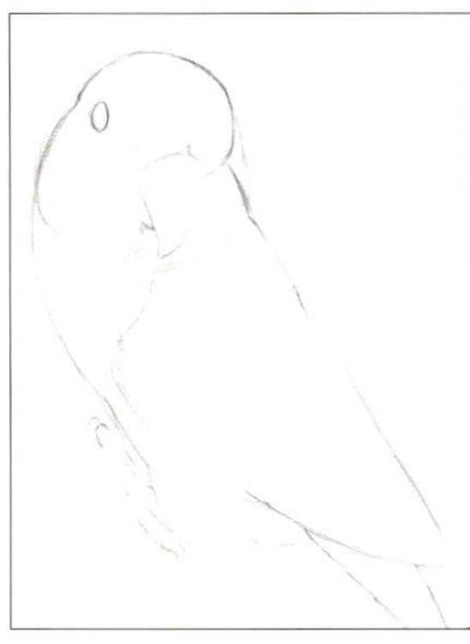

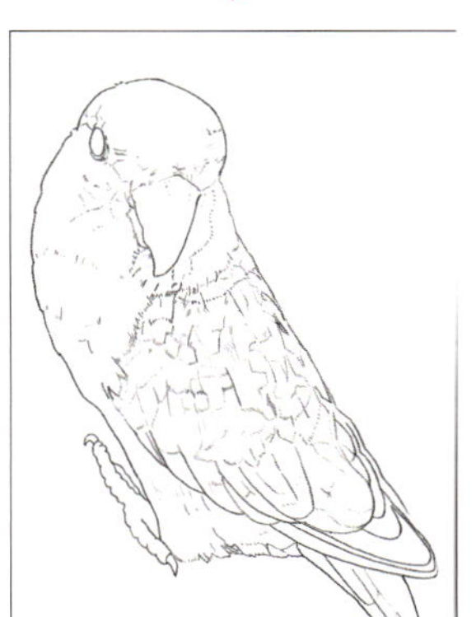

Begin your preliminary drawing by establishing the overall balance of the subject. Pay close attention to the size, position, and orientation of the head and body as you shape the form. Once the proportions are in place, add the finer details. Erase any unnecessary lines to complete the preliminary drawing.

Reference Photo

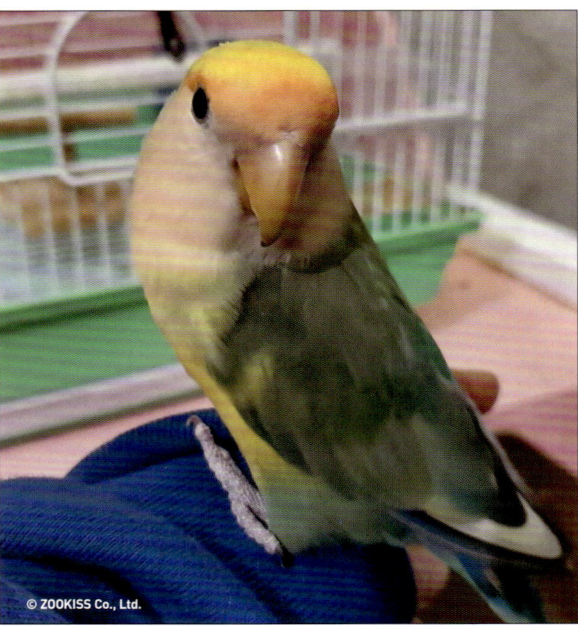

This lesson features a colorful peach-faced lovebird as the subject. To make it easy to follow even with a limited set of colored pencils, we'll reduce the number of colors used and mainly rely on the three primary colors (red, blue, and yellow) to create complex hues. We'll apply the grisaille technique (p.11) early on to preserve the shade and shadow, resulting in a piece that is both vibrant and full of three-dimensional depth.

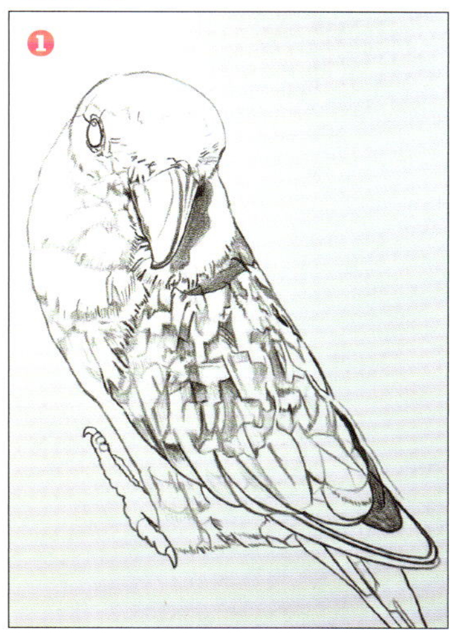

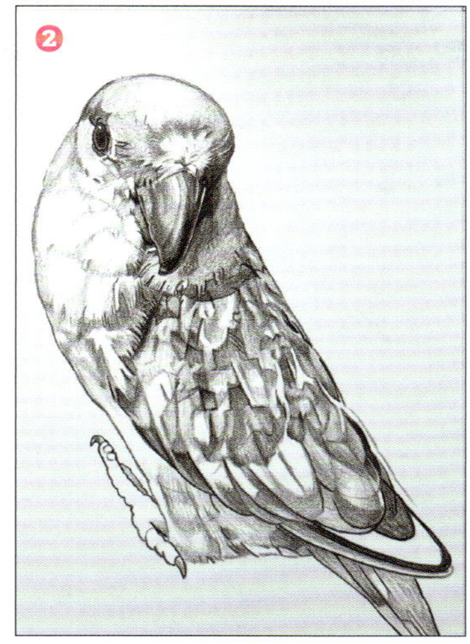

1 Apply the grisaille technique (see p.11). ❶ Start by laying down an undercoat in dark umber, taking into account the overall coloring of the lovebird and the direction of the light source. Begin by tracing the finer details, such as the feather patterns, to avoid losing your place during the coloring process. ❷ Then, gradually build up the shade and shadow. The key is to apply the color lightly without pressing too hard. Darken areas by layering the color multiple times.

■ Dark umber

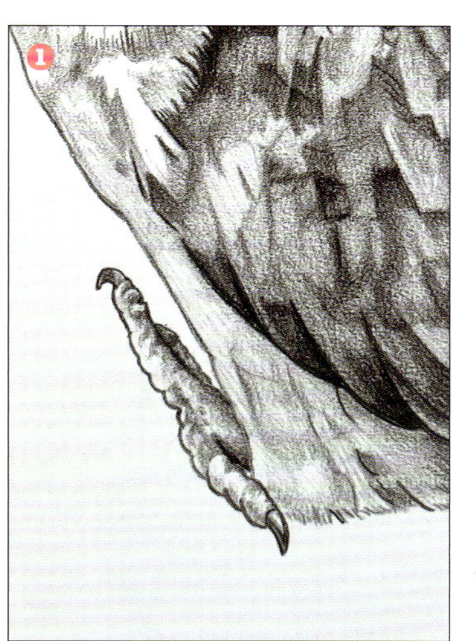

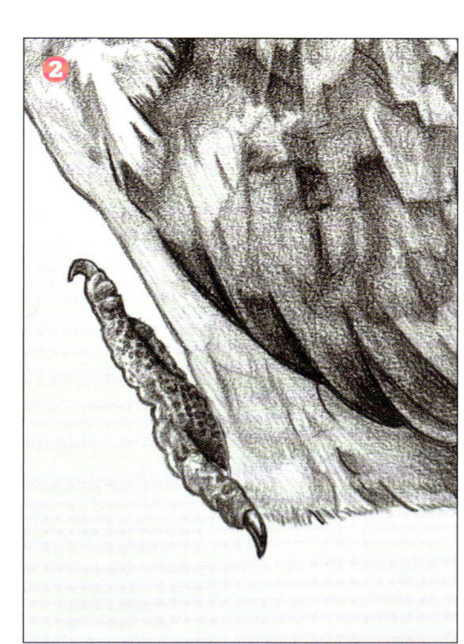

2 Color the legs. ❶ Use dark umber to roughly shade the entire area with broad shade and shadow. ❷ Then, use a sharpened dark umber pencil to draw in the scales.

■ Dark umber

Overall sense of shades and shadows

If you start by coloring the fine patterns first, you may end up lacking an overall sense of shades and shadows on the bird. Your top priority should be to thoroughly apply shades and shadows across the whole bird. The undercoat is complete once the overall shading and shadowing outstrips the shading and shadowing of fine patterns.

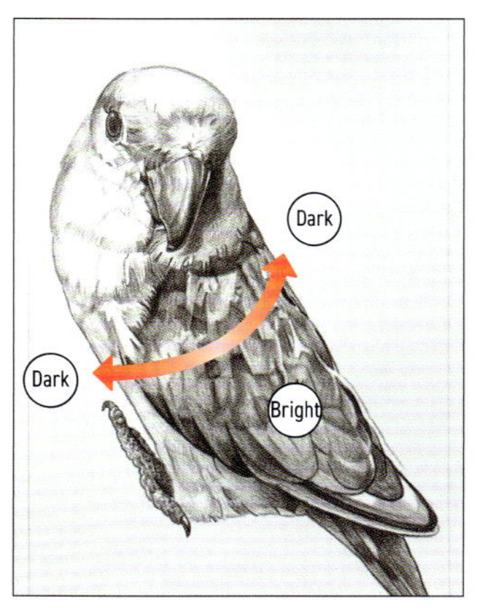

Blending the three primary colors

By blending red, blue, and yellow, you can achieve a wide range of colors. For example, mixing yellow and blue creates green, and by adjusting the balance between them, you can shift the result toward blue-green or yellow-green. Mixing all three colors in equal strength produces a color close to black or brown. Try testing your blends on a separate sheet before applying them to your final paper.

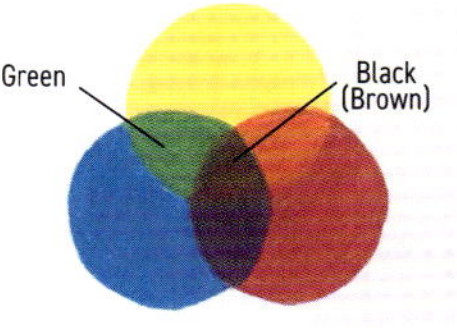

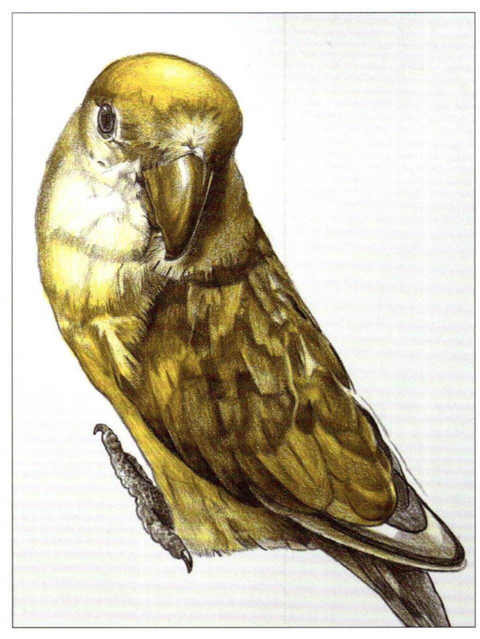

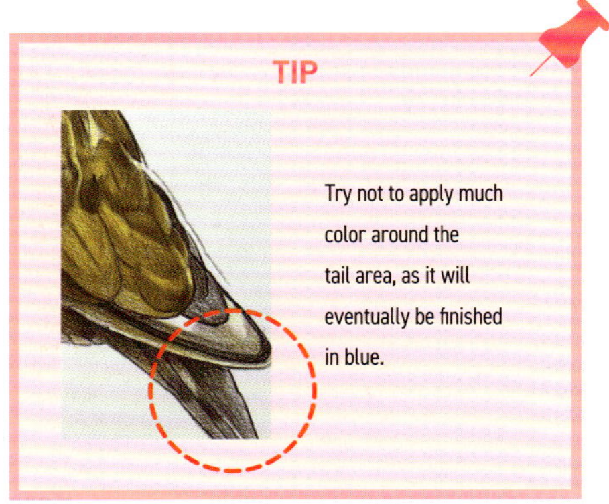

3 Start by applying canary yellow, since it covers the largest area. All coloring should be done with light layers, but it's a good idea to apply slightly more pressure in the darker shaded areas. Focus on coloring the areas where yellow is the most prominent.

▭ Canary yellow

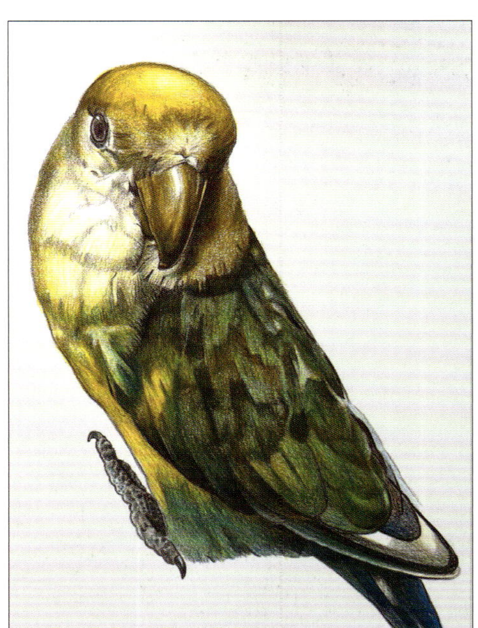

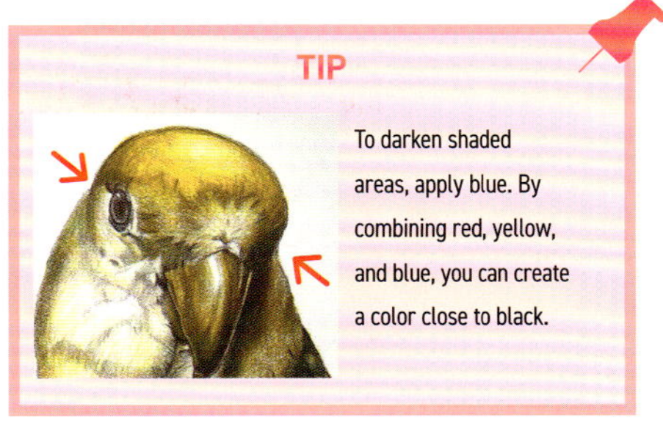

4 Layer true blue over the previous colors, blending mainly in the areas from the back to the tail where the true blue tones are strongest.

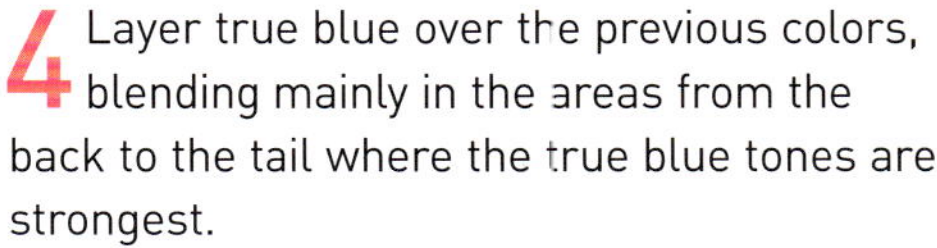
▭ True blue

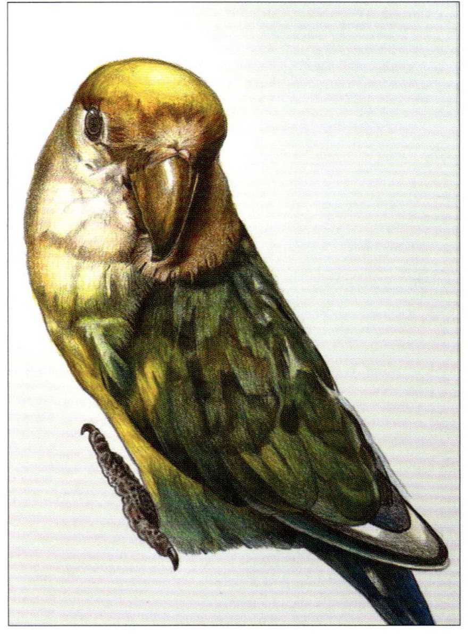

5 Finally, apply a layer of poppy red to finish the first stage of coloring.

▭ Poppy red

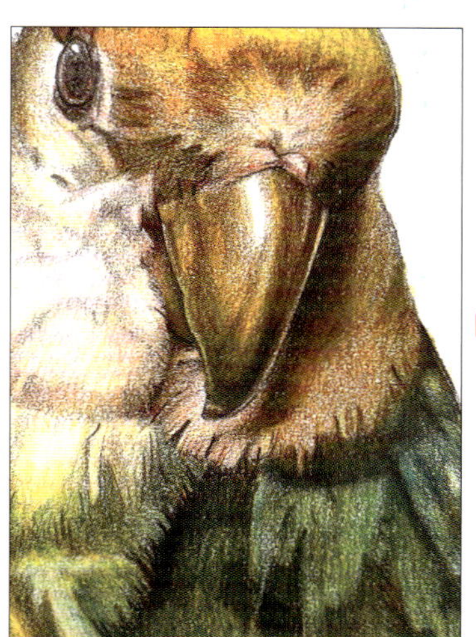 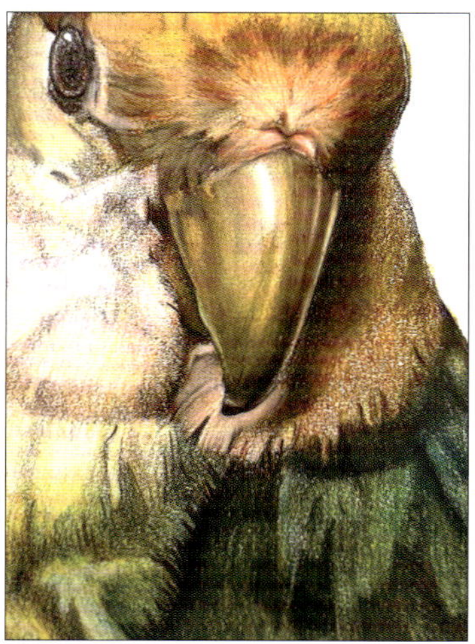

6 Firmly go over all the colors applied so far to create a burnished finish. Use white for areas you want to brighten and soften. For example, while the beak is mostly canary yellow overall, use more white near the highlight, and more dark umber or true blue toward the tip where it falls into shadow. Adjust the colors you apply more heavily depending on each specific area.

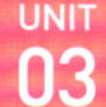

Burnishing (p.12): Up to **Step 4**, the colors have only been applied lightly, so the texture of the paper is still visible, giving the surface an overall rough appearance. To fix this, press firmly to layer and blend the colors from above, creating a smooth, even sheen across the surface.

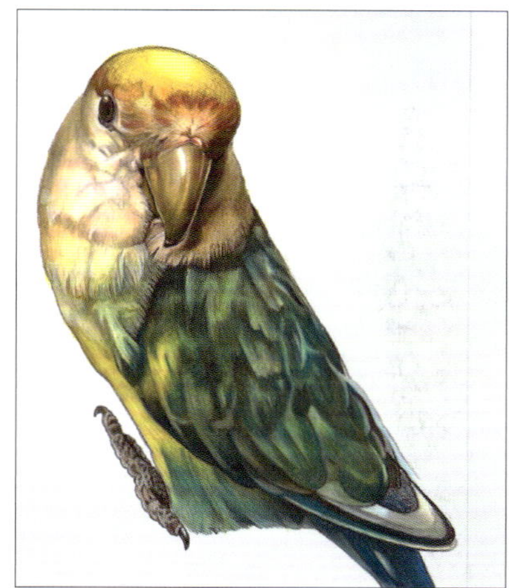

7 Following the same method as in **Step 6**, burnish the entire surface. After that, refine the details of each part.

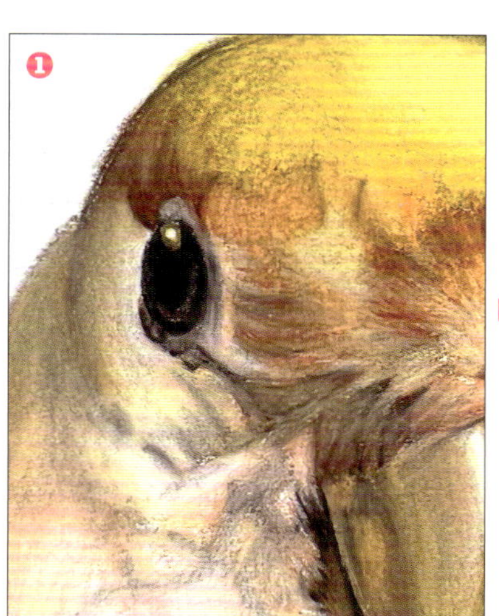
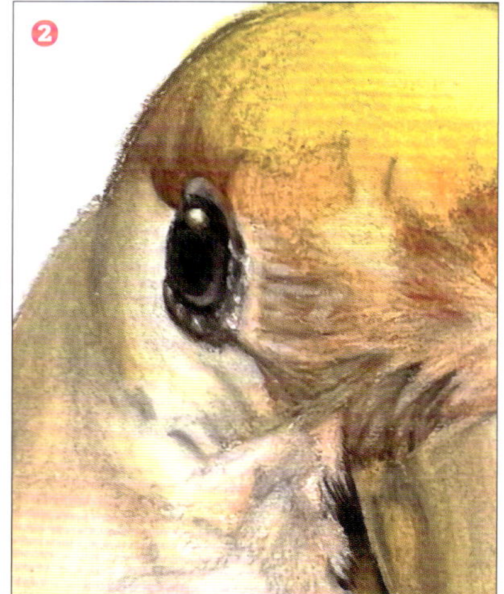

8 Color the eye. ❶ Fill in the pupil with black, and surround the highlight with canary yellow to create a natural light effect.
❷ Add shading to the eyelid around the eye using a sharpened pencil. For the bright areas, use a design knife to scrape the surface and create highlights.

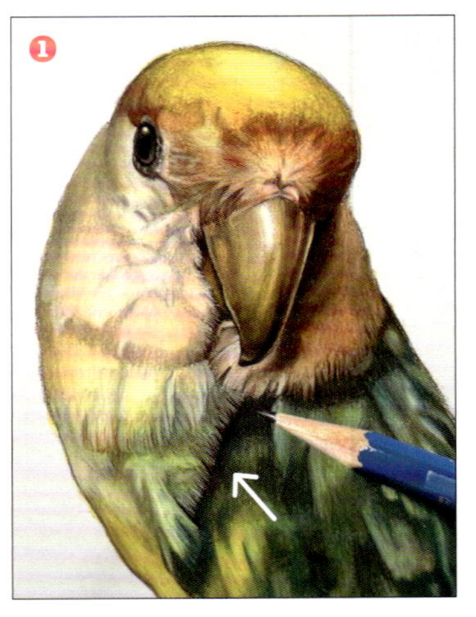

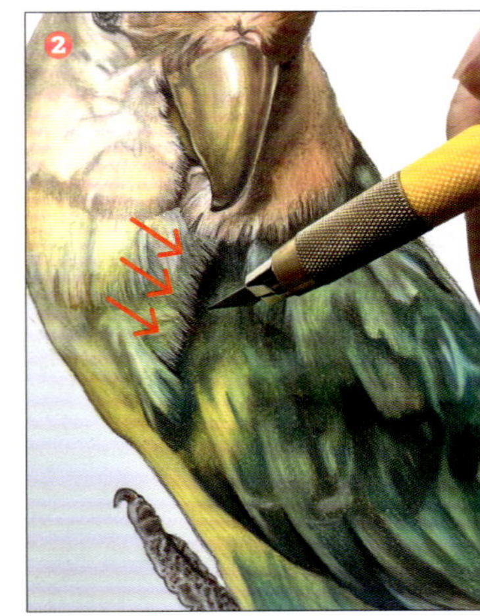

9 Color the neck area. **❶** Since the feathers here stand out more than in other areas, use a sharpened pencil to add shadow. Start from the darker areas and draw quick, light strokes, easing up the pressure as you go. **❷** For the feather tips, lightly use a design knife to scrape the surface. This time, draw gentle lines from the lighter areas toward the shadows.

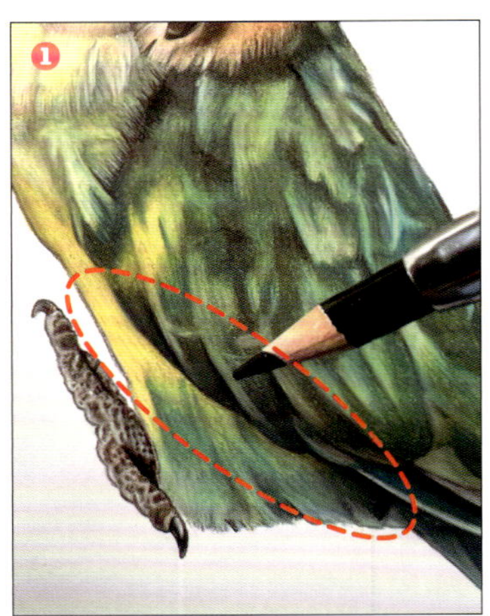

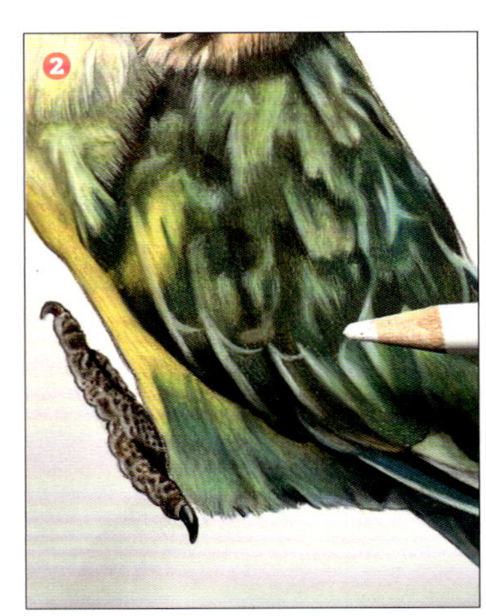

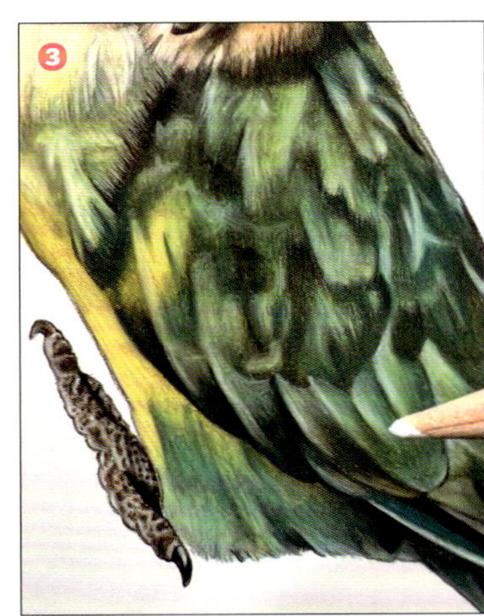

10 Color the wing. **❶** Since the divisions between each feather are clearly defined, use black to add shade and make the edges stand out. **❷** In the bright areas, use soft white (as a final layer) to draw in fine lines. **❸** Then, use regular white to blend and spread the color, creating broader surfaces.

■ Black ☐ Soft white ☐ White

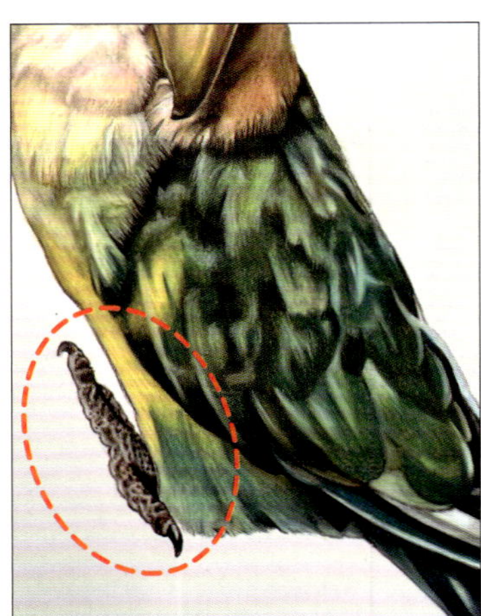

11 For the legs, use black to color the shade between the toes and around the claws.

■ Black

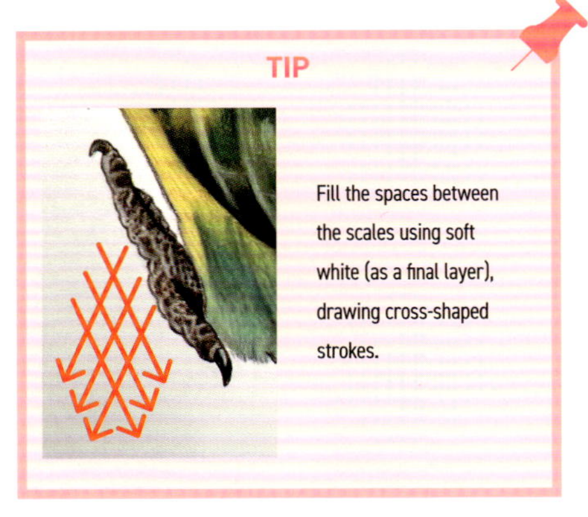

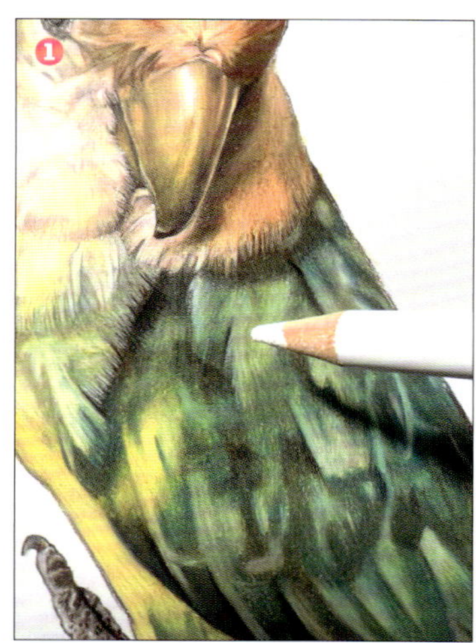
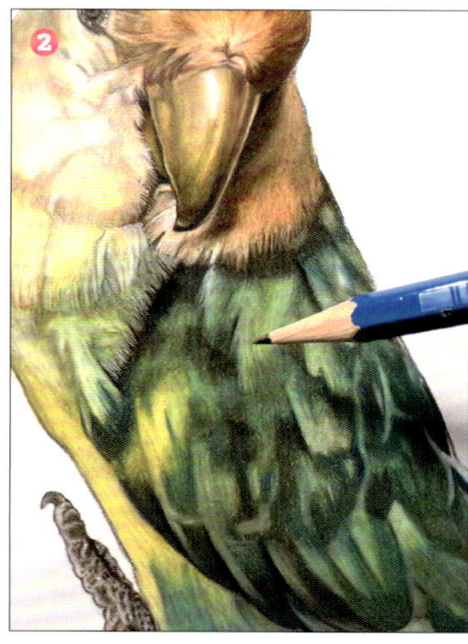

12 ❶ For the lighter areas of the feathers, quickly layer soft white (as a final layer) with light strokes. ❷ For the fine feathers within the shaded areas, use a sharpened pencil to draw thin, faint lines.

Soft white

COMPLETE

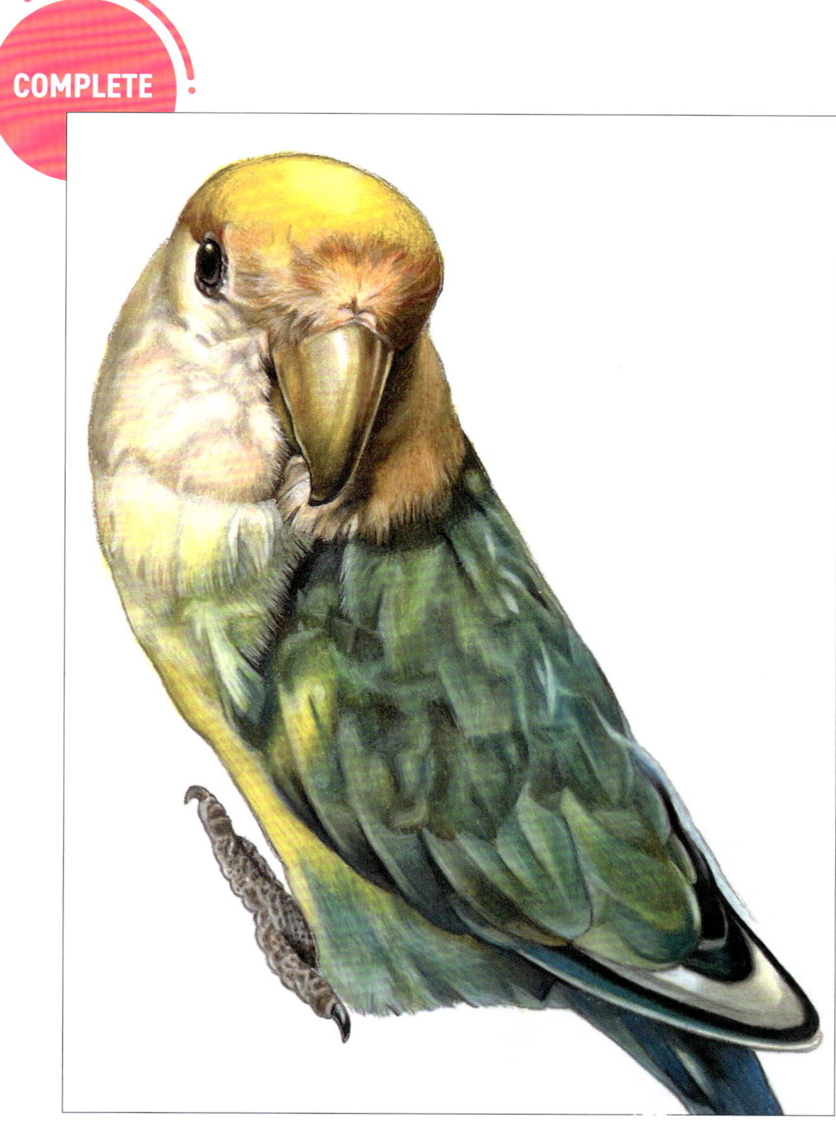

Draw a Labrador Retriever

Colored pencils: Prismacolor
Paper: Smooth White Drawing Paper
Drawn by Ishikawa @ Iroenpitsu

Coloring Key Points

1. You can create a rich and natural-looking coat by being mindful of the fur's length and layering color along the direction of the hair growth (p.15).

2. You can convey the softness of the fur by applying a base layer of white or cream.

Colors Used

▬ PC943 Burnt Ochre		▬ PC914 Cream	
▬ PC948 Sepia		▬ PC942 Yellow Ochre	
▬ PC935 Black		▬ PC941 Light Umber	
▬ PC1069 French Grey 20%		▬ PC946 Dark Brown	
▬ PC938 White		▬ PC997 Beige	

Preliminary Drawing

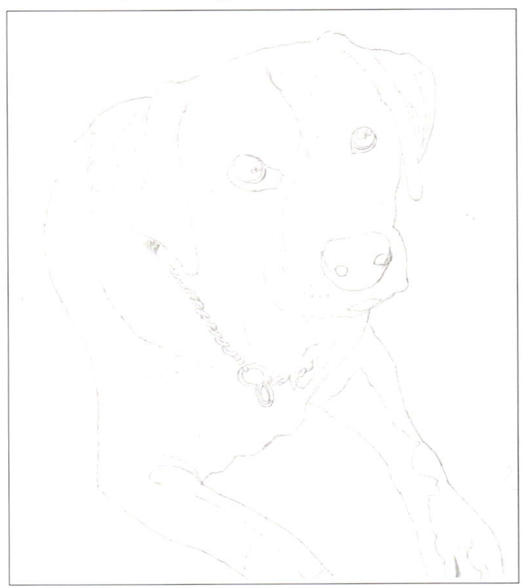

Since the fur color is often light, like cream or white, and tends to blend into the background, keep your sketch lines faint enough that they can be erased later. Draw lightly so the lines don't remain visible after coloring.

Reference Photo

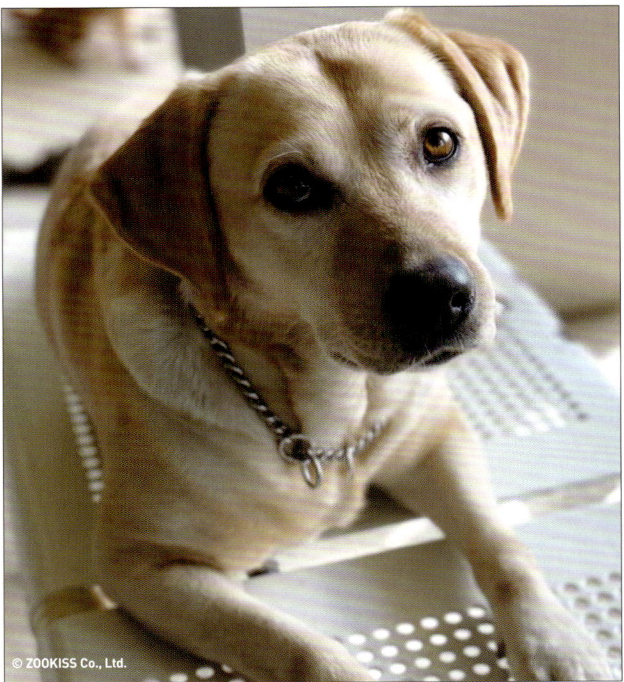

The subject is a Labrador retriever. The key points are how to express the different lengths of fur and how to capture the soft texture of the fur around the belly. Keep these two aspects in mind as you draw. As the lighting is not very strong, you should also make sure that the shading is subtle enough to convey the dog's facial expression.

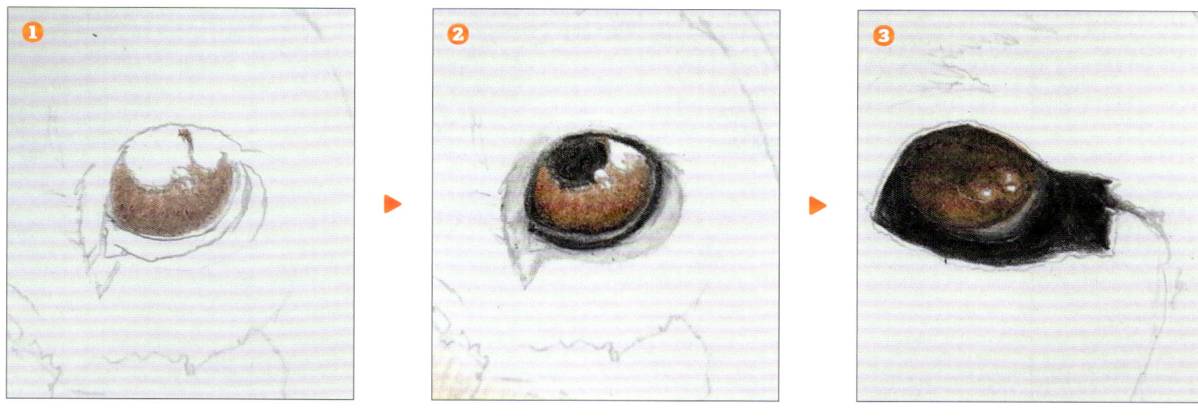

1 Draw the eyes. **❶** Layer burnt ochre followed by sepia, avoiding the highlight areas. **❷** Use black to fill in the rim and the pupil, and French grey 20% for the area around the eye. **❸** Color the other eye in the same way.

▰ Burnt ochre ▰ Sepia ▰ Black ☐ French grey 20%

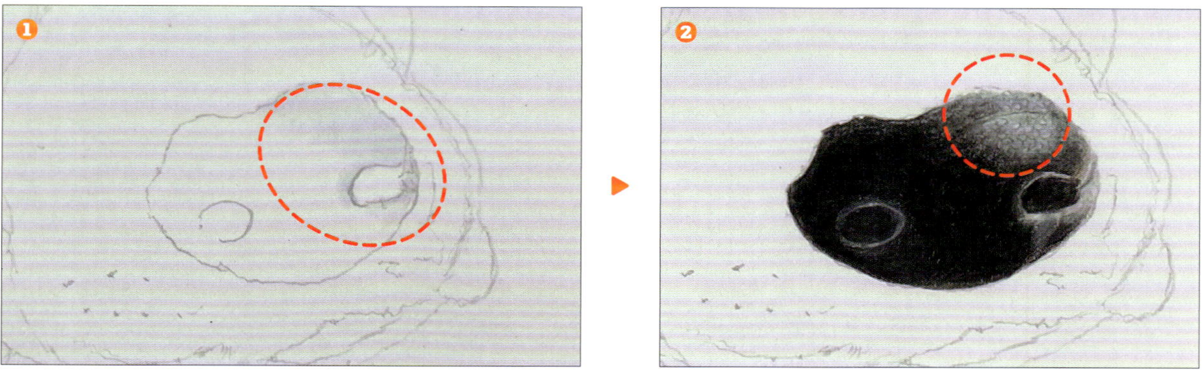

2 Color the nose. **❶** Fill in the red-circled area with white. **❷** Then, color the entire nose with black, and draw a small French grey 20% circle inside the red-circled area that you filled with white.

☐ White ▰ Black ☐ French grey 20%

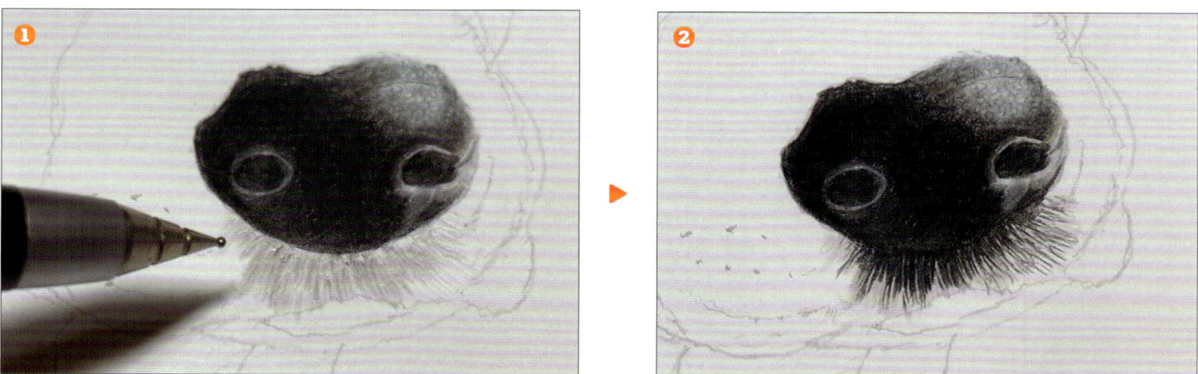

3 **❶** Shade under the nose with French grey 20%, following the direction of the hair, and use a stylus to draw straight lines over it. **❷** Then, apply a strong layer of black on top.

☐ French grey 20% ▰ Black

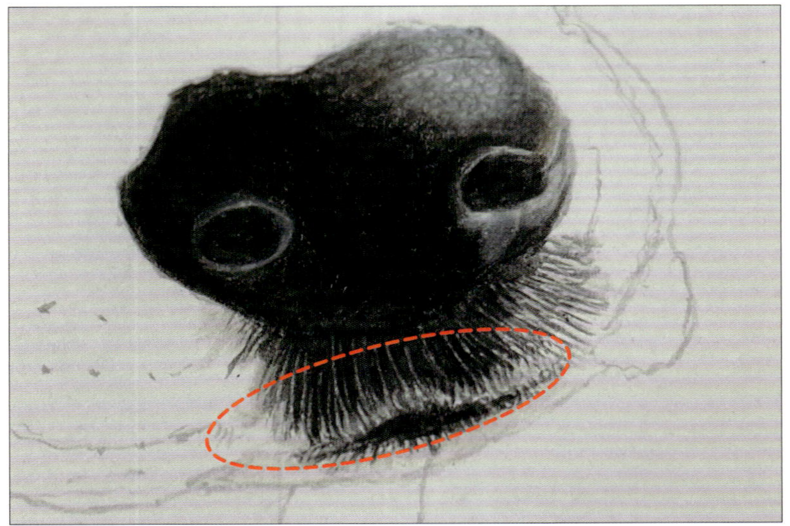

4 Color around the mouth in French grey 20% following the direction of the fur, draw straight lines over it with a stylus, and then color it in black.

▭ French grey 20%
▮ Black

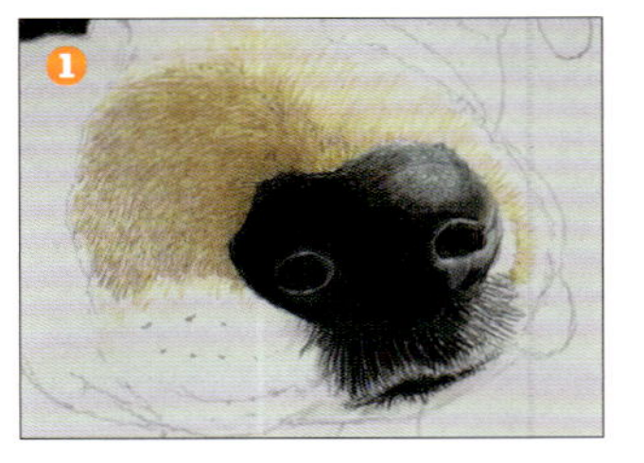 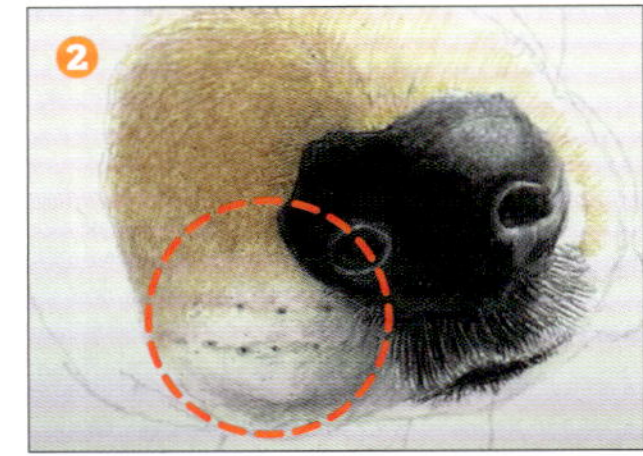

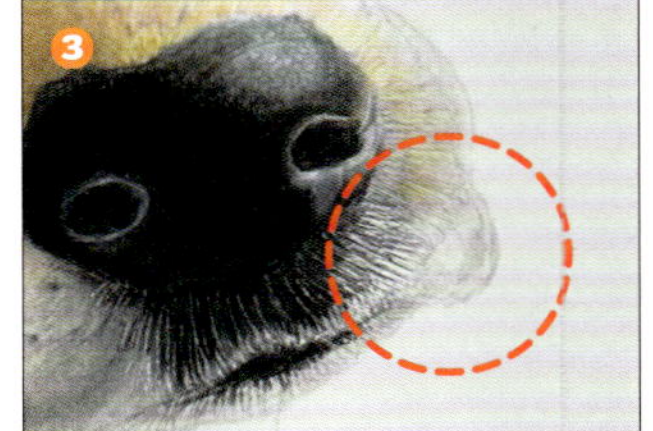 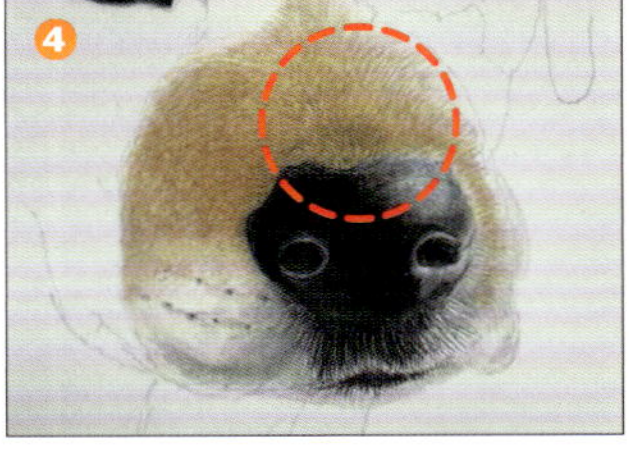

5 Color the muzzle. **1** Be mindful of the hair length and draw each strand individually, Heavily layer cream, yellow ochre, and light umber on the left side of the face as if you are drawing each strand of hair individually. Pay attention to the length of the hair. **2** Fill the entire red-circled area with cream, French grey 20%, and then black to create a sense of three-dimensionality. **3** Apply French grey 20%. **4** Apply dark brown following the direction of the fur.

▭ Cream ▭ Yellow ochre
▮ Light umber ▭ French grey 20%
▮ Black ▮ Dark brown

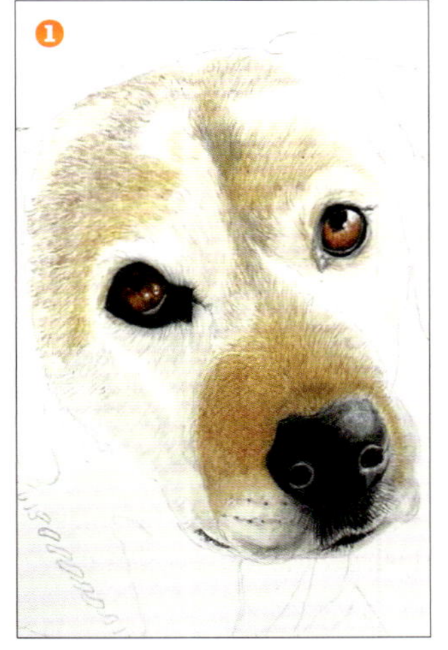 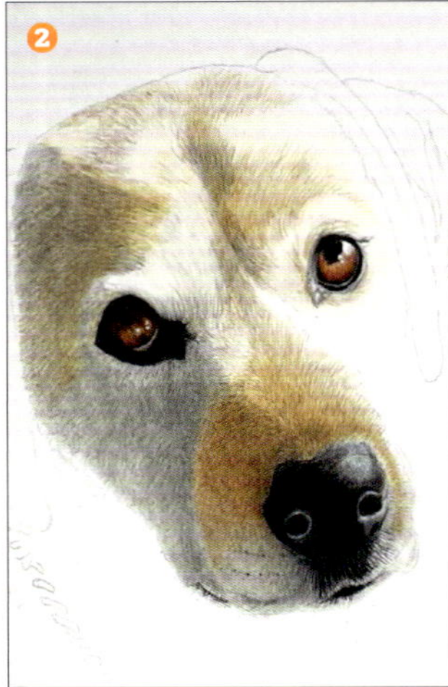

6 **1** Since the fur on the face has a lot of color variation, start by applying a light layer of cream across the entire area. Then, while checking the reference photo, use yellow ochre, dark brown, and French grey 20% to differentiate the tones. Be mindful of the direction and length of the fur as you draw. **2** Use a pencil to add broad shadows across the face.

▭ Cream ▭ Yellow ochre
▮ Dark brown ▭ French grey 20%

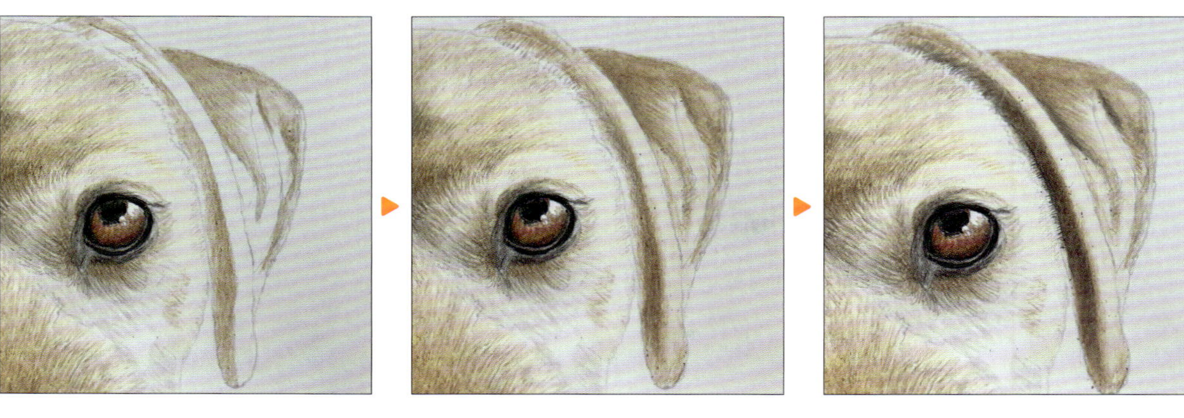

7 For the ears, first apply white over the entire area, then layer dark brown. After that, add beige and use black to deepen the shading. Follow the same steps for the other ear.

▢ White ▣ Dark brown ▢ Beige ▪ Black

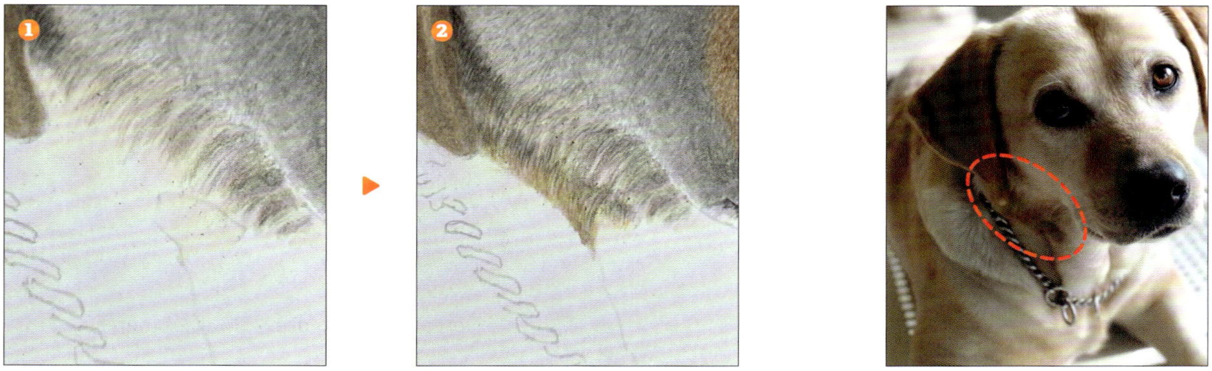

8 The fur around the lower part of the face near the ear (the red-circled area) is colored as follows. **1** Begin with a light layer of cream, then layer beige, sepia, French grey 20%, and black, in that order. The fur is long, so try to draw it in fine lines without obscuring the lower layers. **2** For the base, add yellow ochre to the cream layer that was applied in **Step 1**, and then proceed with the same layering method as in **1**.

▢ Cream ▢ Beige ▪ Sepia ▢ French grey 20% ▪ Black ▨ Yellow ochre

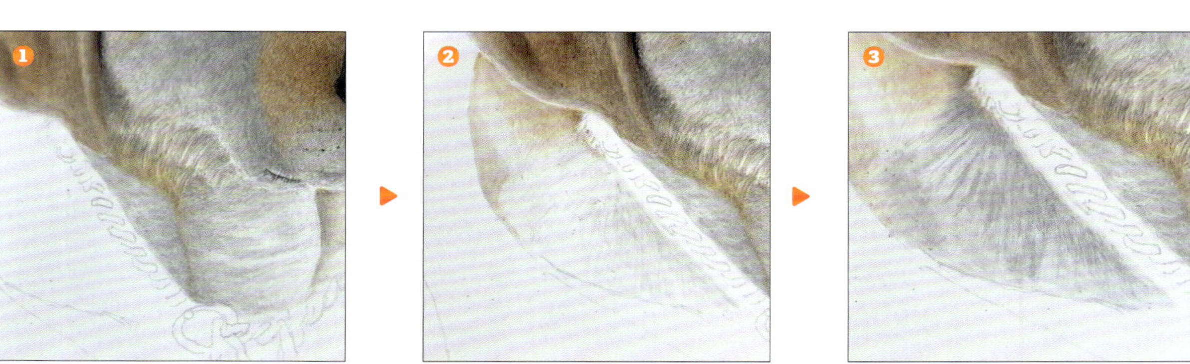

9 **1** For the neck, apply white first, then layer cream over it, and use black to create a sense of three-dimensionality. Keep the structure of the fur clumps in mind. **2** For the fur below the collar, layer white followed by French grey 20%, using the French grey 20% to depict the fur clumps. **3** Then, lightly draw the shadows of the fur clumps with black to add emphasis.

▢ White ▢ Cream ▪ Black ▢ French grey 20%

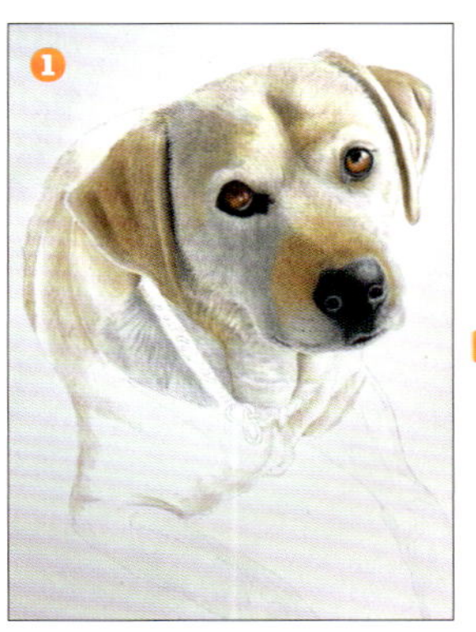 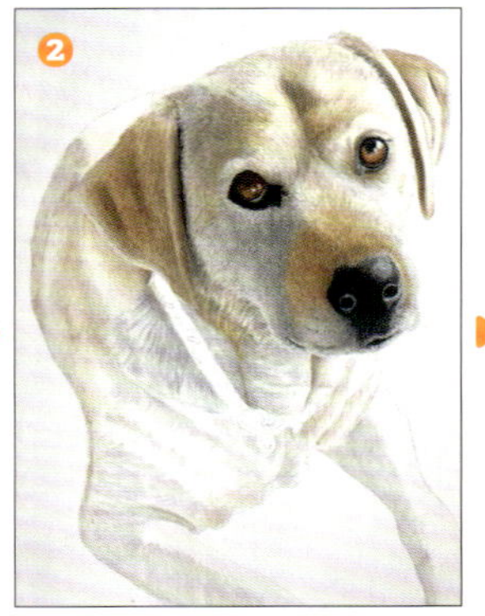 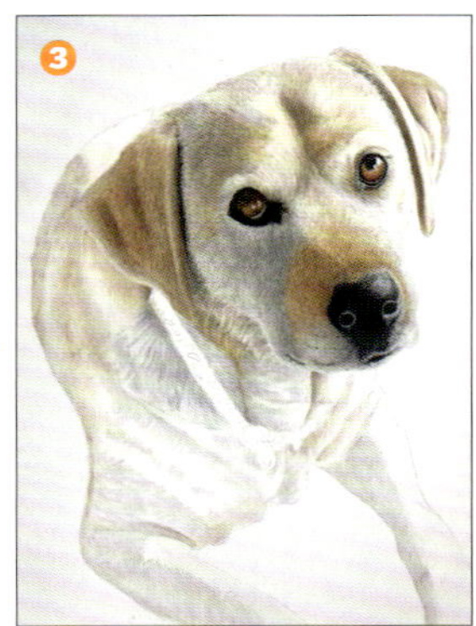

10 For the body, ❶ apply a uniform layer of white, then add light umber in certain areas to establish the overall color. ❷ Color the shaded areas with French grey 20%, following the direction of the fur. ❸ Continue adding shade with a pencil while gradually layering in more light umber.

☐ White
▬ Light umber
☐ French grey 20%

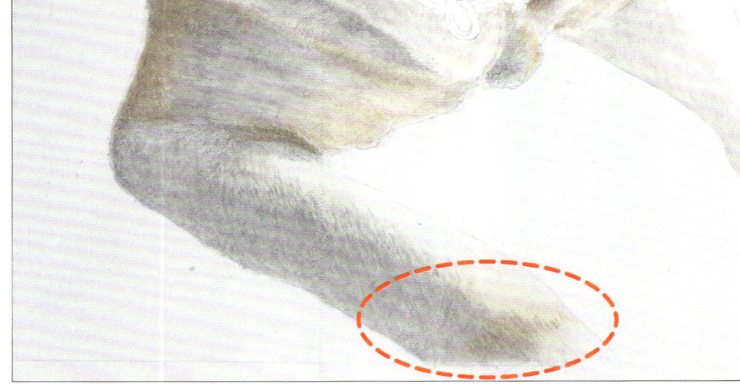

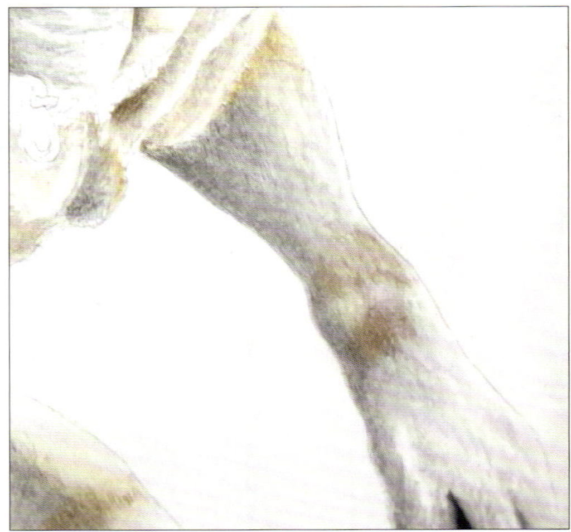

11 Add shadows to the right front leg using a pencil, keeping the direction of the fur in mind as you shade. Then, layer beige followed by dark brown to create the pattern. Use the same approach to color the pattern on the left front leg as well.

☐ Beige ▬ Dark brown

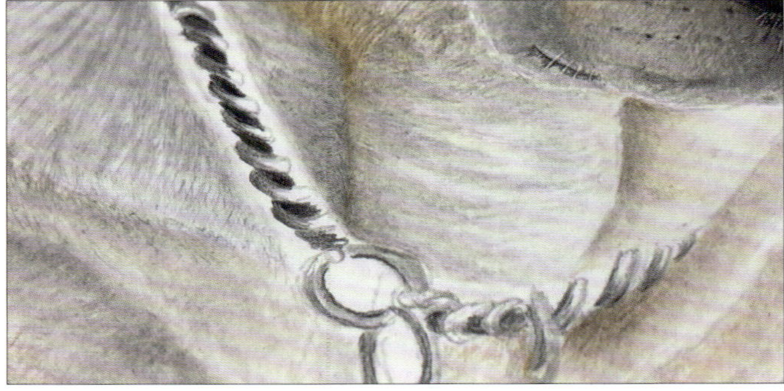

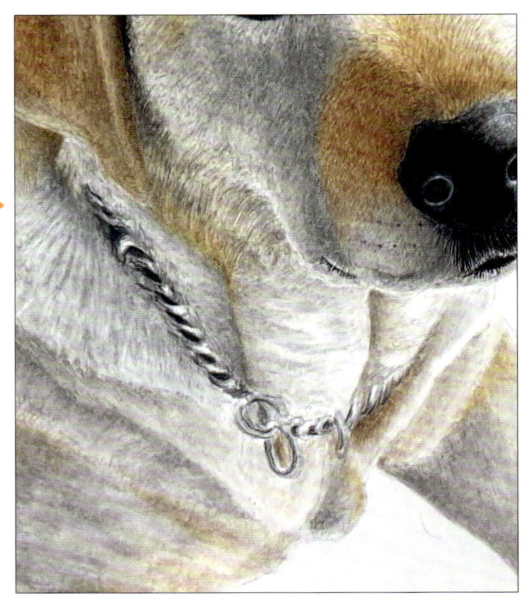

12 For the chain, first use a pencil and black to shade the chain and the gaps between the links, leaving the highlights untouched. Then, fill in the surrounding space with white and French grey 20% to match the nearby fur, and use the pencil to deepen the chain's shadows to enhance the three-dimensional effect.

▬ Black ☐ White ☐ French grey 20%

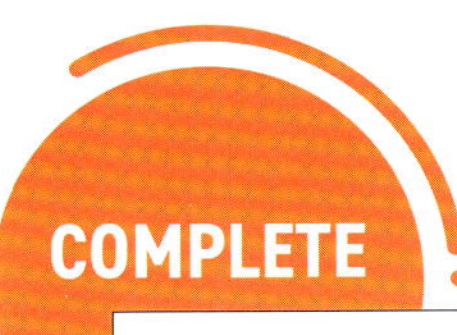

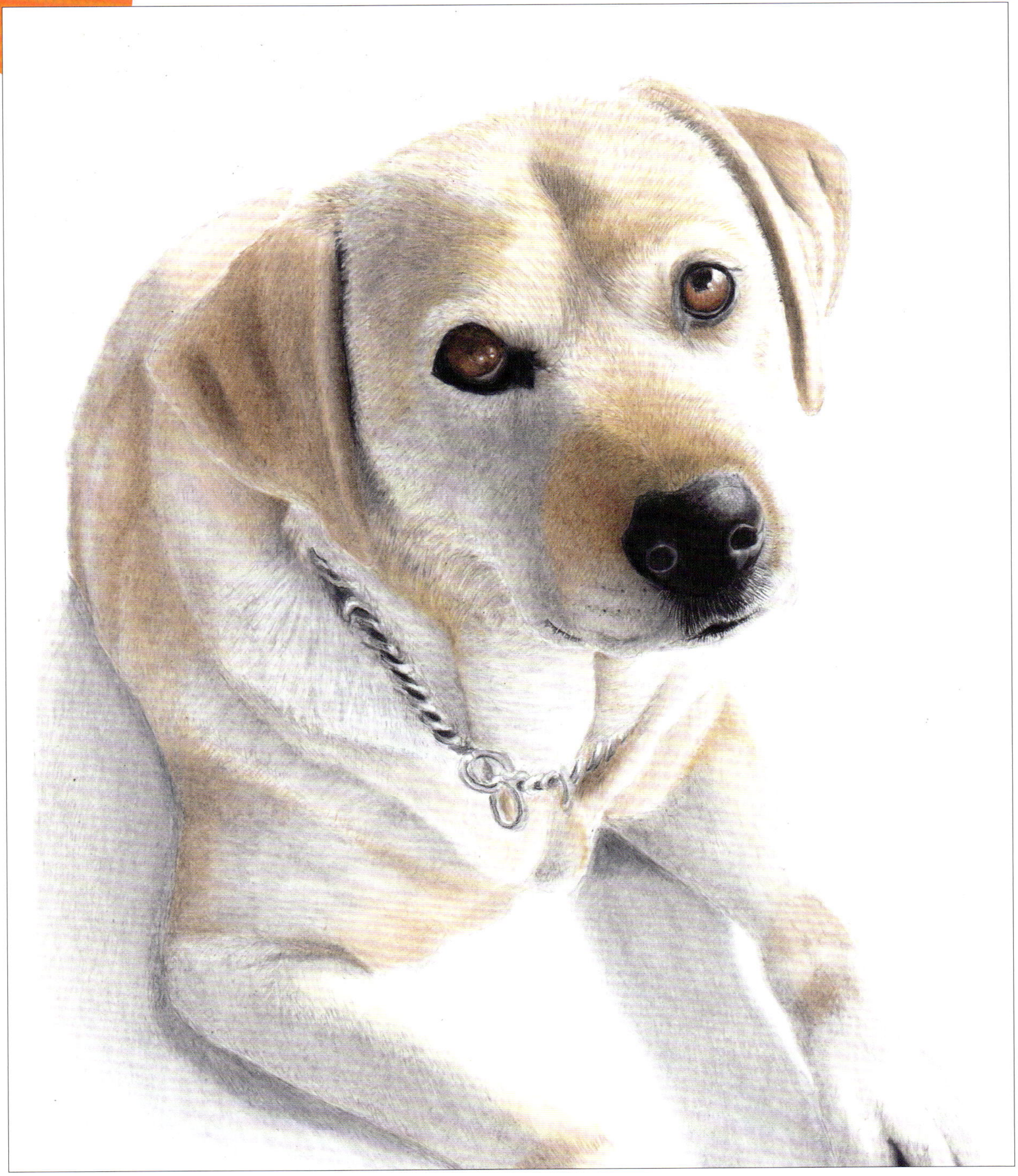

Add the shadows cast by the dog on the ground with French grey 20% and black to complete the drawing.

French grey 20% Black

Draw a Scarab Beetle

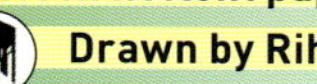

Coloring Key Points

1. Be aware of the shade and shadow created by the light source (p.11).

2. Create a glossy effect by emphasizing contrasts and using highly saturated colors for the boundaries between light and dark areas (p.12).

Colors Used

- ☐ PC914 Cream
- ▉ PC913 Spring Green
- ▉ PC909 Grass Green
- ▉ PC901 Indigo Blue
- ▉ PC930 Magenta
- ▉ PC926 Carmine Red
- ▉ PC918 Orange
- ▉ PC940 Sand
- ☐ PC938 White
- ▉ PC935 Black
- ▉ PC916 Canary Yellow

Preliminary Drawing

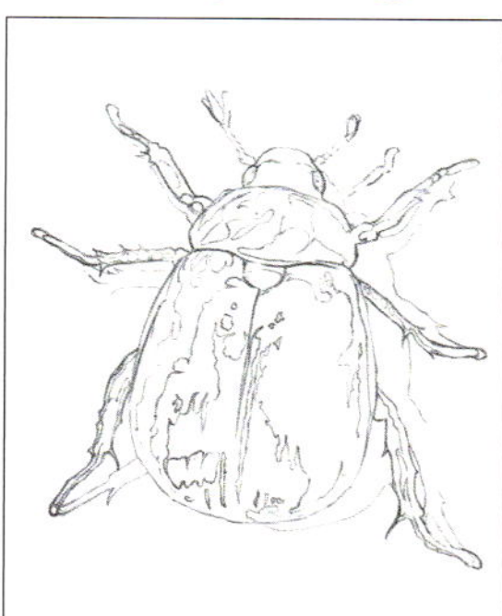

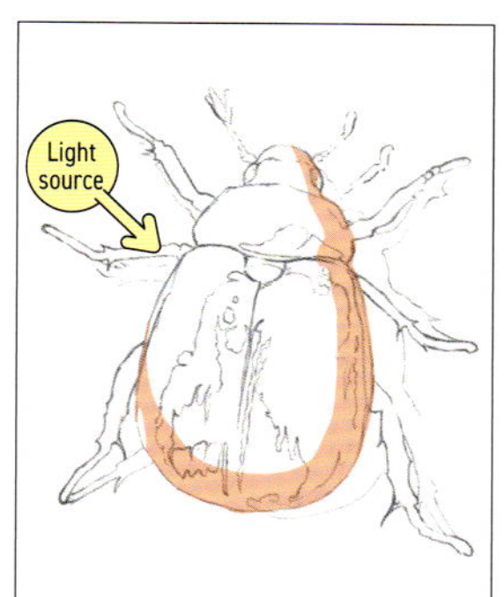

As there's no distinct light source in the reference photo, this time we'll draw as if light were shining on the beetle from above. The light is coming from the upper left of the image, so the shade and shadow will generally appear in the red areas shown in the diagram.

Reference Photo

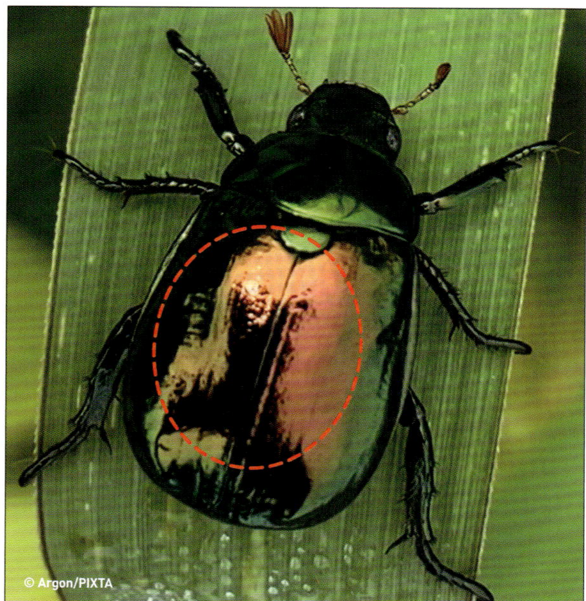

The theme for this drawing is an awareness of three-dimensionality. As you draw, think about the shape of the beetle and where the shade and shadow would fall when light hits it. Consider how to exaggerate those areas to enhance depth. While the glossy surface of the back and legs may catch your attention, be sure to observe the subtle tonal variations as well. The red-circled area in the reference photo is the most protrusive part, so use black or similar colors to create strong contrast there.

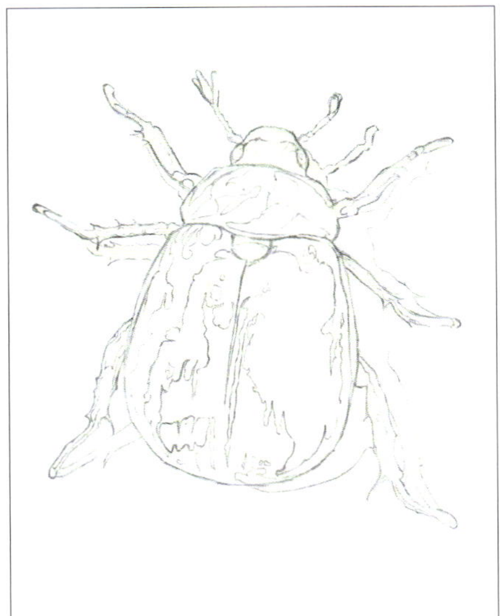

1 Fill in everything except the highlights with cream. Hold the pencil at a low angle and apply the color smoothly to avoid unevenness.

☐ Cream

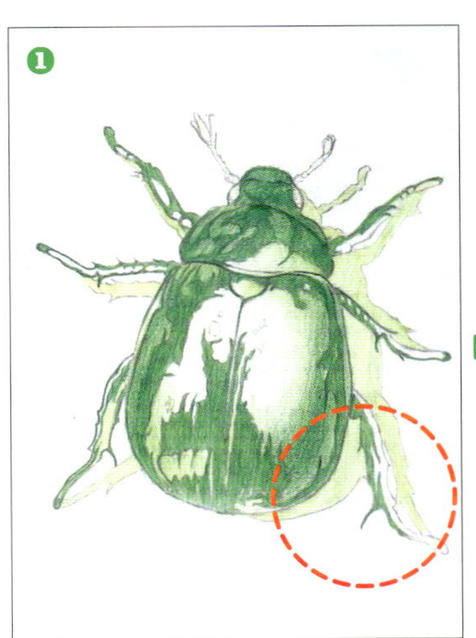

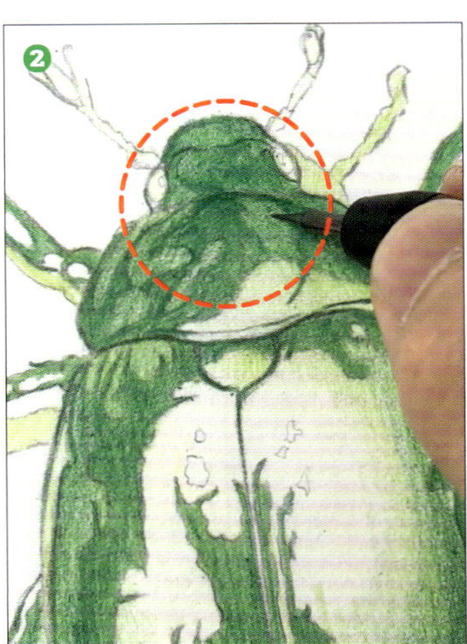

2 ❶ Use spring green and grass green to add tonal variations while being mindful of the gloss and shades and shadows. Be careful to keep the application smooth and even. Increase the contrast in the red-circled area. **❷** Using a stylus, indent the paper around the red-circled area near the head. Hold the stylus slightly upright and tap gently. Be careful not to tap the same spot too many times.

▮ Spring green   ▮ Grass green

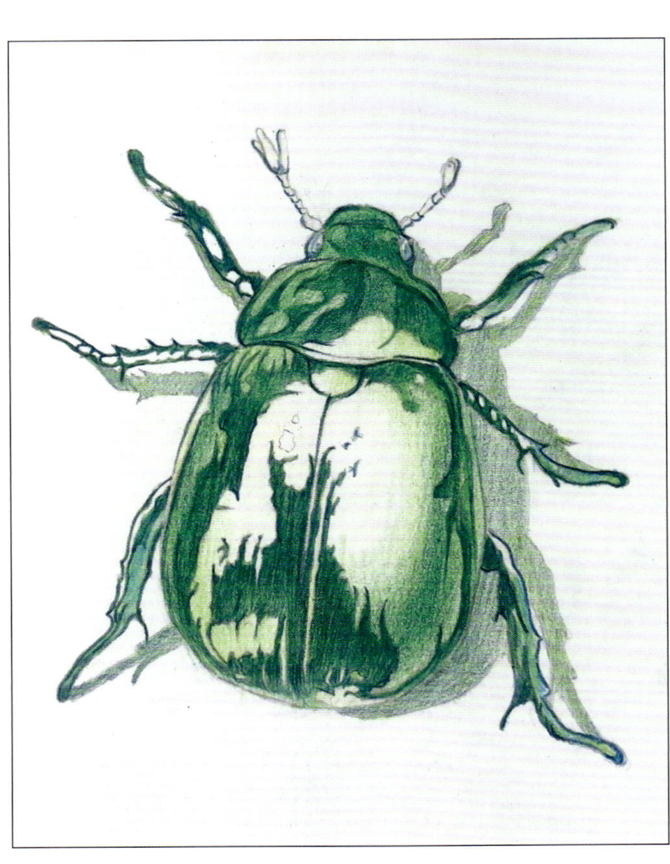

3 While looking at the reference photo, apply indigo blue and darken the dark areas. Add the color to the shadows cast on the ground as well.

▮ Indigo blue

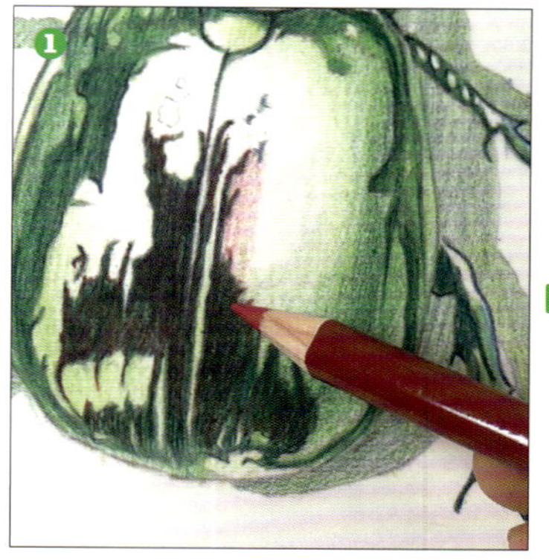 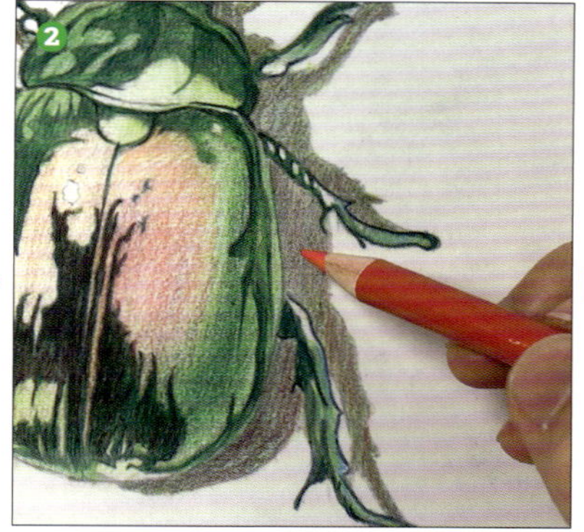 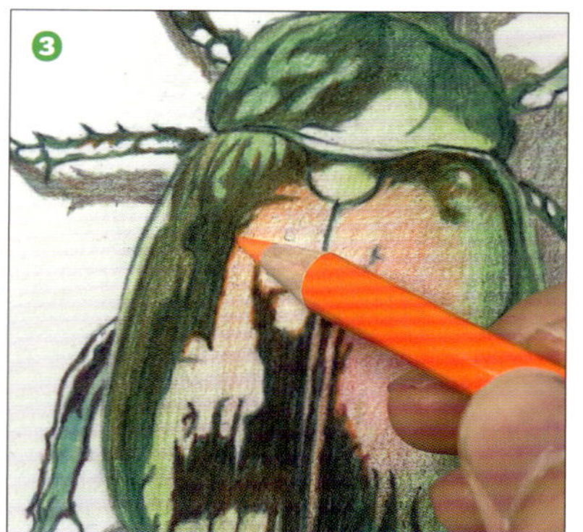

4 **①** Apply magenta. **②** Layer carmine red over the back and the shadows cast on the ground. **③** Apply orange along the border between the light and dark areas. Increasing the saturation at the boundary between light and dark helps create a natural-looking glossy effect.

▬ Magenta ▬ Carmine red ▬ Orange

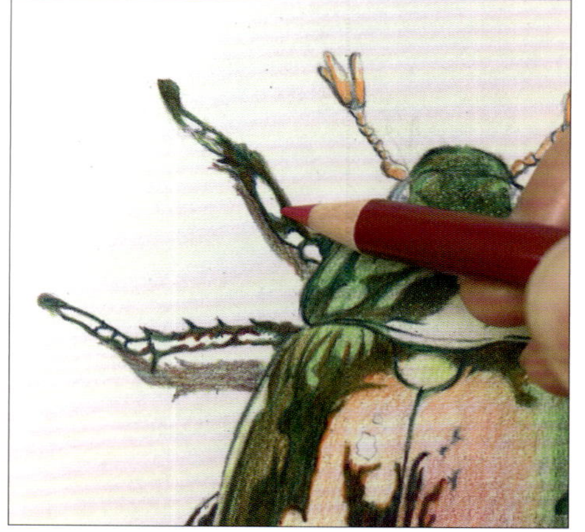

5 Apply magenta to the legs to increase the saturation.

▬ Magenta

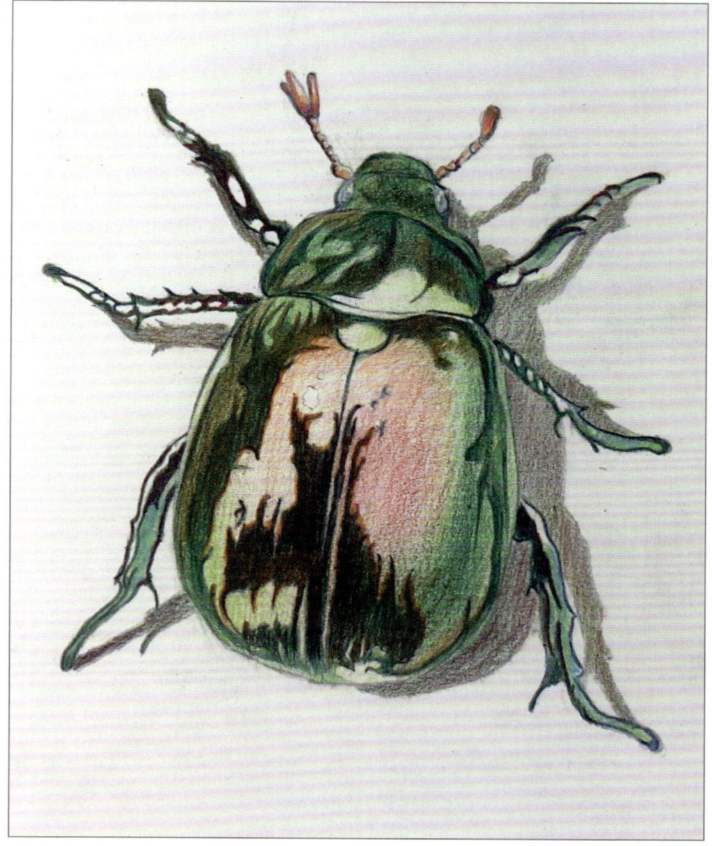

This is what the overall drawing looks like now.

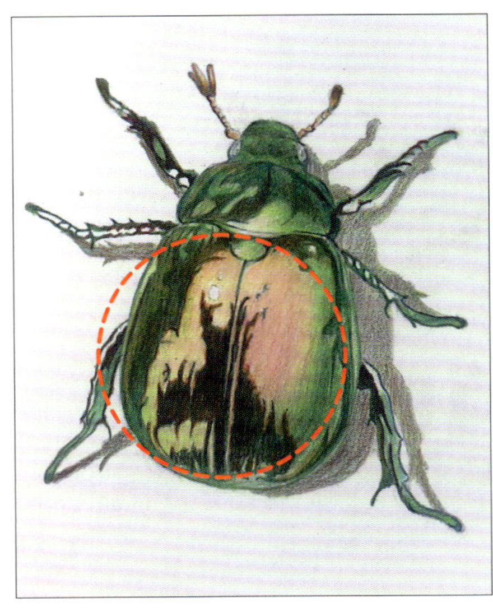

6 Burnish the highlighted areas with the sand color, especially around the red-circled section (p.12). After that, use grass green and spring green to reapply tone across the entire surface.

▭ Sand ▬ Grass green ▭ Spring green

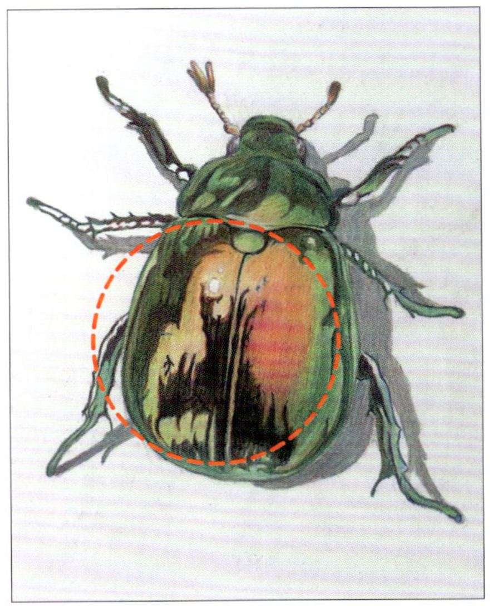

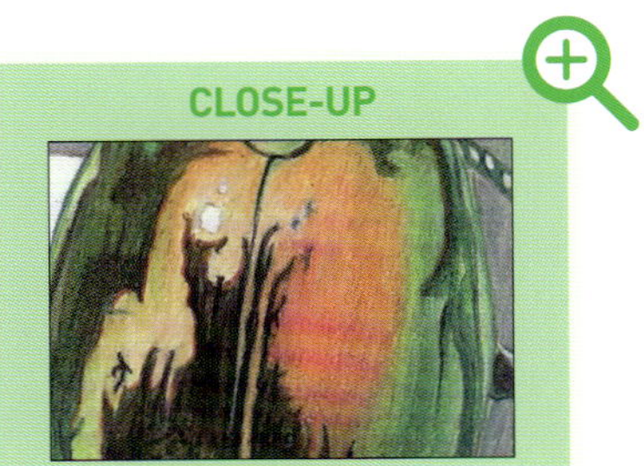

7 Apply carmine red and orange, focusing on the red-circled areas, to increase the chroma. Try adding these colors to areas beyond the red circle as well; this can give the grass green more depth and create the appearance of light interacting across the surface. Use white to burnish the highlight areas and enhance brightness. Also burnish the shadows on the ground with white.

▬ Carmine red ▬ Orange ▭ White

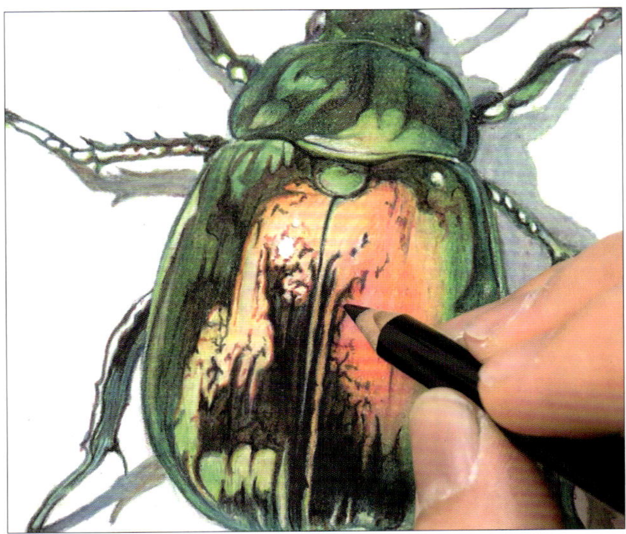

8 Use magenta and black to depict the ridges and grooves on the back that couldn't be fully captured in the preliminary drawing. At the boundary between the light and dark areas, use carmine red and orange to increase the chroma and create a strong accent.

▬ Magenta ▬ Black ▬ Carmine red
▬ Orange

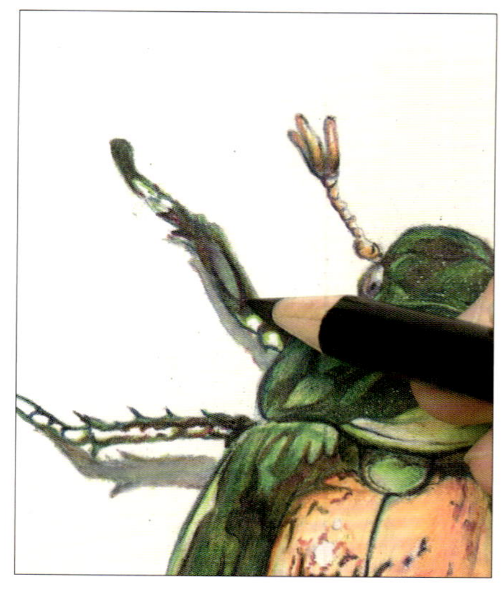

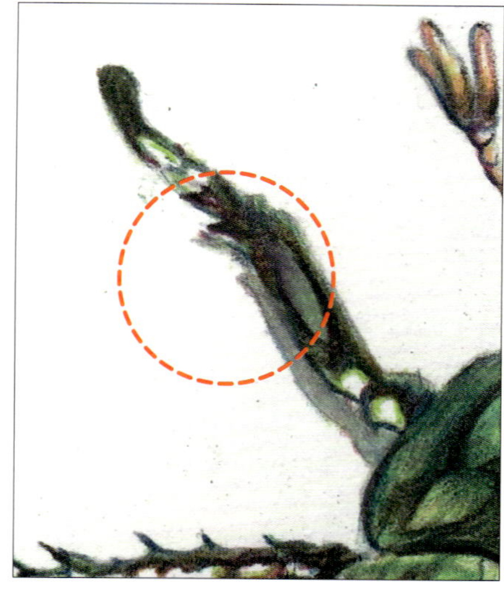

9 Emphasize the center of the legs with black. This helps convey a sense of three-dimensionality.

■ Black

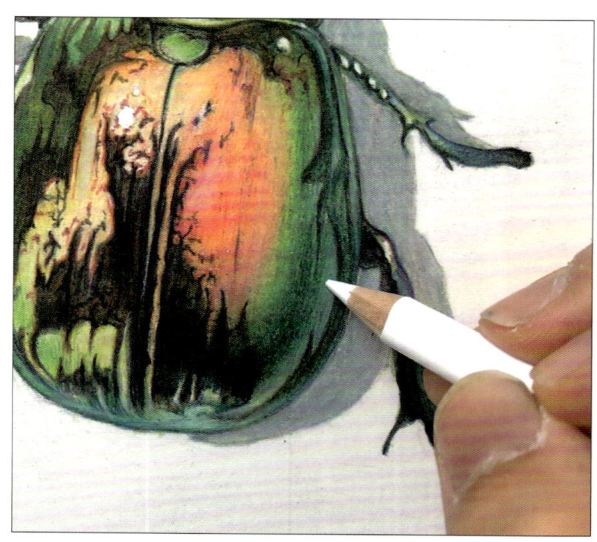

10 Apply white to depict reflected light within the shaded and shadowed areas. As we want a slightly slick texture in these areas, first test with a layer of white, then layer indigo blue or spring green on top. After that, apply another layer of white over everything—this creates a rich, low-saturation reflected light effect.

☐ White   ■ Indigo blue   ▨ Spring green

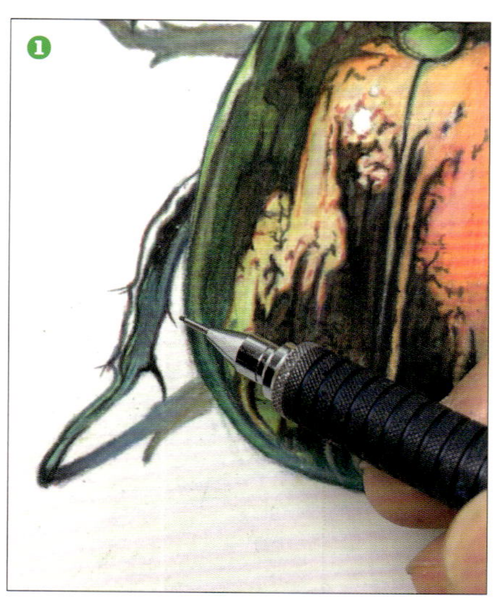

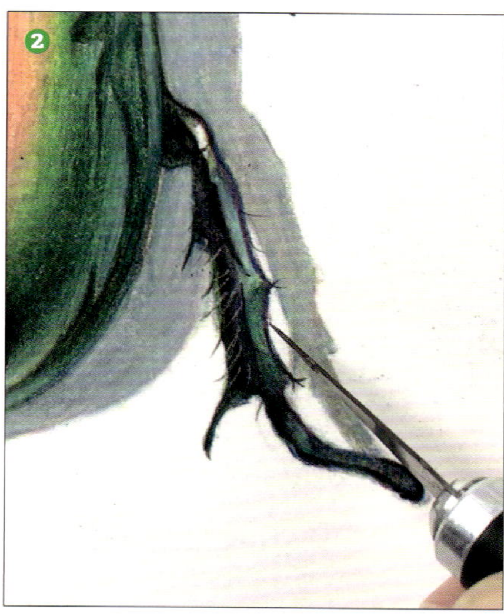

11 ① Use a mechanical pencil to draw the hairs on the legs. ② Then use a design knife to gently scrape the surface and express the leg hairs. You can also use the knife to emphasize the grooves on the back.

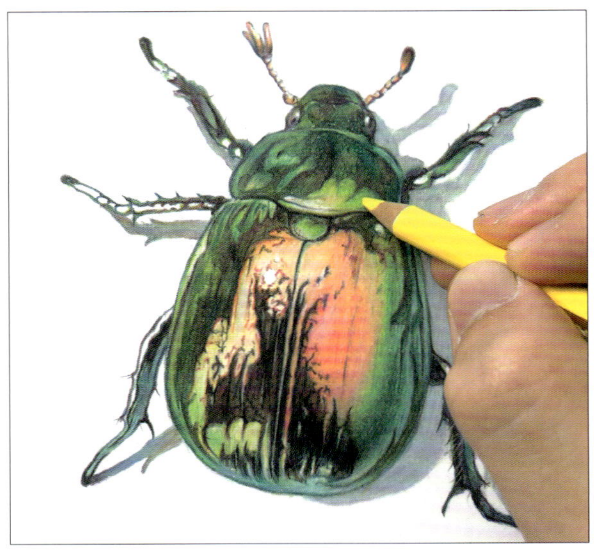

12 Finally, add a touch of canary yellow, focusing on the boundaries between light and dark. Take a step back and look at the whole piece. If anything stands out or feels off, make adjustments as needed. In this case, the color of the shadows on the ground felt a bit flat, so I added grass green, indigo blue, and canary yellow to enrich them.

▢ Canary yellow   ▩ Grass green
▬ Indigo blue

COMPLETE

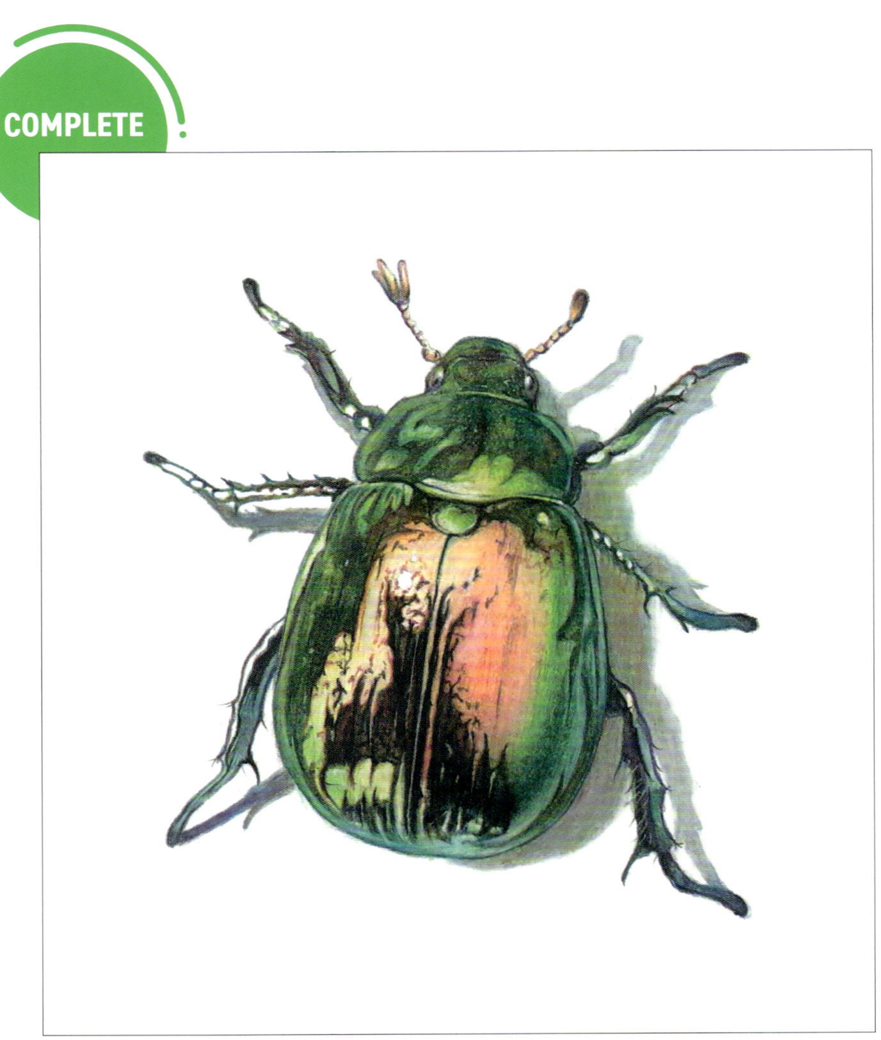

Draw a Penguin

Coloring Key Points

1. Simplify the subject into basic shapes to better understand and express its overall three-dimensionality (p.11).

2. Depict the feathers using colored-pencil strokes (p.15).

Colors Used

- PC1074 French Grey 70%
- PC942 Yellow Ochre
- PC916 Canary Yellow
- PC928 Blush Pink
- PC935 Black
- PC941 Light Umber
- PC938 White
- PC1006 Parrot Green
- PC932 Violet

Preliminary Drawing

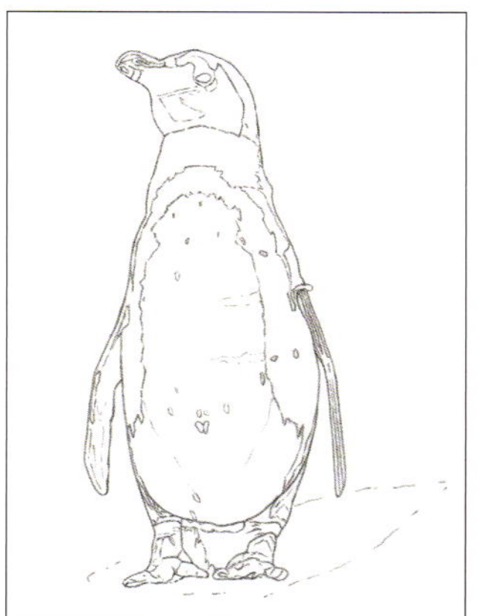

Pay close attention to the size of the head and body when you create the preliminary drawing. Since the fin on the right side (from the viewer's perspective) was hidden, I drew it based on my own imagination.

Reference Photo

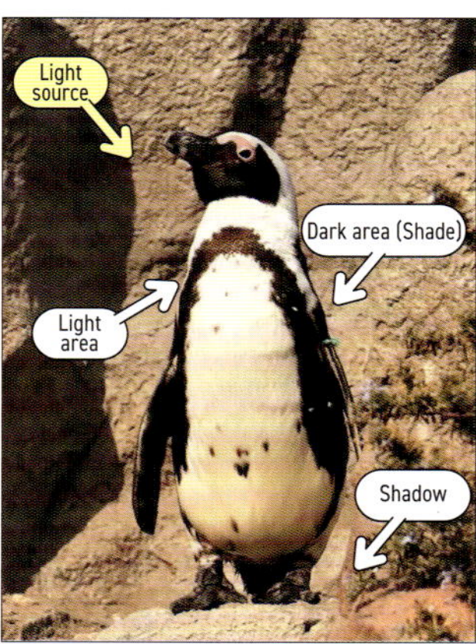

The light is coming from diagonally above and to the left, so the left side of the penguin is bright and the right side is dark.

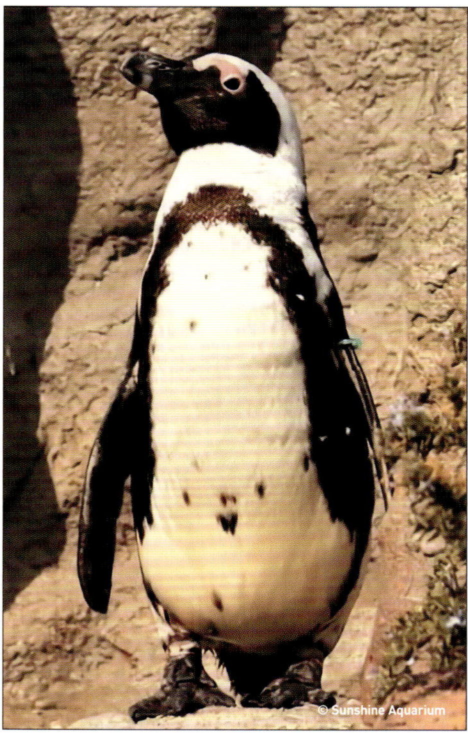

The theme for this drawing is depicting feathers and three-dimensionality. Feathers will be rendered using only colored-pencil strokes, without relying on tools like a stylus. Also, rather than getting caught up in the details, try to stay focused on the overall sense of form and volume as you draw.

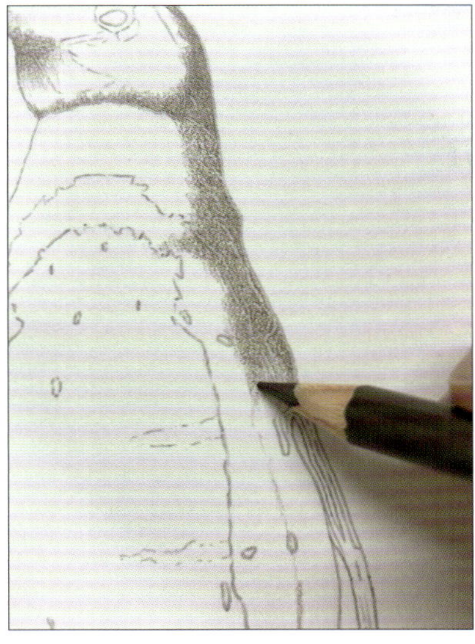

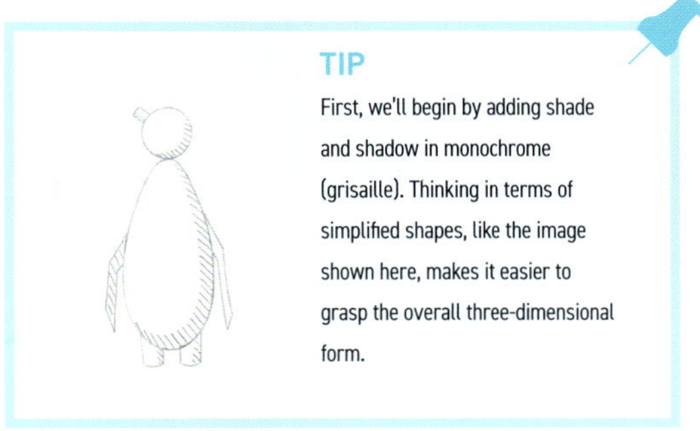

TIP

First, we'll begin by adding shade and shadow in monochrome (grisaille). Thinking in terms of simplified shapes, like the image shown here, makes it easier to grasp the overall three-dimensional form.

1 Use French grey 70% to add shade and shadow. It's important to clearly separate the light and dark areas at the beginning, so apply slightly stronger pressure when coloring in the dark areas (the area with diagonal lines in the **TIP** diagram).

▬ French grey 70%

**UNIT
06**

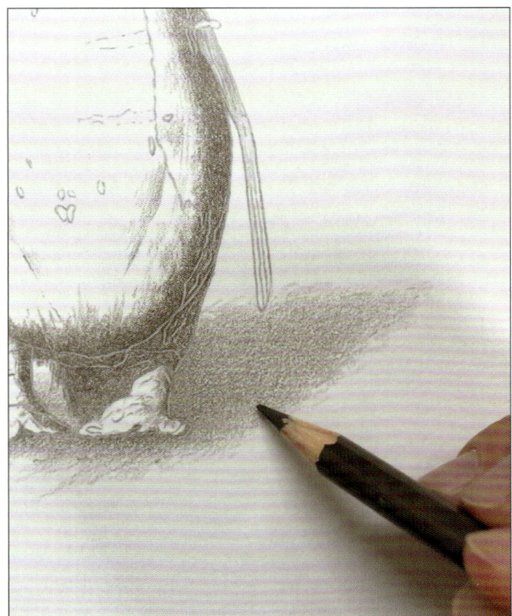

2 Paint the shadows cast on the ground in the same way.

▬ French grey 70%

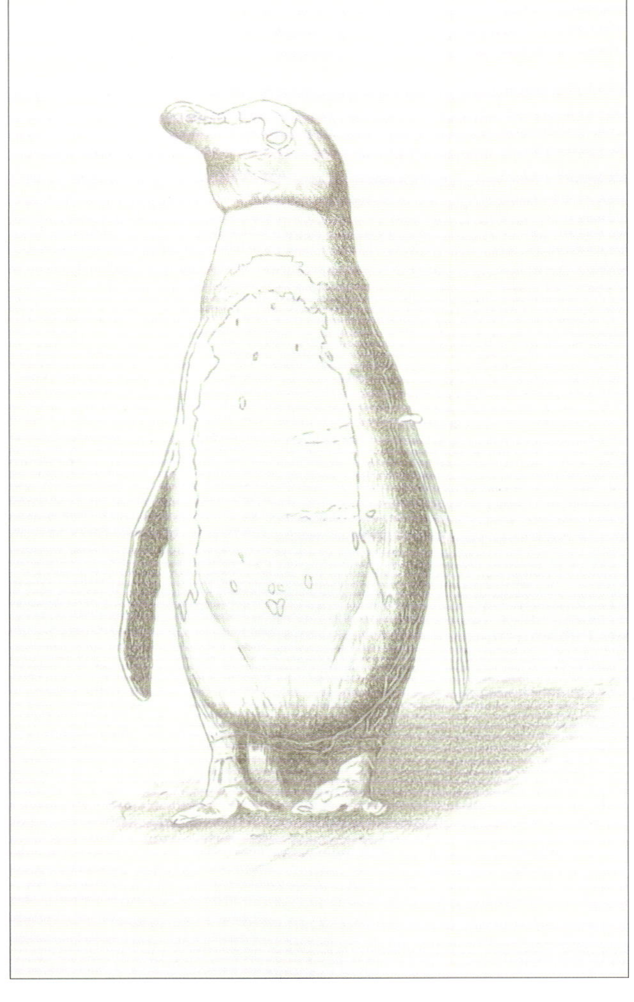

This is the overall drawing so far.

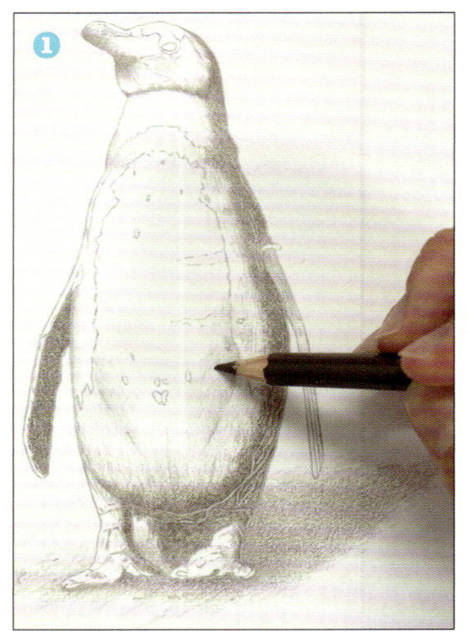 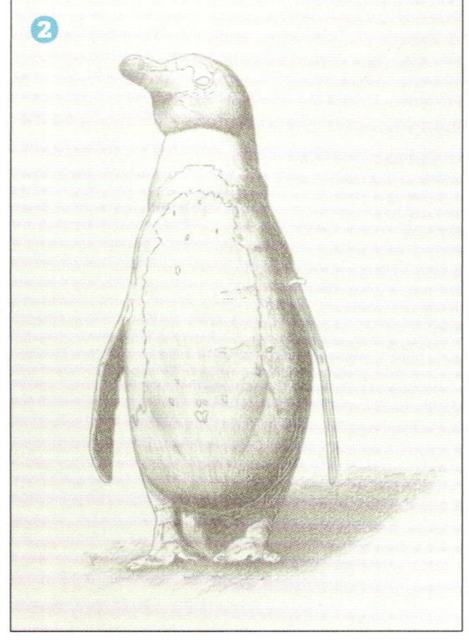

3 ❶ Without disrupting the overall light and dark areas established in **Step 2**, begin adding finer shade and shadow. ❷ This shows the completed shading using French grey 70%.

■ French grey 70%

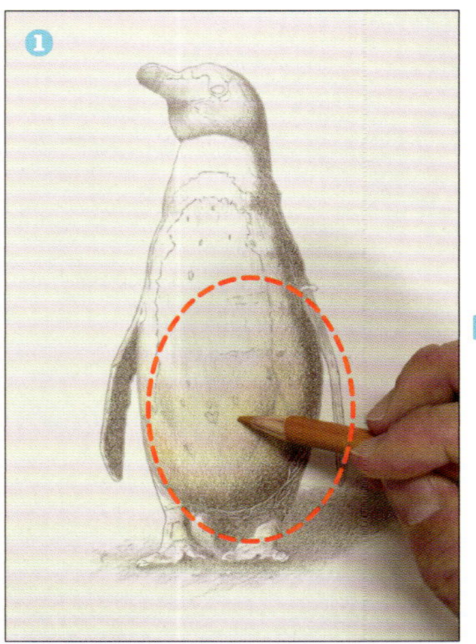 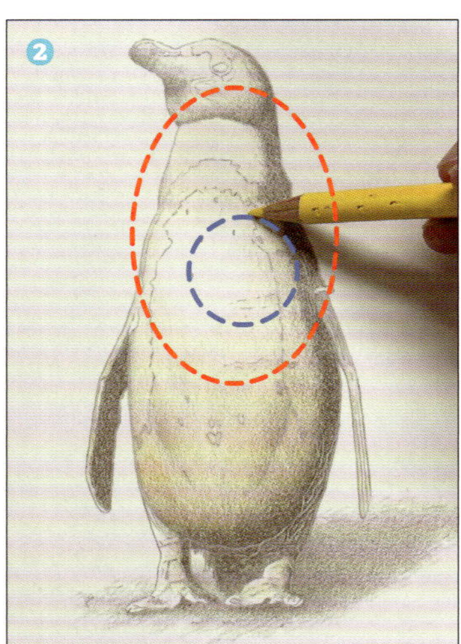

4 Now add color based mainly on the subject's unique color (the color unique to the penguin). ❶ Lightly apply yellow ochre to the lower half of the body (red-circled area). At this stage, you don't need to worry too much about capturing the texture of the feathers. ❷ For the upper half of the body (red-circled area), lightly apply the brighter color of canary yellow. However, make sure to leave the highlight (blue-circled area) as white paper.

▨ Yellow ochre
▨ Canary yellow

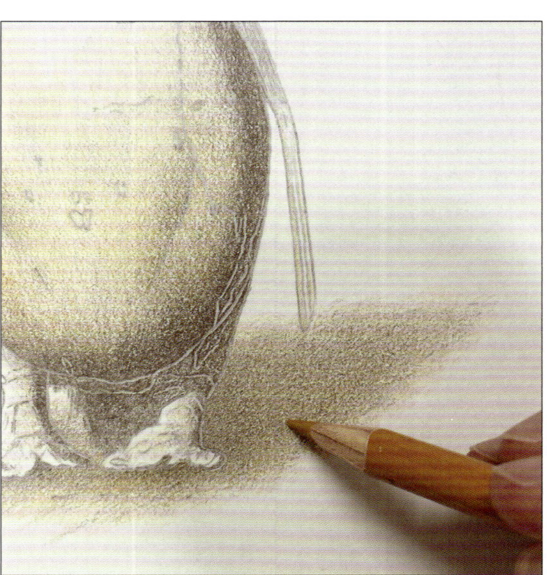

5 You should also add a bit of yellow ochre to the shadow on the ground.

▨ Yellow ochre

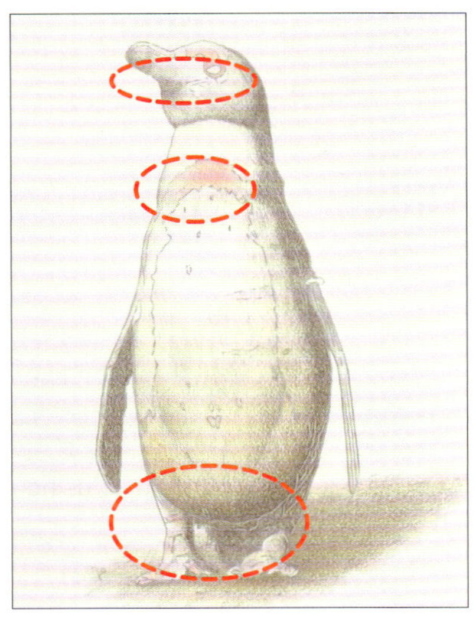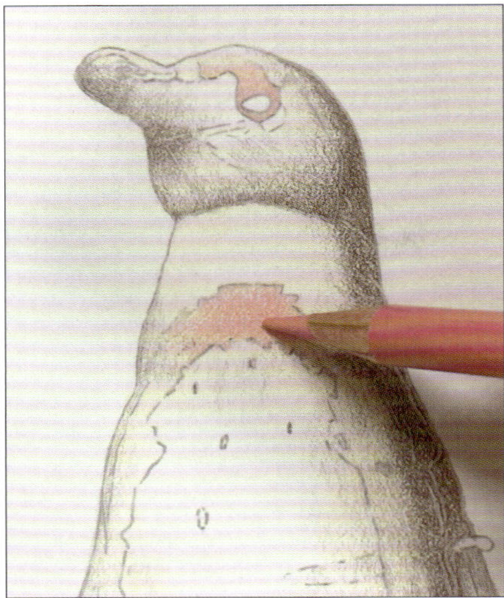

6 Apply blush pink to the red-circled area. As you can later scratch in fine highlights using a design knife, it's okay to apply the color fairly solidly at this stage.

■ Blush pink

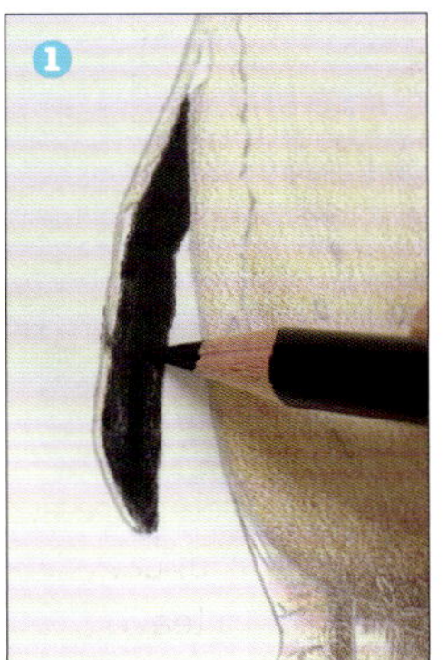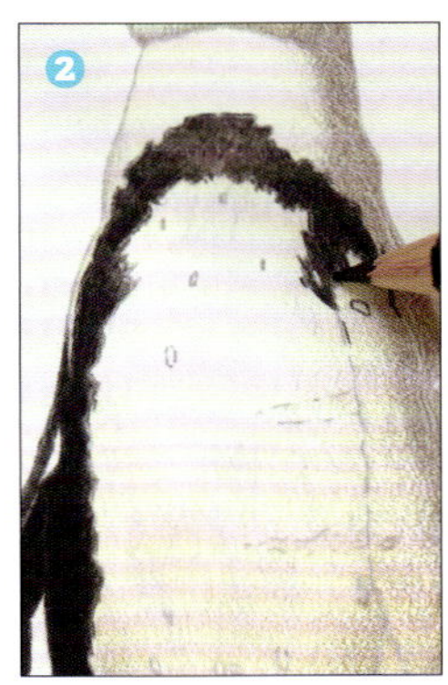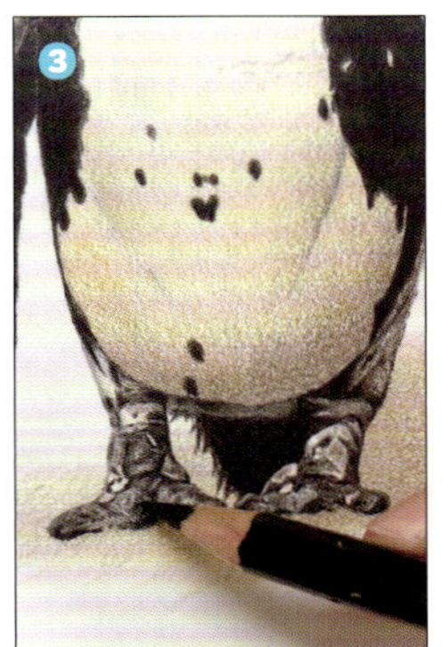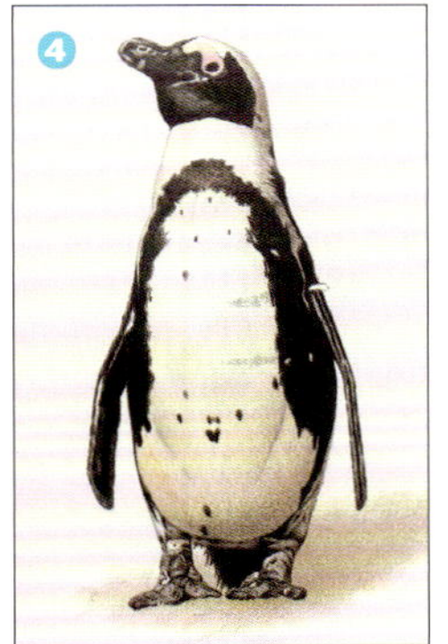

7 ❶-❸ Color the black areas, such as the head, body, wings, and feet, with black. In general, apply strong pressure to get a solid fill, but be mindful of subtle tonal variations as you go. The finer details, like the feet, can be a bit challenging, so take your time and study the reference photo closely as you work. ❹ This shows the drawing after all the black areas have been colored.

■ Black

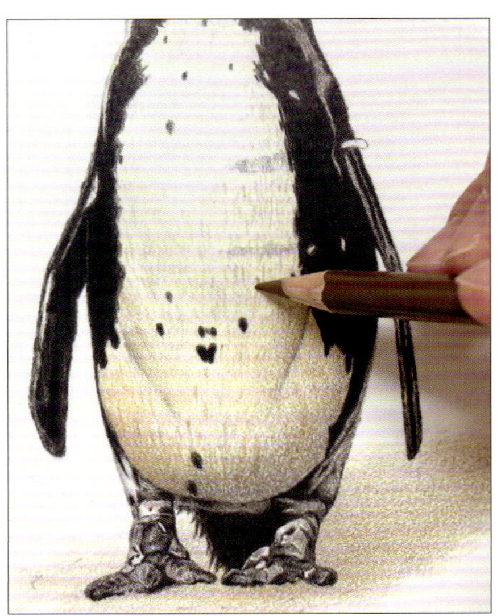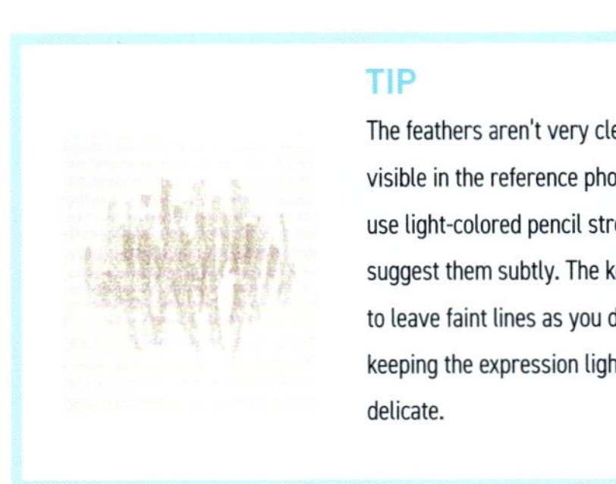

TIP

The feathers aren't very clearly visible in the reference photo, so use light-colored pencil strokes to suggest them subtly. The key is to leave faint lines as you draw, keeping the expression light and delicate.

8 Now it's time to depict the feathers. Using the strokes described in TIP, apply light umber mainly to the lower half of the body. Be careful not to overdo it, as too much detail can make the image feel heavy or overworked.

■ Light umber

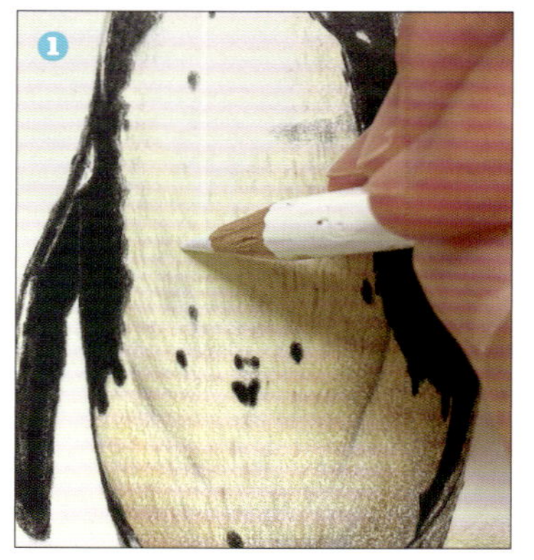 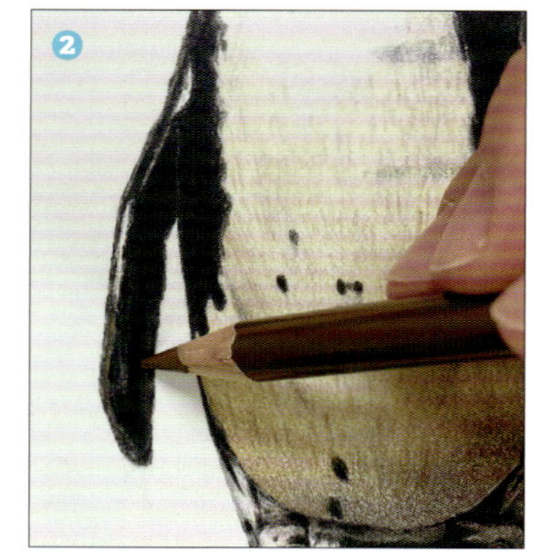 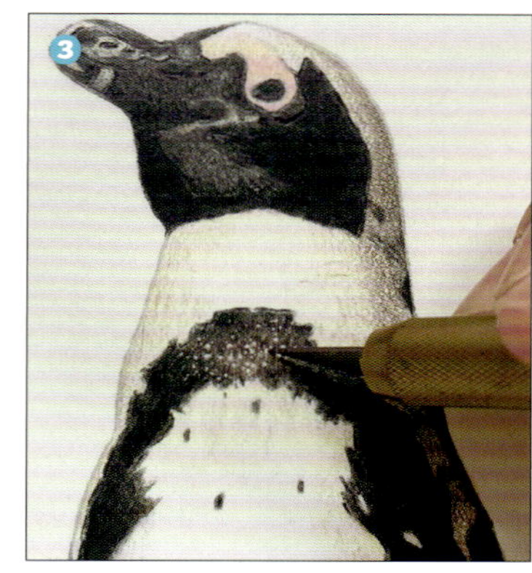

9 Now for the finishing touches. **❶** Lightly blend the light umber feathers from **Step 8** using white. **❷** Try adding a bit of light umber to the black areas for more depth. **❸** Use a design knife to scratch in the fine highlights.

▢ White ▰ Light umber

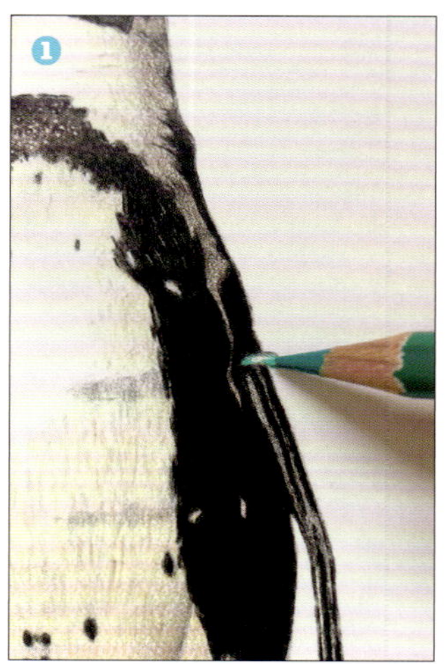 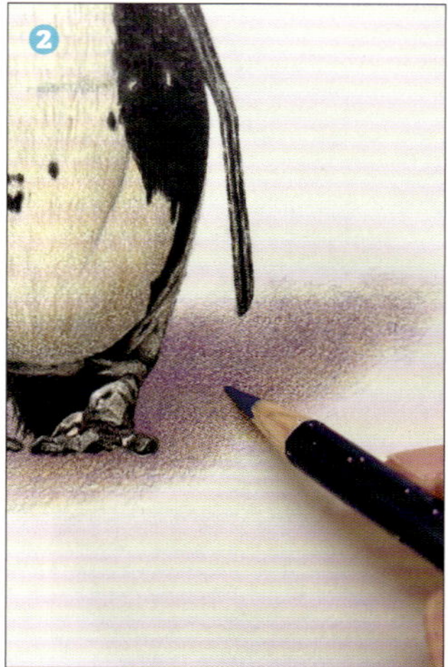

10 **❶** The parrot green of the penguin's ID band serves as an unexpectedly important accent. **❷** As a yellowish tone was added to the cast shadow in Step 5, incorporating a complementary violet adds depth to the shadow.

▰ Parrot green
▰ Violet

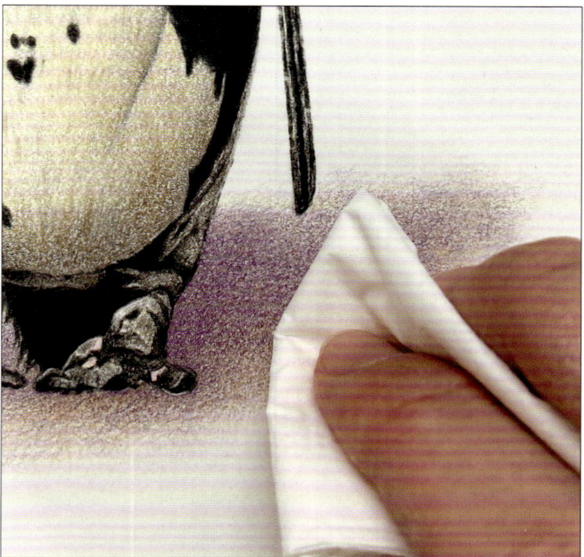

11 You should also blur the outline of the shadow of the shadow on the ground by rubbing it with your finger or a tissue.

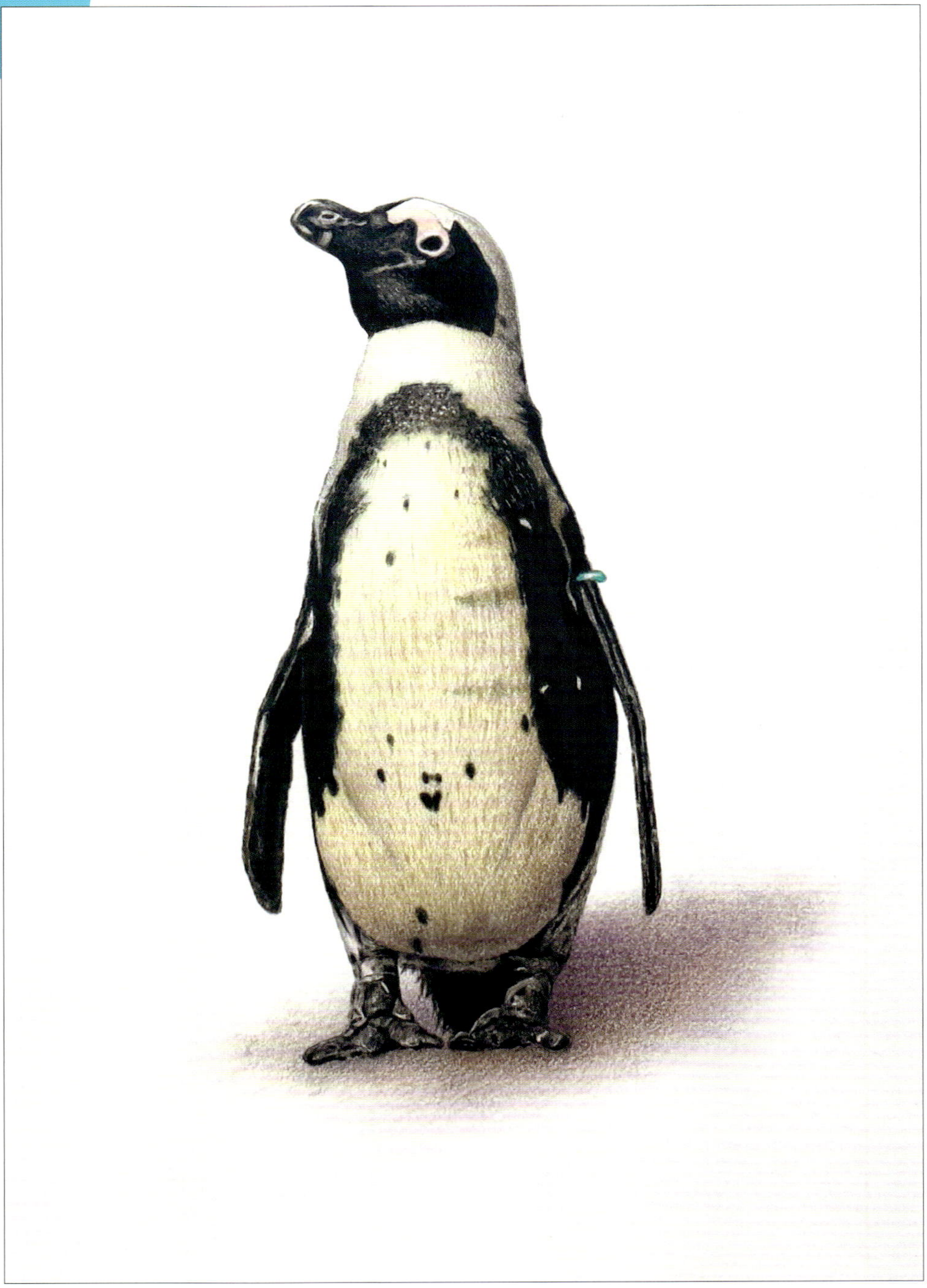

If you think that any color is lacking at this final stage, it's fine if you add it now to complete the drawing.

Draw a Scottish Fold Cat

Colored pencils: Mitsubishi Polycolor
Paper: Pure Kent
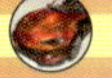
Drawn by Miyakawa

Coloring Key Points

1. Leave the highlight in the eye clearly white to make it shine (p.13).

2. Layer brown tones to create fur texture and patterns (p.15).

3. Use grey tones to depict white fur (p.15).

Colors Used

Yellow Ochre 19		Light Orange 54	
Russet Brown 30		Warm Grey 37	
Black 24		Grey 23	
Brown 21		Cream Yellow 27	
Vandyke Brown 22		Lilac 34	

Preliminary Drawing

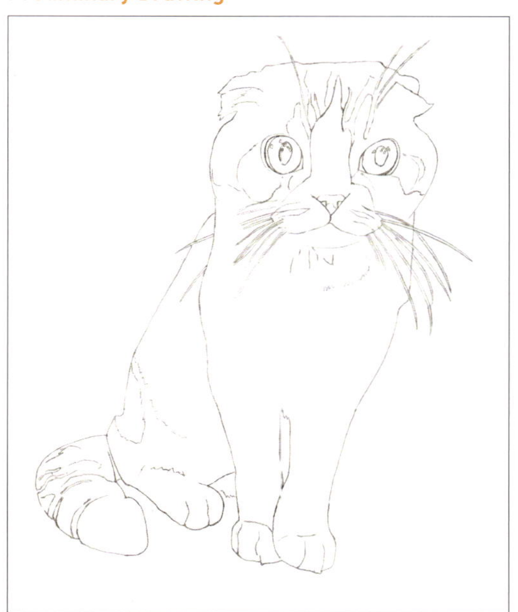

I kept the sketch to a minimum because the fur texture will be depicted during the coloring process.

Reference Photo

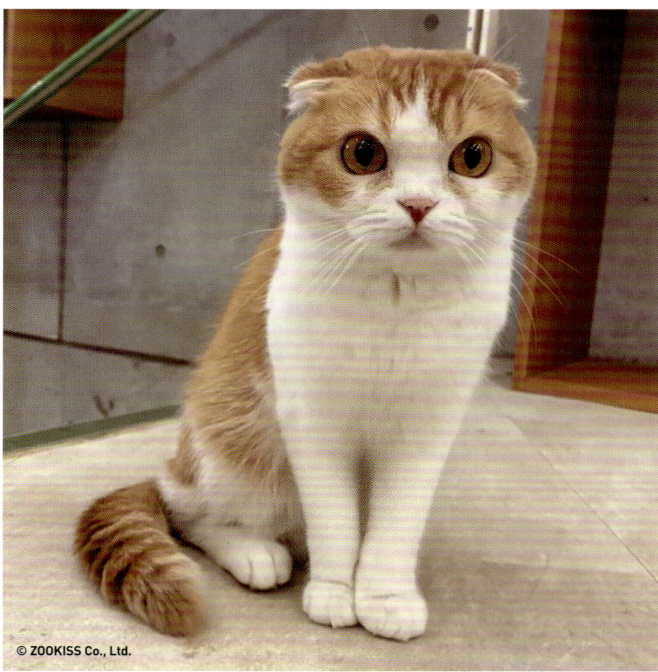

This is a full-body illustration of a Scottish fold cat. The goal is to depict the gloss of the eyes and the texture of the fur. As the image is viewed from a distance, we'll depict the fur using only colored pencils, without relying on a stylus. By layering several shades of brown in fine strokes, we'll depict both the pattern and three-dimensionality. Rather than focusing on extremely detailed rendering, we'll prioritize the overall impression when viewed at a distance, specifically emphasizing the fur pattern and the play of shade and shadow.

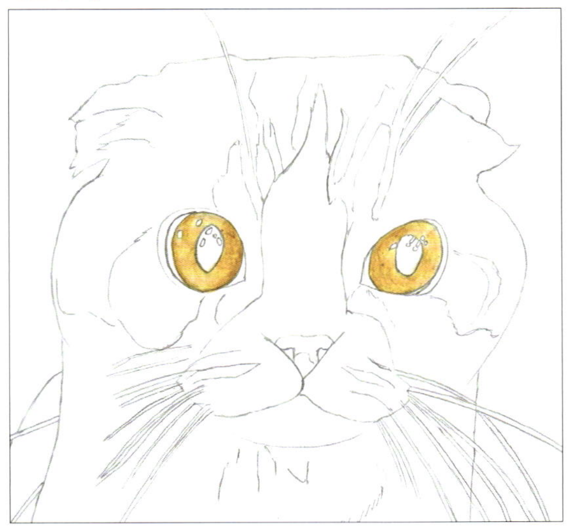

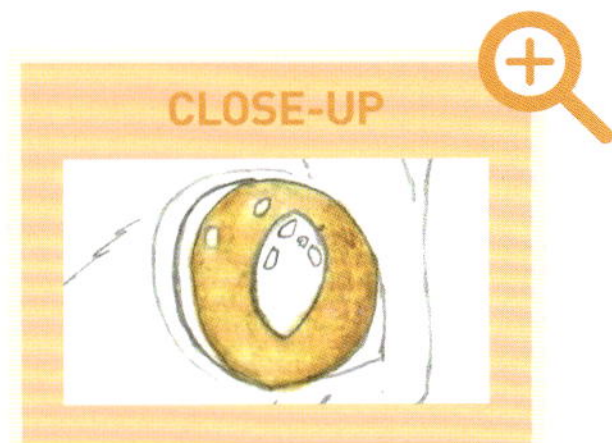

1 You can start with the fur if you like, but for this piece, we'll begin with the eyes. First, use yellow ochre to color the iris. Since the area near the upper eyelid will be in shadow, apply the color slightly more heavily there. Be careful not to color over the highlight! (You can also use something like a dotting tool to press in the paper and preserve the highlight.)

▮ Yellow ochre

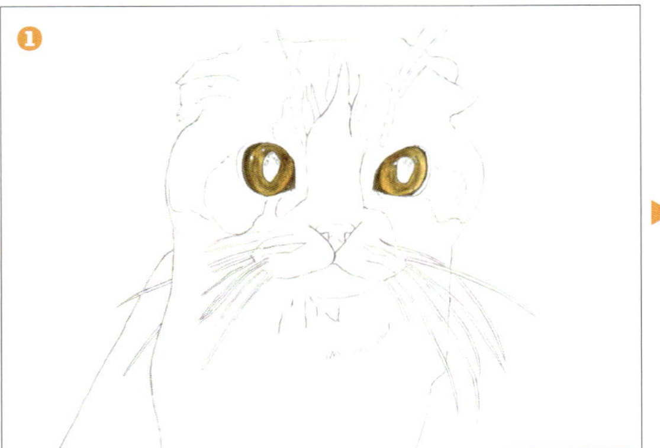

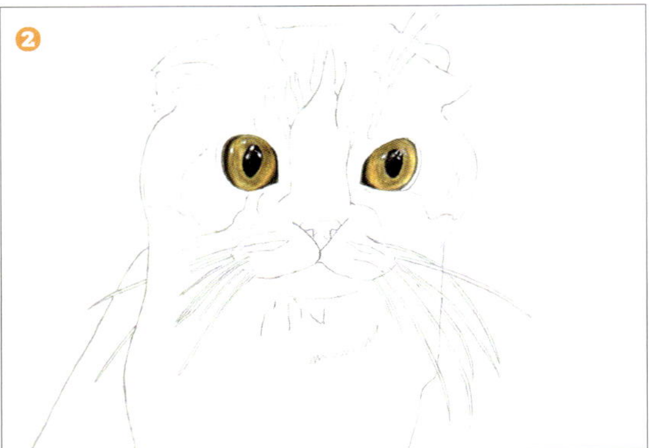

2 **❶** Layer the iris with russet brown, adding patterns that encircle the pupil. Also apply a base layer of russet brown at the inner and outer corners of the eye. **❷** Use black to fill in the pupil, the outer corner, and the inner corner. As long as you preserve the highlight, the eye will already appear to shine at this stage.

▮ Russet brown ▮ Black

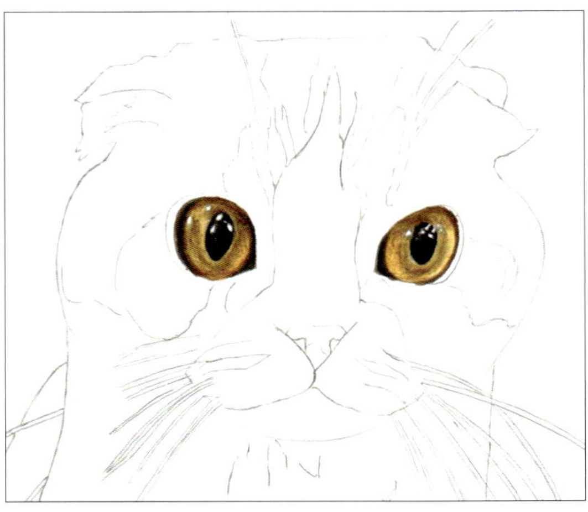

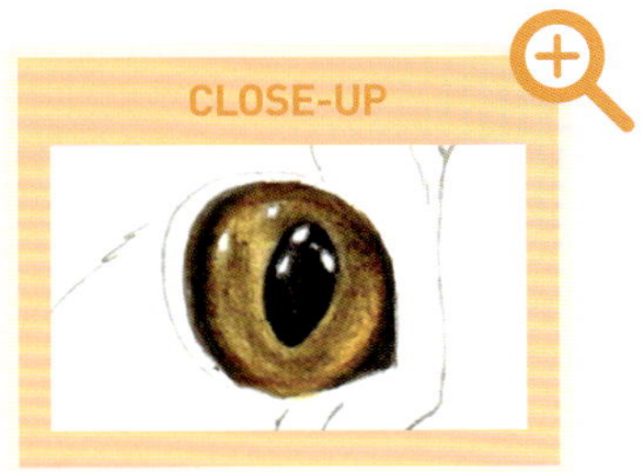

3 Adjust with brown. Emphasize the pattern around the pupil from **Step 2 ❶**, as well as the shaded area just beneath the upper eyelid.

▮ Brown

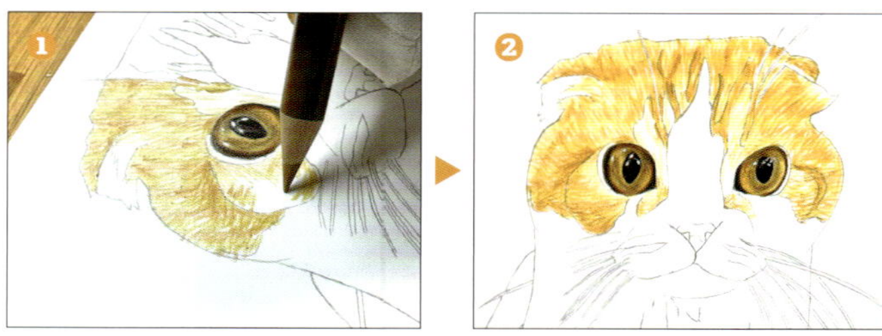

4 Color the fur, starting with yellow ochre. ❶ Using a sharpened pencil held upright, draw many fine lines as if sketching individual strands of fur. Pay attention to the direction of hair growth, drawing from the roots toward the tips. ❷ For example, on the face, draw radiating outward from the nose. Use the density of the lines to express the fur pattern. There's a patch of white fur on the left foreleg and around the belly, so be sure to leave that area uncolored.

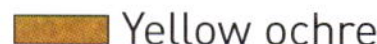 Yellow ochre

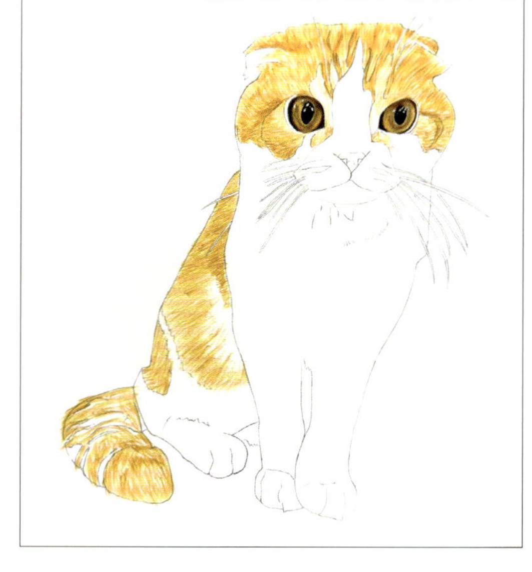

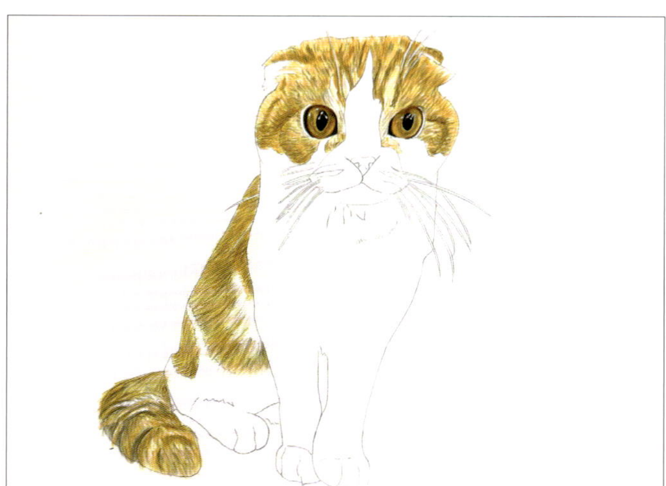

5 Using russet brown, layer fine strokes just like in **Step 4**. Add more strokes to the darker areas of the fur to make the pattern stand out. When drawing the tail, try to create a striped pattern while referring to the reference photo.

Russet brown

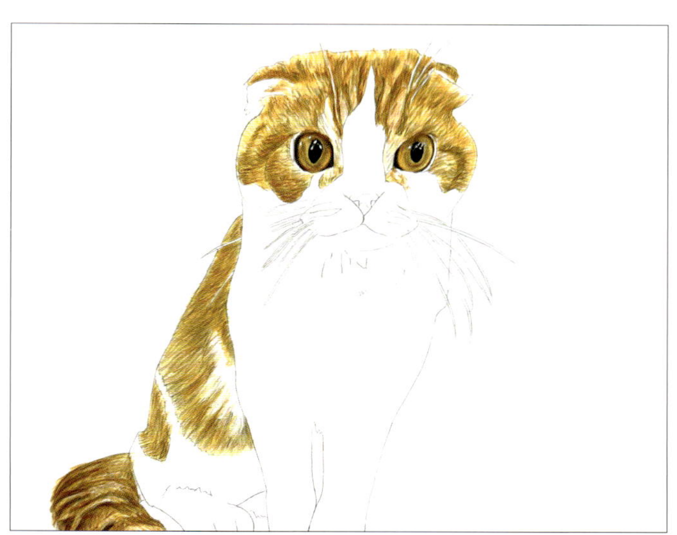

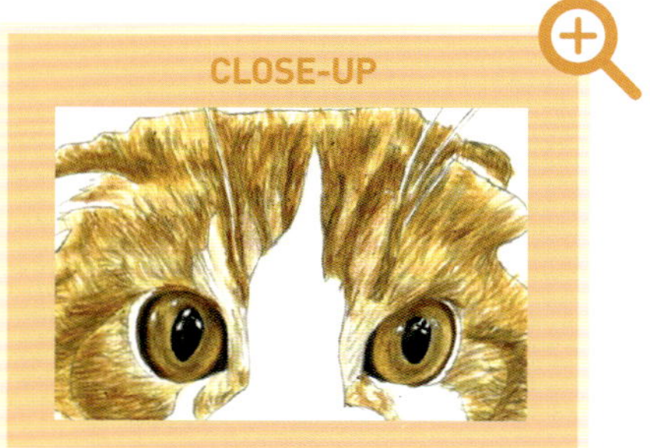

6 Just like in **Steps 4** and **5**, layer with brown. At this stage, the pattern should be made clearly visible. In particular, focus on applying more color over the areas that were colored with russet brown in **Step 5**.

Brown

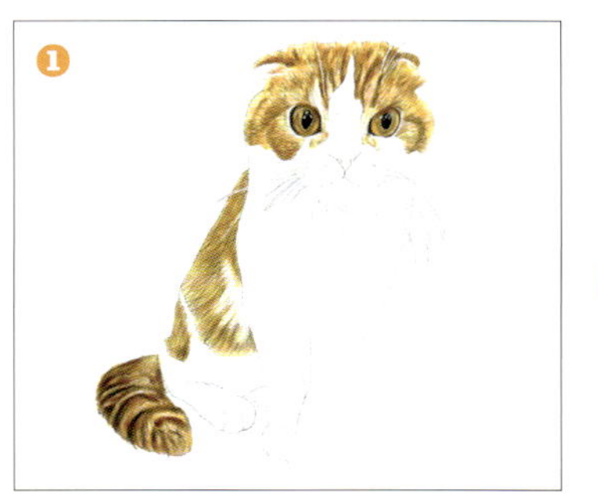

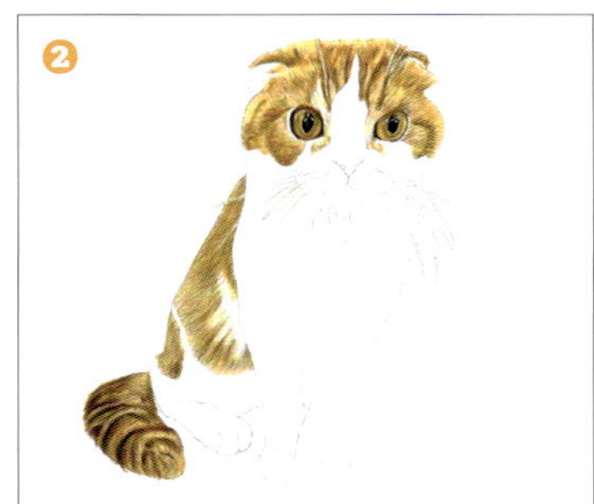

7 **❶** Adjust using Vandyke brown. Make the stripes on the tail more distinct. **❷** At this stage the fur lines look too well-defined, which makes the drawing seem stiff. You should therefore soften the whole area by applying a thin layer of light orange over it.

▰▰ Vandyke brown
▱ Light orange

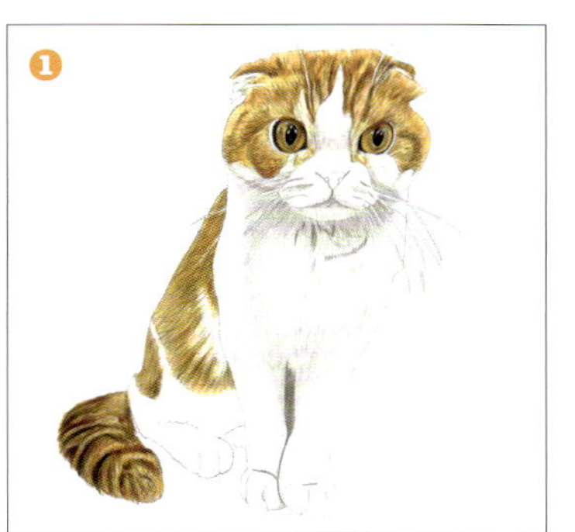

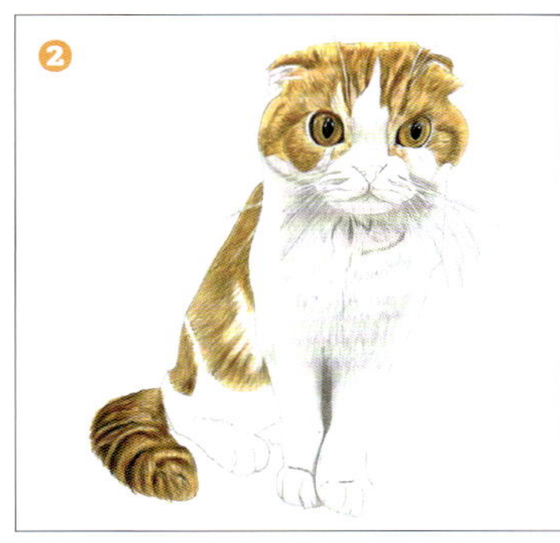

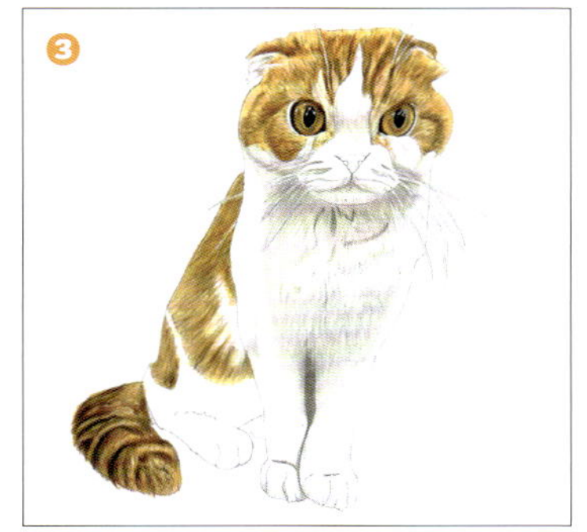

8 **❶** Use warm grey to color the face and body (from the back to the belly). For the face, shade the area between the eyes and mouth, and for the body, move the pencil vertically along the direction of the fur, from the chin down to the front legs. Shade more heavily under the face and slightly darker around the base of the legs. Be careful not to color over the whiskers (it's also fine to leave them slightly indented). Add some shade around the base of the neck as well. **❷** Using grey, layer over the same areas as in **Step 8 ❶**. At this stage, drawing fine fur lines will help give a realistic fur texture. Also color the shaded area near the tips of the legs. **❸** Add a touch of cream yellow around the neck and the base of the front legs. Brush it on loosely to slightly soften the fur lines drawn in **Step 8 ❷**.

▰▰ Warm grey ▰▰ Grey ▱ Cream yellow

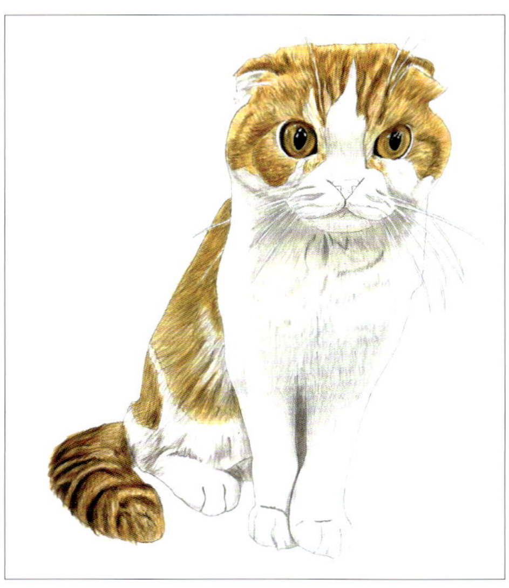

9 Draw the white fur using warm grey. Just like with the upper body, move the colored pencil along the direction of the fur. Don't hesitate to shade darker in areas where the fur is in shadow. For the white fur on the belly, also follow the flow of the hair as you shade. To give it a more realistic white-fur texture, leave some of the paper showing through by drawing slightly rough, sketchy strokes.

▰▰ Warm grey

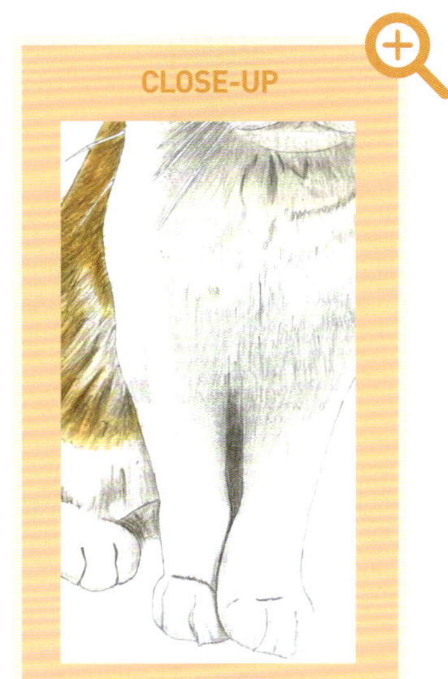

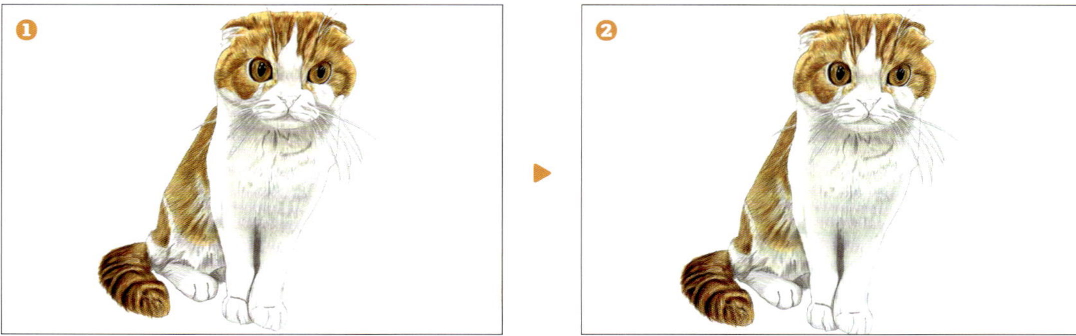

10 ❶ Apply a top layer of grey over the white fur areas, in the same way that you did for the cat's back.
❷ Then soften it by layering cream yellow over the top. That completes the drawing of the fur.

▬ Grey ▭ Cream yellow

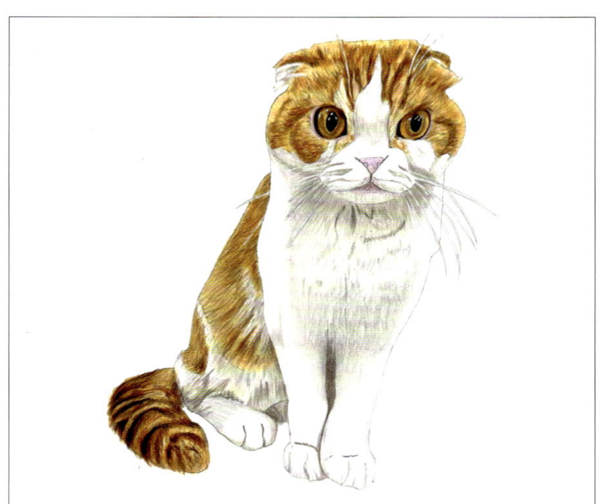

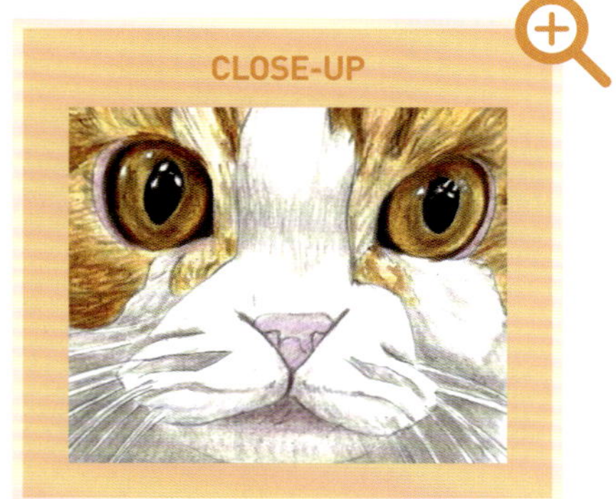

11 Lightly color the edges of the eyes, the nose, and the mouth area with lilac.

▬ Lilac

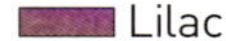

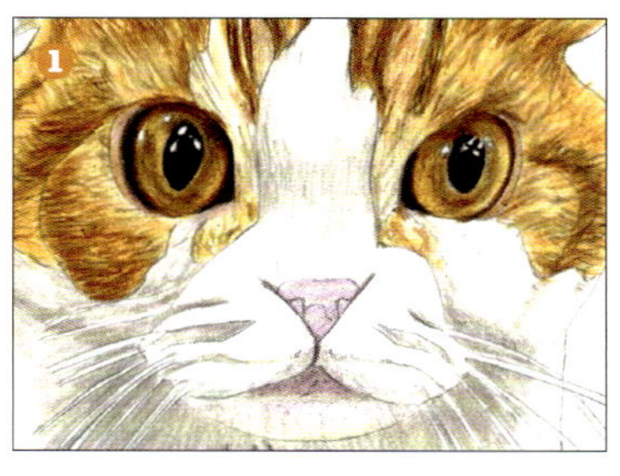

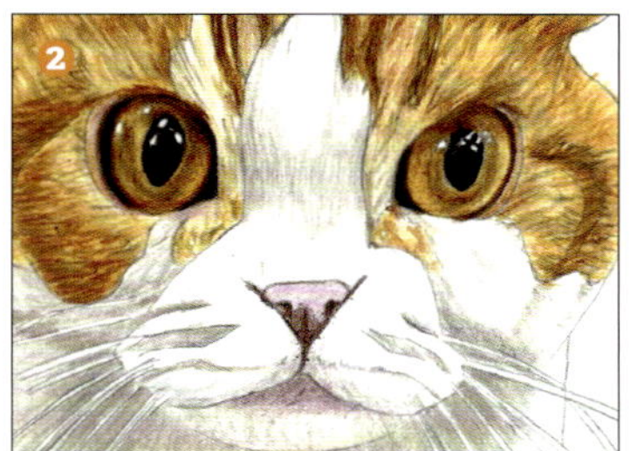

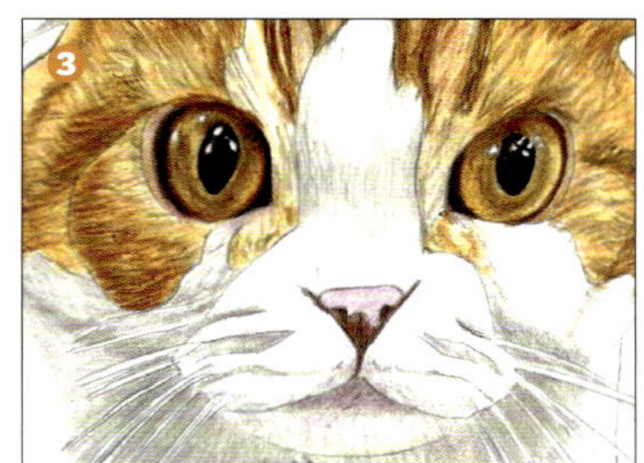

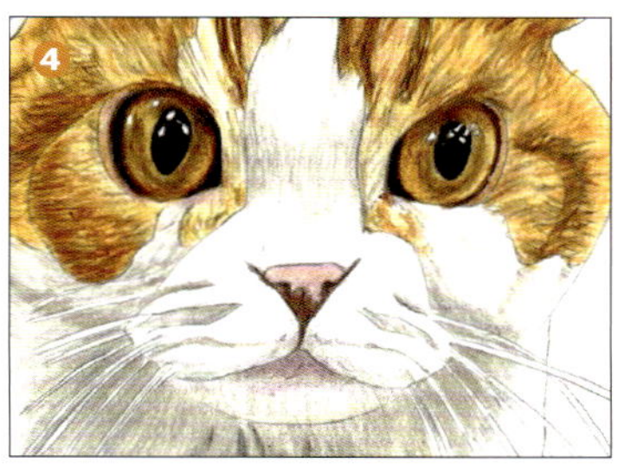

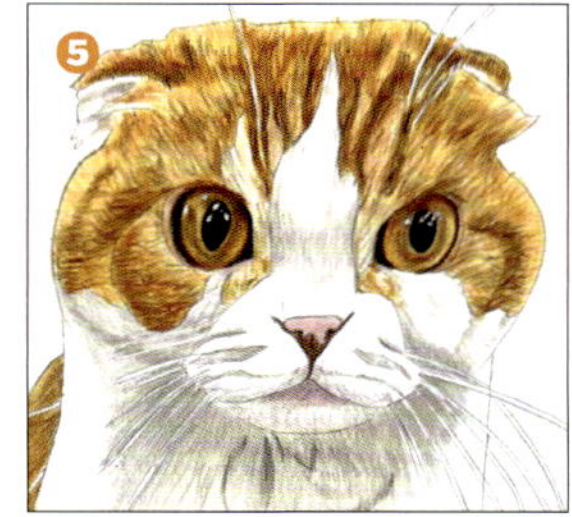

12 ❶ Color the edges of the eyes with yellow ochre. ❷ Lightly color the shade on the nose with Vandyke brown. ❸ Apply a thin layer of brown over the Vandyke brown–colored area. ❹ Color the tip of the nose with light orange to give it a slightly pinkish tone. ❺ This is the final drawing of the face.

▬ Yellow ochre ▬ Vandyke brown
▬ Brown ▭ Light orange

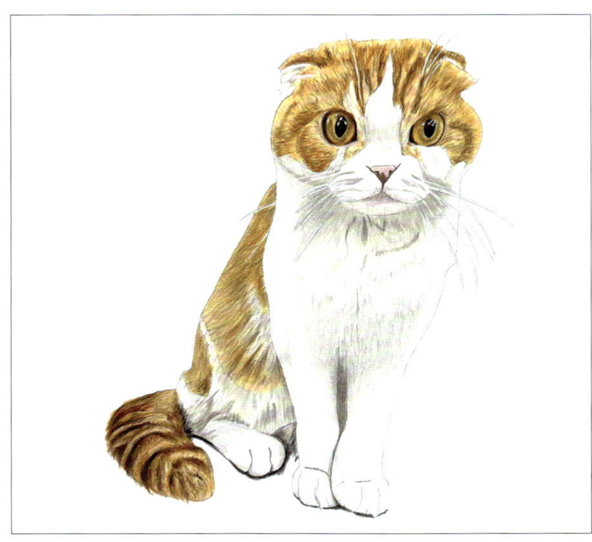

13 Color the shadows cast on the ground. Use black to depict the shadows, almost as if you are tracing around the cat's feet.

███ Black

COMPLETE

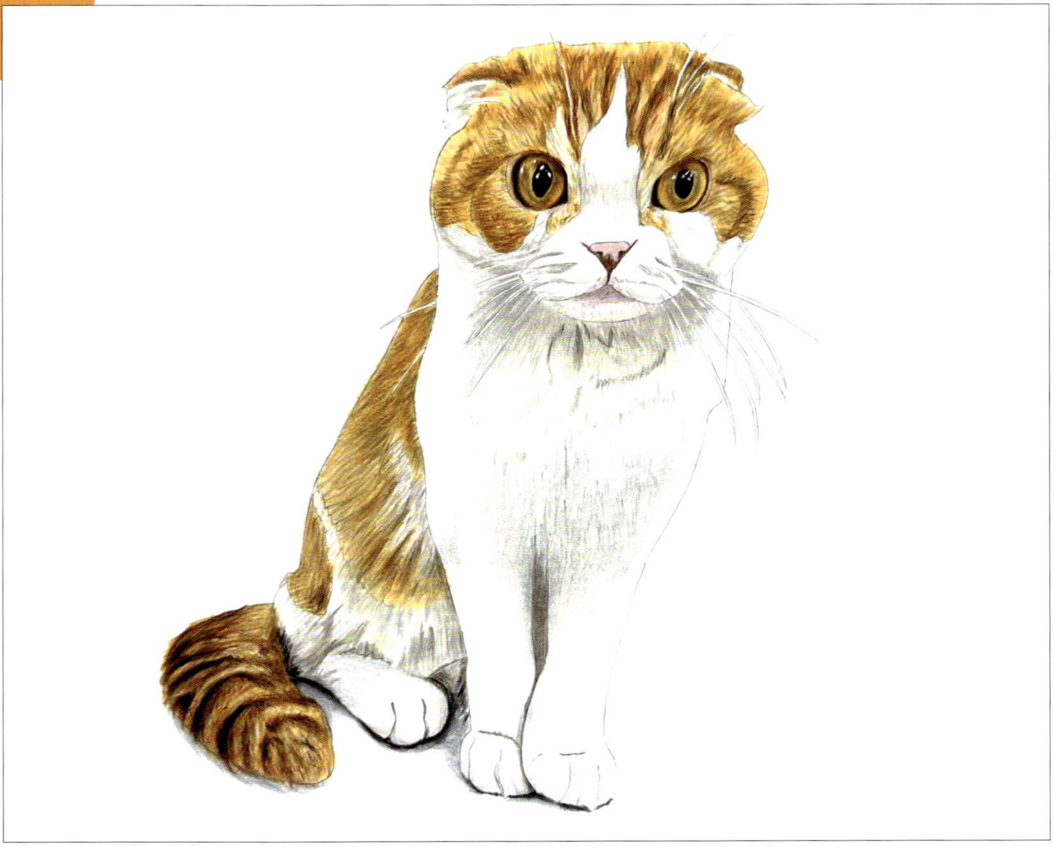

Expand the shadows from **Step 13** by applying grey. This completes the drawing.

███ Grey

Draw a Red-Eyed Tree Frog

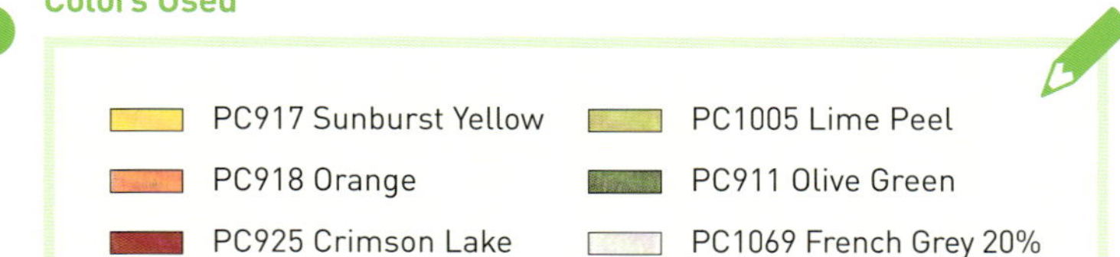

Coloring Key Points

1. Add shading so that the protruding eye appears spherical.

2. Use burnishing to make the body surface appear smooth (p.12).

3. Depicting shades and shadows with red, blue, and green creates more variation than just using black by itself.

Colors Used

PC917 Sunburst Yellow		PC1005 Lime Peel	
PC918 Orange		PC911 Olive Green	
PC925 Crimson Lake		PC1069 French Grey 20%	
PC935 Black		PC901 Indigo Blue	
PC908 Dark Green		PC938 White	

Reference Photo

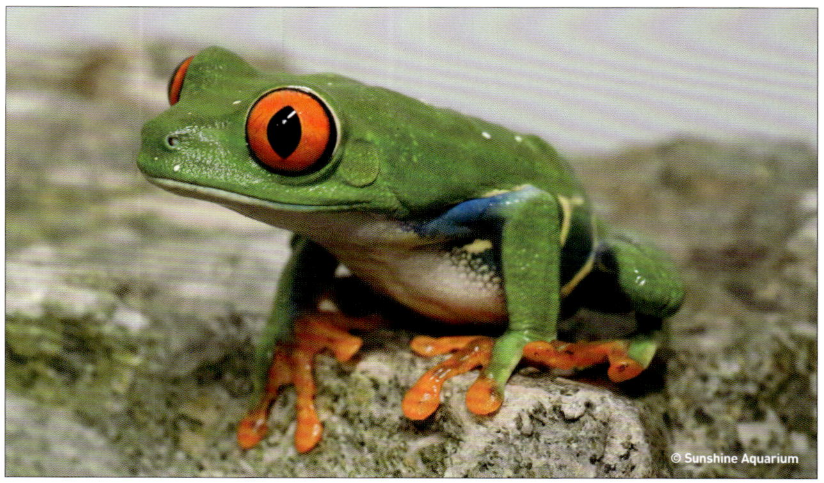

The red-eyed tree frog is known for its large, glossy eyes. By carefully preserving highlights, you can effectively depict the smooth texture of the eyes and body. Also, by using a blend of red, blue, and green to add shadows, you can express a more nuanced sense of three-dimensionality than by simply layering black over the shadows.

Preliminary Drawing

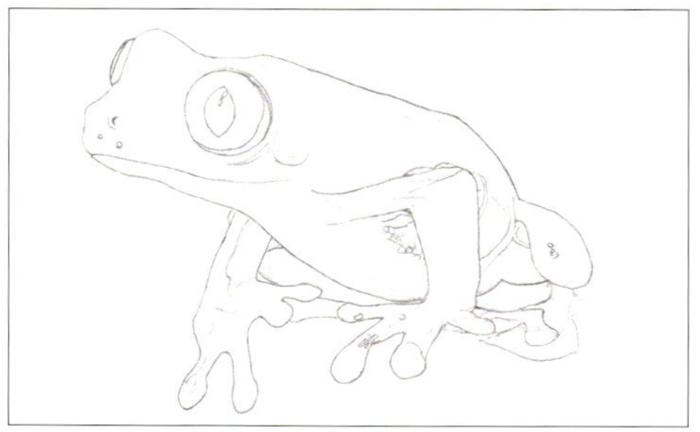

Sketching in where the highlights will go makes it easier to grasp the shape of the body.

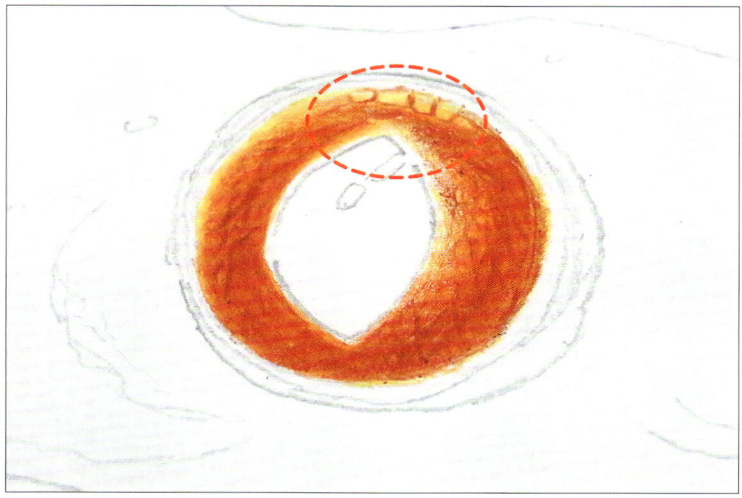

1 Color the eye by layering sunburst yellow, then orange, and finally crimson lake around the pupil, deepening the tone as you go. Use red to perform burnishing (p.12), and draw the blood vessels and highlights (red-circled area) in the eye.

▢ Sunburst yellow
▢ Orange ▢ Crimson lake

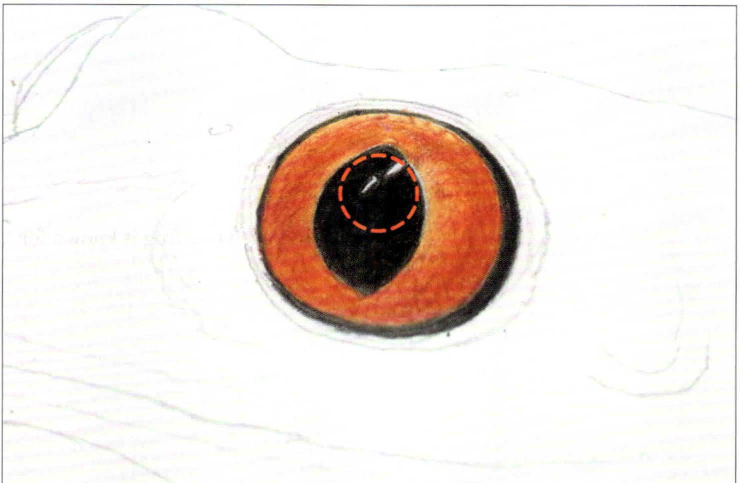

> **TIP**
>
> If the highlight is clearly defined, the surface of the eye will appear smooth.

UNIT 08

2 Use black to fill in everything around the highlight and the area around the edge of the eye. Apply it darkly so that the highlight (indicated by the red circle) stands out clearly.

▢ Black

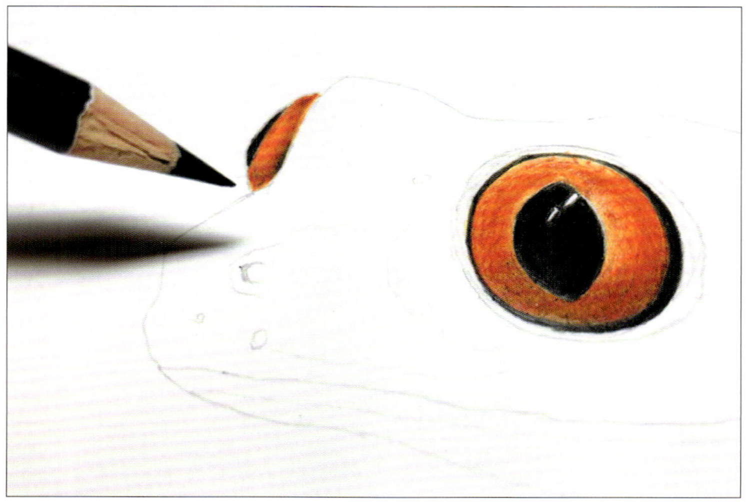

> **TIP**
>
> The highlight should have a crisp, well-defined shape to convey a smooth surface. A shape that rises like a small hill makes the surface appear more rounded and glossy.

3 Color the right eye in the same way as **Steps 1** and **2**, then add shading to the lower part using dark green

▢ Sunburst yellow ▢ Orange
▢ Crimson lake ▢ Dark green

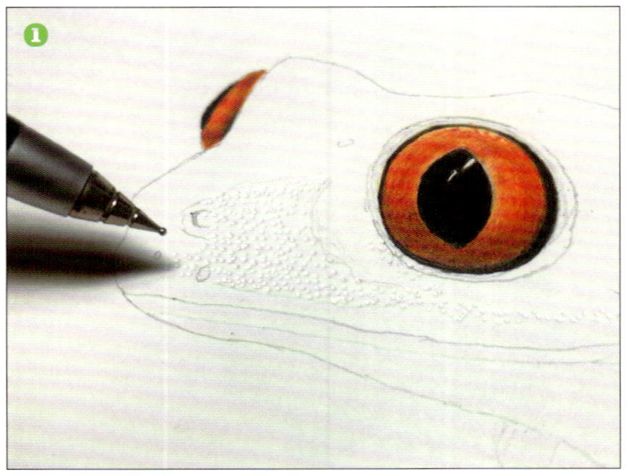

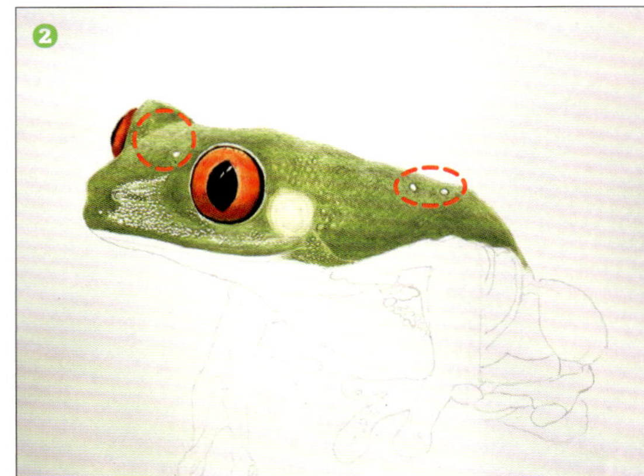

4 ❶ Draw the face. Use a stylus to create indentations on the paper. By stopping color sticking to the paper in these areas, you will end up creating fine highlights. ❷ Color the upper body, starting with lime peel and then layering olive green on top. Be sure to draw in the small spots. If you outline the spots (red-circled areas) in advance, it will make coloring easier.

☐ Lime peel ☐ Olive green

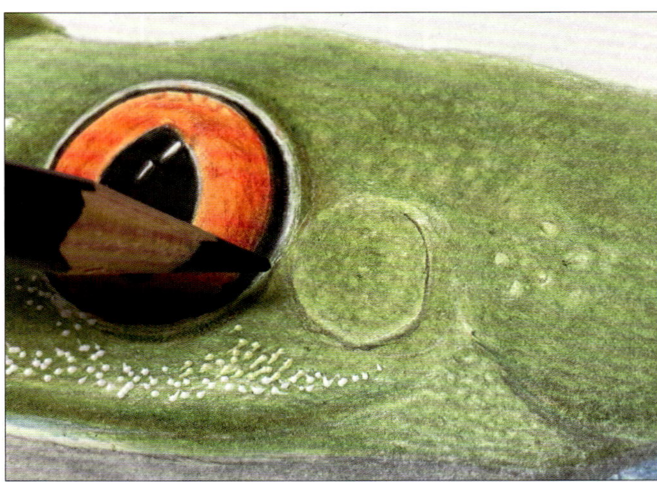

5 Color the ears by applying first lime peel and then olive green. Then draw a line along the edge with black.

☐ Lime peel ☐ Olive green ☐ Black

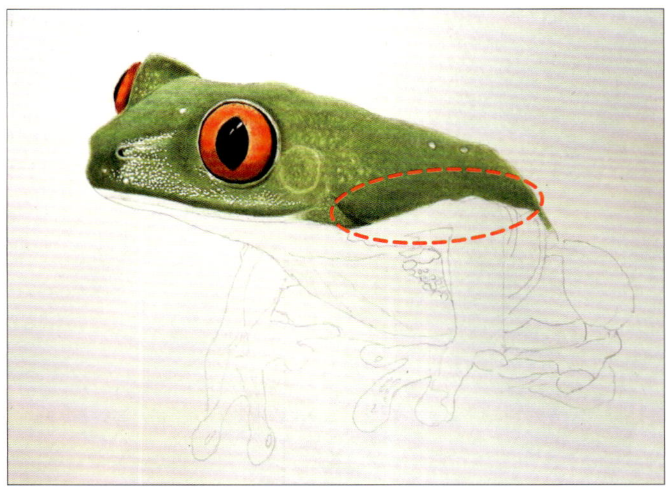

6 Apply orange to the red-circled area in layers to create shadows and enhance the three-dimensionality.

☐ Orange

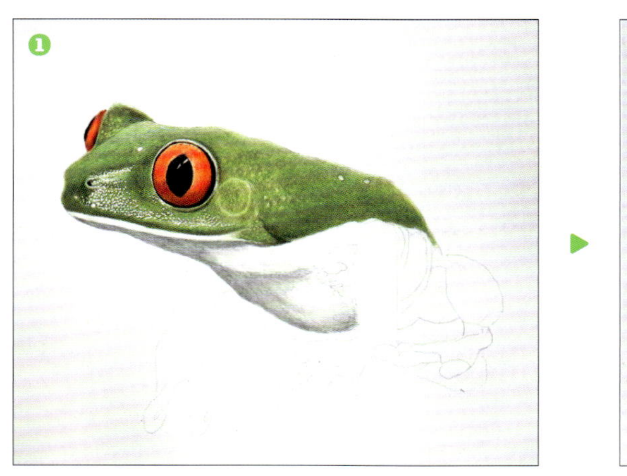 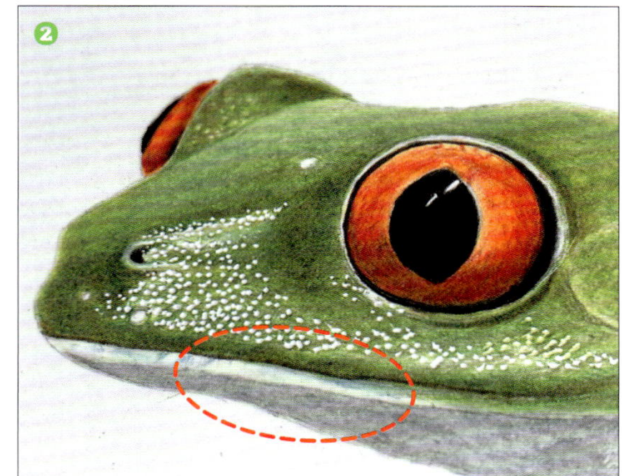

7 ❶ Color the lower half of the body. For the shaded areas on the lower part, apply French grey 20% first, then layer black on top. ❷ For the mouth, lightly draw the pattern (red-circled area) in indigo blue, then outline it with black.

☐ French grey 20% ■ Black ■ Indigo blue

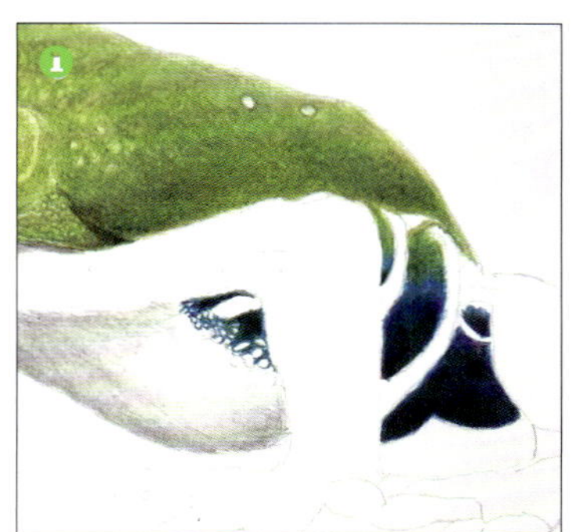 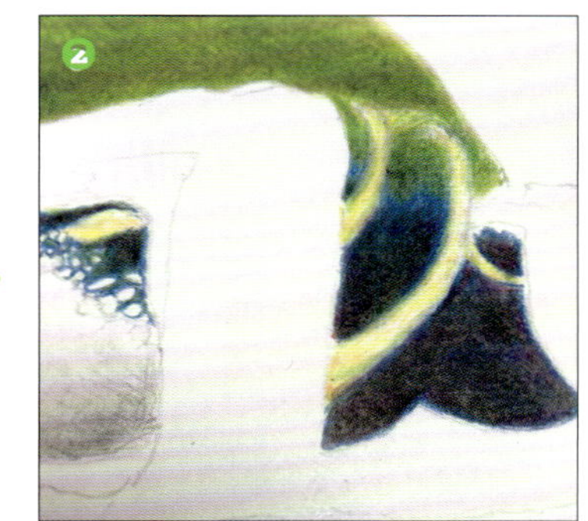 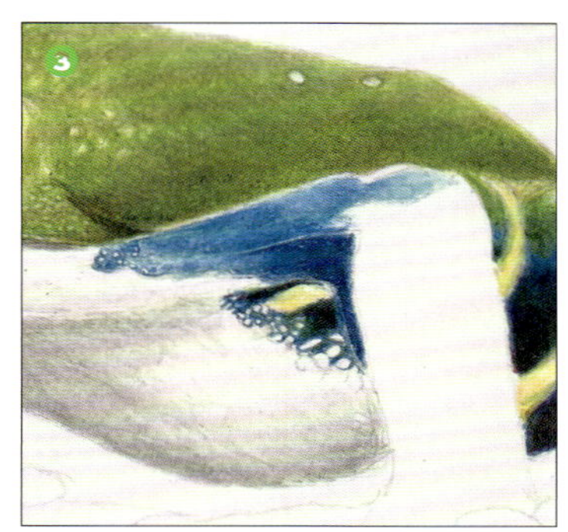

UNIT
08

8 ❶ Color the belly with indigo blue, then darken the shaded areas using deep green and crimson lake. ❷ For the belly pattern, layer white first, then sunburst yellow. ❸ Color the legs in indigo blue, starting with the left front leg first. Remember that you can use a mixture of light and dark tones to create a sense of three-dimensionality.

■ Indigo blue ■ Dark green ■ Crimson lake ☐ White ☐ Orange

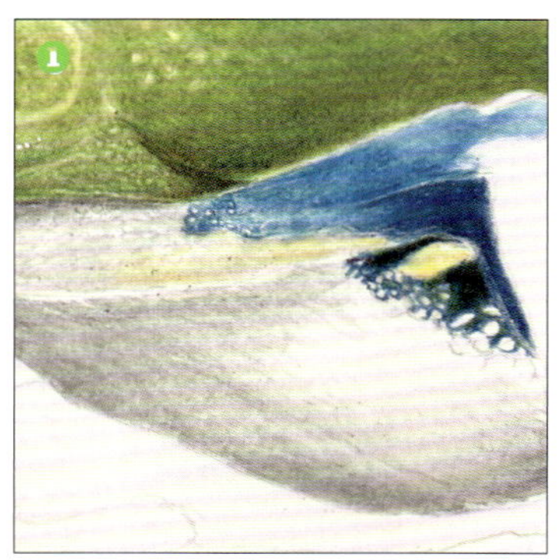 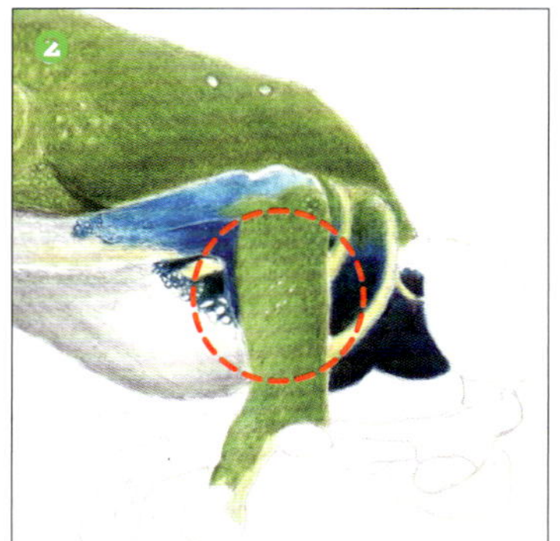 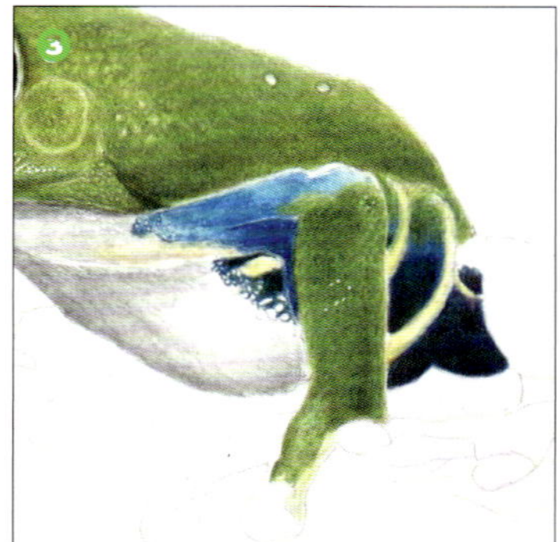

9 ❶ Lightly apply sunburst yellow. ❷ Color the legs. First, use a stylus to indent the small white spots, then apply lime peel followed by olive green, brushing in the direction of the skin's flow. ❸ Layer orange on top to create shadows and enhance the sense of three-dimensionality

☐ Sunburst yellow ☐ Lime peel ■ Olive green ■ Orange

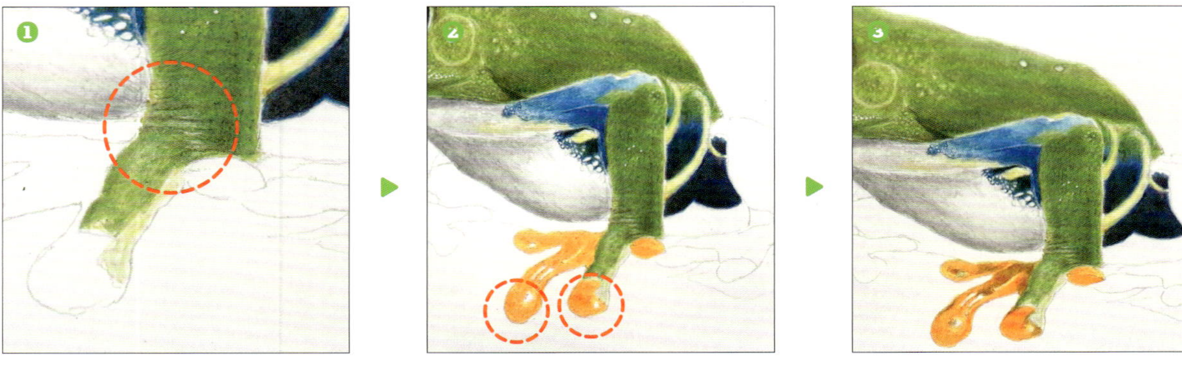

10 ❶ Use black to draw the wrinkles in the skin, and layer white over the raised areas on the skin to emphasize the texture. ❷ Paint the toes by layering sunburst yellow and then orange on all areas except the highlights. For the blurred highlight areas marked with red circles, use white around the edges to soften them. ❸ Lightly apply black to draw the pattern on the foreleg.

▨ Black ▭ White ▨ Sunburst yellow ▨ Orange

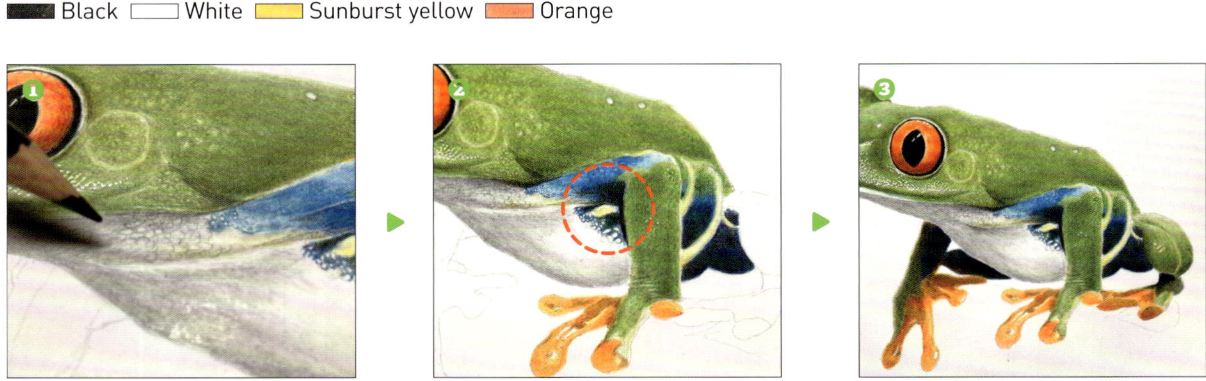

11 ❶ Draw the wrinkles on the skin with black. For the raised areas on the skin, apply white to highlight them. ❷ Draw the shadow of the arm using a mixture of crimson lake and olive green. Color the fingers by layering sunburst yellow followed by orange on all areas except the highlights. In the red-circled area where the highlight is blurry, soften it by applying white around its edges. ❸ Lightly apply black to draw the patterns on the forelimbs.

▨ Black ▨ Crimson lake ▨ Olive green ▨ Orange ▨ Sunburst yellow ▭ White

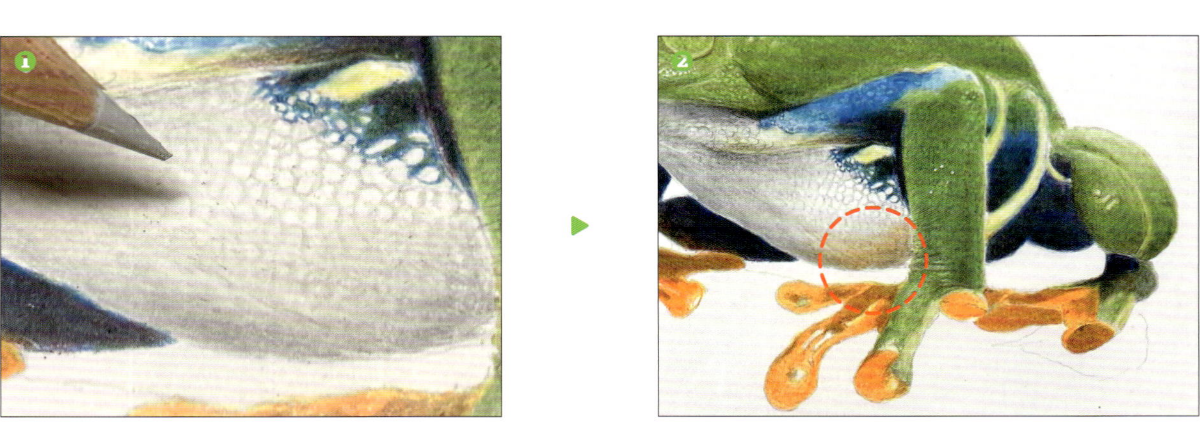

12 ❶ Draw the patterns on the belly using French grey 20%. ❷ Lightly apply orange to depict the color of the forelimbs reflected on the belly.

▭ French grey 20% ▨ Orange

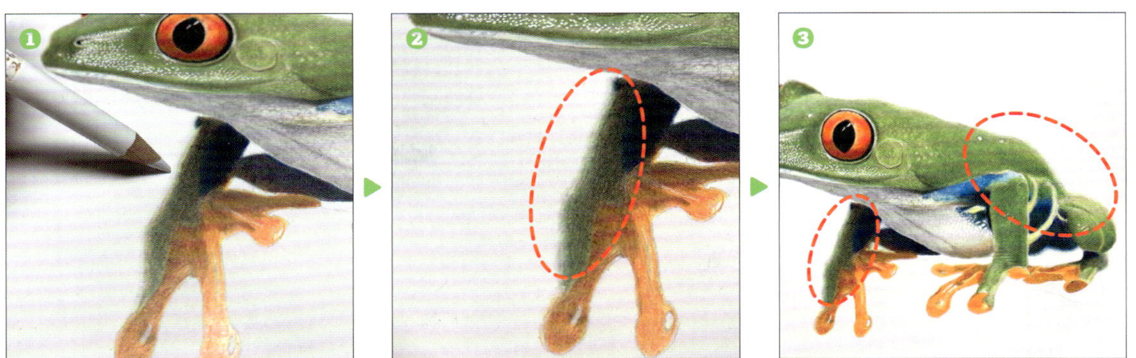

13 ❶ Use white pencil to softly blur the edges and surrounding areas where the subject appears out of focus in the reference photo. ❷ After laying down white, gently apply the intended color over it to create a hazy transition. ❸ Repeat this process for all blurred areas across the image, using the same technique.

☐ White   ☐ Lime peel   ☐ Olive green   ☐ Indigo blue   ☐ Orange

COMPLETE

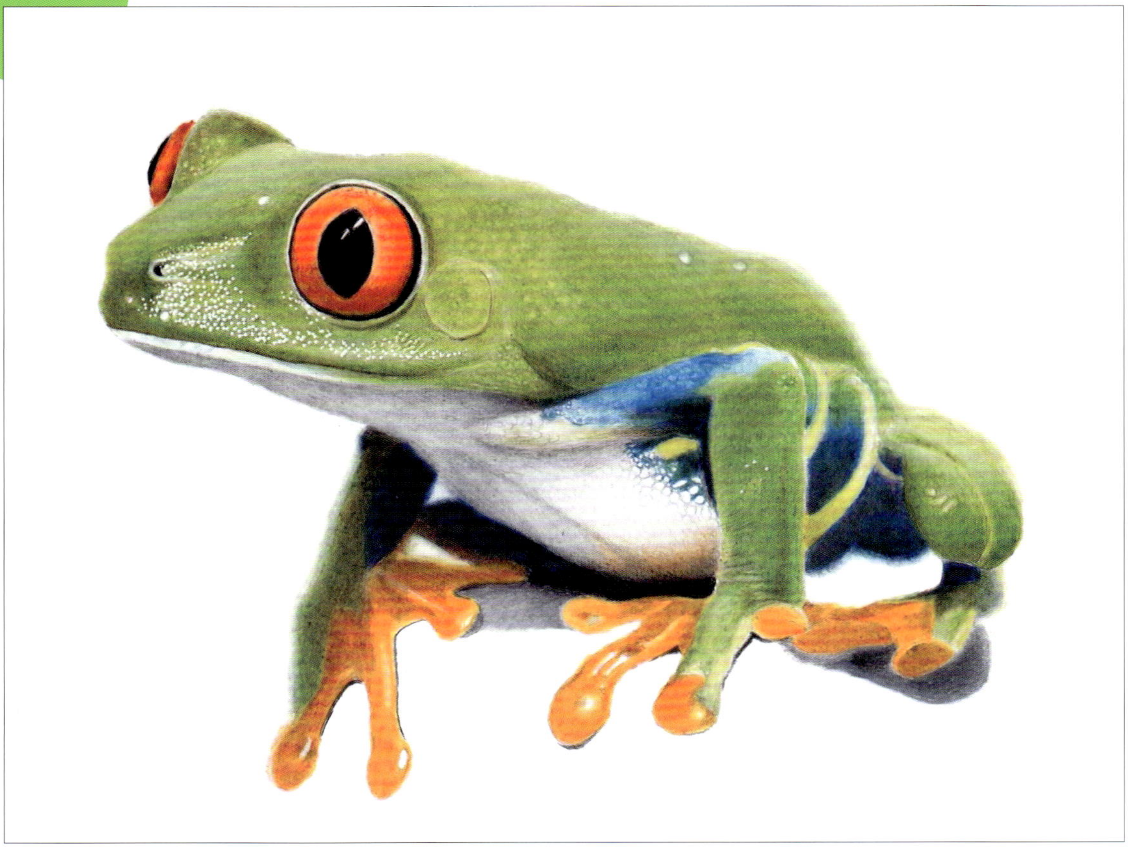

Draw the cast shadow using black, then apply French grey 20% with a burnishing technique to finish.

☐ Black   ☐ French grey 20%

Draw a Dolphin

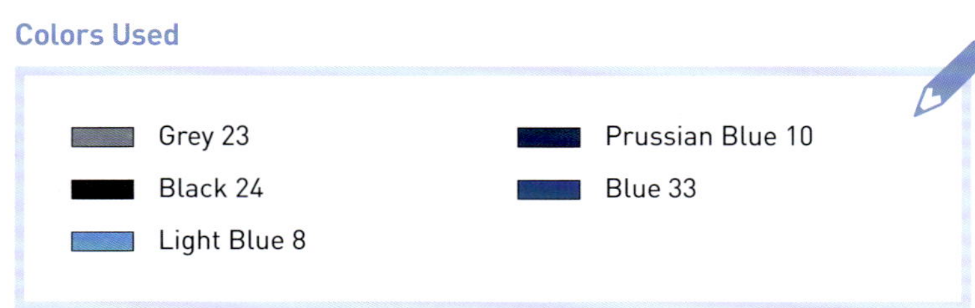

Coloring Key Points

1. This drawing is basically created using just grey and blue.

2. The reflection of the water on the dolphin is depicted by using light blue.

3. It's up to you how to convey the patterns of the waves.

Colors Used

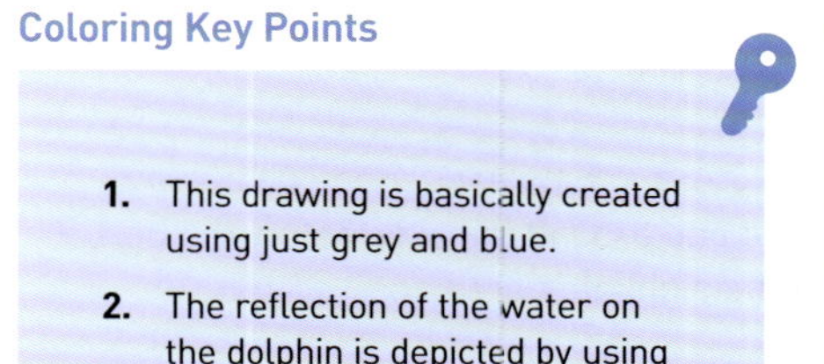

- ▬ Grey 23
- ▬ Black 24
- ▬ Light Blue 8
- ▬ Prussian Blue 10
- ▬ Blue 33

Reference Photo

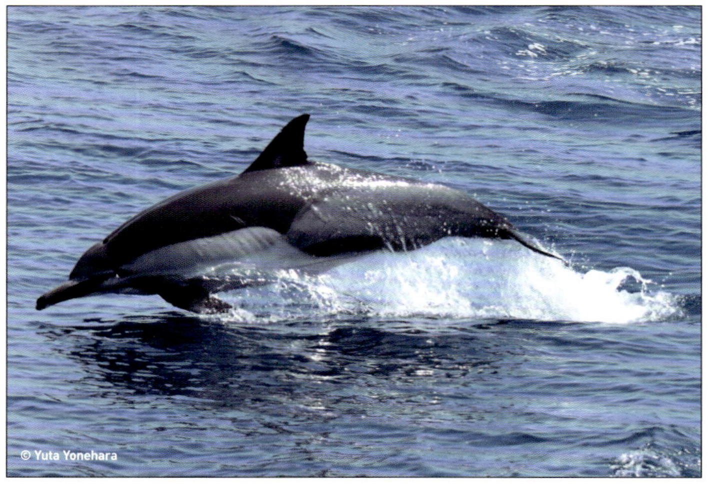

This is a wild spinner dolphin captured at the moment it leaps. You'll be depicting the glossy, wet texture, the smooth three-dimensional form of its body, and also the water surface. The basic process involves shading and shadowing with grey and black, then repeatedly applying blue tones to represent reflections and water splashes. The subtle handling of light and shadow will determine the dolphin's sense of presence, so observe carefully as you work.

Paint the dolphin's distinctive markings in the order of darker areas → lighter areas. Also, pay close attention to the area around the face, where the blue reflections from the water surface are especially noticeable.

Preliminary Drawing

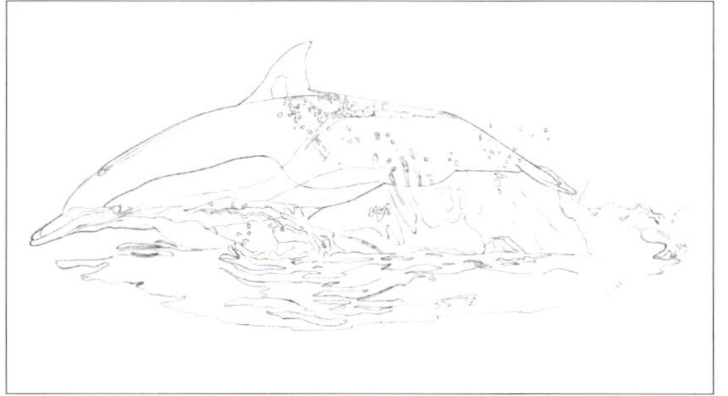

For this preliminary drawing, you should sketch the body of the dolphin, the splashes, and some of the surface of the water.

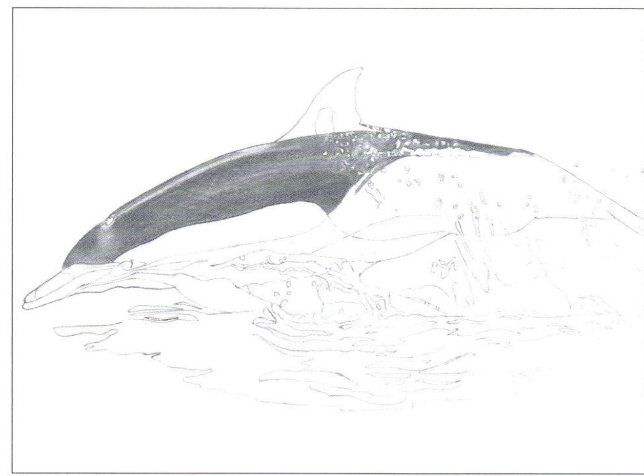

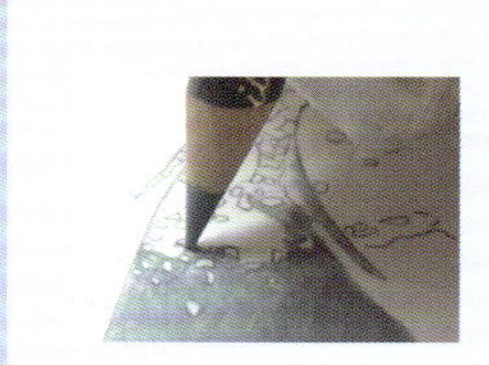

1 Observe the dolphin's markings carefully and begin coloring the darker areas with grey, starting from the upper part. There's a stripe running from the blowhole to the dorsal fin, so use variations in grey to express it. Similarly, shade lightly under the blowhole and around the area below the dorsal fin, where the highlights are concentrated.

▮ Grey

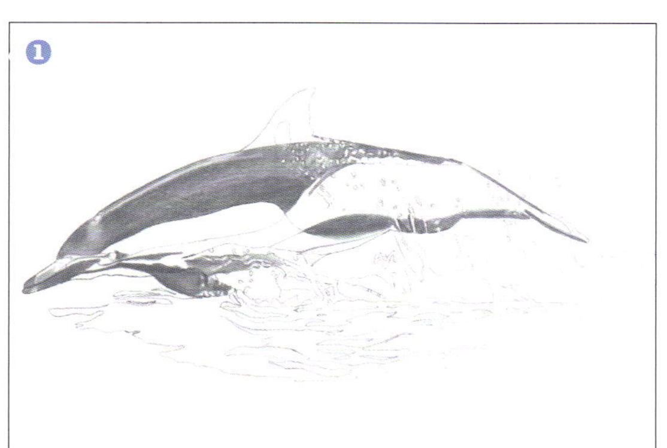

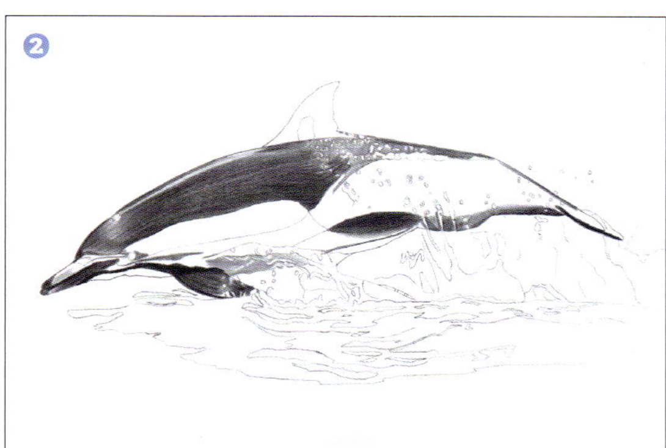

2 ❶ Underpaint the darker areas of the head, pectoral fins, and rear body using grey. ❷ Then, apply a layer of black over the areas that were colored in **Step 2** ❶. The goal is to enhance the contrast by deepening the parts that were colored more heavily in grey.

▮ Grey ▮ Black

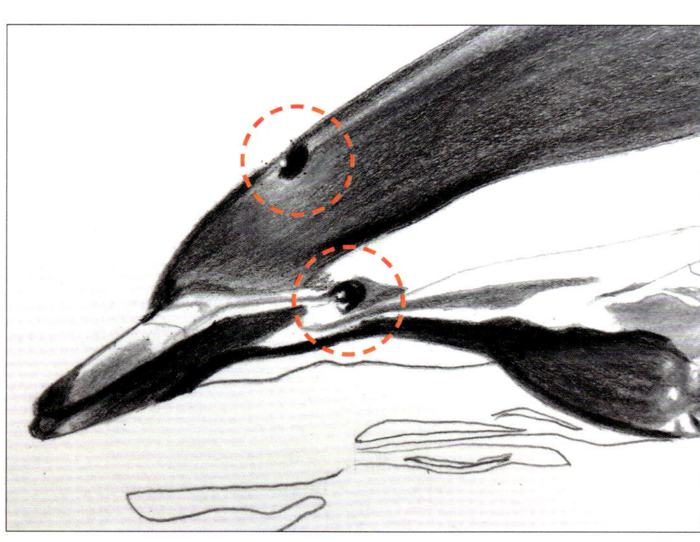

3 Color in the eye and blowhole using black. Be sure to clearly preserve the small highlights.

▮ Black

UNIT 09

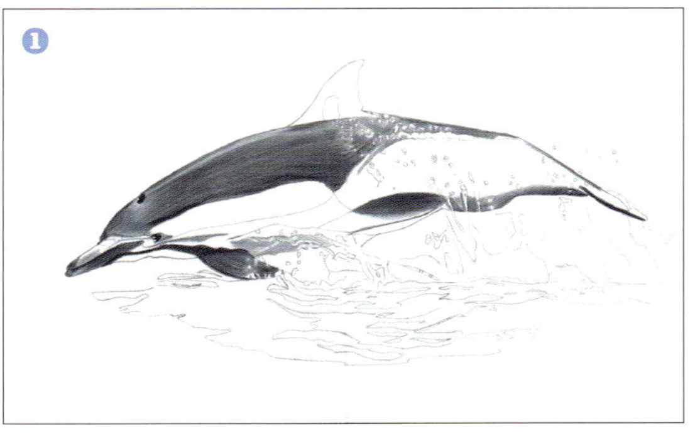

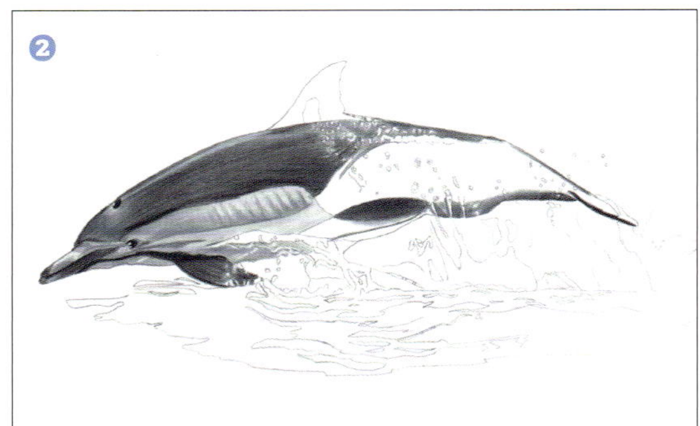

4 ❶ Color the area below the blowhole and the streak along the back, both from **Step 2**, using light blue. ❷ Shade the lighter areas of the upper body with grey. For the parts where the rib cage protrudes, first draw several thick lines, then adjust the shad ng so that the lower parts become darker.

▬▬ Light blue ▬▬ Grey

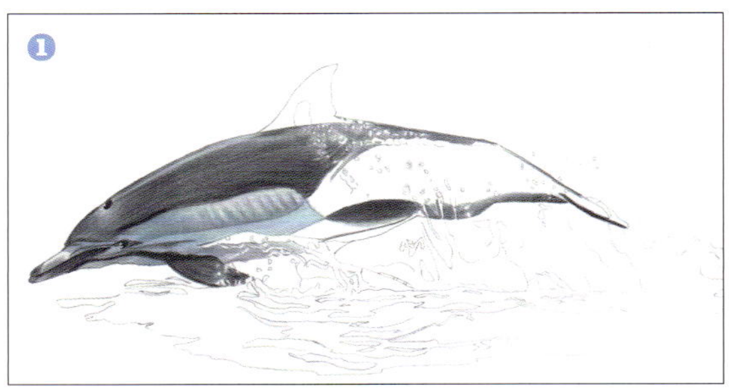

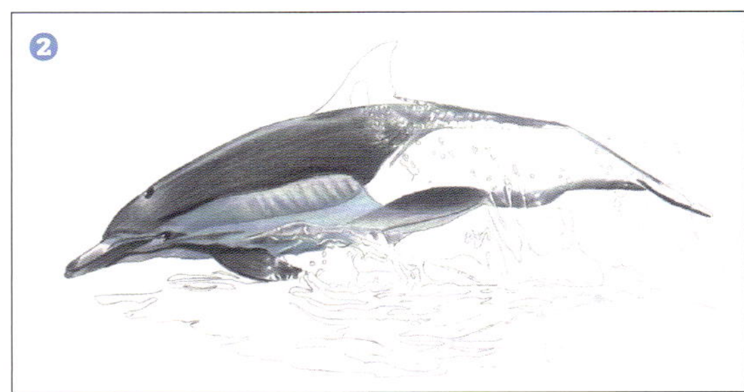

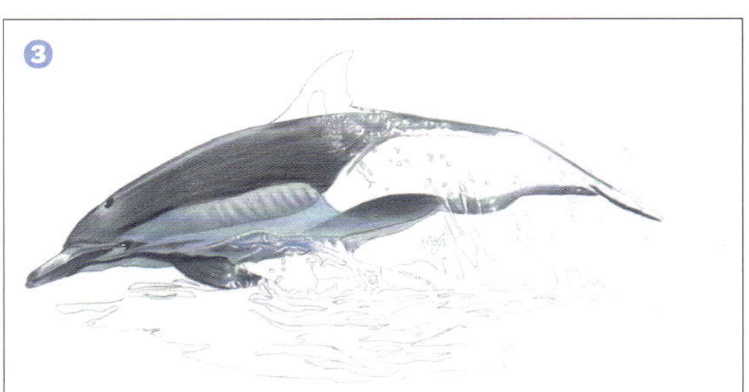

5 ❶ Apply light blue to the areas that were colored in **Step 4** ❷. While a real dolphin would normally appear whitish-grey, this is the reflected light from the water surface, so don't hesitate to apply it boldly. ❷ Shade the lower part of the body with grey, paying attention to the shadows so that the new color blends naturally with the areas already painted. ❸ Similarly, use light blue to depict the reflected color from the water.

▬▬ Light blue ▬▬ Grey

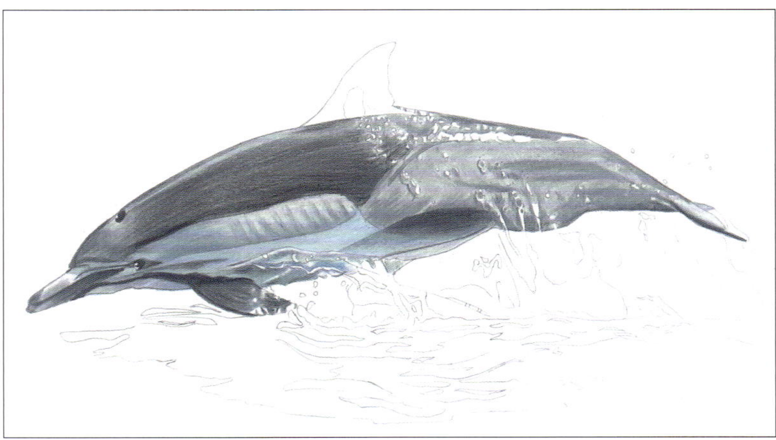

6 Fill in the remaining lower body with grey. Leave the highlights on the upper part and the bubbles along the dolphin's side white. When you do this, pay close attention to the shades and shadows and also depict the dolphin's distinctive markings.

▬▬ Grey

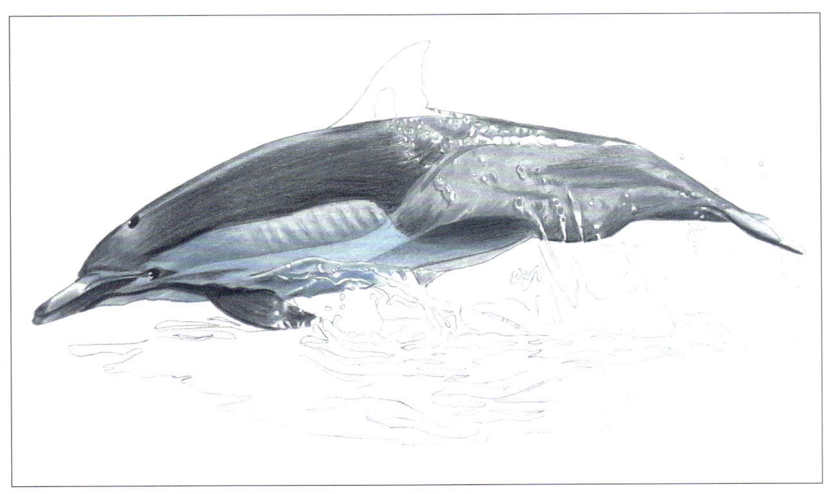

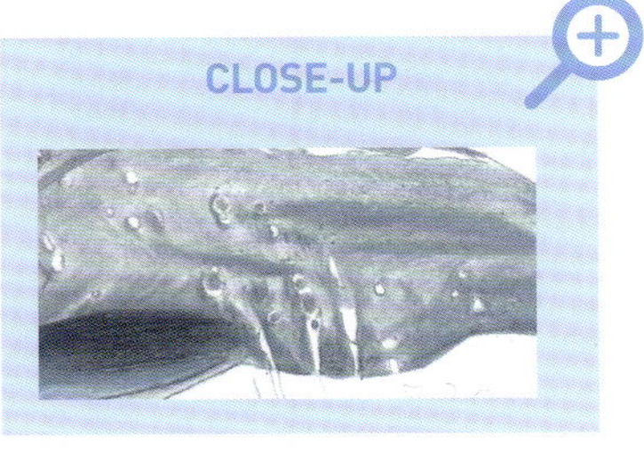

7 Lightly layer black over the areas to emphasize the shadows. It's fine to do this only on the parts that were darkened with grey in **Step 6**.

███ Black

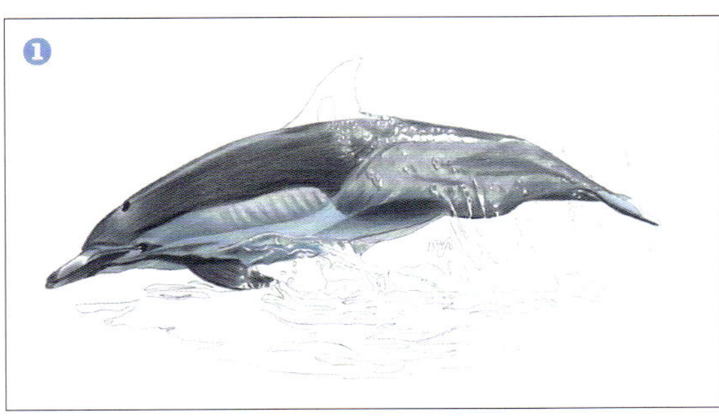

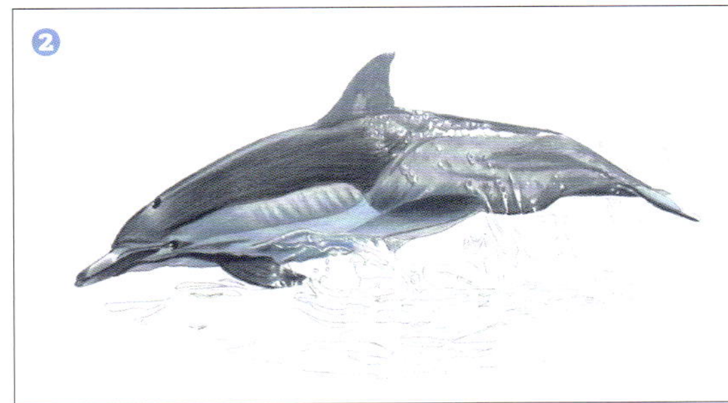

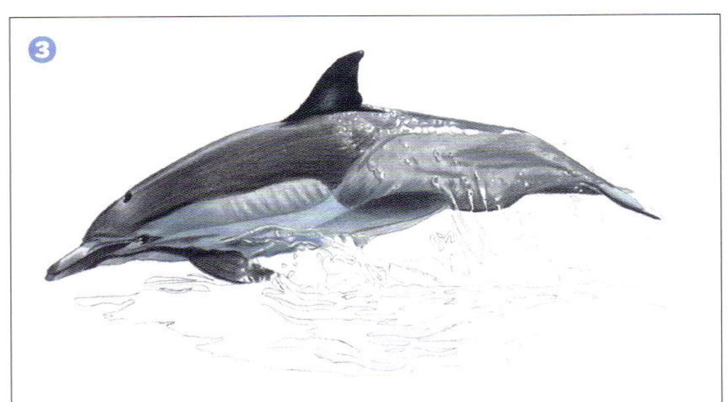

8 ❶ Add light blue to the areas colored in **Step 7**.
❷ Using only grey, color over the entire dorsal fin while leaving the central marking visible.
❸ Darken the dorsal fin with black. Then, tint the faintly preserved central area with light blue. The dolphin itself is now complete.

███ Light blue ███ Grey ███ Black

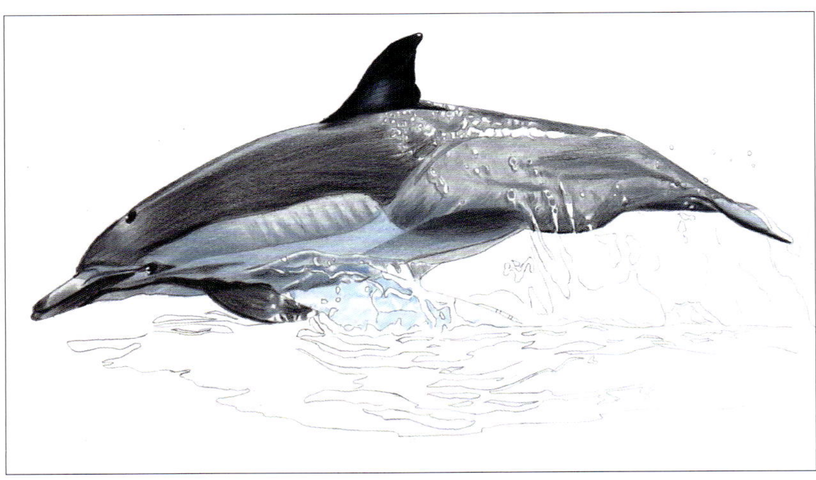

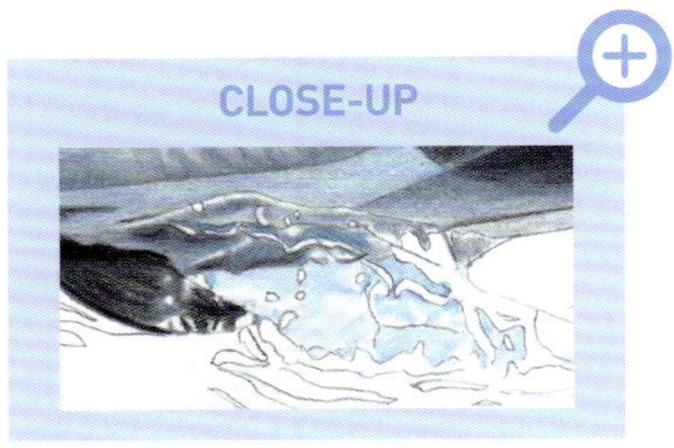

9 Color the splashes of water. Start by lightly applying light blue around the pectoral fin area. Be sure to leave the highlights uncolored.

███ Light blue

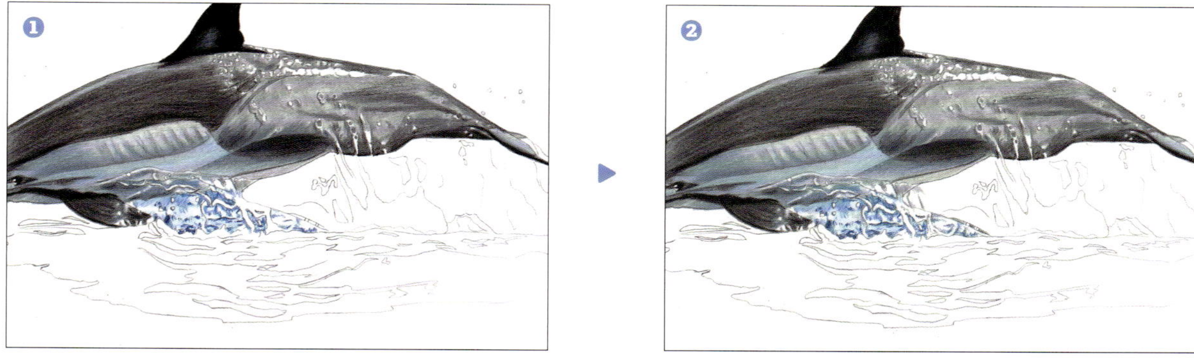

10 ❶ Layer Prussian blue from the top down, using fine strokes to color as if drawing in the patterns. ❷ Use grey to slightly enhance the shading. Be careful not to make it too dark, as it might lose its watery feel. Keep it light.

▰▰ Prussian blue ▰▰ Grey

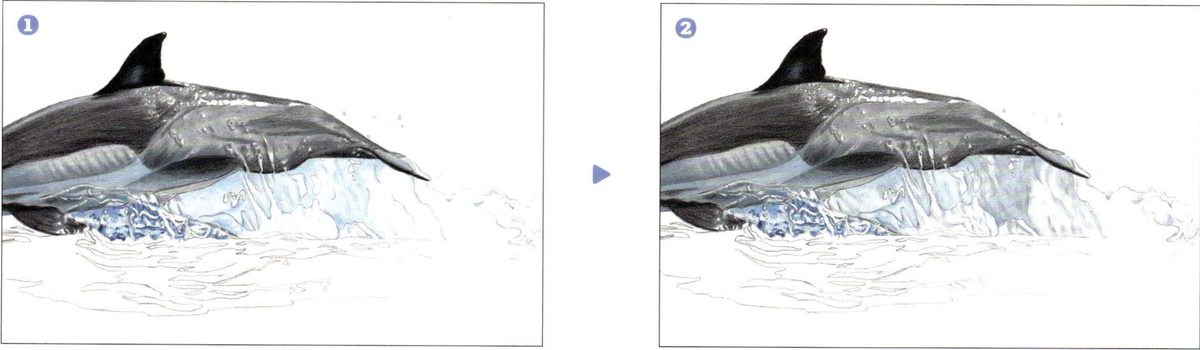

11 ❶ Paint the white spray near the tail fin by following the preliminary drawing lines and lightly shading with light blue. Leave the white areas unpainted. ❷ Then add a light layer of grey over it to enhance the shading.

▰▰ Light blue ▰▰ Grey

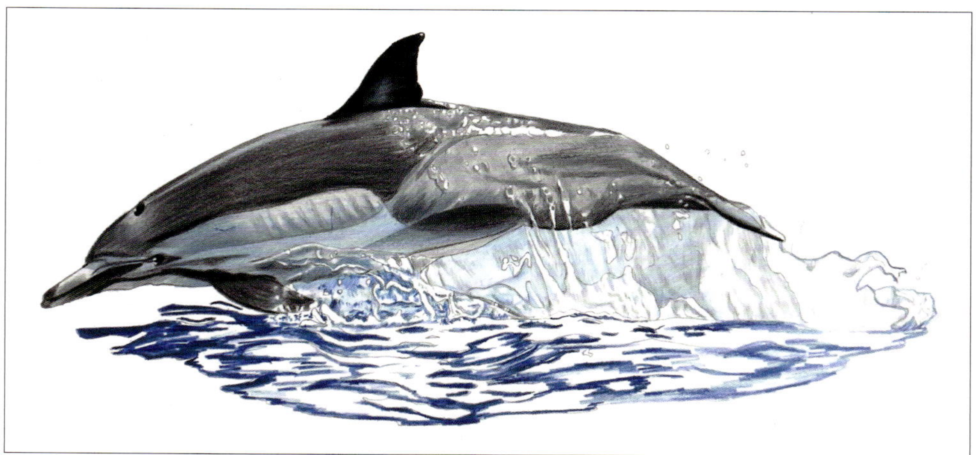

12 Draw the water surface by roughly adding wave patterns in Prussian blue below the dolphin. Feel free to draw the wave patterns as you wish. They will look convincing as long as you preserve the shadows and highlights. While you're at it, trace the outlines of the white spray as well.

▰▰ Prussian blue

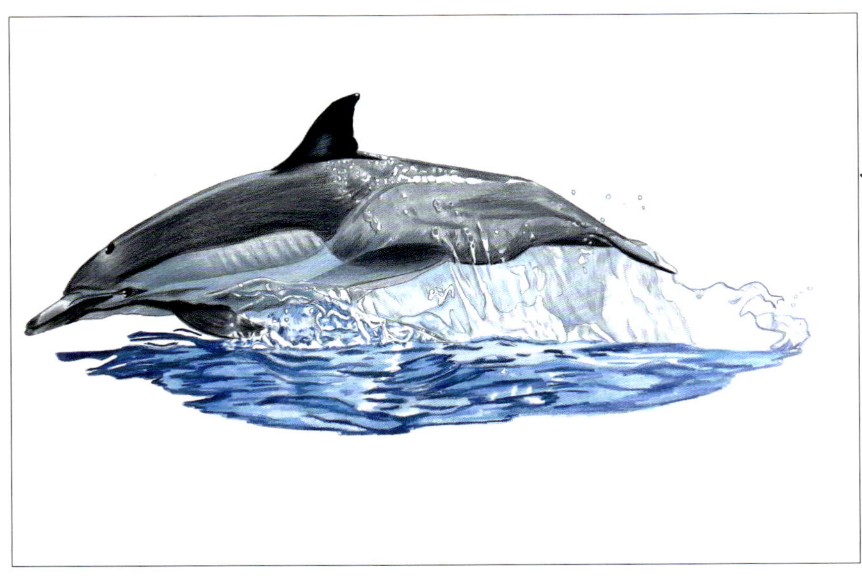

13 Layer light blue over the surface, again keeping shadows and highlights in mind. Be sure to leave the highlights clearly white. The water surface on the left side near the dolphin's head can be shaded in quite darkly.

■ Light blue

COMPLETE

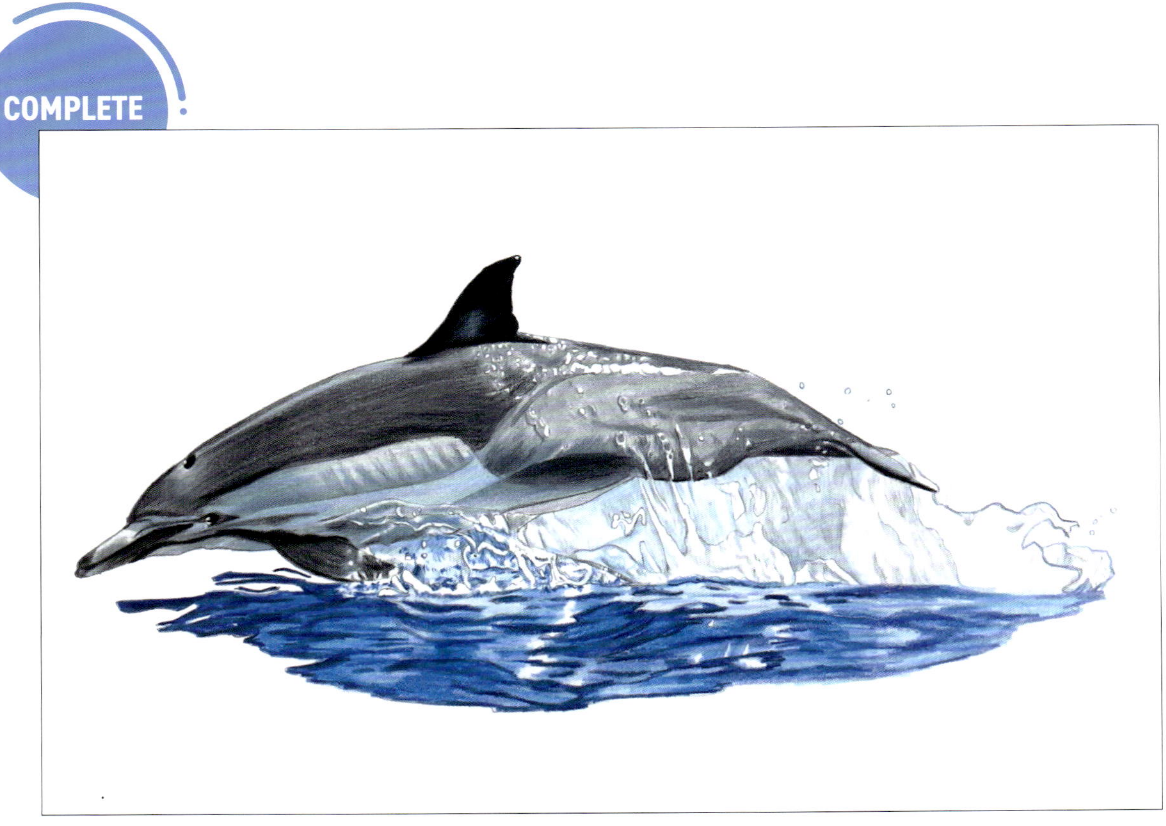

Adjust with blue, emphasizing the shadows already created with the light blue. You can add greenish tones if you like, but as I prefer a deep blue sea, I'll consider it finished at this point.

■ Blue

Draw a Rabbit

Colored pencils: Prismacolor
Paper: New TMK Poster Paper (A4)
Drawn by Ryosuke Mika

Coloring Key Points

1. Simplify the forms and focus on capturing the overall three-dimensional structure (p. 11).

2. By putting extra effort into the eyes, you can enhance the rabbit's sense of life and presence (p.14).

3. Depict the fur texture primarily through colored-pencil strokes, with minimal use of a stylus (p.15).

Colors Used

PC1063 Cool Grey 50%	PC1051 Warm Grey 20%
PC914 Cream	PC935 Black
PC942 Yellow Ochre	PC938 White
PC928 Blush Pink	PC932 Violet
PC956 Lilac	

Reference Photo

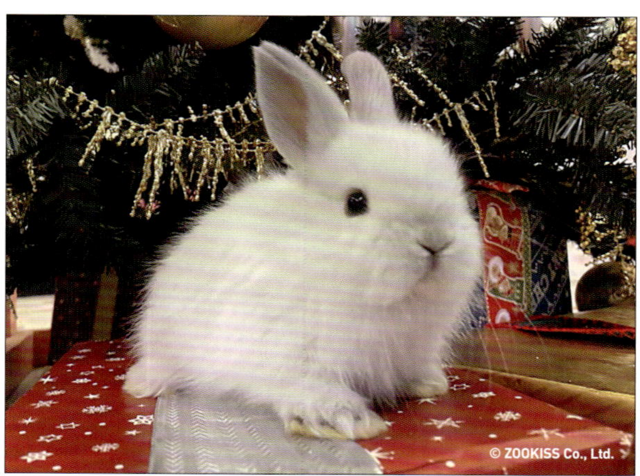

The theme for this drawing is the depiction of the eyes, fur texture, and three-dimensional form. The eyes are the most important part of conveying the animal's sense of life, so special care should be taken with them. The fur texture will be rendered using colored-pencil strokes. A key point is to stay mindful of the overall sense of three-dimensionality and form while drawing. As the light source in the reference photo is a bit unclear, we'll proceed with the assumption that the light is coming from the upper left.

Preliminary Drawing

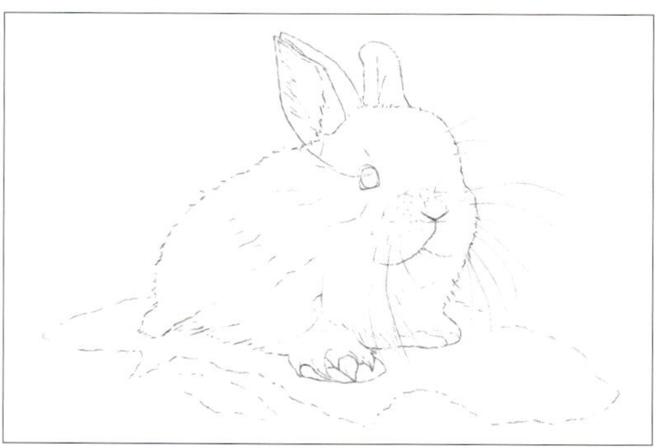

Pay close attention to the size and proportions of the head and body as you create the preliminary drawing. At this stage, be sure to clearly draw the eye, nose, and mouth as well.

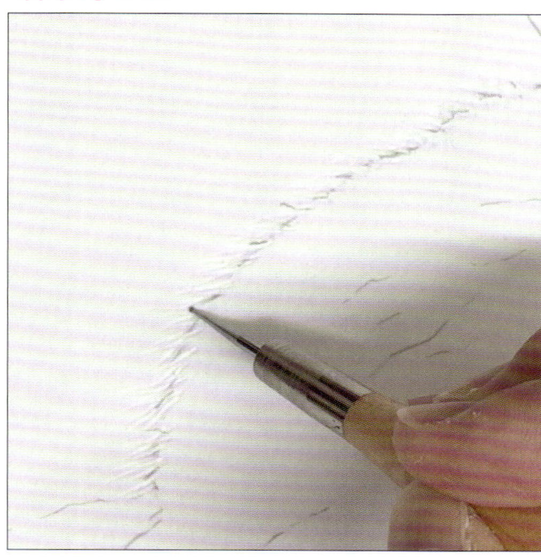

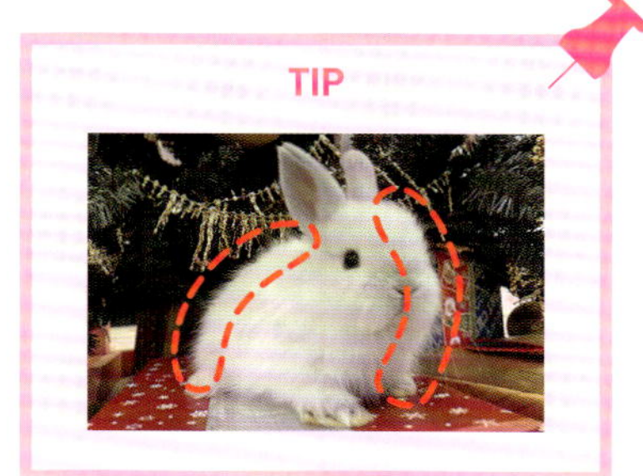

1 In this drawing I hardly ever use a stylus. However, as it's difficult to depict the fine fur along the rabbit's outline (in the red-marked areas in **TIP**) with colored pencils alone, it would be a good idea to use it here. Styluses come in various thicknesses, but a relatively fine one is easier to use for this area. Since the background will be lightly shaded at the end, the grooves made with the stylus will stand out at that stage.

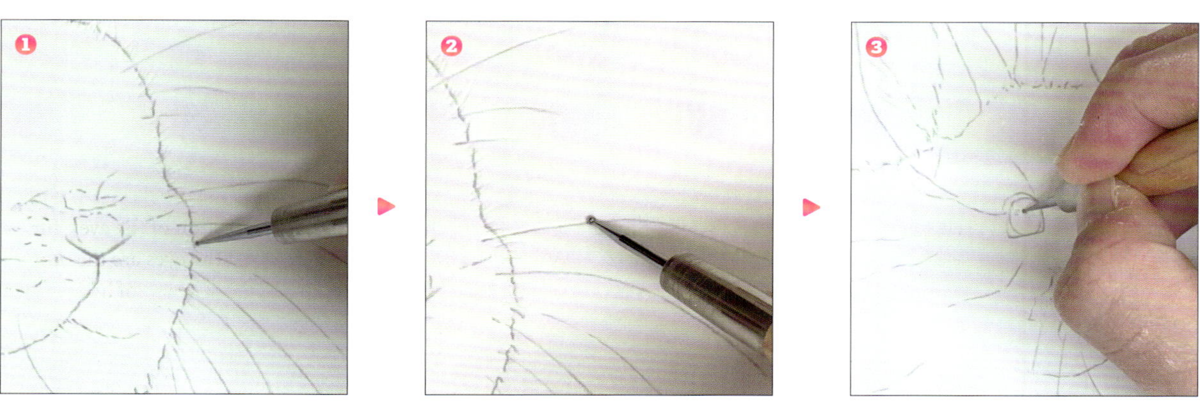

2 ❶ When using the stylus, the key is not to move it in a single direction, but rather to move it irregularly in various directions. ❷ Use the stylus for the whiskers as well. For this area, a relatively thicker stylus works better. ❸ Finally, use the stylus to create the highlight in the eye. The trick is to press it in firmly from directly above.

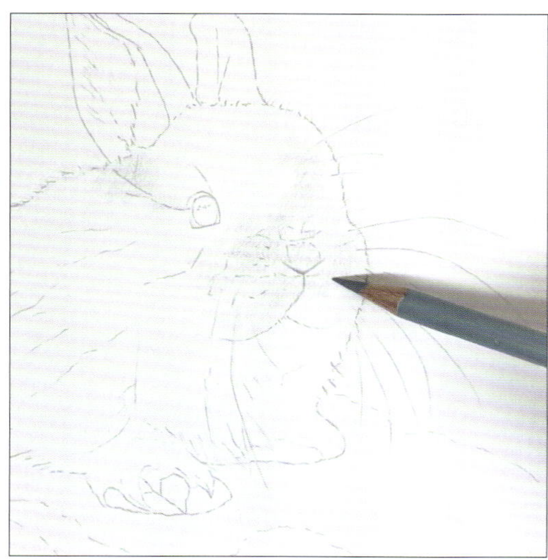

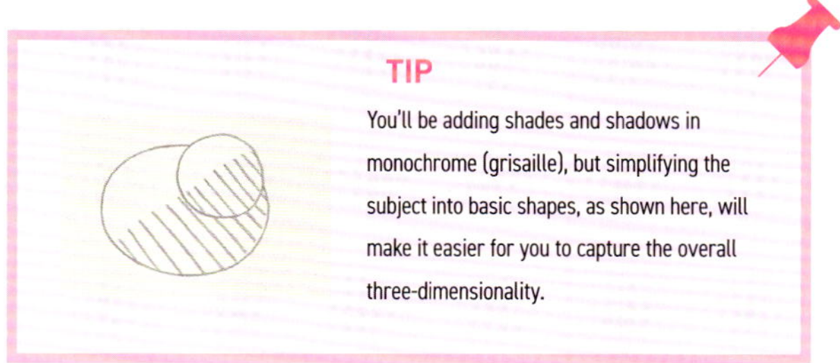

3 First, use cool grey 50% to roughly block in the shades and shadows, focusing on the hatched areas in **TIP**. The key is to hold the colored pencil at a slight angle and apply the color gently.

▬▬ Cool grey 50%

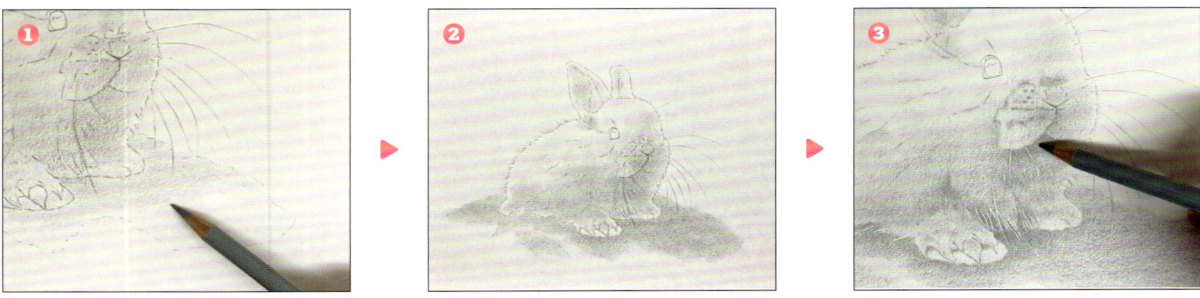

4 **①** Add cool grey 50% to the cast shadows as well. **②** If the outlines feel a bit too harsh, gently dab them with a kneaded eraser. **③** Once the basic shading is in place, begin adding more detailed shades and shadows.

▬ Cool grey 50%

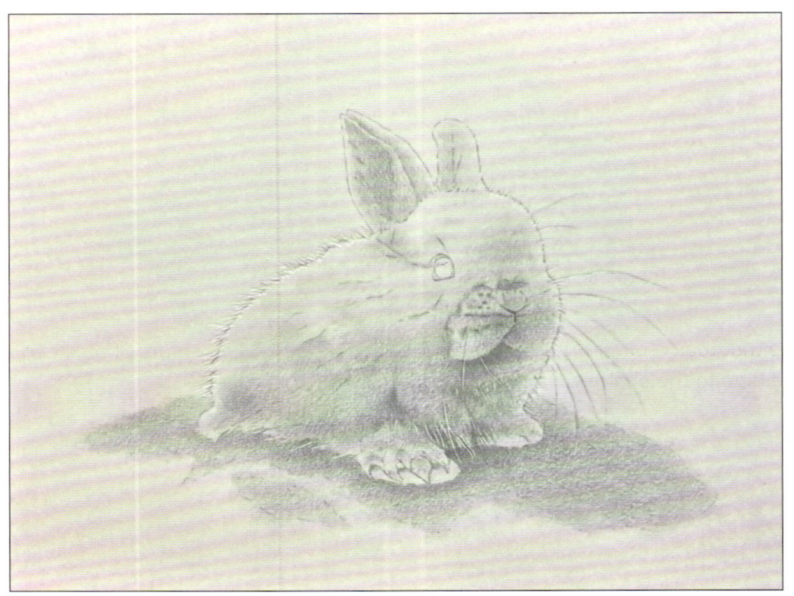

The drawing after you've finished adding the shades and shadows with cool grey 50%.

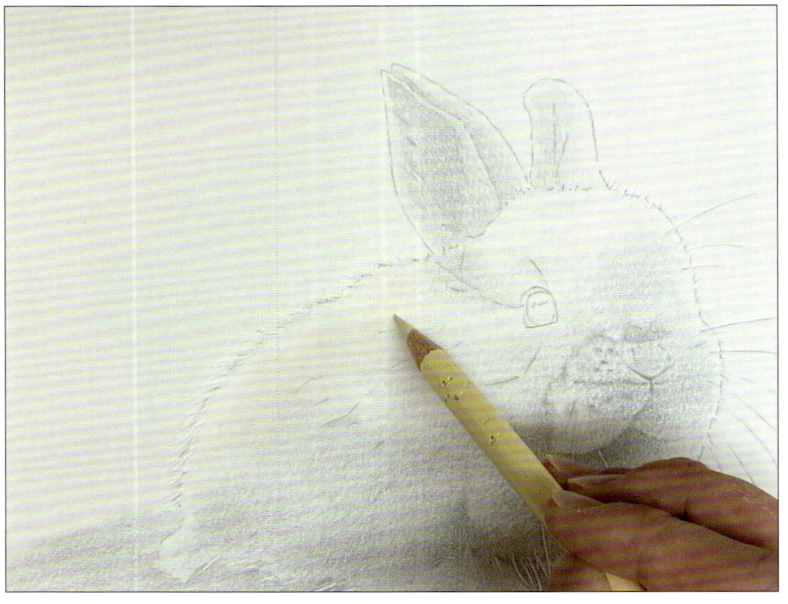

5 Start by applying the base colors of the rabbit. Although it may appear white at first glance, a closer look reveals subtle variations in color. Observe carefully and color what you see. At this stage, you don't need to worry about fur texture—just focus on getting the rabbit's true colors down. Begin by covering the entire area with a light cream tone.

▭ Cream

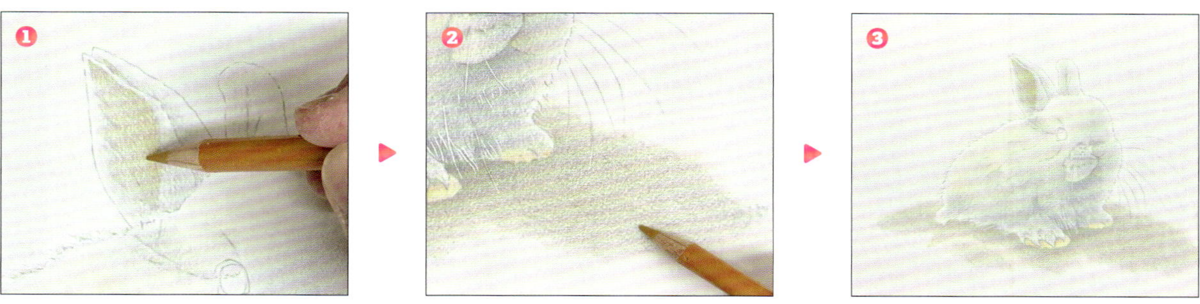

6 ❶ Next, add touches of yellow ochre in certain areas. ❷ It's also a good idea to apply some yellow ochre to the shadows cast on the ground. ❸ This is what the drawing looks like after applying the cream and yellow ochre.

▧ Yellow ochre

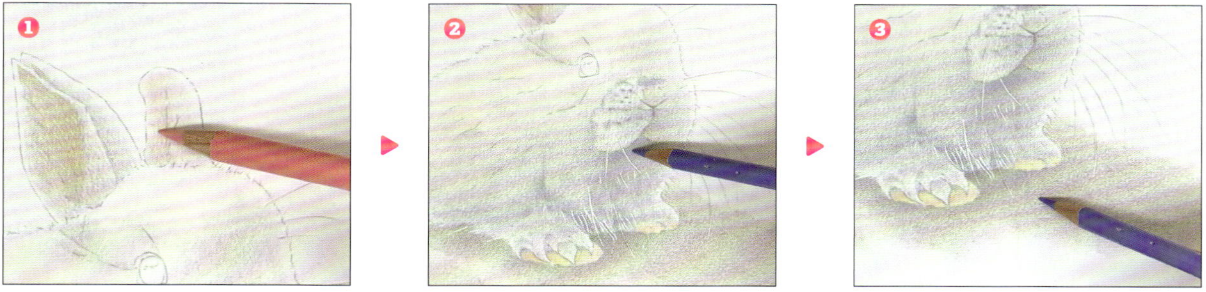

7 ❶ Gently apply blush pink to the areas that look a bit pink, such as around the ears. ❷ Adding hints of lilac can also be effective. ❸ I also added some lilac to the shadows on the ground.

▧ Blush pink ▧ Lilac

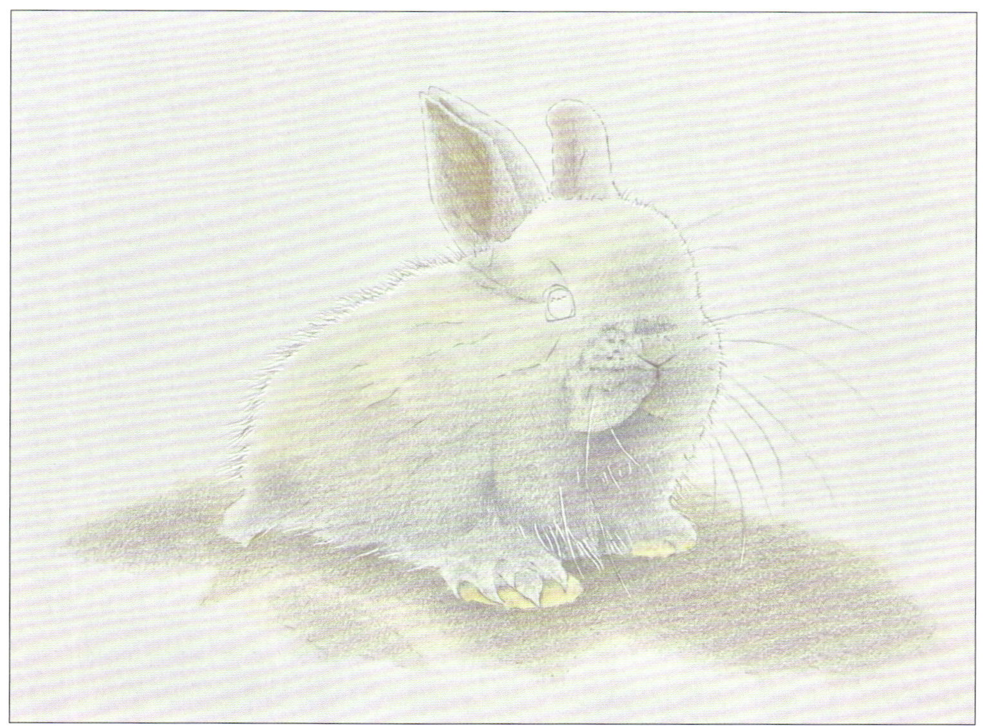

The drawing after the base colors have been added.

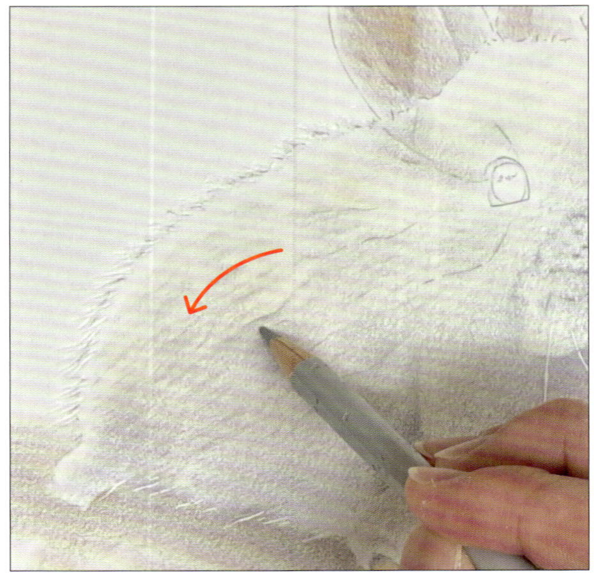

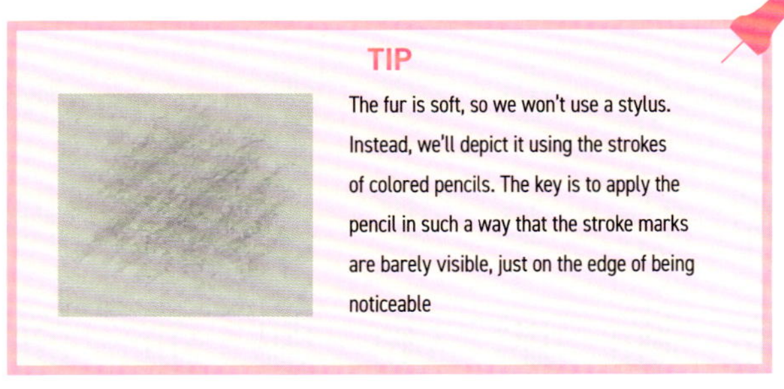

8 Now we begin depicting the fur texture. Using warm grey 20%, draw while keeping in mind the technique shown in the **TIP** section. You don't have to reproduce the reference photo exactly. Instead, focus on the direction and flow of the fur as you work.

▬ Warm grey 20%

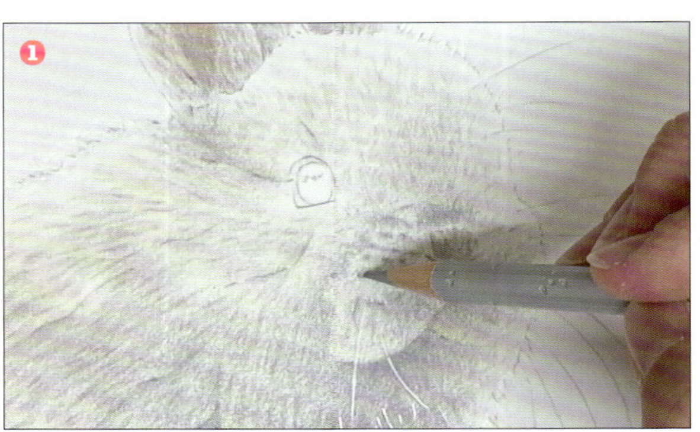

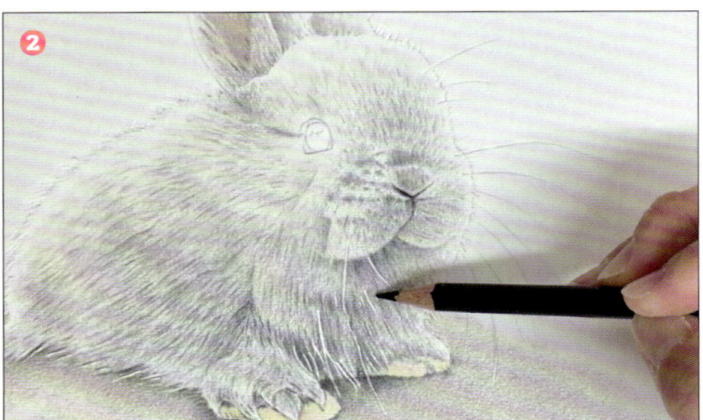

9 ❶ For fine details like the whiskers, use warm grey 20% and carefully observe the reference photo as you draw. ❷ Then, selectively add some black to give the drawing a bit more contrast. Be careful not to overdo it, as using too much black can easily muddy the colors.

▬ Warm grey 20% ▬ Black

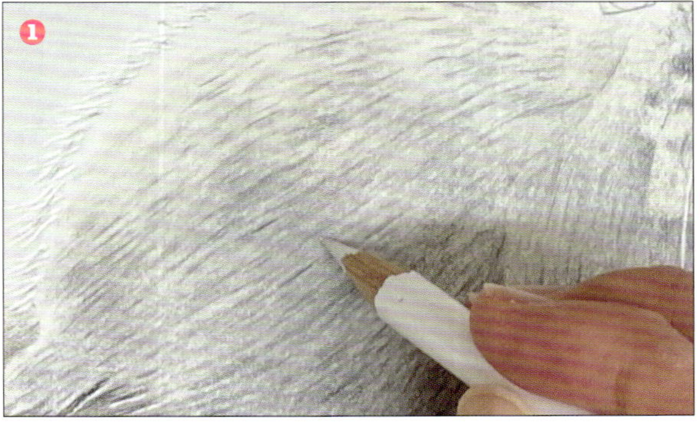

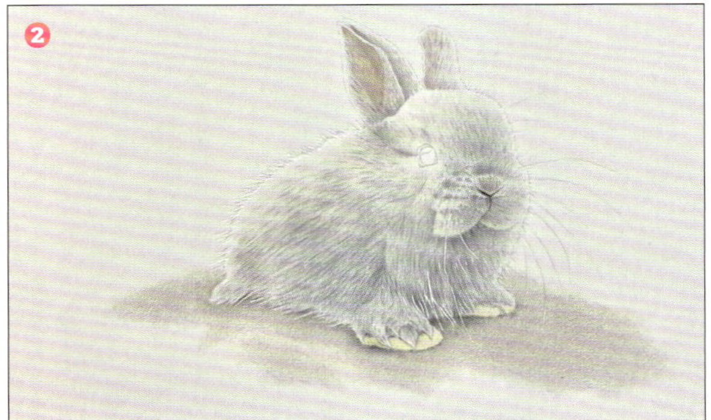

10 ❶ Use white to gently blend the fur texture you created in **Steps 8** and **9**—think of it as a light vanishing (burnishing) process. ❷ This completes the fur rendering.

▭ White

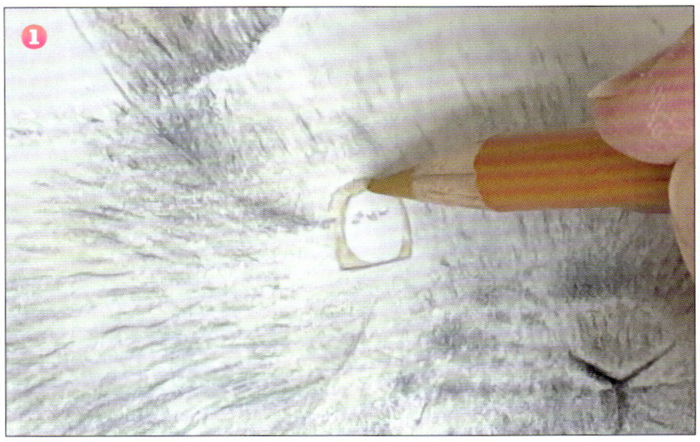

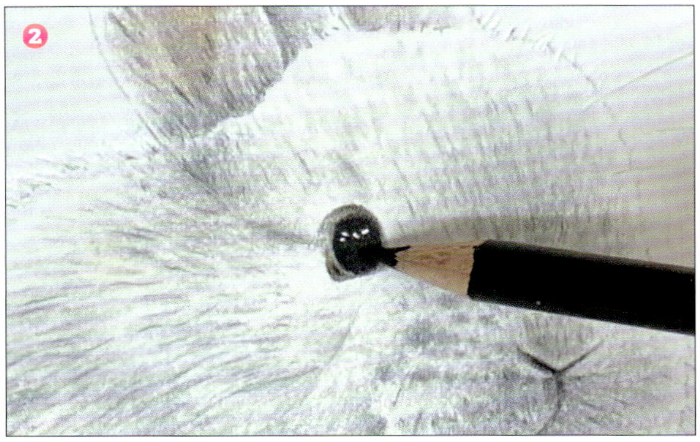

11 Draw the eye. It's one of the most important parts when drawing animals, so give it extra attention. ❶ First, use yellow ochre to shade the rim of the eye. ❷ Then, fill in the eyeball with black. The indentations made earlier in **Step 2** ❸ with the stylus should now come into play.

Yellow ochre Black

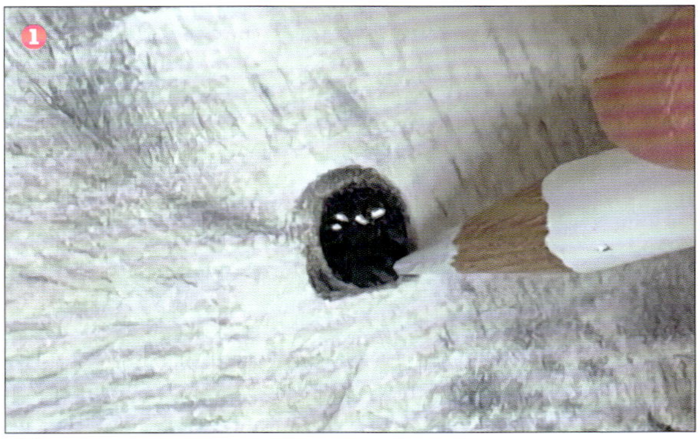

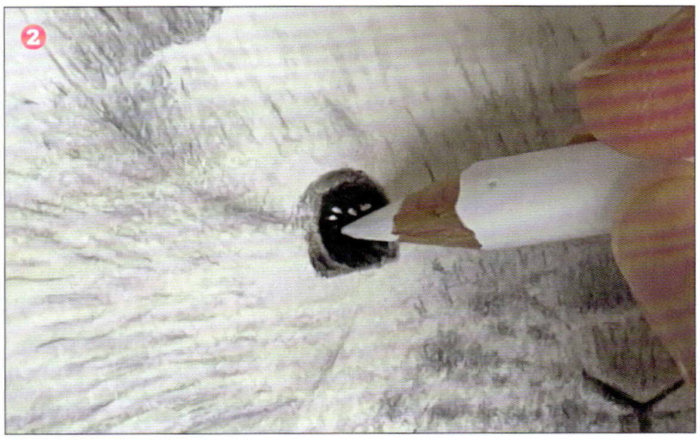

UNIT 10

12 ❶ For areas where fur overlaps the eye, draw over the black with white. ❷ It's also a good idea to add a bit of white to the eyeball to enhance its look.

White

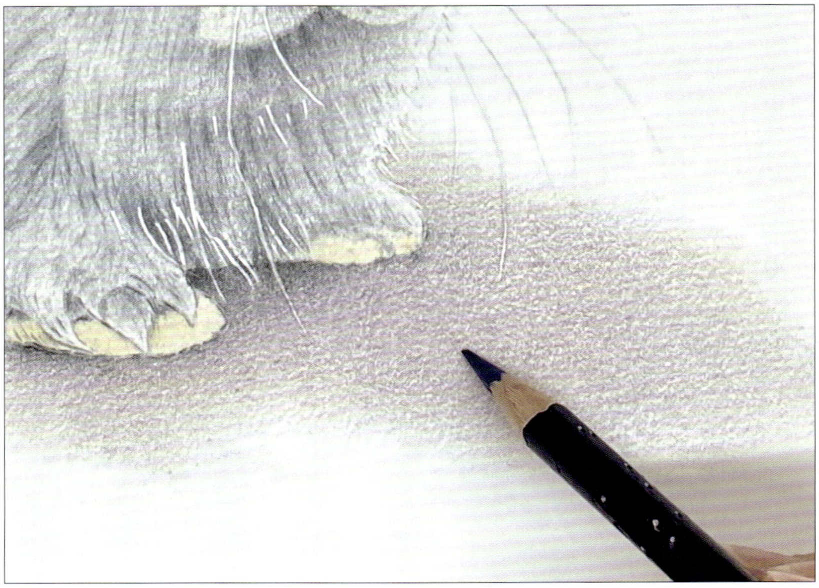

13 Now for the final touches. As yellow ochre was added to the cast shadow in **Step 6** ❷, adding its complementary color, violet, will now give the shadow more depth.

Violet

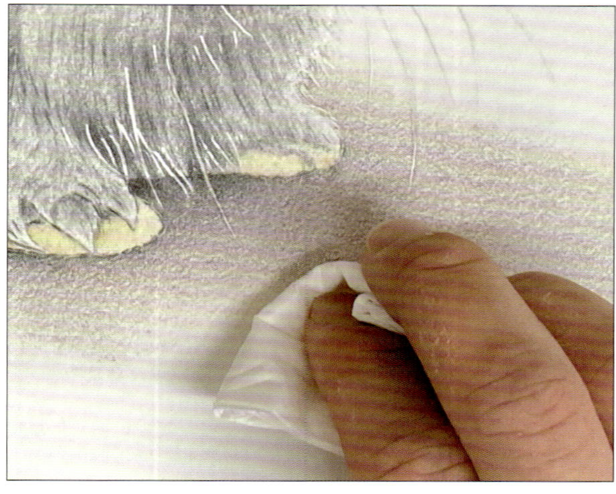

14 You can soften the edges of the cast shadow by gently rubbing them with a tissue.

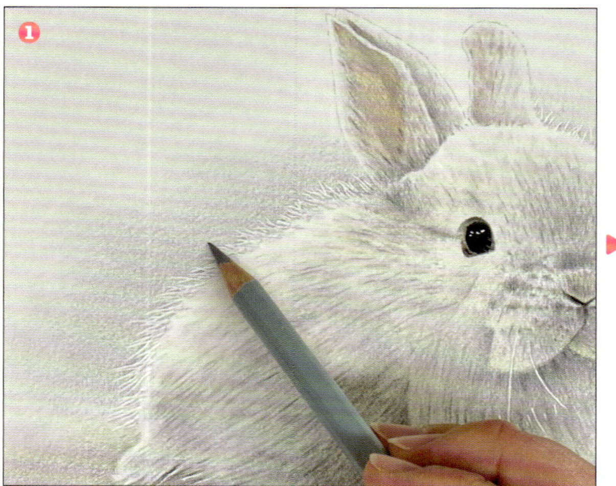

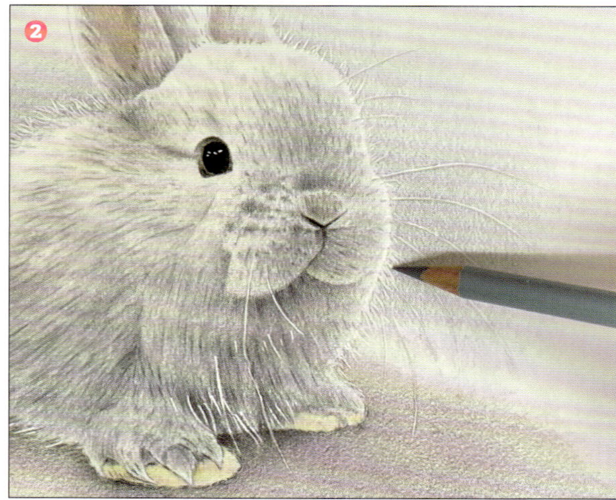

15 ❶ By lightly shading the background with cool grey 50%, you can enhance the presence of the rabbit.
❷ The indentations made with the stylus in **Steps 1** and **2** should now become more visible.

▬ Cool grey 50%

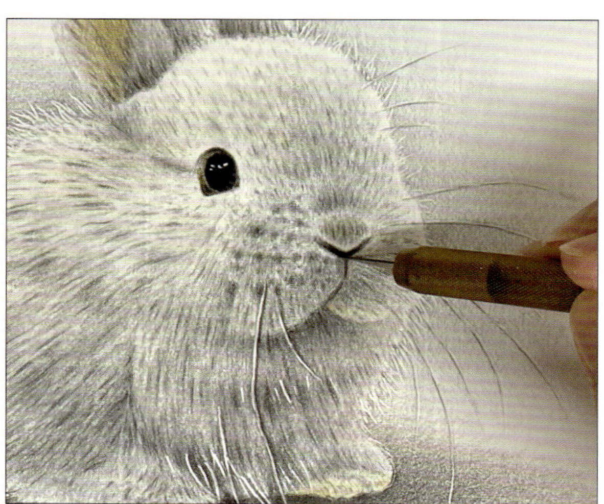

16 Finally, add any missing colors. If you've overdrawn in some areas, you can gently scrape them away with a design knife.

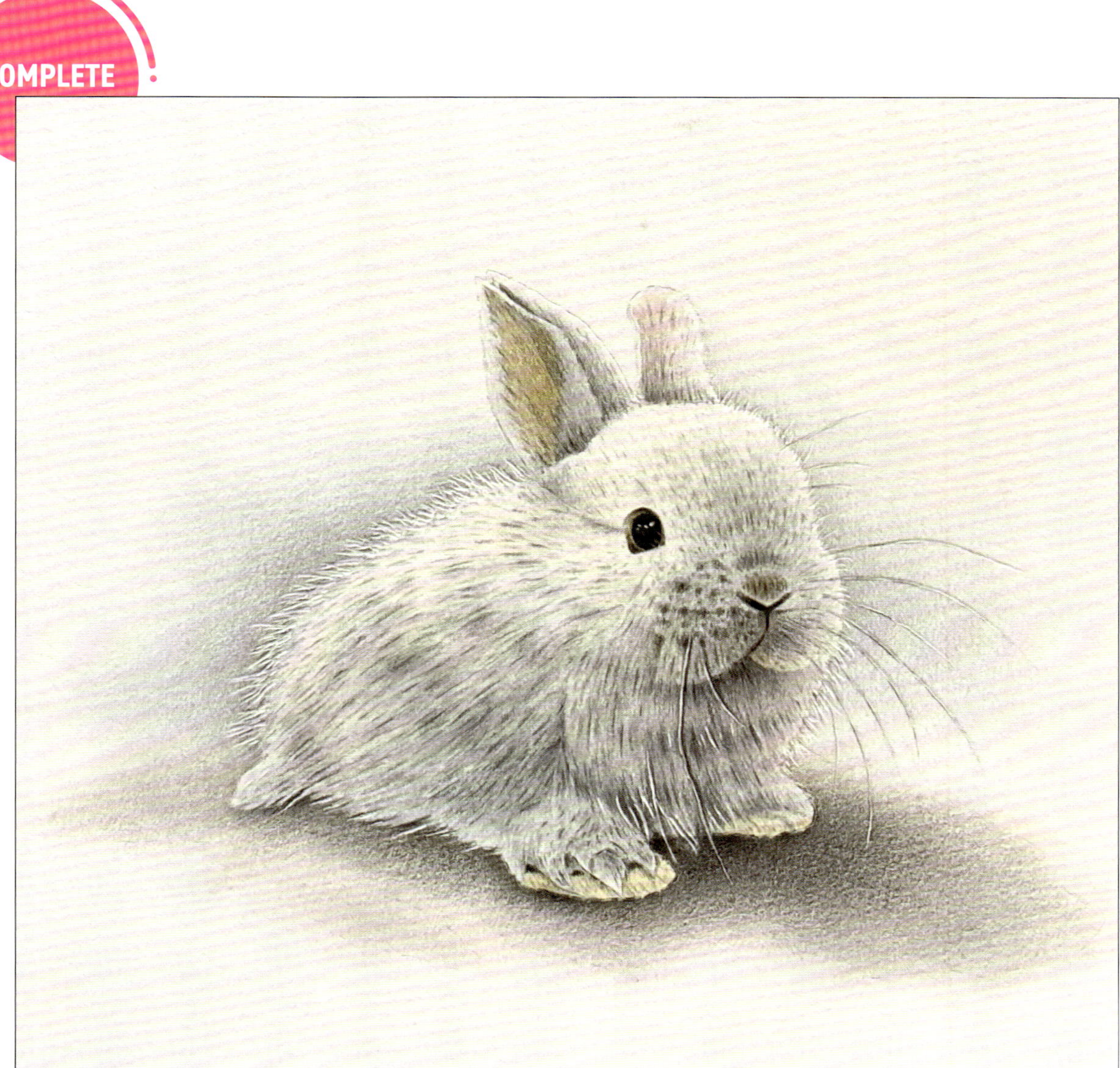

Stand back and take a look at the drawing. If everything looks okay, you've finished!

Draw a Shiba Inu

Colored pencils: Prismacolor
Paper: Daigen Thick Kent Paper
 **Drawn by Bonbon**

Coloring Key Points

1. Depict the subtle "light" visible within the pupil to suggest an outdoor setting (p.14).

2. Use highly opaque, light-colored pencils to depict the fur (p.15).

3. Emphasize the strength of the sunlight by using strong contrasts in light and shadow to enhance the sense of three-dimensionality (p.11).

Colors Used

■ PC935 Black	■ PC922 Poppy Red
▢ PC997 Beige	■ PC947 Dark Umber
▢ PC1024 Blue Slate	▢ PC916 Canary Yellow
■ PC1032 Pumpkin Orange	▢ OP501 Soft White*
■ PC902 Ultramarine	■ PC1056 Warm Grey 70%
▢ PC929 Pink	*Holbein

Preliminary Drawing

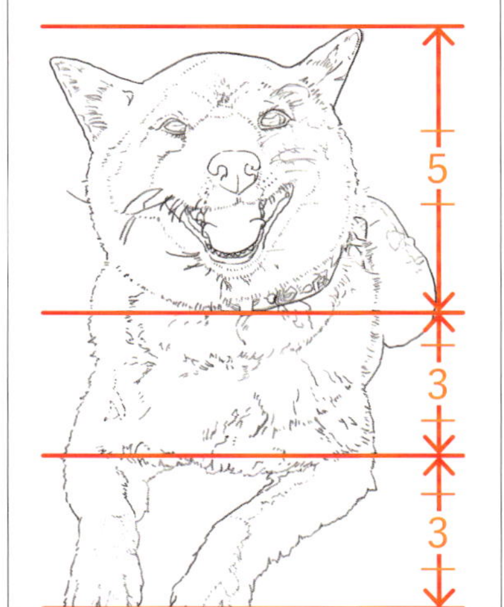

This is a frontal angle that makes it easier to capture the form. Because the photo is taken from a slightly high angle, pay attention to the relative heights of the head, chest, and front legs (approximately 5:3:3). Try not to overcomplicate the details. It's best to suggest just some fur texture and give a rough indication of the boundaries between light and shadow.

Reference Photo

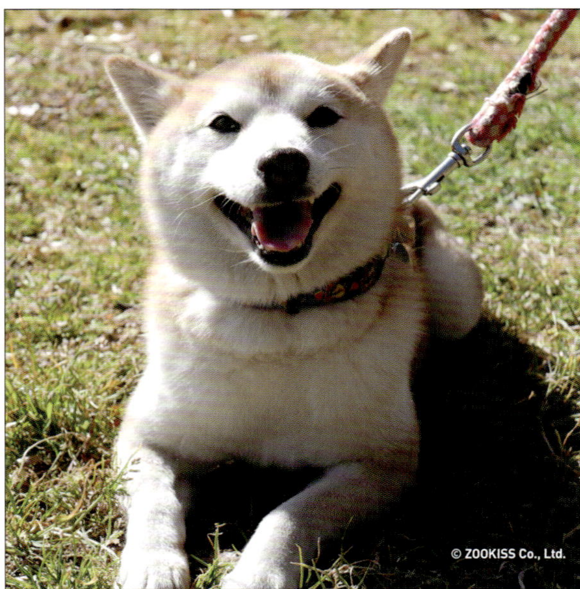

The subject is a Shiba Inu basking in the sun. The key point is how to depict the sunlight. By using black for the grisaille, you can heighten the contrast in the shading and emphasize the intensity of the sunlight. Also, by adding blue tones to the shadowed areas, you can create a color scheme that conveys the presence of strong sunlight.

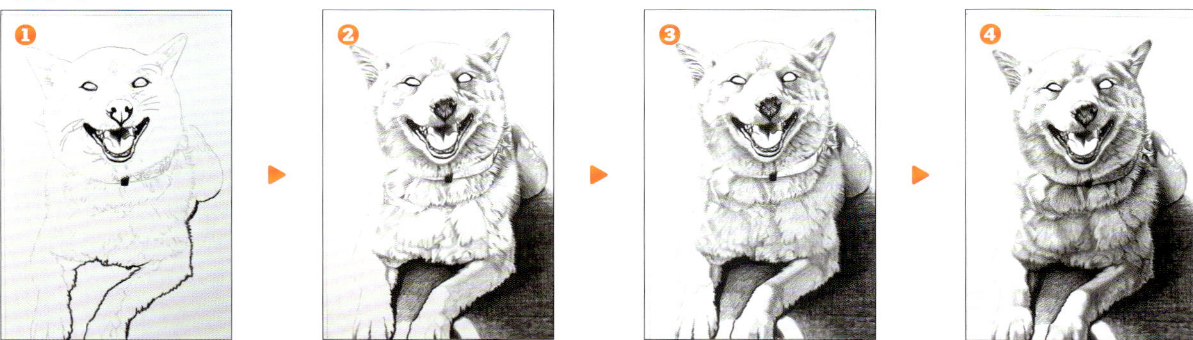

1 This is the grisaille stage (p.11). **1** First, trace the really dark areas using black with firm pressure to make the boundaries easy to see. **2** Then, color in the main fur texture as if you are drawing it. The key is to keep a light touch and apply the color thinly. **3** Once the fur texture is somewhat established, lightly shade the shadowed areas overall to clearly separate the light and dark areas. **4** When the contrast between light and shadow is established, deepen the shading on the fur and other shadowed areas to complete the grisaille.

▮ Black

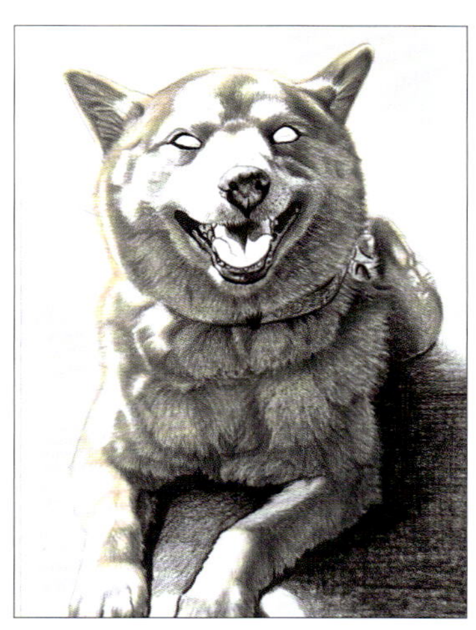

2 Use beige to add color to the brownish areas. Also lightly apply beige to the white fur on the face, chest, and legs to create a sense of overall color harmony.

▭ Beige

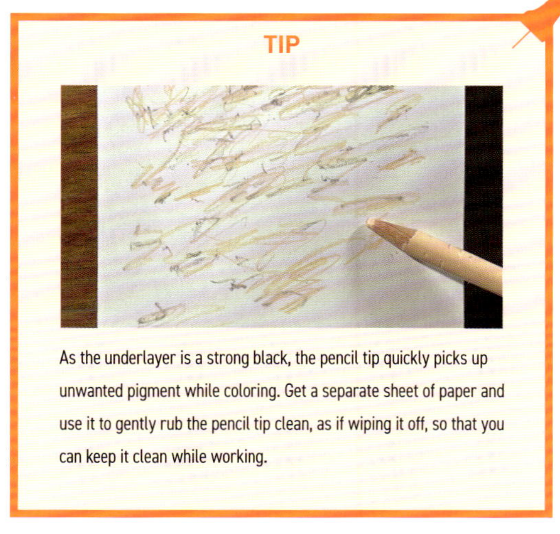

TIP

As the underlayer is a strong black, the pencil tip quickly picks up unwanted pigment while coloring. Get a separate sheet of paper and use it to gently rub the pencil tip clean, as if wiping it off, so that you can keep it clean while working.

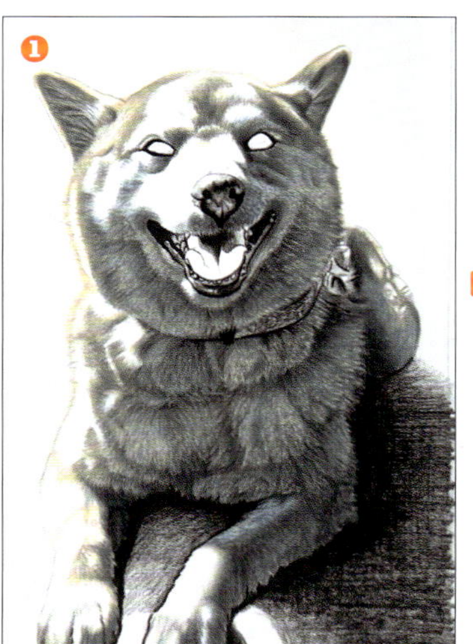 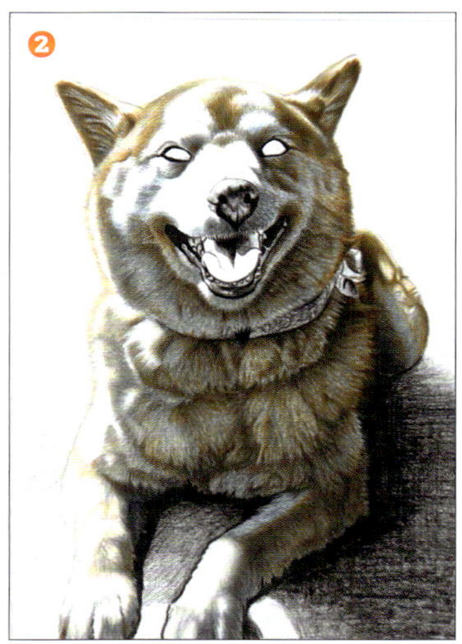

3 **1** Because sunlight has a high color temperature, bluish tones stand out strongly, particularly in shaded areas. For that reason, you should apply layers of blue slate mainly to the shadows in the white fur. **2** In the shaded areas of the brown fur, apply layers of pumpkin orange to deepen the shade.

▭ Blue slate ▮ Pumpkin orange

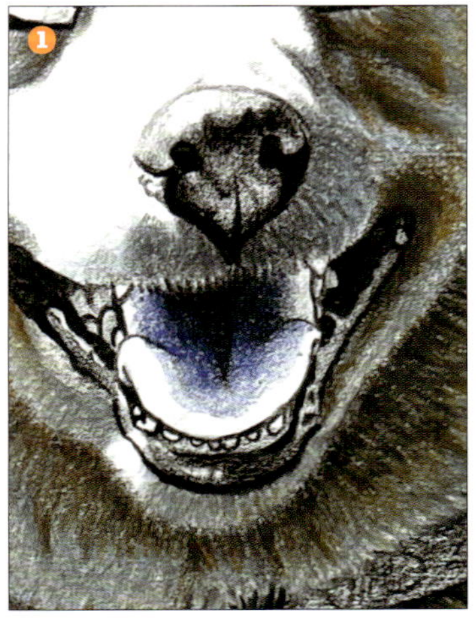 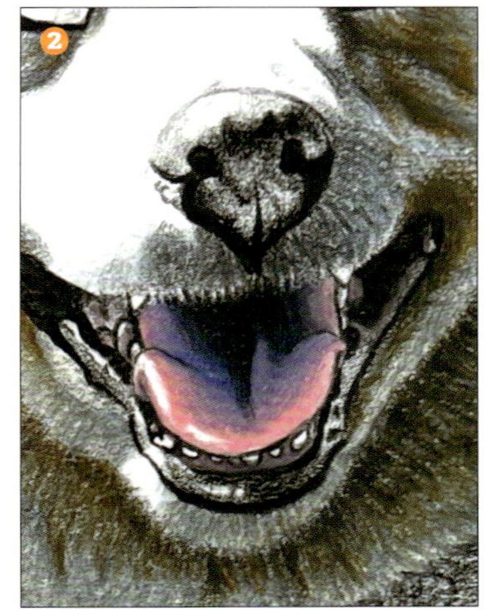 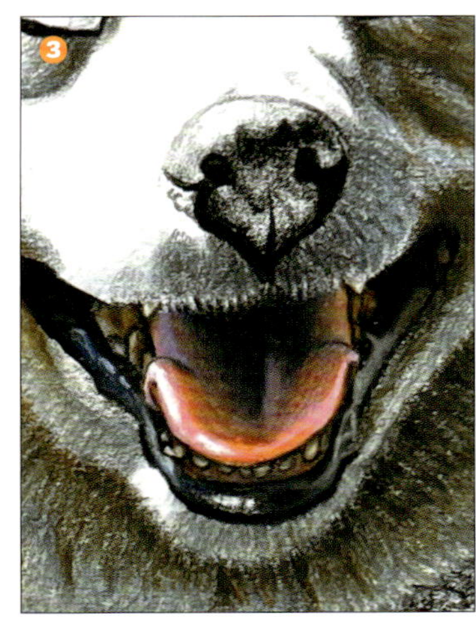

4 Color the mouth as follows. **❶** Apply ultramarine as the shade color for the tongue. **❷** Layer pink over the entire tongue. **❸** Use poppy red to adjust the overall tone of the tongue. For the teeth, use beige for the teeth and dark umber for their shaded areas. Apply layers of ultramarine around the highlights on the lip to depict the reflection of sunlight.

■■ Ultramarine ■■ Pink ■■ Poppy red ■■ Dark umber

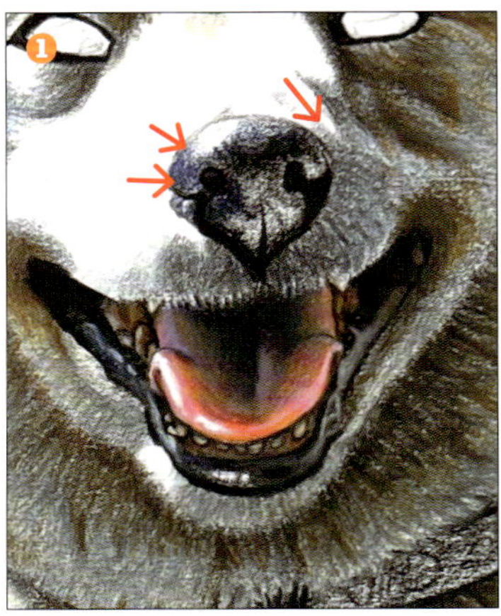 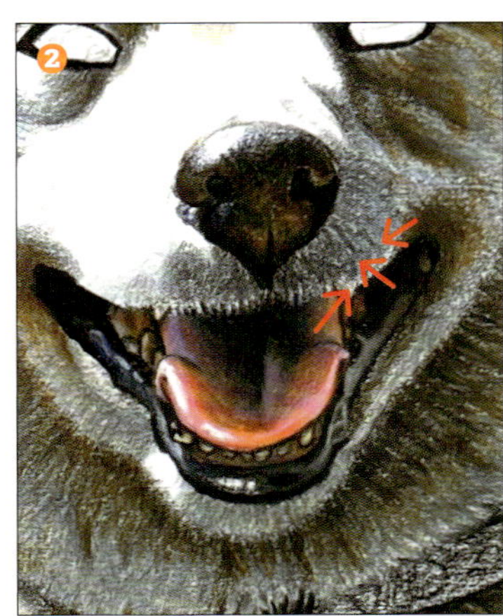

5 Color the nose as follows. **❶** Apply ultramarine around the highlights. **❷** Apply layers of pumpkin orange to represent the reflected light coming from the lower right.

■■ Ultramarine
■■ Pumpkin orange

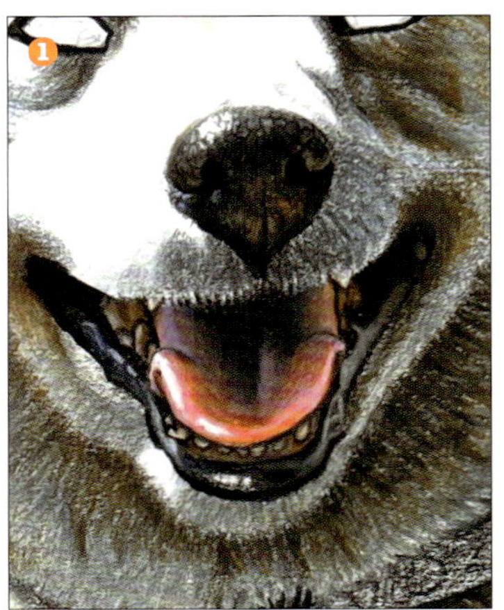 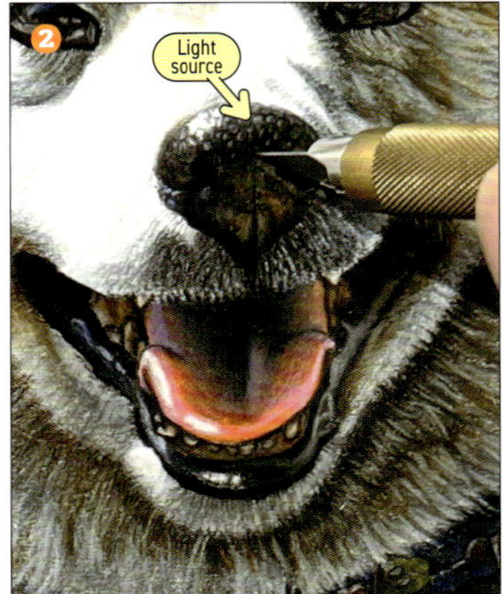
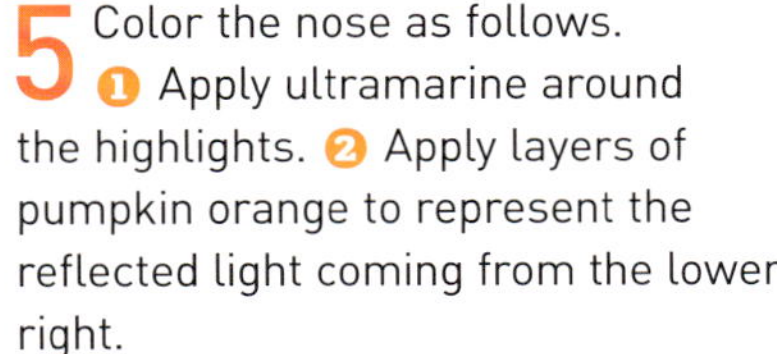

6 **❶** Use a sharpened regular pencil (not a colored one) to draw the textured, keratin-like pattern on the nose. This allows for cleaner, sharper lines. **❷** For the finishing touch, lightly scrape along the direction of the light source on the keratin texture using a design knife. Hold the blade parallel to the paper so that it gently scrapes off just the surface layer of the colored pencil, creating a subtle scratched effect.

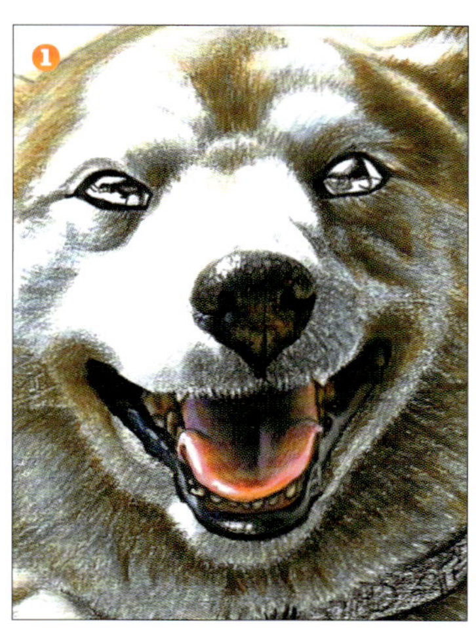 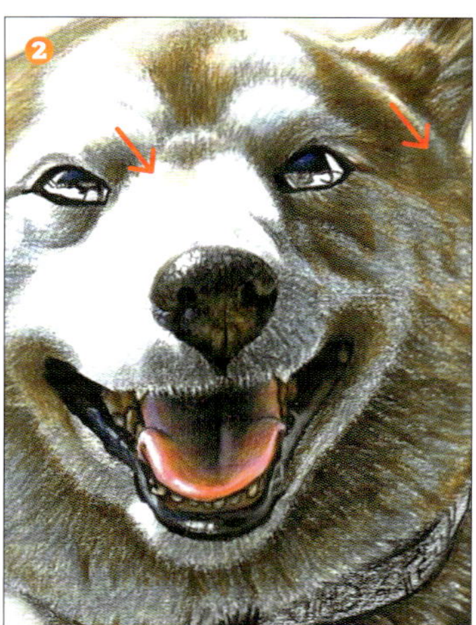 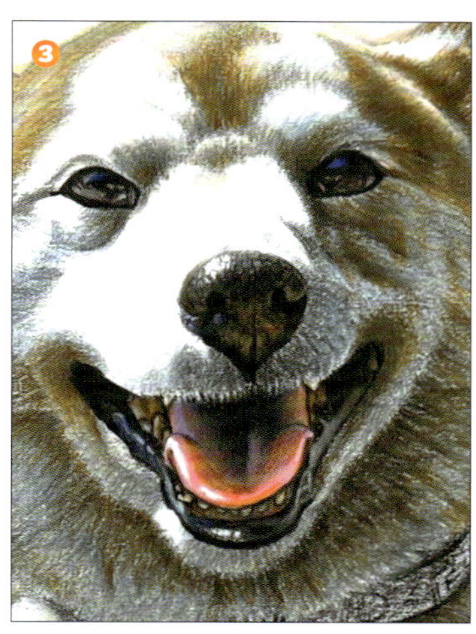

7 Color the eyes. **❶** First, fill the entire eyes with black, paying close attention to variations in tone and pressure to add depth. **❷** As the sky is reflected in the part of the eyes hit by the light source, you should apply layers of ultramarine over the appropriate areas. **❸** Finish the eyes by applying layers of beige to the parts of the eyes that are brightened by ground reflections from the lower right, and of dark umber to the eyes in their entirety. Just like with the nose, it's best to use a sharp pencil for drawing fine lines.

▮ Black ▮ Ultramarine ▯ Beige ▮ Dark umber

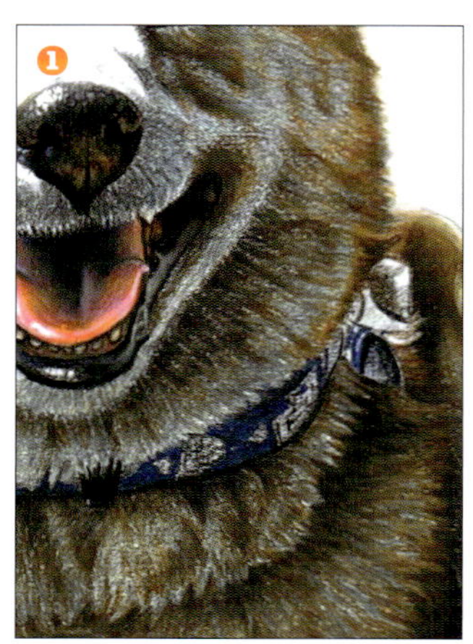 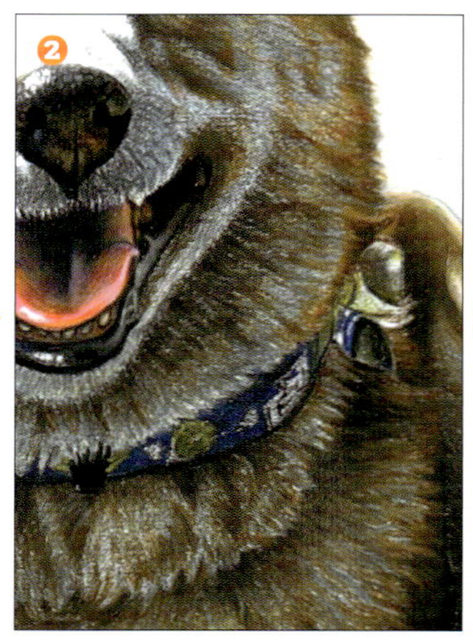 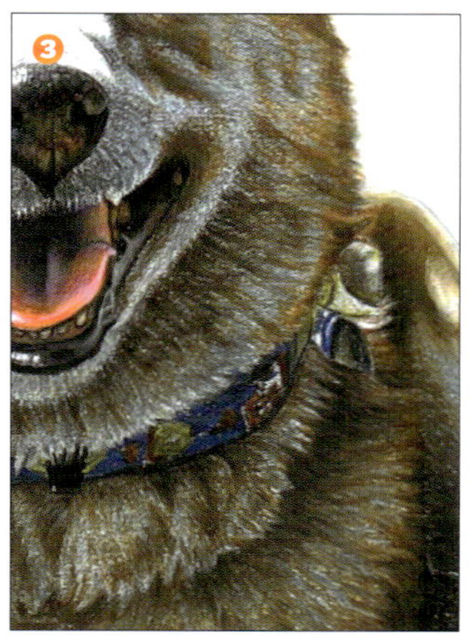

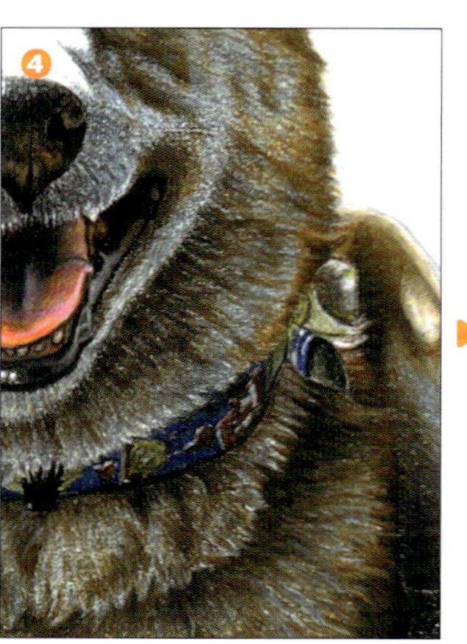 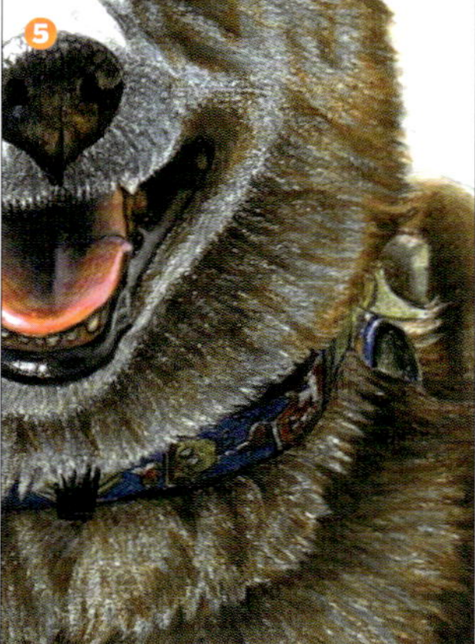

8 Color the collar as follows. **❶** Begin by applying ultramarine as the base color. As the area is very small, suggest the pattern by intentionally leaving some parts uncolored. **❷** Next, fill in the pattern with canary yellow. **❸** Then, add poppy red to enhance the design. **❹** For the bright areas that appear white, use beige to give them a subtle tone. **❺** Finally, use black to define and tighten the edges. As with earlier steps, a sharpened regular pencil is effective for drawing fine lines.

▮ Ultramarine ▯ Canary yellow
▮ Poppy red ▯ Beige ▮ Black

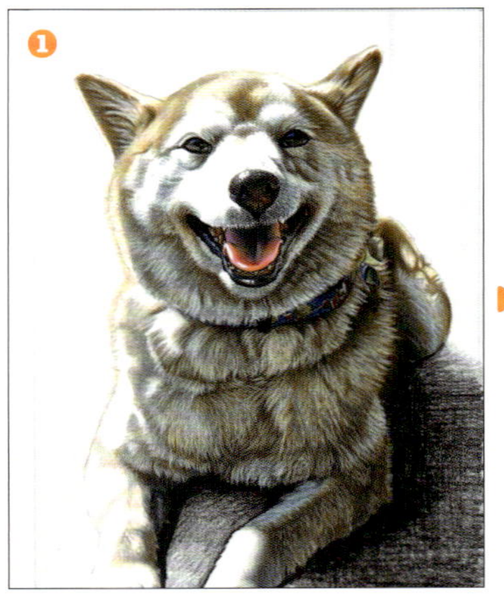

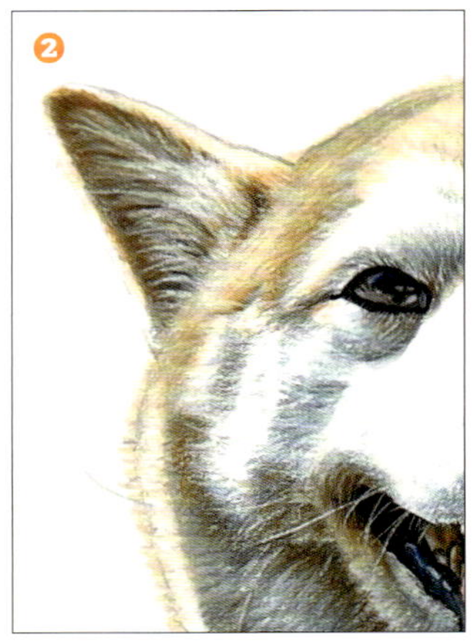

9 Depict the fur. **❶** Focus on the shaded areas and draw the fur using white. Rather than drawing each strand individually, try rendering them more in small clumps or tufts. Stroke from the base of the fur toward the tip with a flicking motion. Since applying bright white over dark areas can be difficult, it's best to use a colored pencil with high opacity (in this case, Holbein's soft white). **❷** Use the same technique to add fur inside the ears.

☐ Soft white (Holbein)

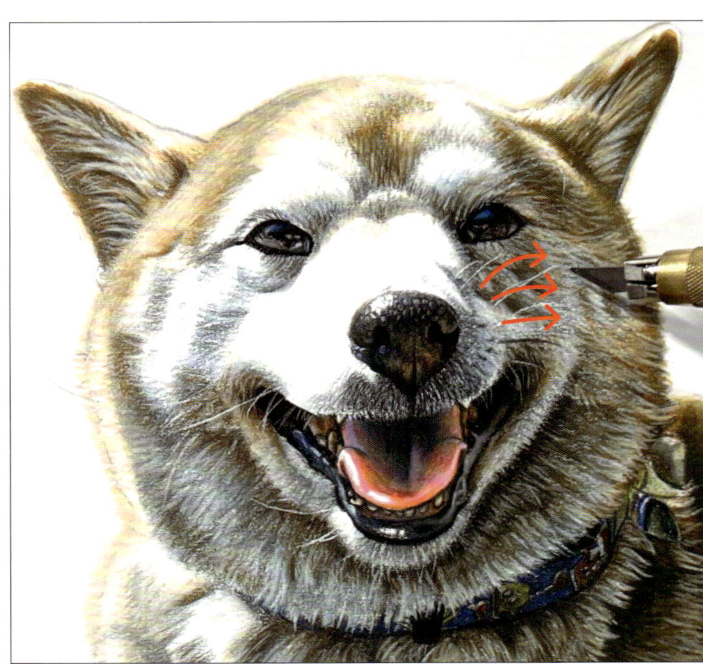

10 Depict the whiskers by scraping with a design knife. As this can't be undone, carve carefully in a single, steady motion. Scrape from the base of the whisker toward the tip with a smooth flick to create a natural look. Practicing on a separate sheet beforehand is highly recommended.

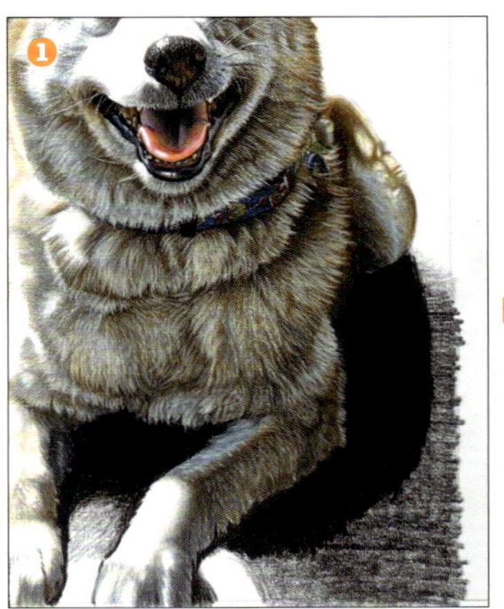

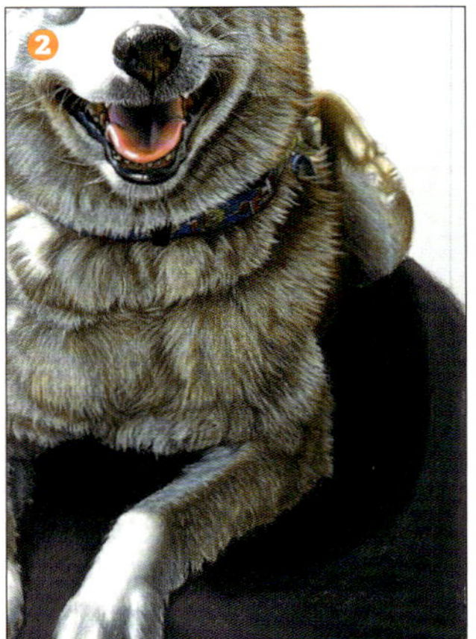

11 Color the shadows on the ground. **❶** Fill in the darkest part of the cast shadow using black. **❷** Then expand the shadow outward with warm grey 70%. Take care with how you apply the warm grey 70% to ensure a natural gradient from the black applied in **STEP 11 ❶**.

■ Black ▰ Warm grey 70%

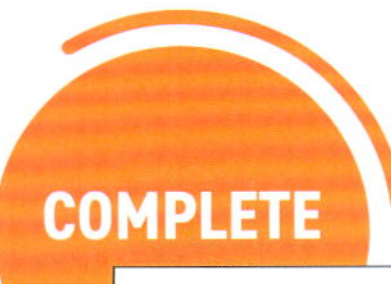
COMPLETE

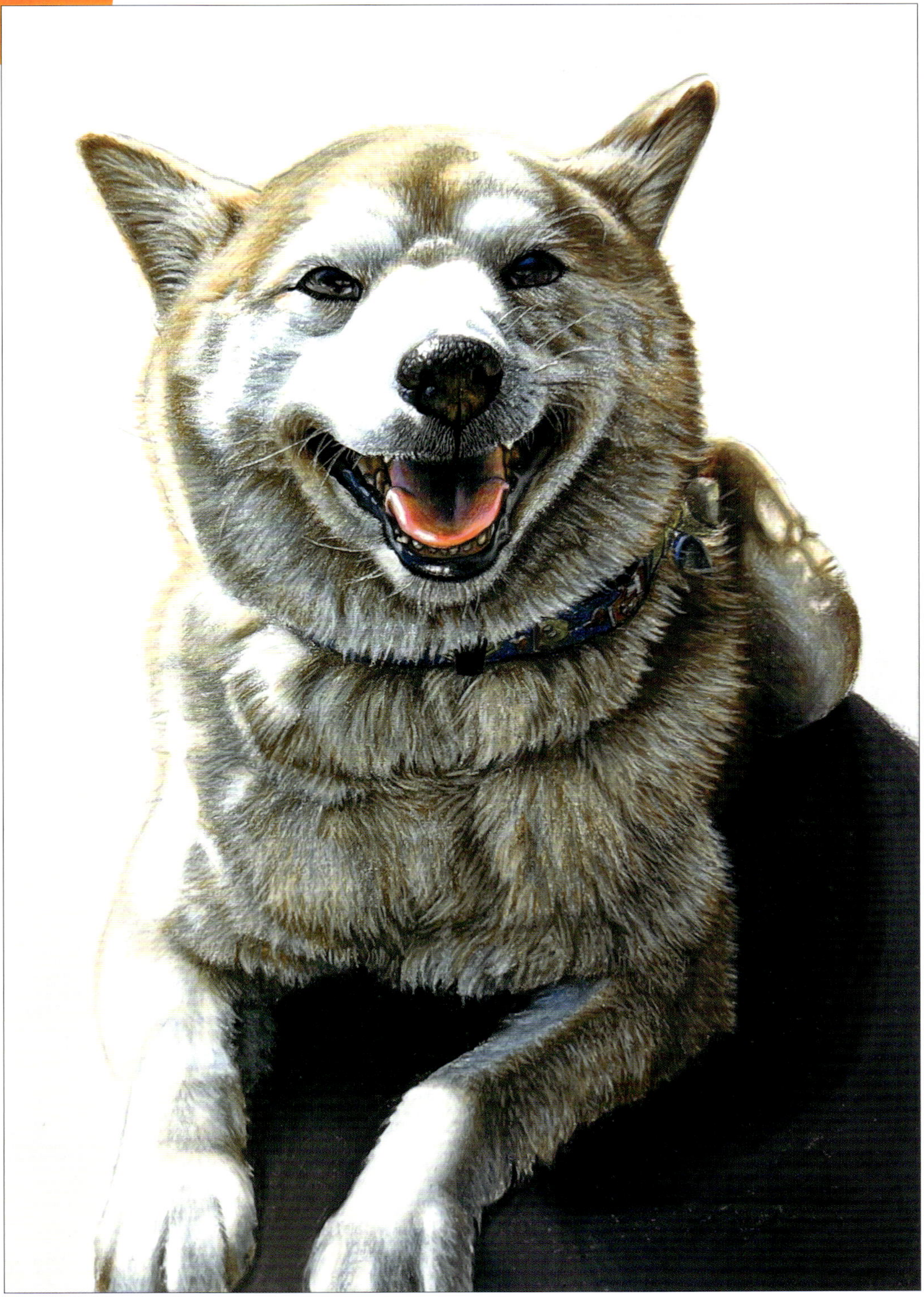

UNIT
11

Draw a Blue Mountain Swallowtail Butterfly

Colored pencils: Prismacolor
Paper: Smooth White Drawing paper
 **Drawn by Ishikawa @ Iroenpitsu**

Coloring Key Points

1. Use a stylus to depict the speckled texture of the wings.

2. When you applying dark or highly opaque colors like black later on, they won't stick if you have already indented the surface beforehand with a stylus.

Colors Used

PC914 Cream		PC1007 Imperial Violet	
PC913 Spring Green		PC922 Poppy Red	
PC910 True Green		PC935 Black	
PC1054 Warm Grey 50%		PC924 Crimson Red	
PC903 True Blue		PC916 Canary Yellow	
PC992 Light Aqua		PC938 White	

Reference Photo + Preliminary Drawing

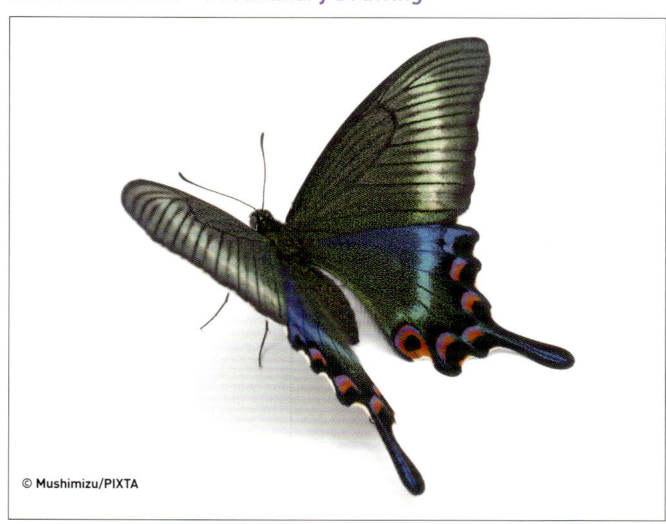

© Mushimizu/PIXTA

The blue mountain swallowtail butterfly is often thought of as a black butterfly, but its wings have a vivid, speckled surface. This effect is created using a stylus. You need to first apply the wing color with a colored pencil, then create indentations in the paper with a stylus and finally apply warm grey 50% or black over it.

I'll divide the wings into four sections for explanatory purposes. The upper-right part of the wing will be labeled **A**, the lower-right part **B**, the upper-left part **C**, and the lower-left part **D**.

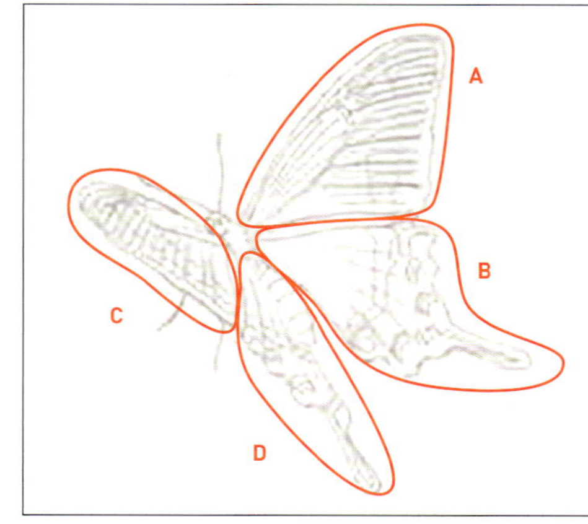

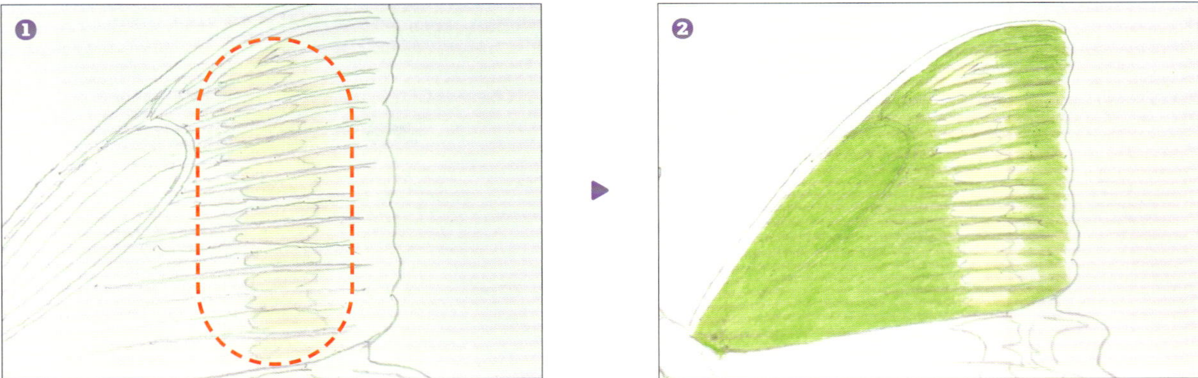

1 Color the upper-right part of the wing (**A**). **❶** Lightly apply cream to the areas within the red oval. **❷** Then, apply spring green thickly to the area that was not colored in **Step 1 ❶**.

☐ Cream ▦ Spring green

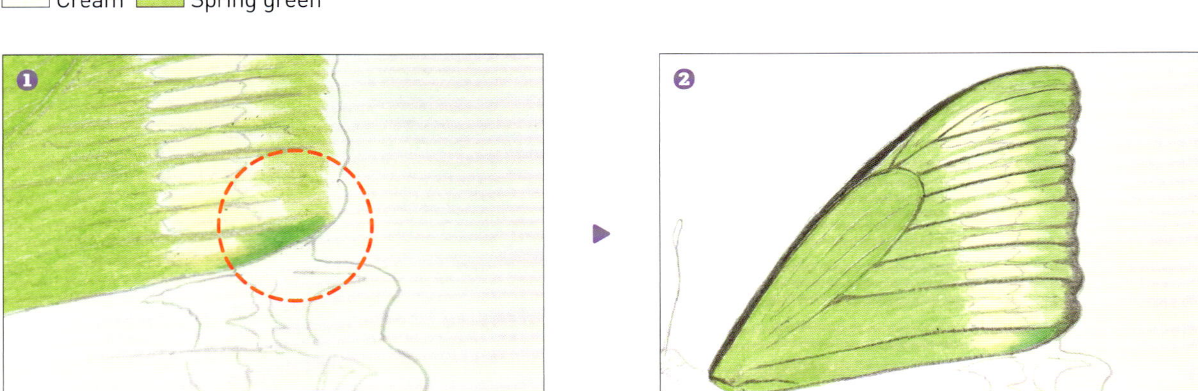

2 **❶** Apply true green to the lower-right area (marked with a red circle). **❷** Use warm grey 50% to color the outline and some of the lines that were sketched into the preliminary drawing.

▦ True green ▦ Warm grey 50%

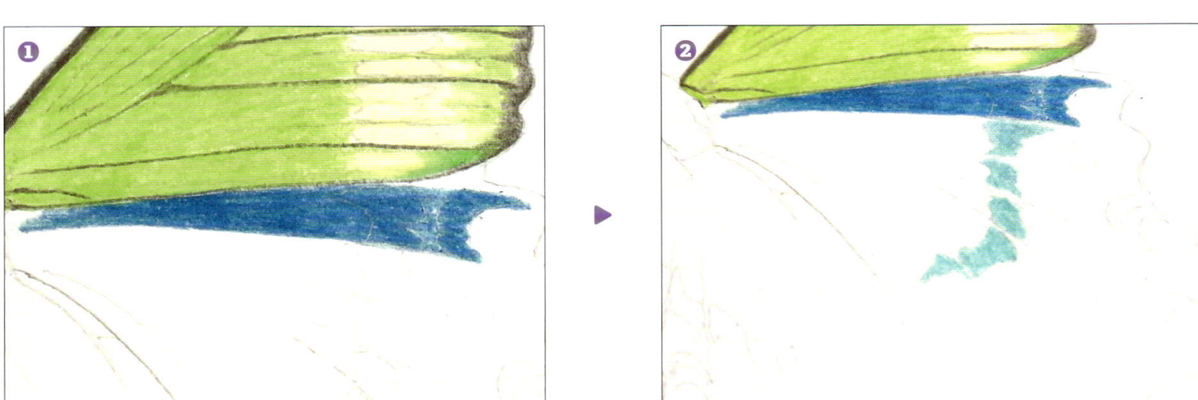

3 Color section **B** (lower-right wing). **❶** First, apply true blue thickly over the entire area. **❷** Then, referring to the reference photo, use light aqua to color the wing's patterns.

▦ True blue ▦ Light aqua

UNIT
12

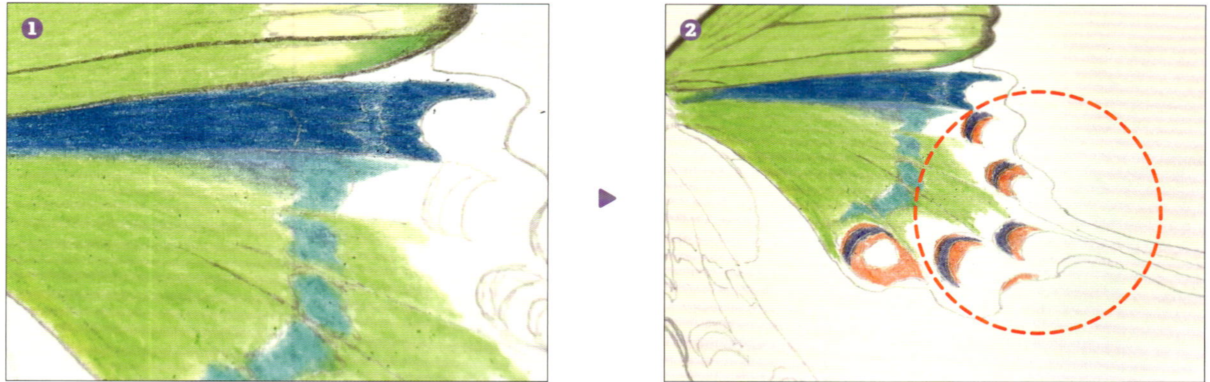

4 ❶ Apply spring green to the areas that were left uncolored in **Step 3**. ❷ In the red-circled area, draw the patterns with light strokes of imperial violet and poppy red.

▧ Spring green ▧ Imperial violet ▧ Poppy red

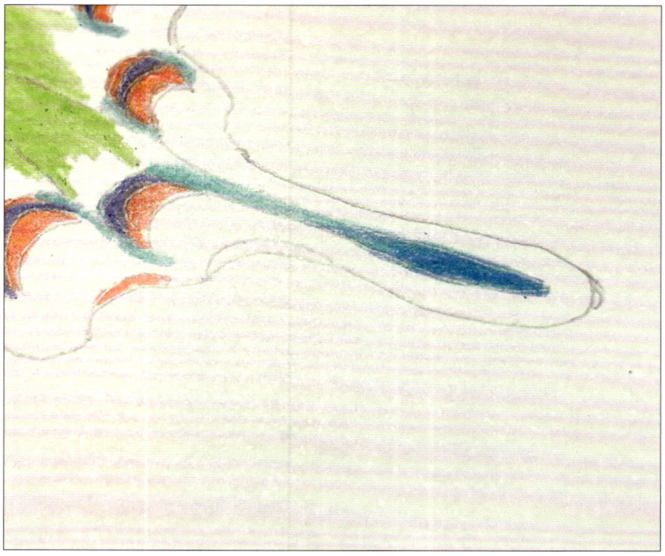

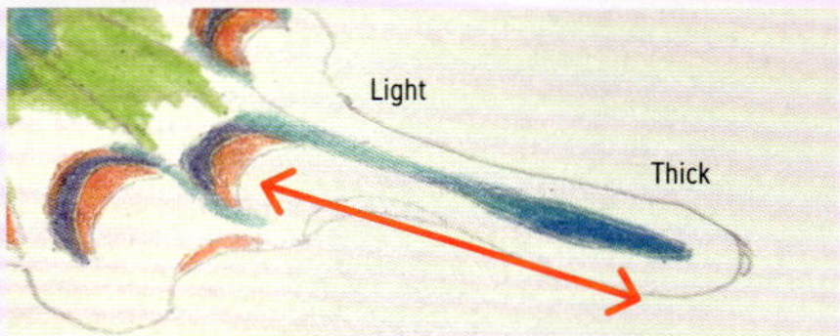

5 Apply true blue to the areas on either side of the patterns drawn in **Step 4** ❷, as well as to the extended lower part of the wing.

▧ True blue

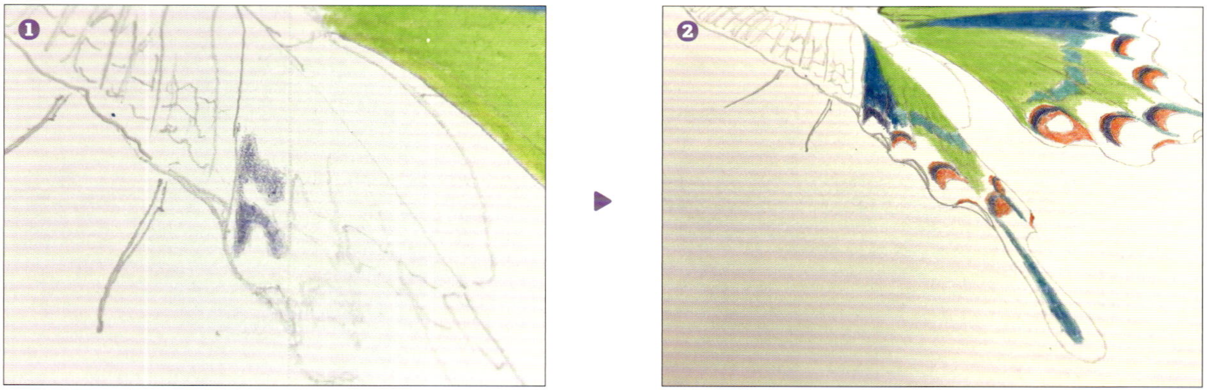

6 Paint the lower-left part of the wing section **D**. ❶ Lightly apply imperial violet. ❷ Then continue coloring the lower-left part of the wing, following the same process as in **Steps 3** to **5**.

▧ Imperial violet ▧ True blue ▧ Light aqua ▧ Spring green ▧ Poppy red

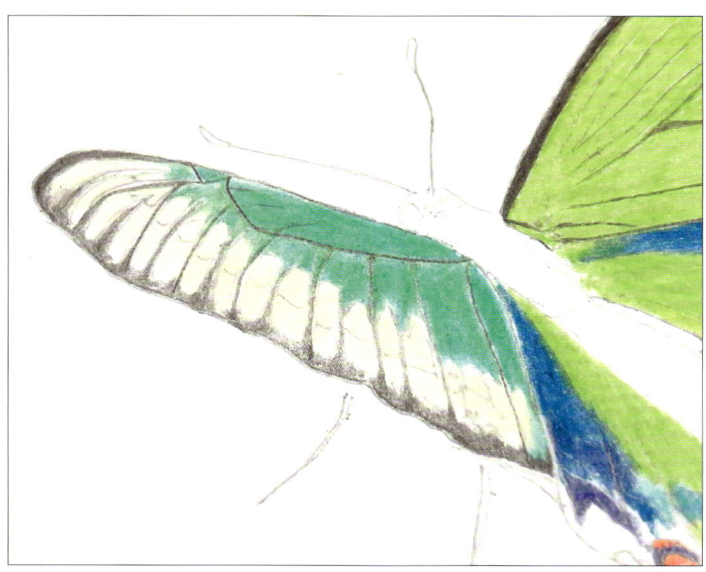

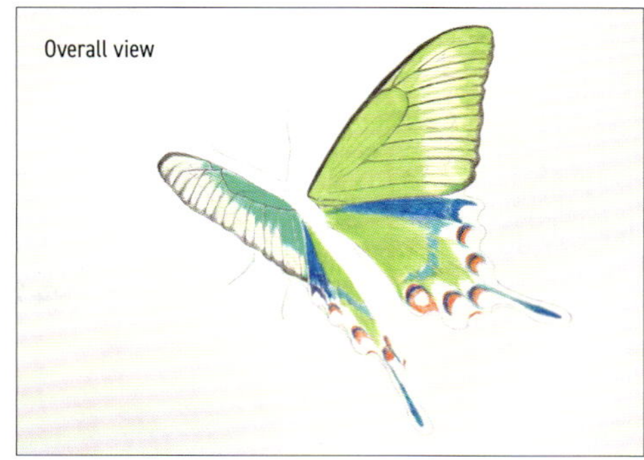

7 Paint the upper-left part of the wing section **C** using the same method as in **Step 1** and **Step 2** ❷ with cream, light aqua, and warm grey 50% in that order.

☐ Cream ▨ Light aqua
▨ Warm grey 50%

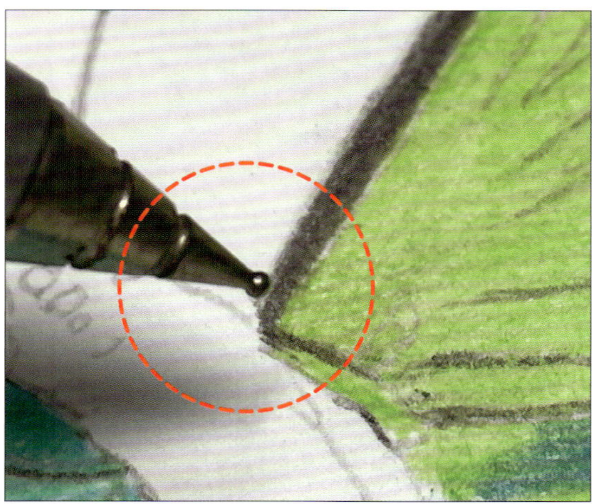

8 Color the upper-right section of the wing (Area **A**). Place about three sheets of paper underneath, then gently tap the entire wing with a stylus to create slight indentations in the paper.

UNIT
12

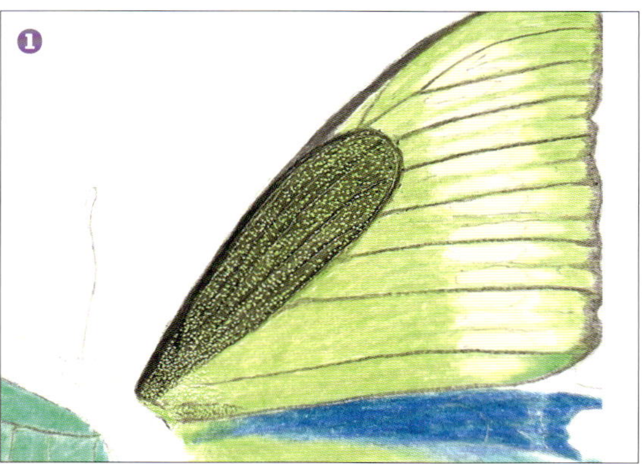

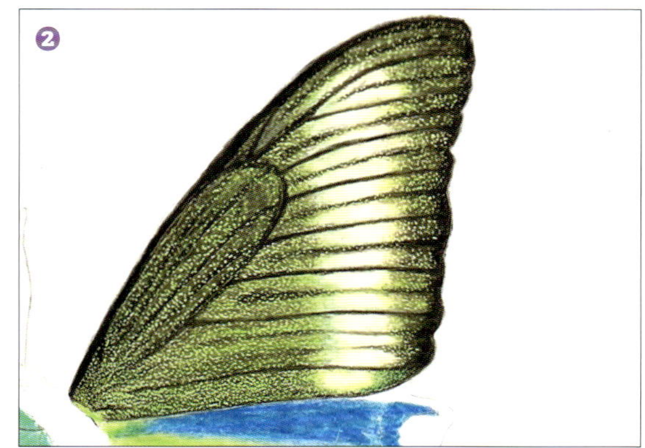

9 ❶ When you color over the area with black, only the indentations made by the stylus will retain the spring green color. ❷ Repeat **Step 8** and **Step 9** ❶ to continue coloring the entire surface. If you overdo the coloring, it's better to gently scrape with a design knife rather than using an eraser. This helps preserve the small indented dots without flattening them.

▨ Black

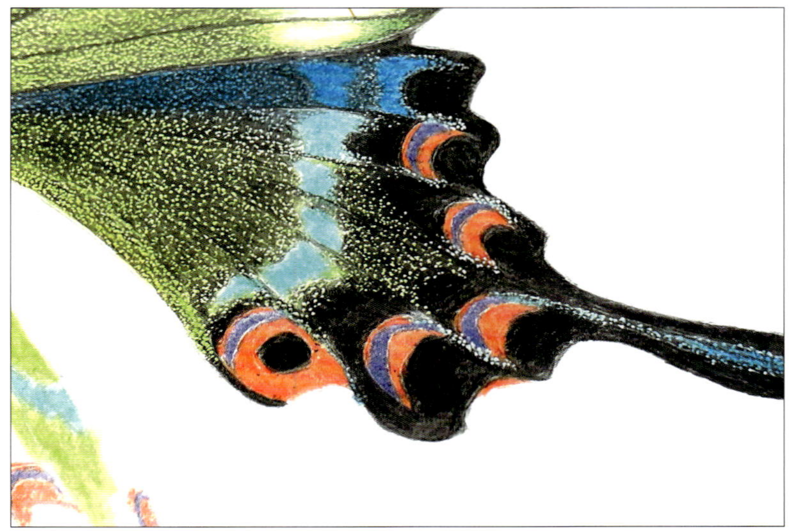

10 Color the lower-right wing section **B**. Just like in **Steps 8** and **9**, first use a stylus to press small indentations into the paper, then apply black over the entire area.

▬ Black

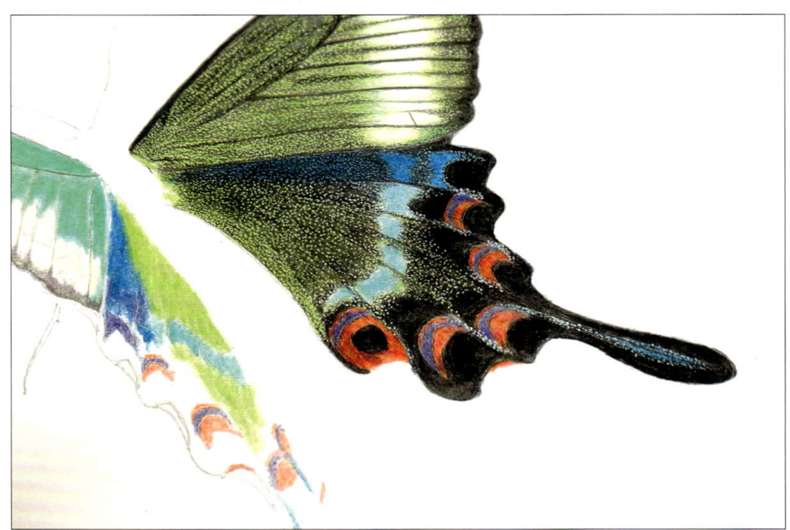

11 Apply layers of crimson red over the areas where poppy red was applied in **Step 4 ❷**.

▬ Crimson red

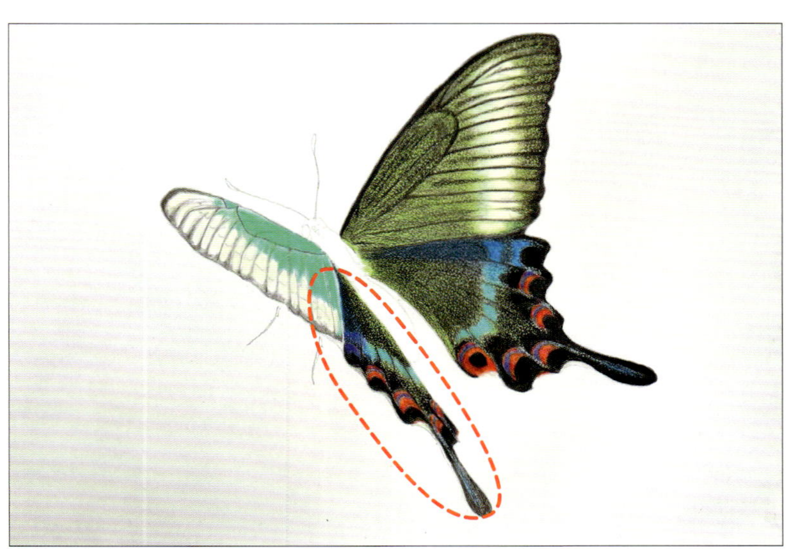

12 As in **Steps 8** and **9**, continue layering black and crimson red while using the stylus tool to indent the surface.

▬ Black ▬ Crimson red

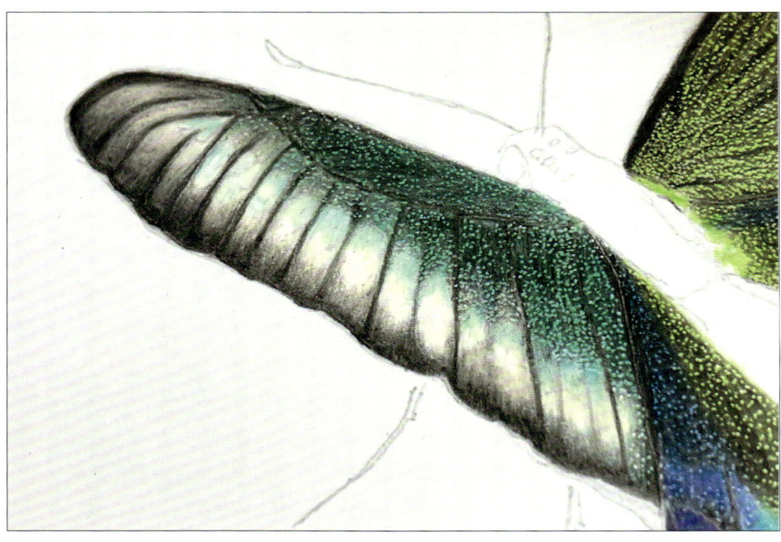

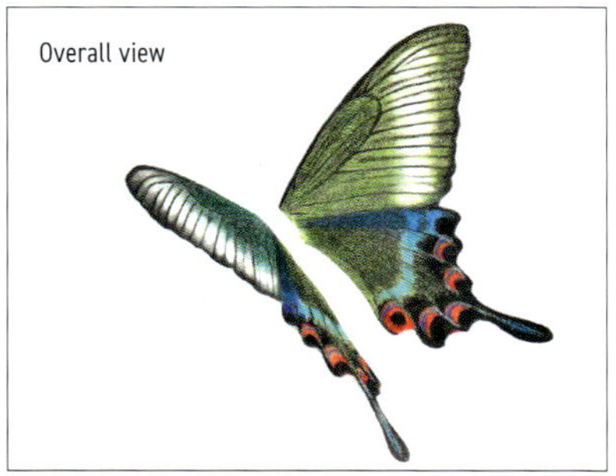

Overall view

13 Color the upper-left section of the wing **C**. As in **Steps 8** and **9**, apply black using a stylus.

▬▬ Black

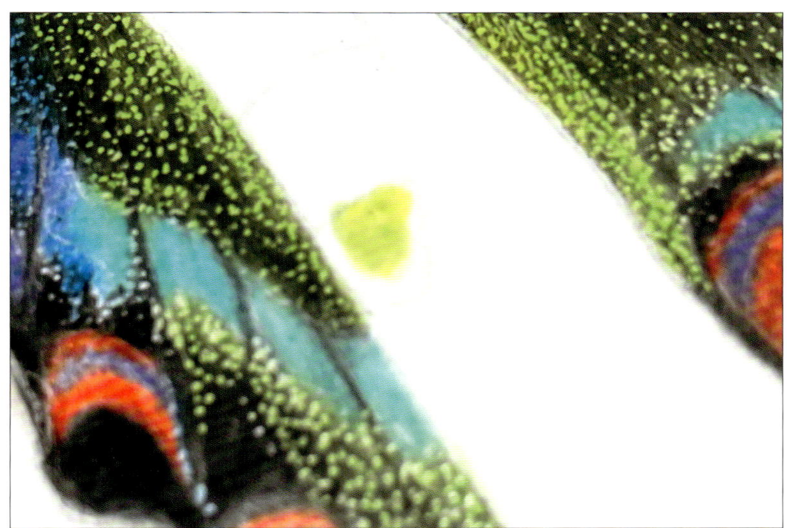

14 Color the body by first applying a base layer of canary yellow to the center area, then roughly layering spring green on top of it.

▭ Canary yellow
▭ Spring green

UNIT
12

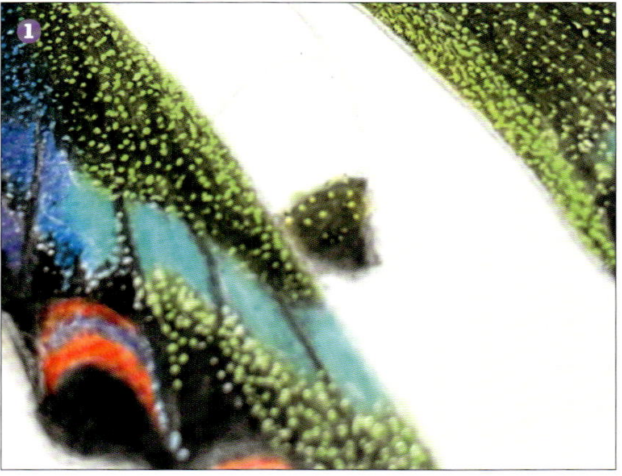

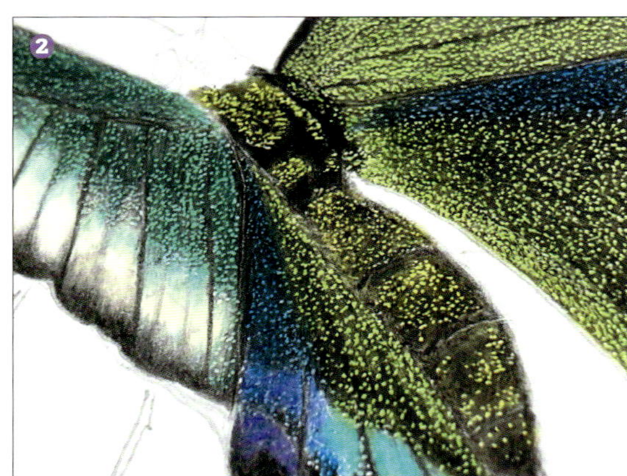

15 ❶ As with the wings, use a stylus to indent the surface before applying black. ❷ Repeat **Step 14** and **Step 15** ❶ to gradually color the entire body

▬▬ Black ▭ Canary yellow ▭ Spring green

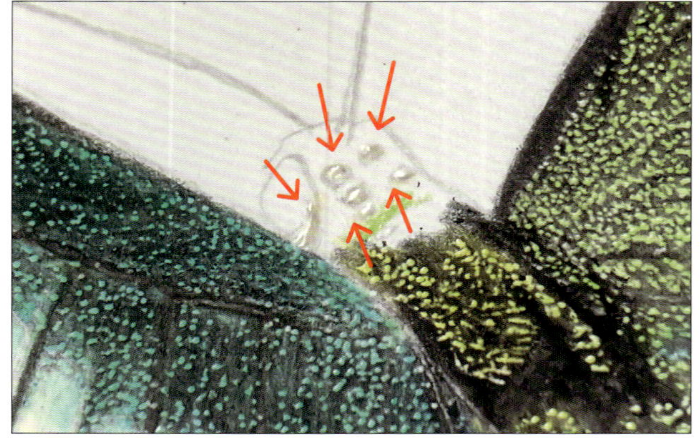

16 Color the head by first applying a base layer of cream color, and then indenting the surface with a stylus.

☐ Cream

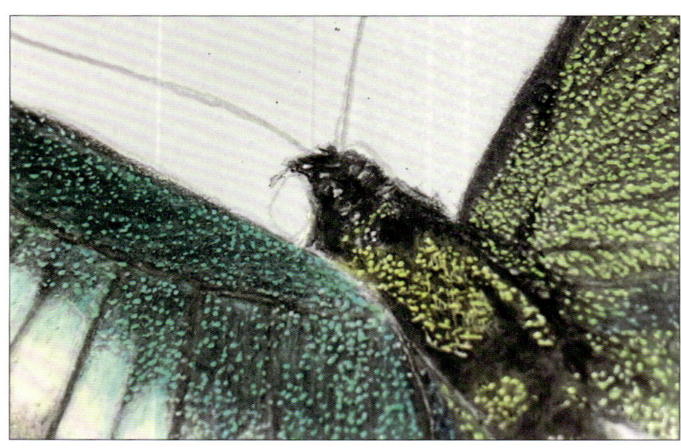

17 Apply black over the entire head. Although black is a highly opaque color, the cream-colored areas remain visible because they were indented with a stylus beforehand.

■ Black

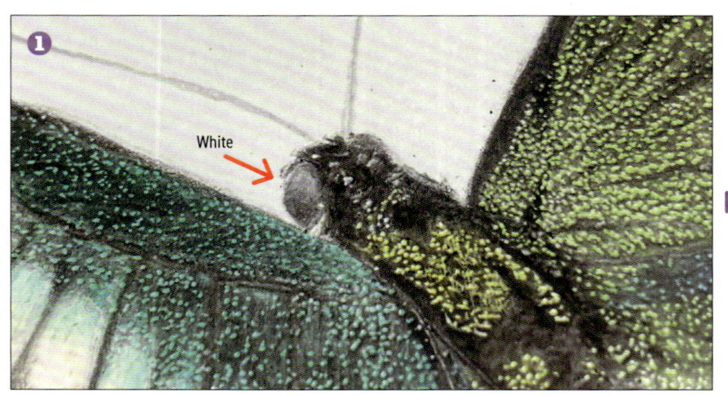

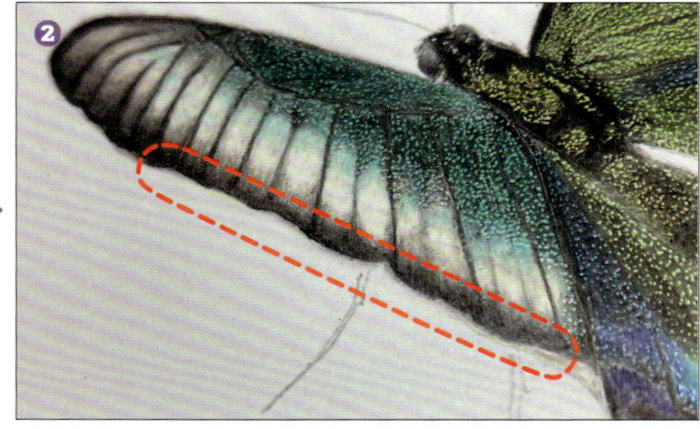

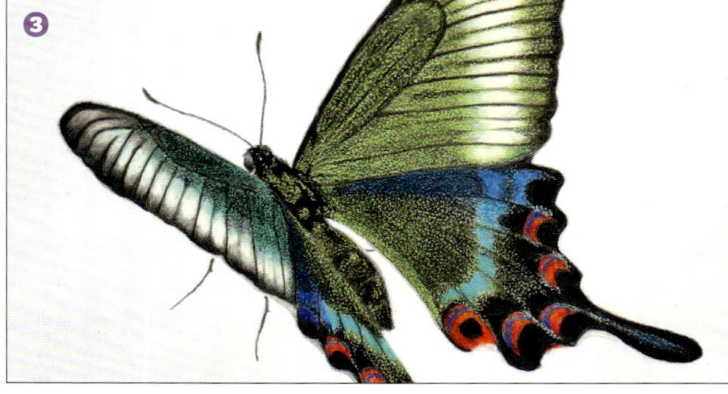

18 Color the eye as follows. ❶ Lightly apply black, then use white on the upper part to create a sense of three-dimensionality. ❷ In the red oval area, apply cream and burnish it for a smooth finish. ❸ Use warm grey 50% to draw the antennae and legs.

■ Black ☐ White ☐ Cream
▨ Warm grey 50%

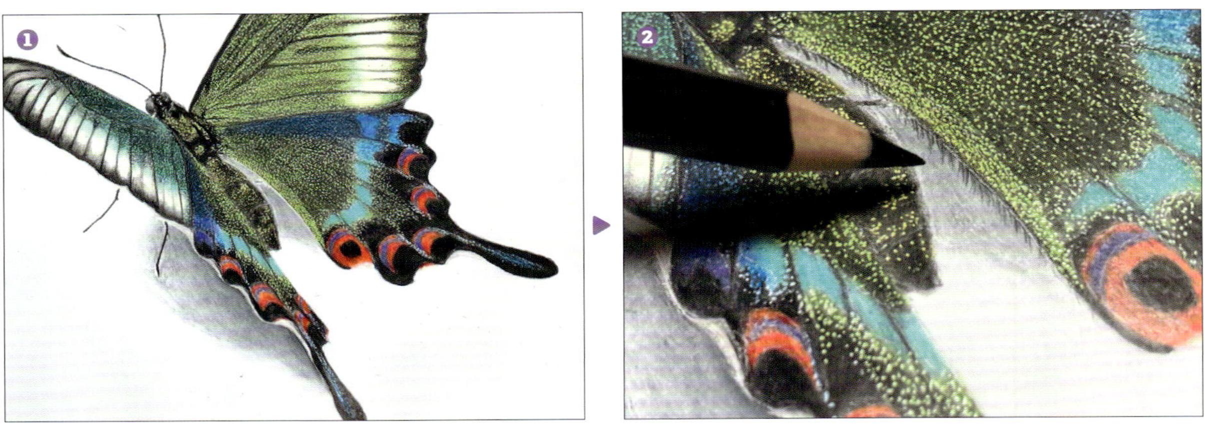

19 Draw the shadows as follows. ❶ Lightly apply black, then draw the shadow while burnishing with white.
❷ Use black to draw the hairs on the lower-right wing section B.

⬛ Black ⬜ White

COMPLETE

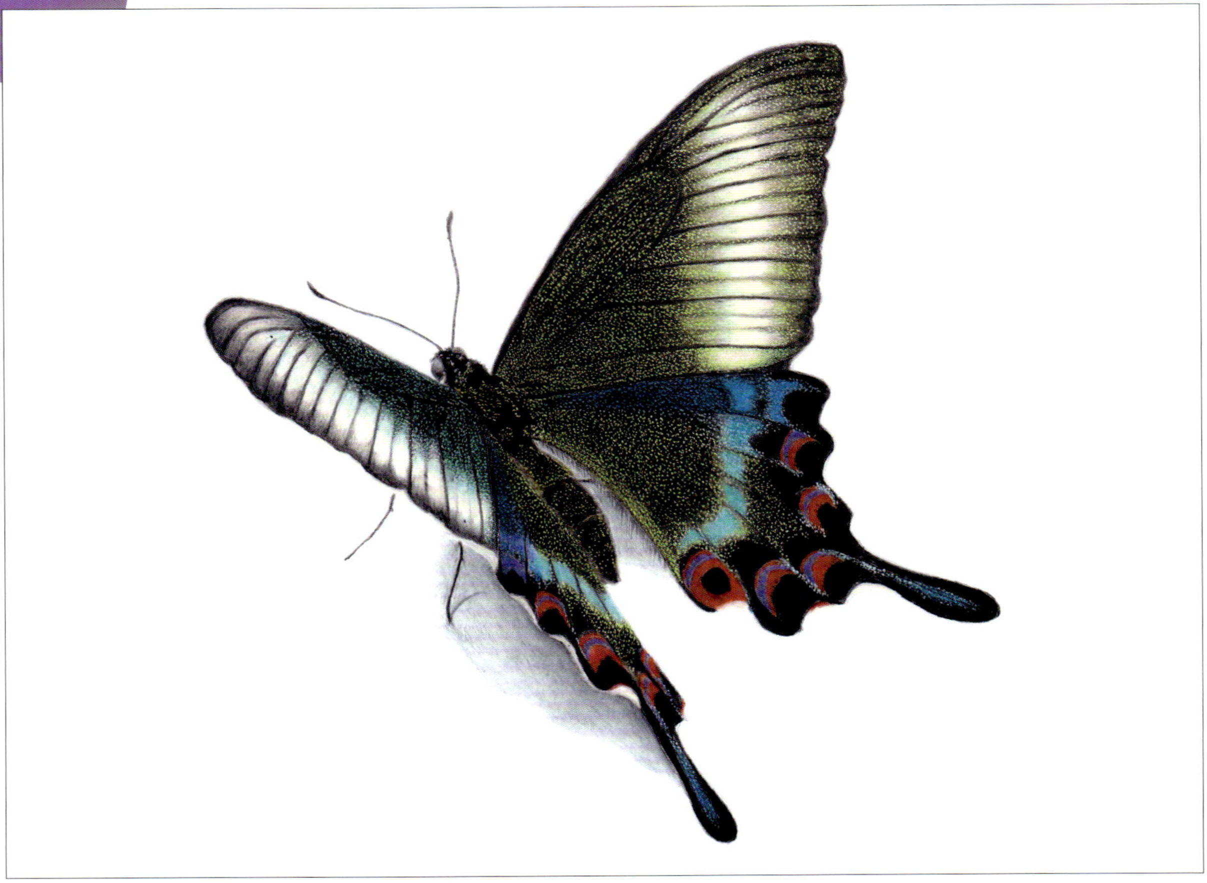

Because the true green is too strong, apply layers of black all over to complete the drawing.

Draw a Hamster

Colored pencils: Mitsubishi Polycolor
Paper: Pure Kent
Drawn by Miyakawa

Coloring Key Points

1. By adjusting the density of the lines used to draw the body hair, you can convey both the pattern and the structure of the body (p.15).

2. For the white areas of fur, rather than drawing the hairs themselves, think of it as drawing the shadows between the hairs.

3. The highlights in the eyes are key (p.12).

Colors Used

- Black 24
- Yellow Ochre 19
- Warm Grey 37
- Grey 23
- Russet Brown 30
- Vandyke Brown 22
- Khaki 29
- Cream Yellow 27
- Reddish Brown 20
- Rose Red 36
- Lilac 34

Reference Photo

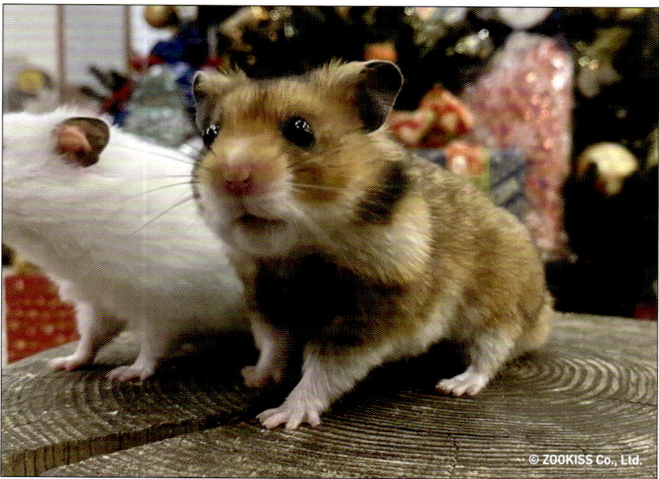

You'll be drawing a palm-sized hamster at a large scale. The basic process involves repeating two main steps: first laying down a base color, then drawing individual hairs on top with darker colors. Use variations in line color, pressure, direction, and density to create the hamster's three-dimensional form. At the same time, consider the overall light and shadow, carefully distinguishing between areas that should be darker and those that should remain lighter. One key point in the reference photo is the slightly loose skin covered with fine fur. Pay close attention to the hair length and the direction it flows.

Preliminary Drawing

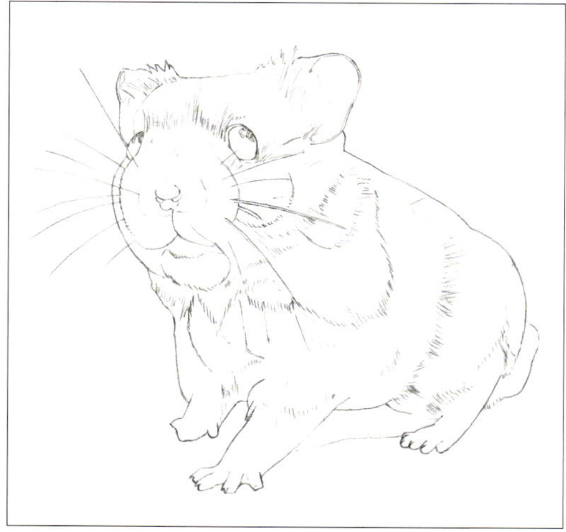

I have roughly drawn the color transitions in the fur. The whiskers on the right side (from the viewer's perspective) are noticeably thicker, so their centers have been left white. These whiskers will remain uncolored throughout the rest of the drawing.

Applying Color

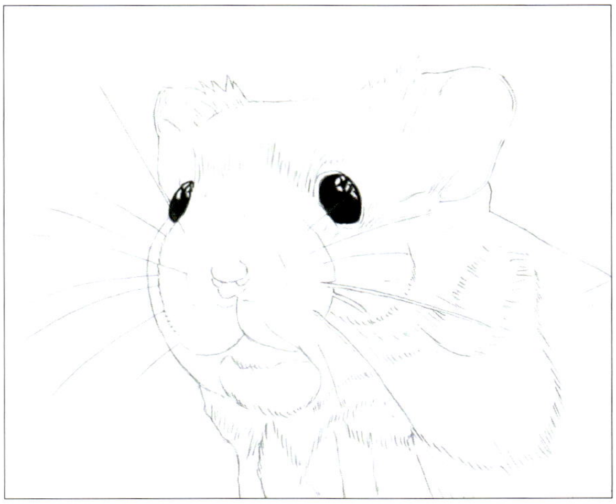

1 Color the eyes with black, leaving distinct highlights uncolored in white.

Black

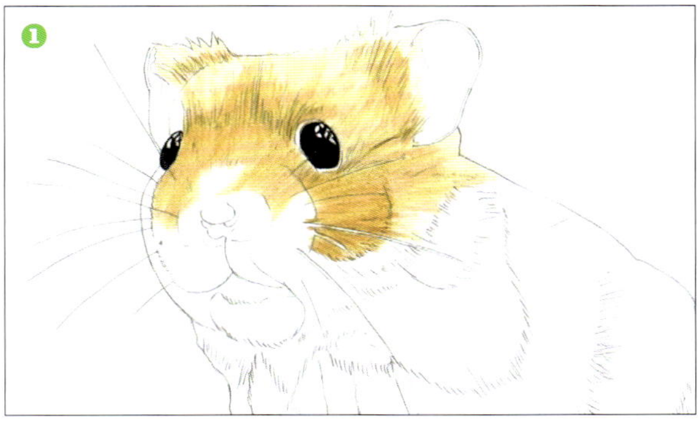

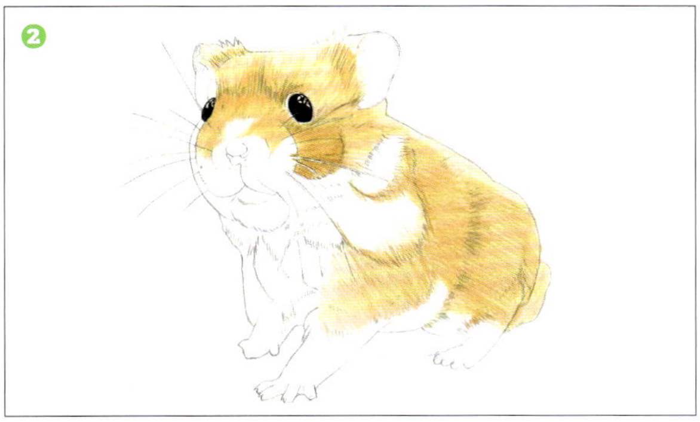

2 ❶ Color the face with yellow ochre. Where there are preliminary lines indicating the fur direction, apply the color more heavily. Rather than drawing individual hairs, focus on covering the entire area with color. ❷ Then, using the same yellow ochre, color the body. Move the colored pencil along the direction of the fur, applying the color with a slightly rough texture.

Yellow ochre

UNIT 13

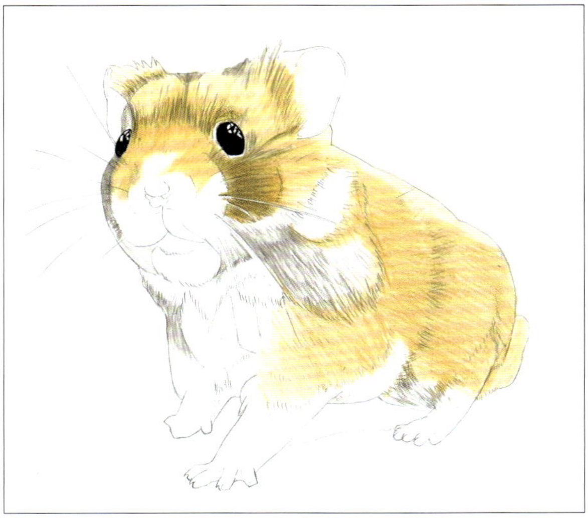

3 Use a warm grey to draw the facial markings, the white fur in the center of the body, and the fur around the base of the hind legs. For areas other than the face, apply the color loosely along the direction of the fur, making sure to leave some white areas to suggest the texture and lightness of the fur.

Warm grey

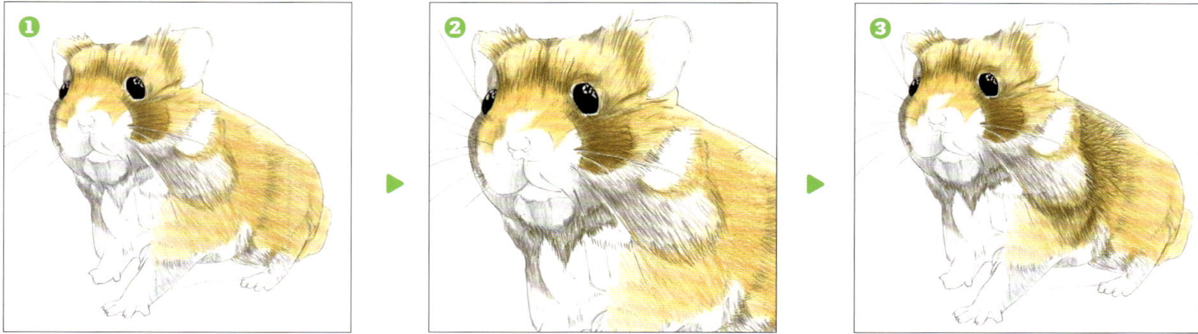

4 ❶ Use a grey to draw the fur under the chin, around the base of the legs, and under the belly. Apply it the same way as in **Step 3**. ❷ Slightly darken the fur under the chin with russet brown. ❸ Still using russet brown, draw the fine fur on the front half of the body. At the borders where the fur color changes, apply the color more heavily to create contrast.

▬▬ Grey ▬▬ Russet brown

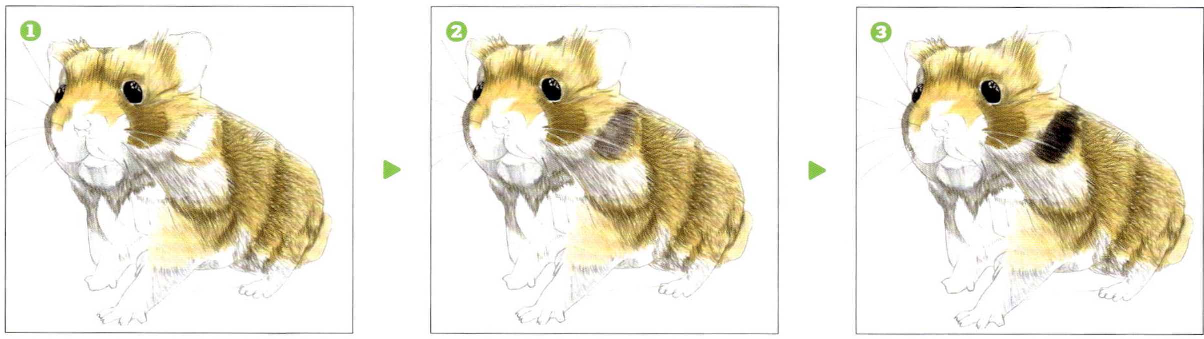

5 ❶ Following the same approach as in **Step 4** ❸, use russet brown to draw the back half of the body. ❷ Next, draw the dark markings on the side of the face. Apply many layers of Vandyke brown in numerous short, horizontal strokes in the direction of the fur. ❸ Over the same area, repeat the same kind of strokes using black to further deepen the shading and detail.

▬▬ Russet brown ▬▬ Vandyke brown ▬▬ Black

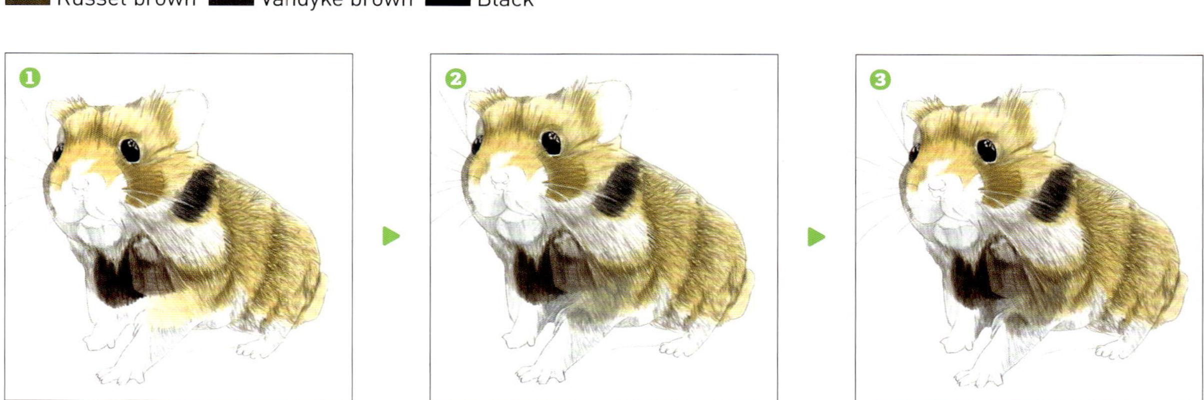

6 ❶ Use Vandyke brown to shade the area under the chin. Follow the preliminary drawing and vary the intensity to create depth. ❷ Using grey, shade the lower part beneath the area from **Step 6** ❶. Also layer this color over the yellow ochre–colored parts of the front legs that have been colored with Vandyke brown. ❸ Deepen the shading in the areas colored in **Step 6** ❷ by layering more Vandyke brown to enhance contrast and definition.

▬▬ Vandyke brown ▬▬ Grey

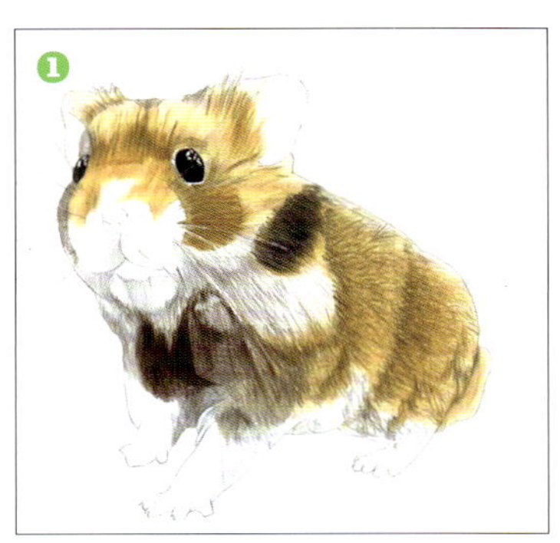 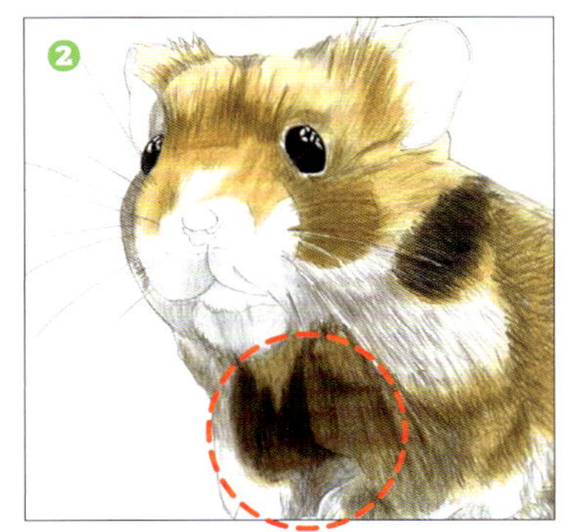 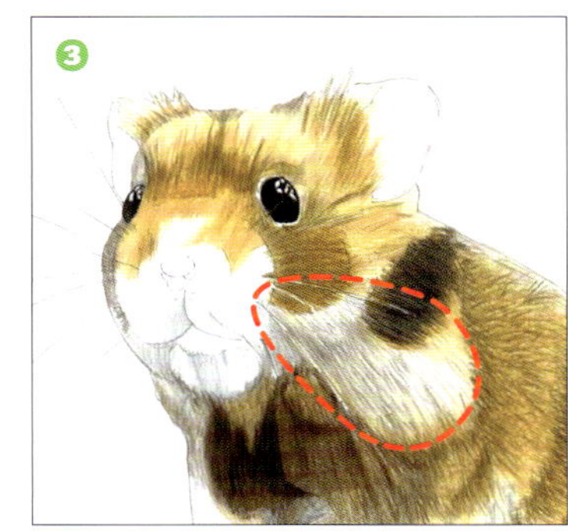

7 ❶ Layer khaki over the areas colored up to **Step 5** (excluding the white areas). Since the goal is to slightly blur the fine hair lines, don't worry about following the direction of the fur. ❷ Similarly, apply khaki under the chin. ❸ Layer cream yellow over the white fur on the side of the face.

▨ Khaki ▨ Cream yellow

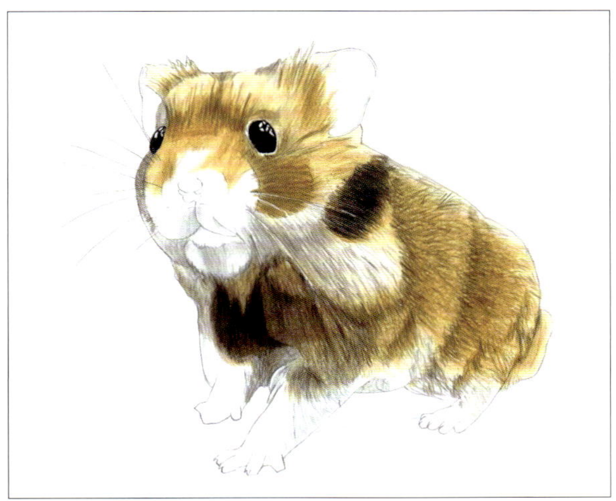

8 Here you should make a quick adjustment. Add a bit of warm grey to the white fur areas.

▨ Warm grey

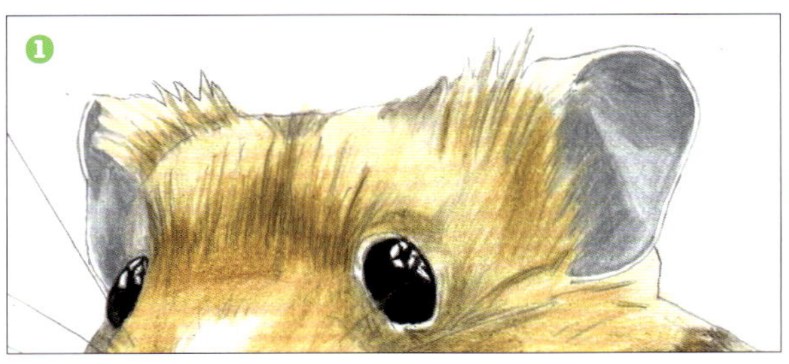 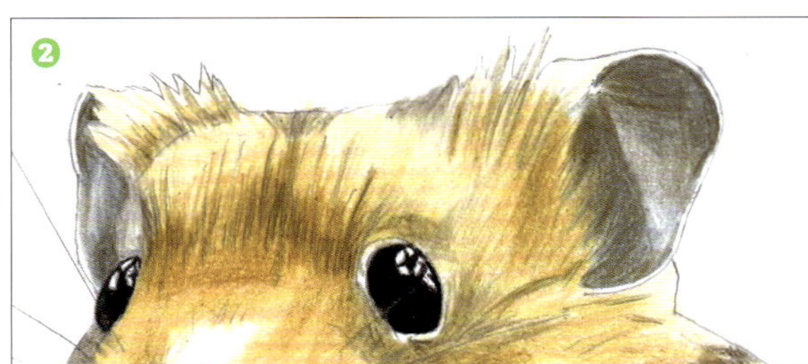

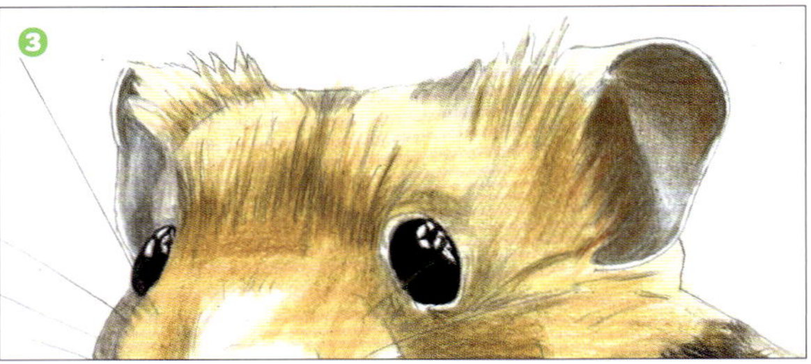

9 ❶ Color the ears, using grey to create light and dark contrast. Be sure to leave the ear fur jagged. ❷ Deepen the color with russet brown in the same way. ❸ Add reddish brown only to the left ear (on the viewer's right side).

▨ Grey ▨ Russet brown ▨ Reddish brown

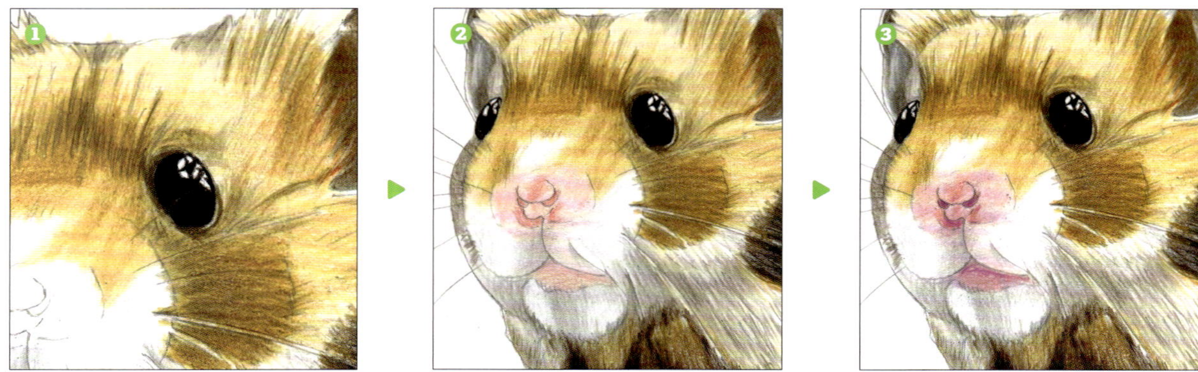

10 ❶ Color the area around the eye with russet brown, leaving a small white area below the eye. ❷ Use rose red to color the nose, the area under the nose, and the mouth. Slightly darken the nostrils and the groove beneath the nose. ❸ Go over the darkened areas from **Step 10** ❷ with lilac, layering the color well around the mouth.

▮ Russet brown ▮ Rose red ▮ Lilac

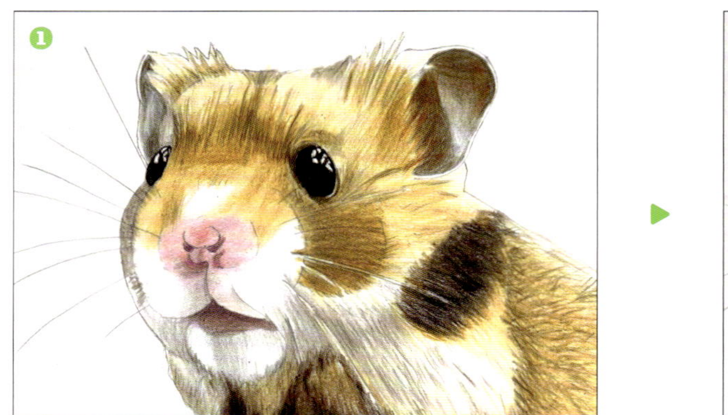
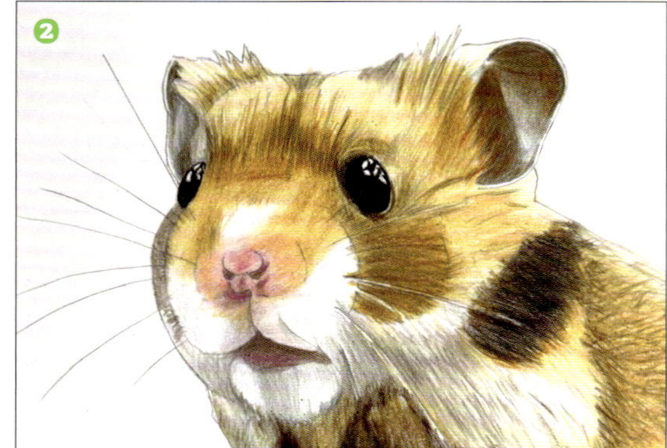

11 ❶ Color the same areas as in **Step 10** ❸ with warm grey. ❷ Apply reddish brown over the light pink areas around the nose.

▮ Warm grey ▮ Reddish brown

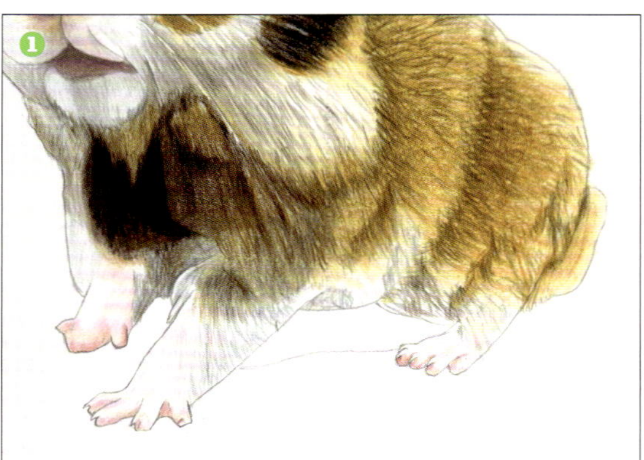
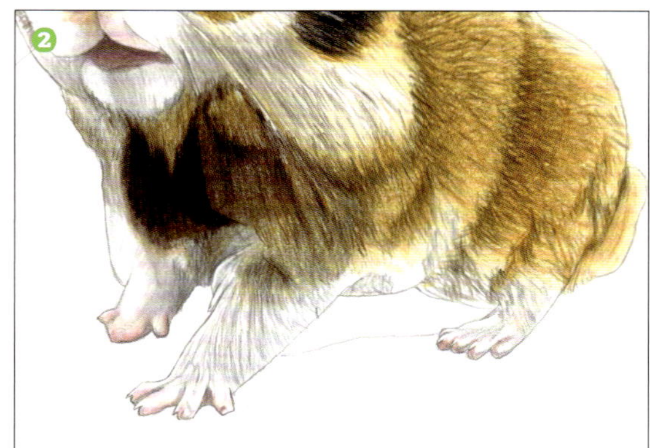

12 ❶ Color the tips of the feet with rose red, extending the color lightly a little higher up. ❷ Use grey to draw the shade and fur on the feet. Try to give the impression of the fur extending outward toward each toe.

▮ Rose red ▮ Grey

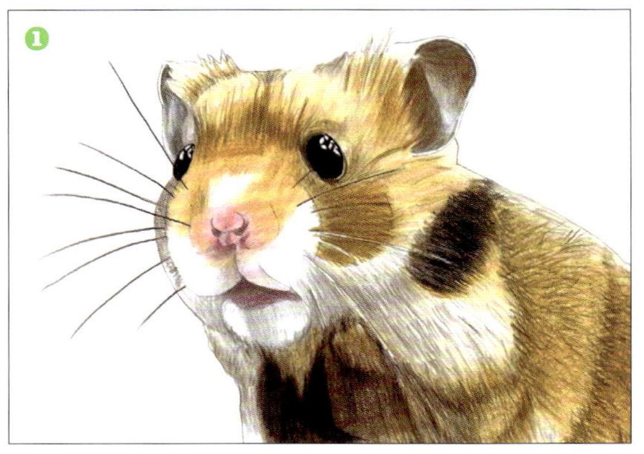 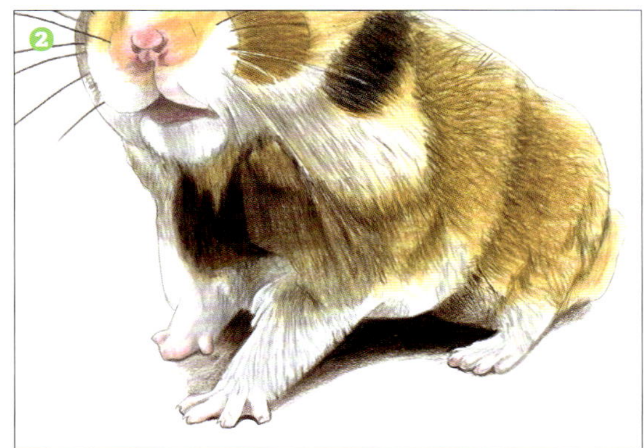

13 ❶ Draw the whiskers by tracing over the lines in the preliminary drawing with Vandyke brown. ❷ Use Vandyke brown to draw the shadow on the ground under the body. Make sure it gets darker the closer it is to the body. Slightly overlapping the outline of the legs will help convey the texture of the fur.

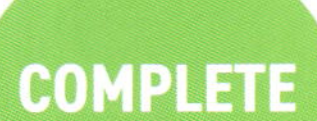 Vandyke brown

COMPLETE

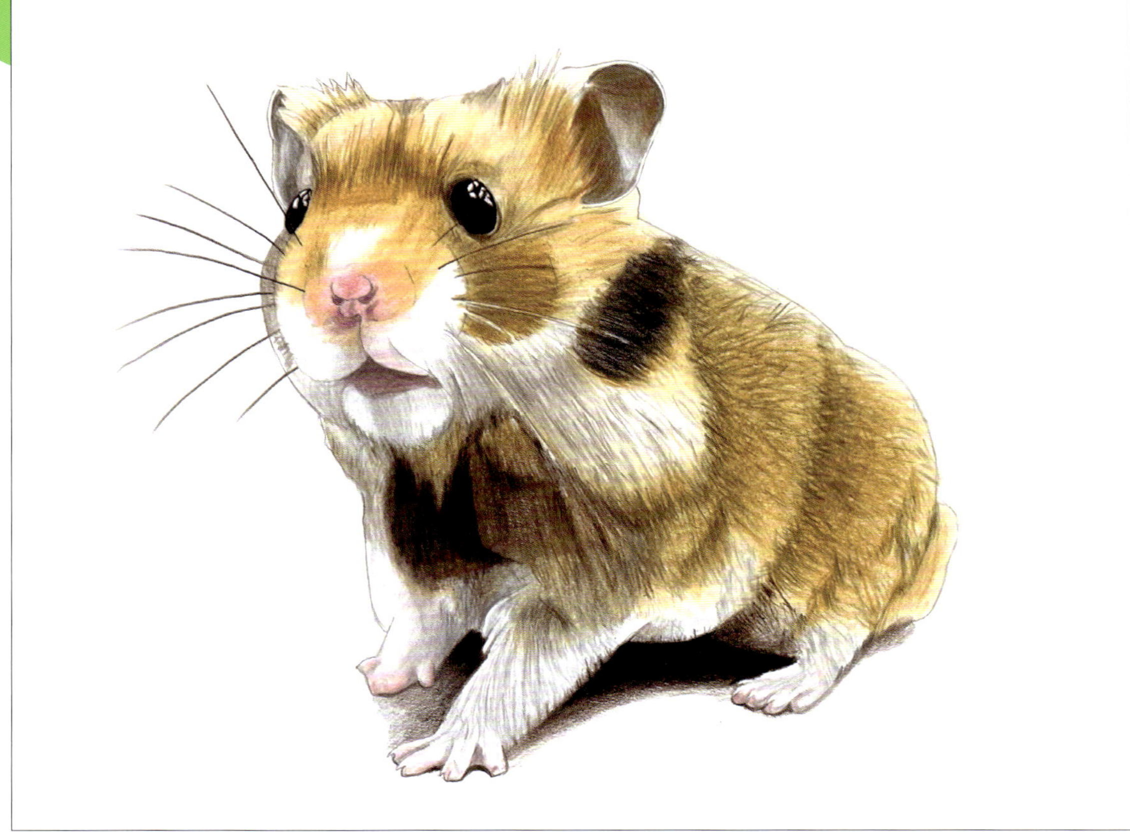

Add another layer of black over the shadows made in **Step 13** to complete the drawing.

■ Black

UNIT
13

Draw a Russian Blue Cat

Colored pencils: Prismacolor
Paper: KMK Kent Paper
Drawn by Rihito

Coloring Key Points

1. Awareness of the transparency of the eyes (p.13).
2. Depiction of fur using a stylus and design knife (p.15).

Colors Used

- PC914 Cream
- PC938 White
- PC910 True Green
- PC903 True Blue
- PC901 Indigo Blue
- PC935 Black
- PC941 Light Umber
- PC946 Dark Brown
- PC1065 Cool Grey 70%
- PC1074 French Grey 70%
- PC1060 Cool Grey 20%
- PC929 Pink
- PC924 Crimson Red

Reference Photo + Preliminary Drawing

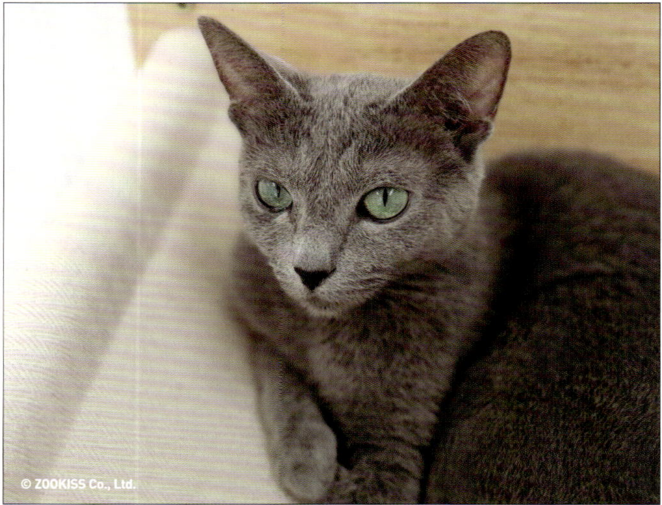

For this drawing, use the design knife not only to express fur and whiskers, but also to lighten areas where too much color has been applied by scraping the paper surface, especially when an eraser doesn't work. In such cases, scrape in the direction of the fur to brighten the area. Also, rather than thinking of it as "coloring," try to approach fur expression with the mindset of drawing and layering fine lines. When you need to blur certain areas, do so relentlessly by burnishing firmly with white or cool grey 20%.

The reference photo is on the dark side, so draw the face a bit brighter and with more detail, gradually reducing the level of detail from the chest and front legs to the body. Leave some of the paper's white visible around the eyes and nose. Since everything apart from the eyes and nose is out of focus, blur by burnishing with cool grey 20% or white.

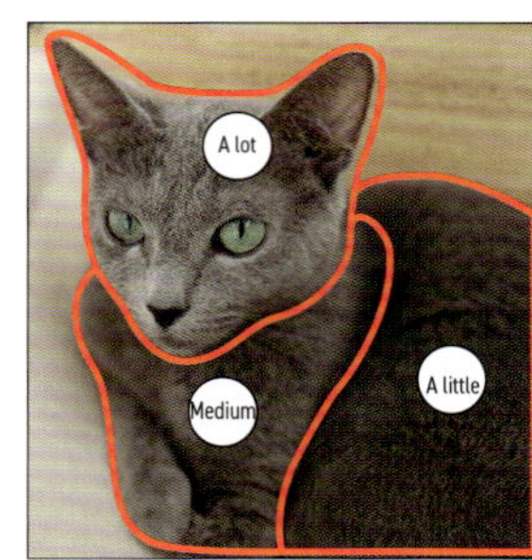

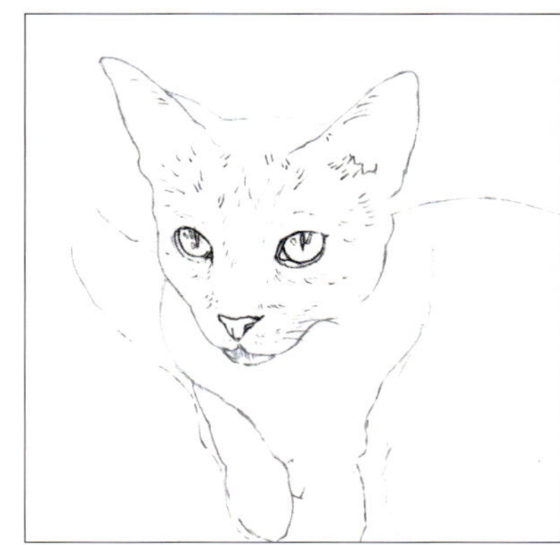

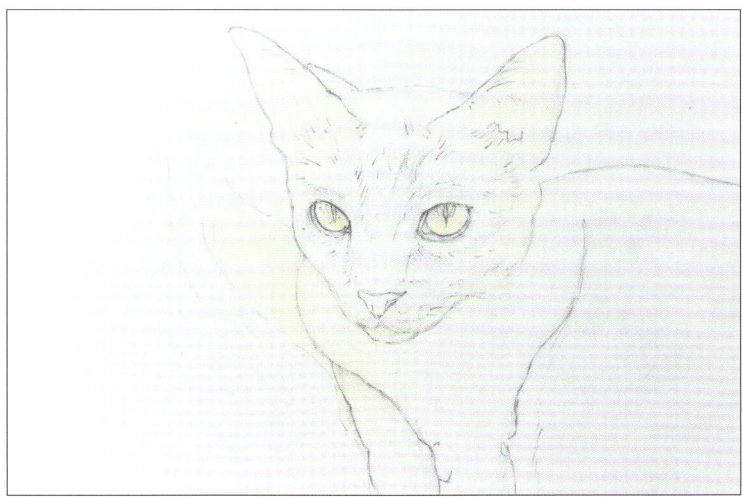

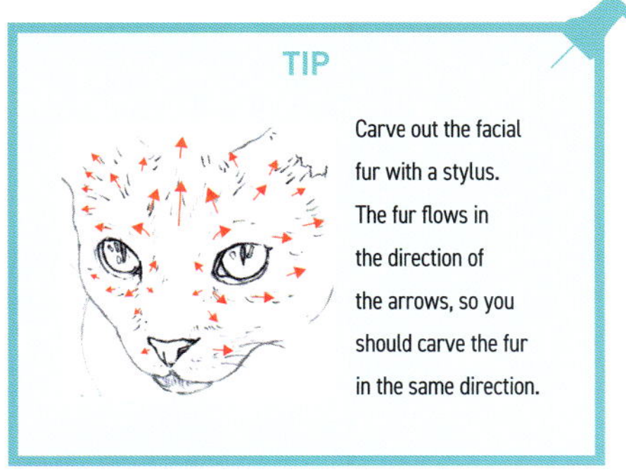

1 Start by carving the fur on the cat's face with a stylus.

2 Apply cream color to the areas that will become darker and around the eyes, and white to the rest of the surface. This helps prevent pencil strokes from standing out too much when drawing the fur later. It also improves color adherence. Be sure to leave the highlights uncolored.

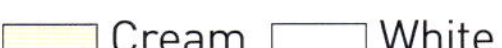

⬜ Cream ⬜ White

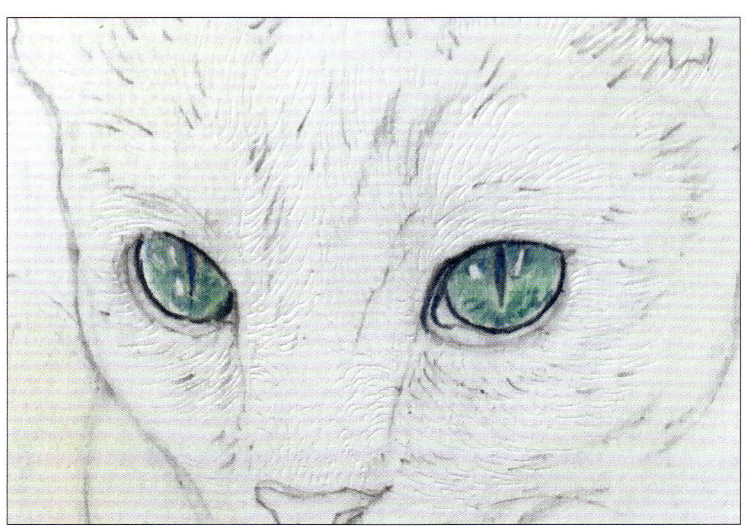

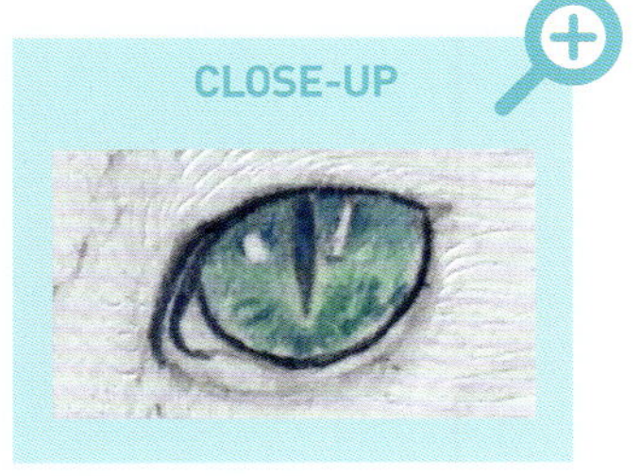

3 Color the eye using true green and true blue. Use indigo blue to outline the eyeball and also fill in the pupil. Be sure to leave the highlights uncolored here as well.

🟩 True green 🟦 True blue
🟦 Indigo blue

UNIT 14

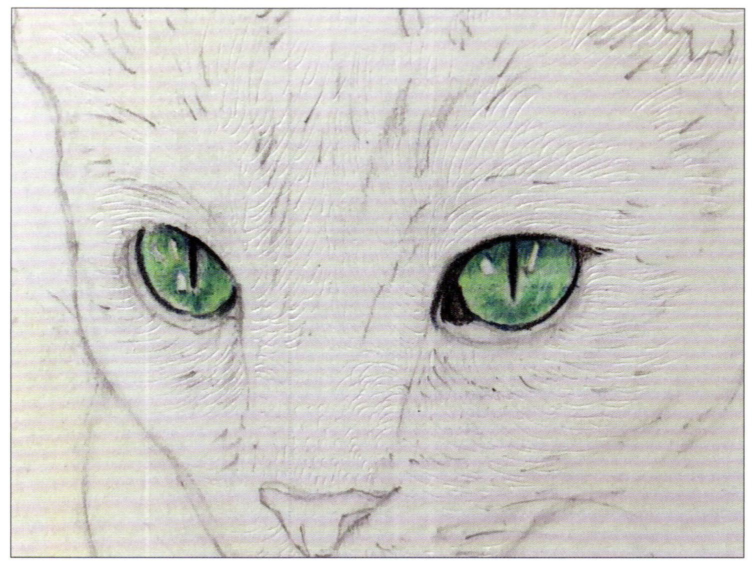

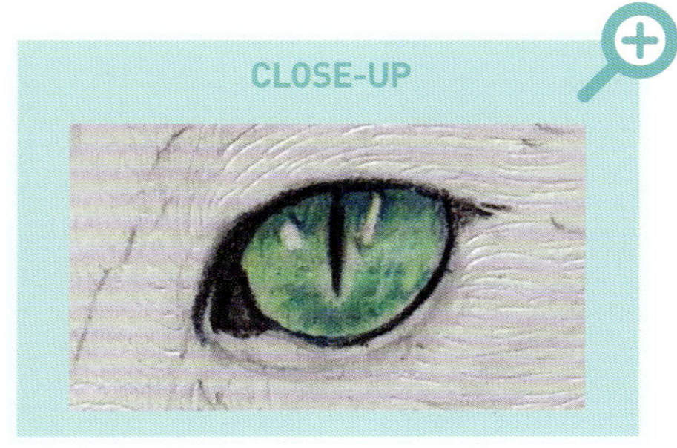

4 Color the pupil, the border between the eyelid and the eyeball, and the inner corner of the eye using black. Then, apply another layer of true green over it. Be sure to leave the highlight uncolored.

■ Black ▥ True green

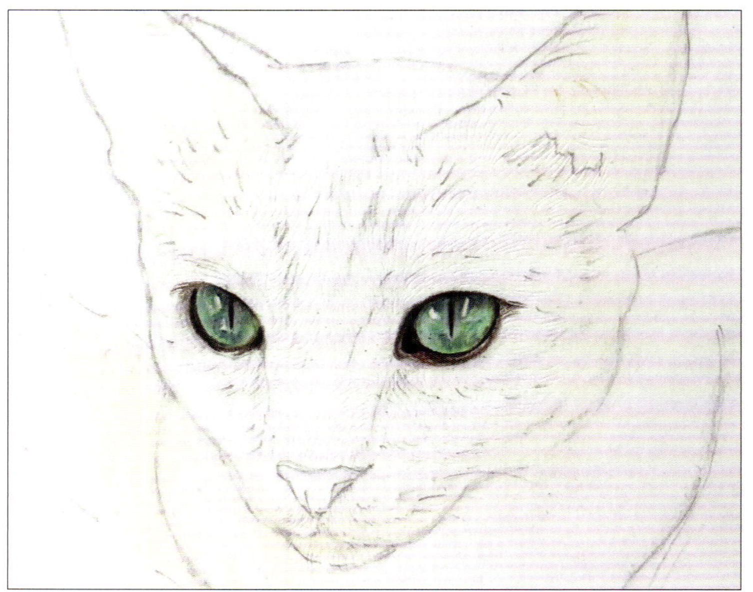

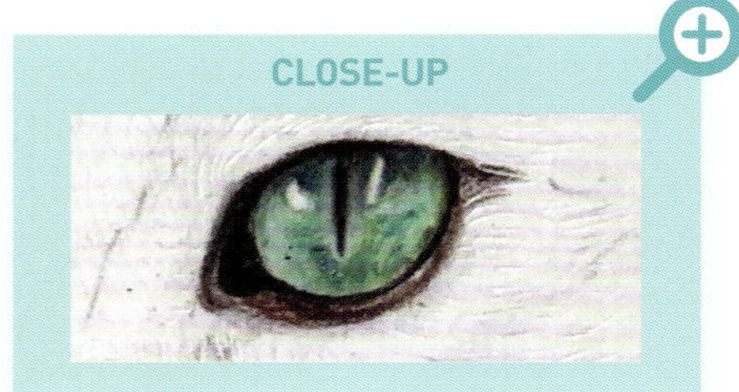

5 After burnishing the entire area except for the highlights with white, shade the part of the eyeball where the eyelid casts a shadow using indigo blue and light umber. For the iris, draw lines with indigo blue. Add true green near the iris as well to increase the saturation. Be sure to leave the highlights unpainted.

▢ White ■ Indigo blue
▥ Light umber ▥ True green

How to Draw Fur

Try applying a coloring technique that uses jagged lines. Although there are obviously some areas where you'll want to avoid leaving any pencil strokes, around the face you should try to focus on this rougher type of application, as shown to the right. Ever without drawing each individual hair, you can still give a sense of the overall fur texture.

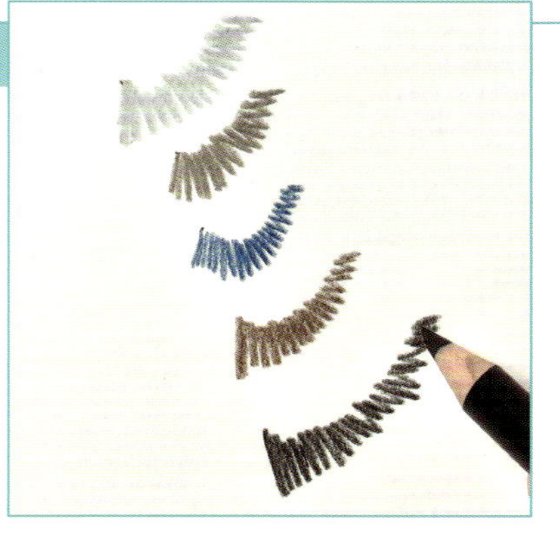

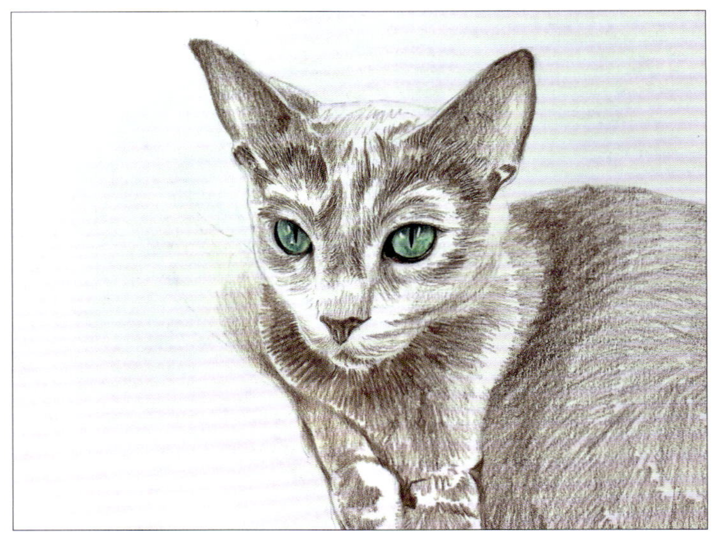

6 Color the whole body with visible strokes of dark brown. Leave the areas under the eyes and around the nose uncolored so that the white of the paper shines though.

■ Dark brown

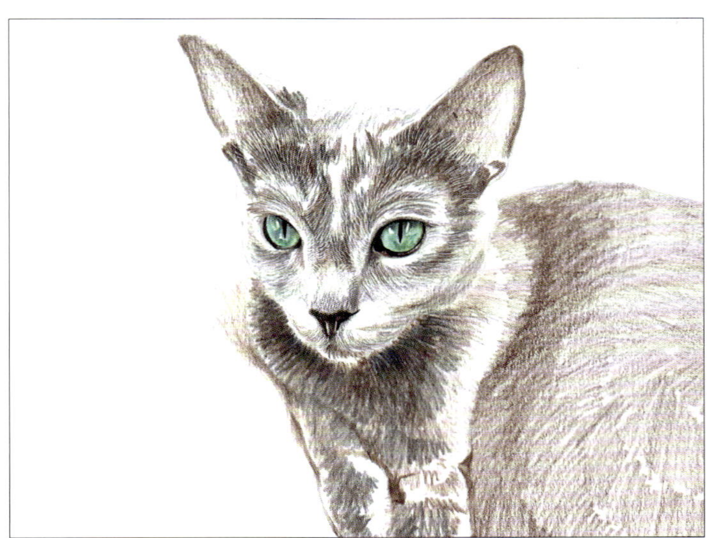

7 Apply a layer of cool grey 70% to the same areas that were colored with dark brown in **Step 6**. Also add some indigo blue to the dark area under the cat's chin.

■ Cool grey 70%　■ Indigo blue

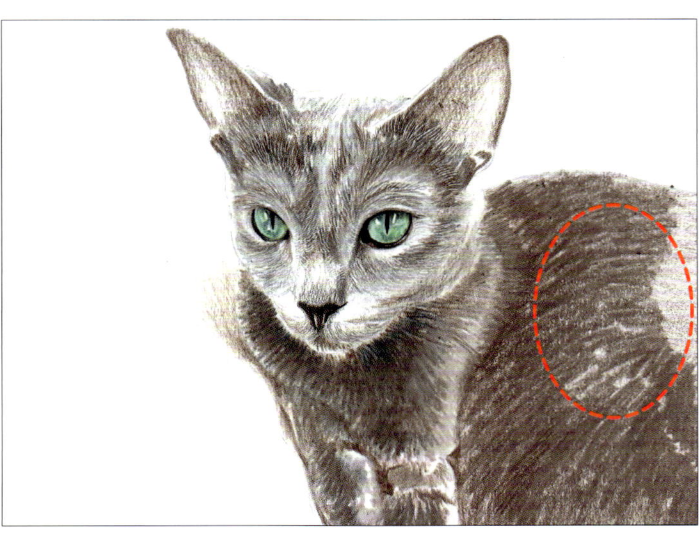

8 Apply layers of French grey 70% and cool grey 20% to the entire body. Use about 60% pressure for both colors. Leave the red-circled area on the right uncolored.

■ French grey 70%　■ Cool grey 20%

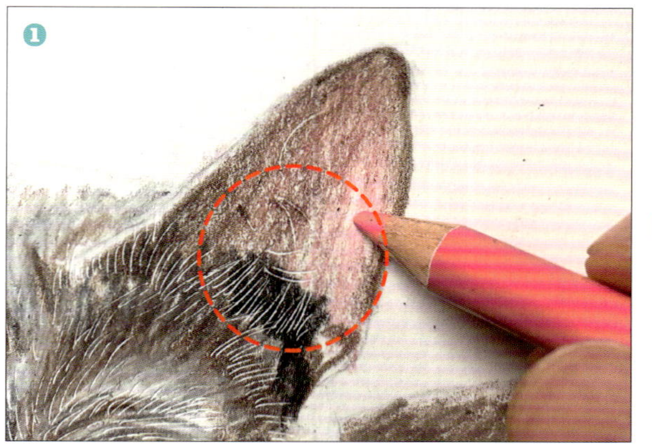 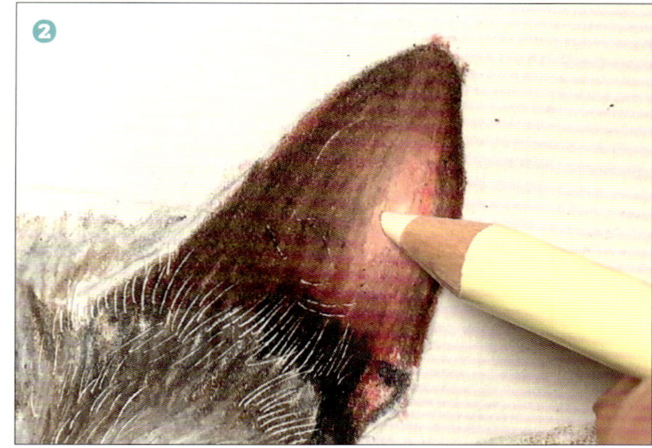

9 ❶ Shade the ears using French grey 70% and pink, creating areas of light and dark. In the particularly dark part of the red-circled area, use black. ❷ Apply layers of crimson red and dark brown and then burnish with cream.

▮ French grey 70% ▮ Pink ▮ Black ▮ Crimson red ▮ Dark brown ▯ Cream

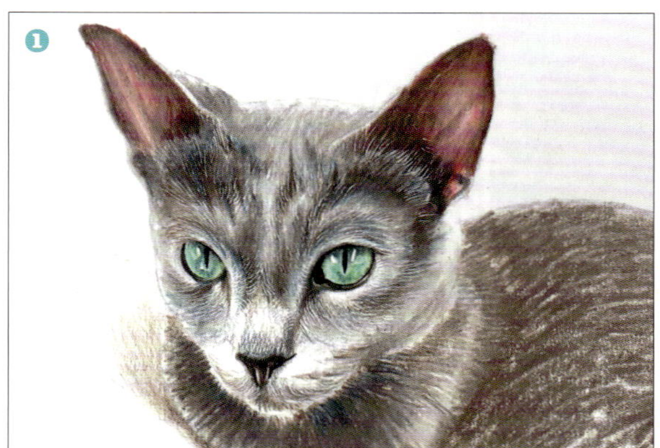 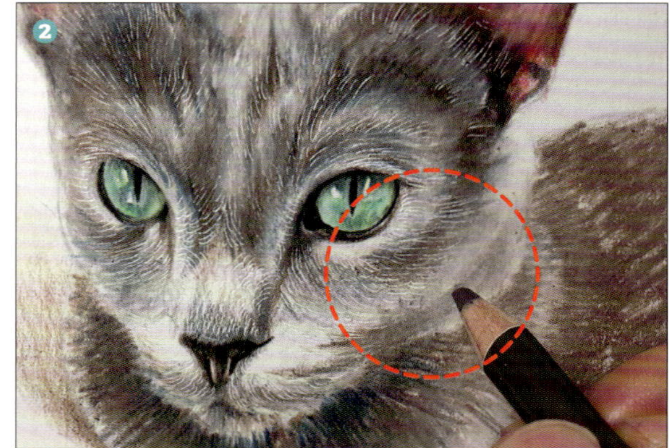

10 ❶ Add indigo blue and dark brown to the facial fur. ❷ Darken the cheek within the circled area with French grey 70%.

▮ Indigo blue ▮ Dark brown ▮ French grey 70%

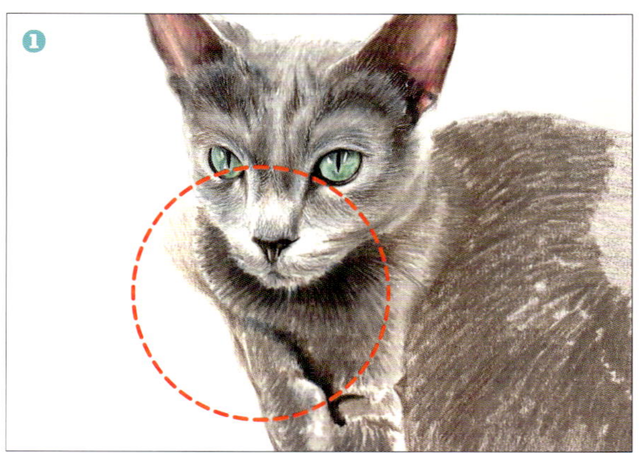 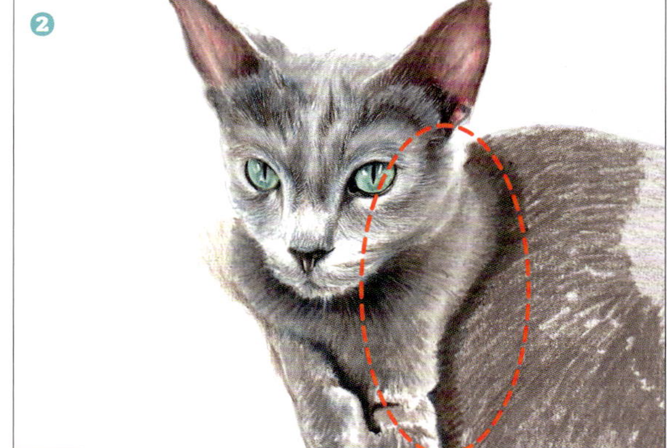

11 ❶ Add dark brown, indigo blue, and black to the facial fur. Be careful not to make it too dark. ❷ Darken the cheek within the circled area with French grey 70%. Add light umber to the circled area.

▮ Dark brown ▮ Indigo blue ▮ Black ▮ French grey 70% ▮ Light umber

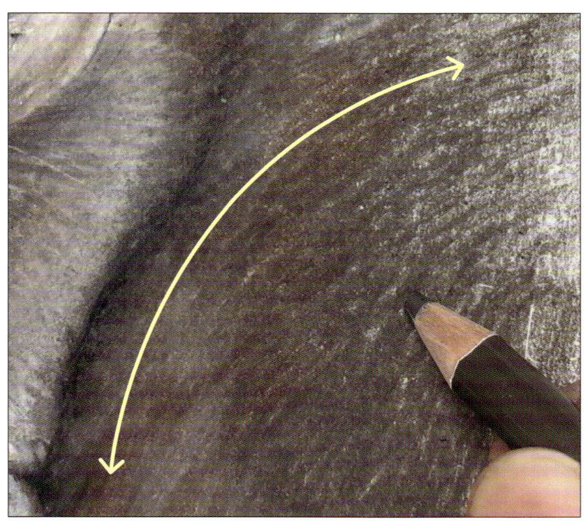

12 Color the body with French grey 70% in the directions of both opposite arrows.

▬ French grey 70%

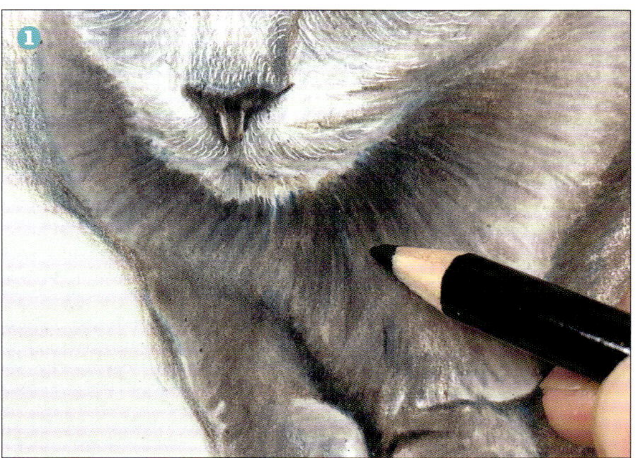
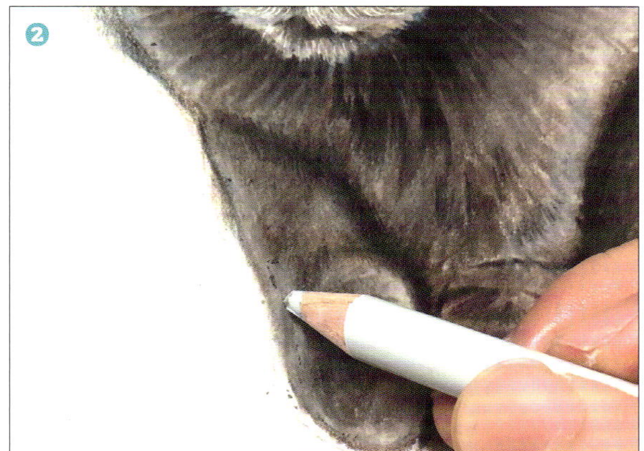

13 ❶ Use black to draw the clumped texture of the fur on the chest. ❷ Use white to add reflected light in the darker areas.

▬ Black ▭ White

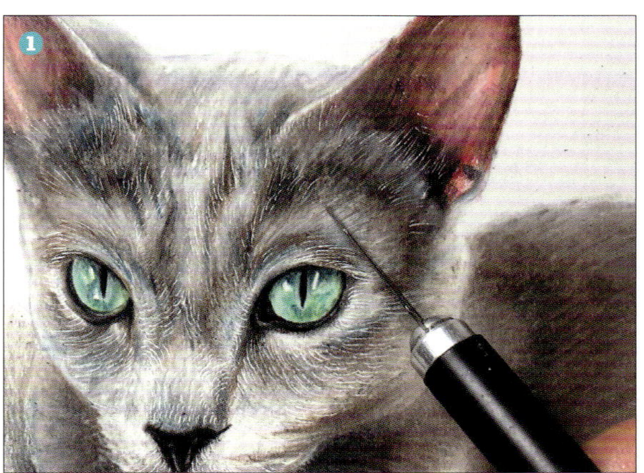
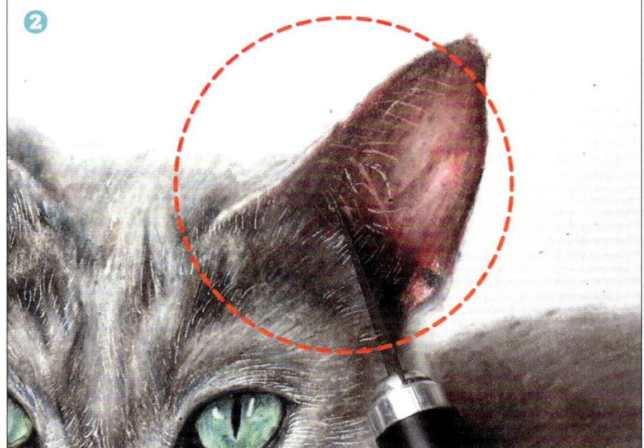

14 ❶ Depict the fur texture by scraping the colored surface with a design knife. Around the eyes and nose, follow the direction of hair growth as explained in the TIP from Step 1. ❷ Do the same for the ears. Depict the fur around them by scraping the colored surface with a design knife.

UNIT
14

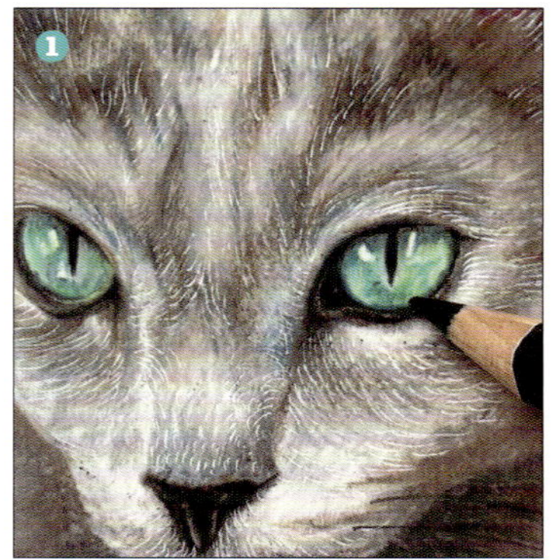 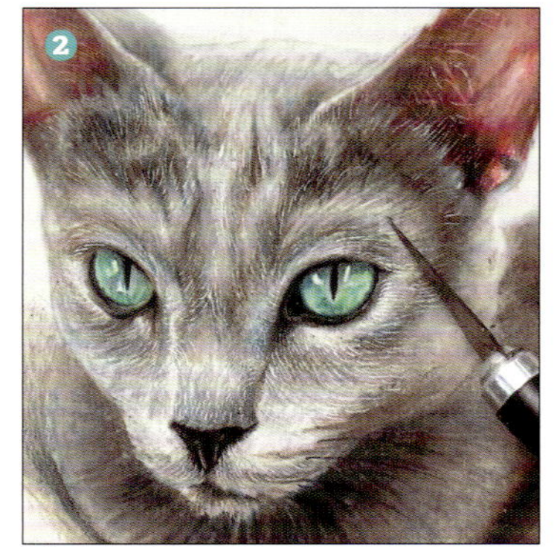 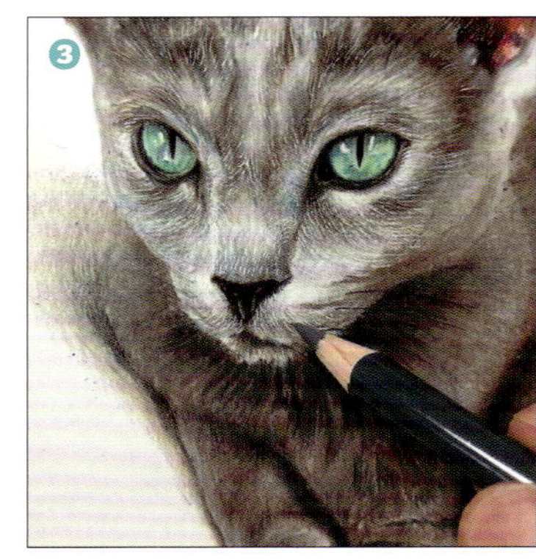

15 Final touches. ❶ Use indigo blue to blur the boundary of the eyeball. ❷ Scrape the surface of the face with a design knife to brighten it. ❸ Add shading with cool grey 70% around the right side of the mouth (from the viewer's perspective). To emphasize the three-dimensional form of the nose, chin, and face, slightly exaggerate the shading compared to the reference photo.

▬ Indigo blue ▬ Cool grey 70%

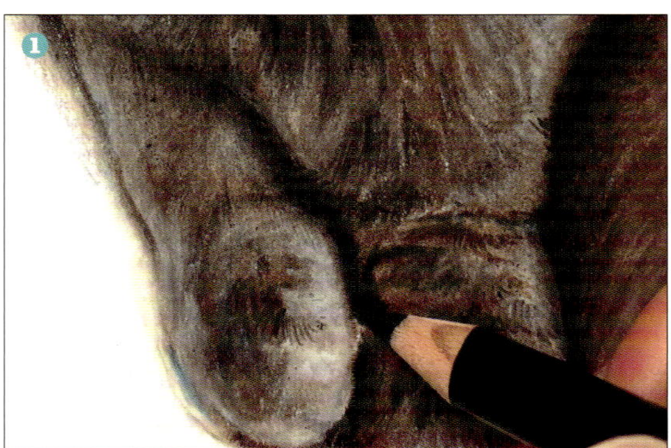 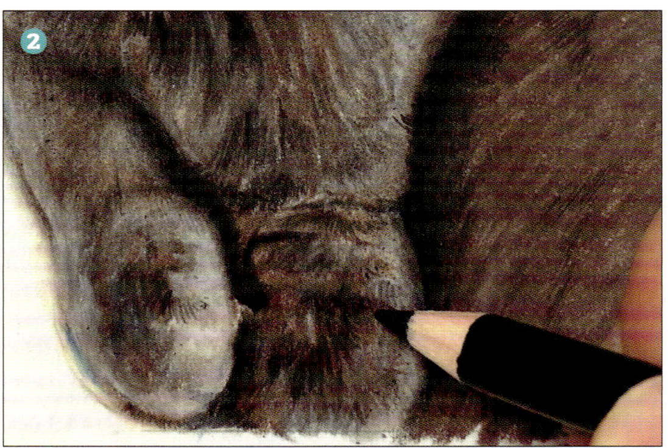

16 ❶ Add black to define the outline of the front legs. ❷ Depict the fur on the front legs with black. Hold the pencil upright and draw as if turning each stroke into a strand of fur.

▬ Black

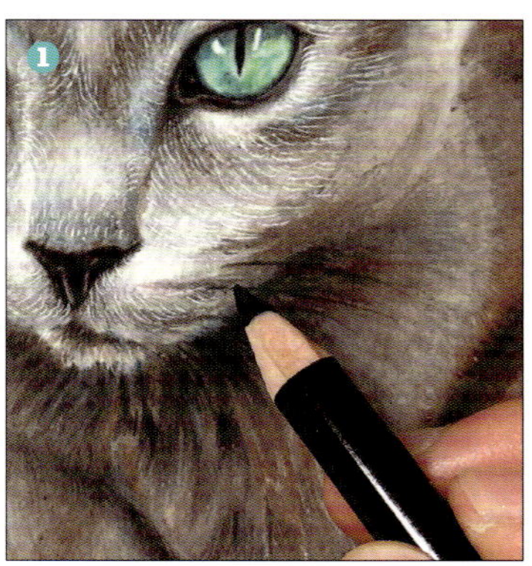 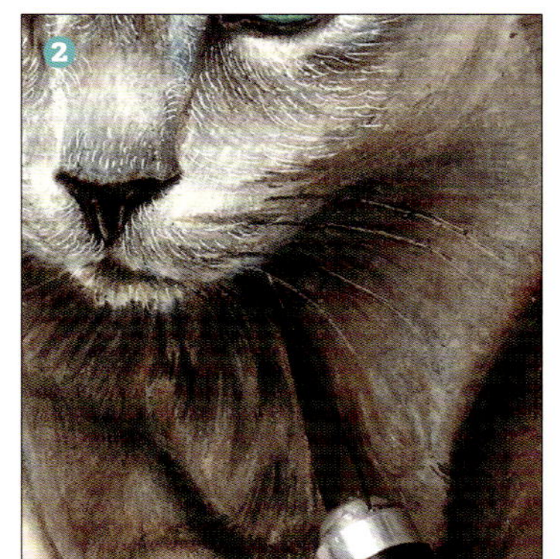 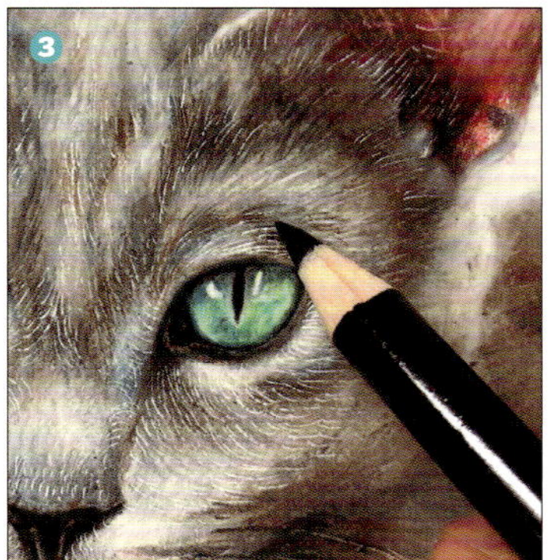

17 ❶ Draw the whiskers with black. ❷ For whiskers in the darker areas, use a design knife to scrape the surface of the drawing. ❸ While carefully observing the reference photo, add black here and there. Rather than thinking of it as coloring, treat it as drawing lines. Don't apply too much pressure.

▬ Black

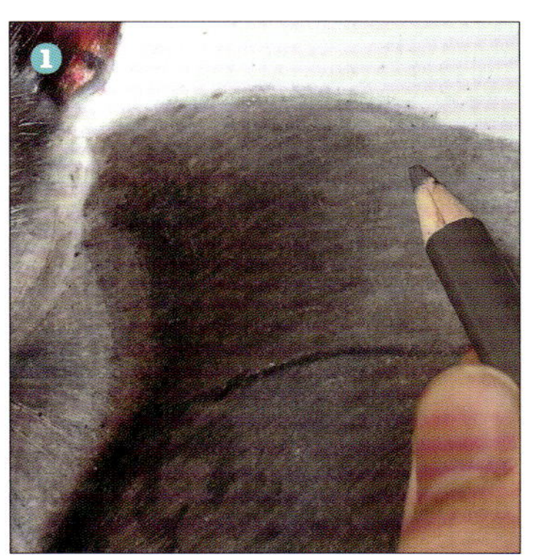 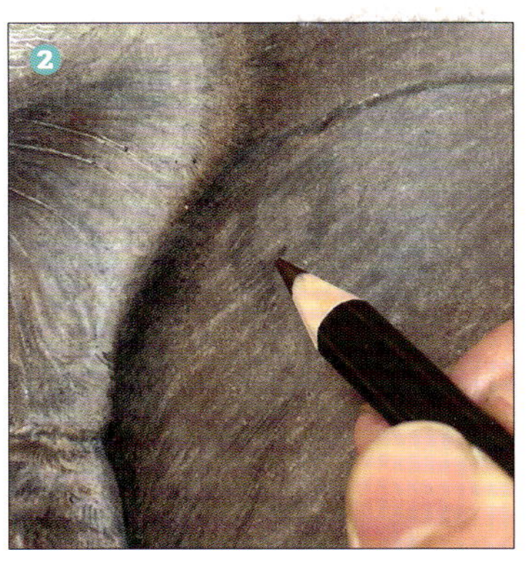 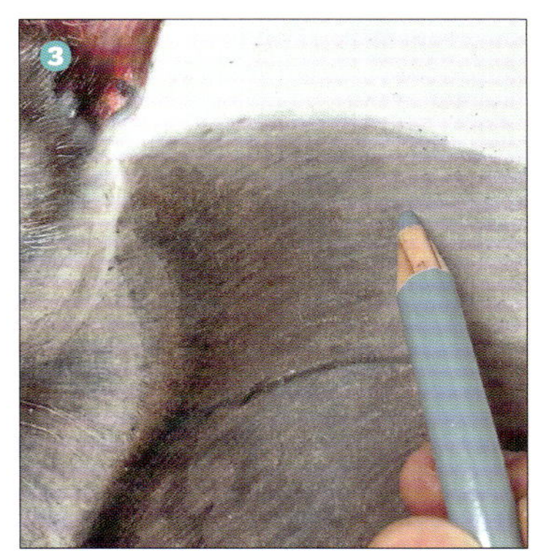

18 ❶ Color the dark areas with French grey 70% to blur them. Apply about 80% pressure with the pencil. ❷ Using dark brown, hold the pencil upright with the fur texture in mind, and make scratchy strokes that leave visible marks. ❸ Blur the uncolored parts of the body by burnishing them with cool grey 20%.

▬ French grey 70%   ▬ Dark brown   ▬ Cool grey 20%

COMPLETE

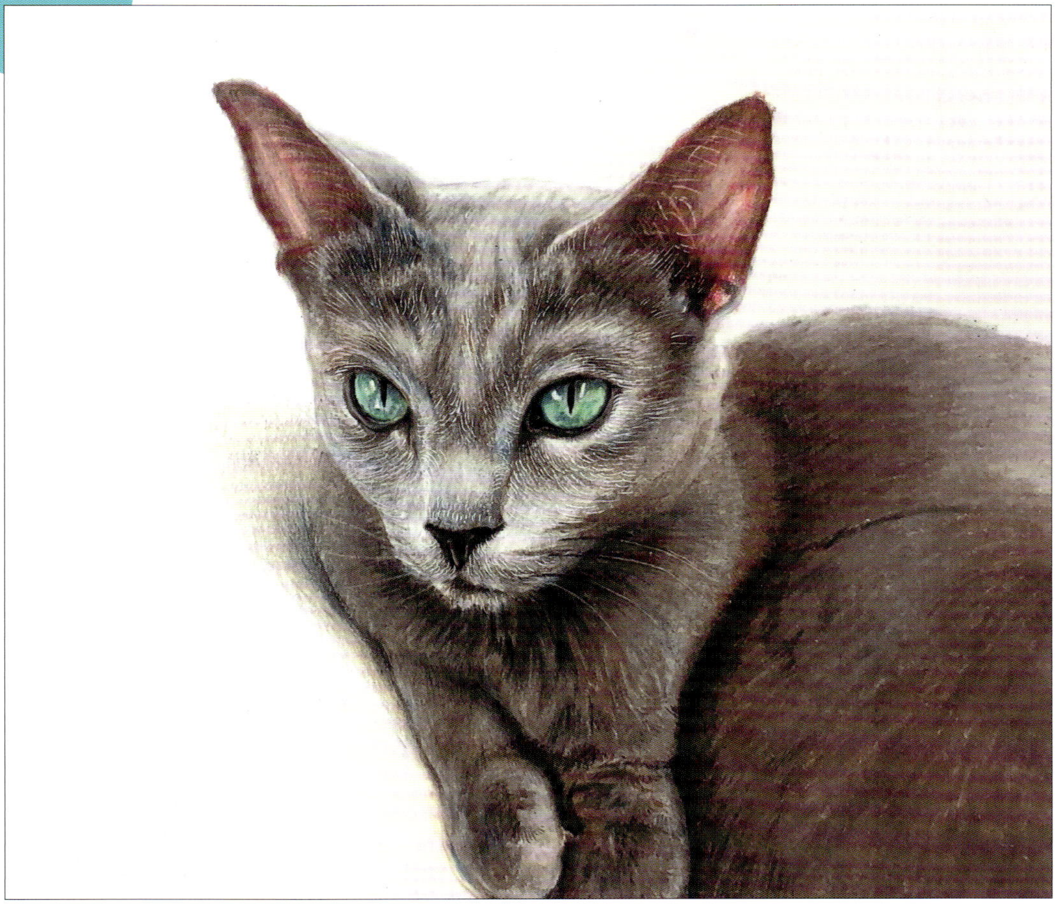

Draw a Pomeranian

Colored pencils: Prismacolor
Paper: Daigen Thick Kent Paper
Drawn by Bonbon

Coloring Key Points

1. Depict the slight charges of color in the small iris (p.14).

2. Capture the different types of fur in this double-coated breed (p.15).

3. Find a suitable balance between the fine shading of single hairs and the overall shading of the coat.

Colors Used

PC935 Black	PC1032 Pumpkin Orange
PC1027 Peacock Blue	PC941 Light Umber
PC947 Dark Umber	PC944 Terra Cotta
PC1050 Warm Grey 10%	PC997 Beige
PC914 Cream	OP501 Soft White*
PC1034 Goldenrod	PC1024 Blue Slate
PC1052 Warm Grey 30%	PC925 Crimson Lake
PC1056 Warm Grey 70%	* Holbein

Preliminary Drawing

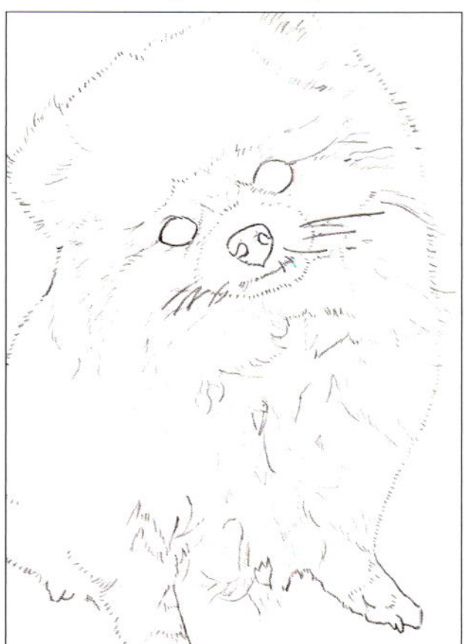

Since the fur is fluffy, it's hard to grasp the overall outline. As you draw, think about the actual size of the body and head, and how far the fur extends.

Reference Photo

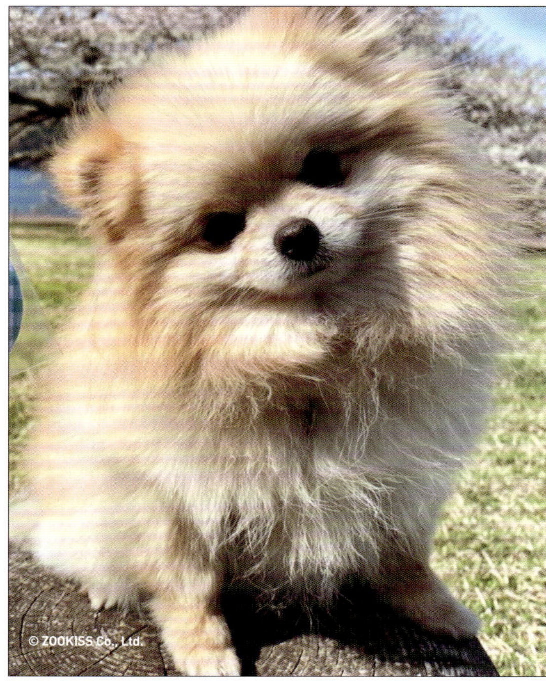

The subject is a long-haired pomeranian. This double-coated breed has both long, straight, stiff outer fur and a soft, downy undercoat. The goal is to distinguish between these two types of fur using colored-pencil strokes, as well as tools like a stylus or design knife. While prioritizing the overall shading created by strong sunlight, be sure to also depict the subtle shadows within the fur texture.

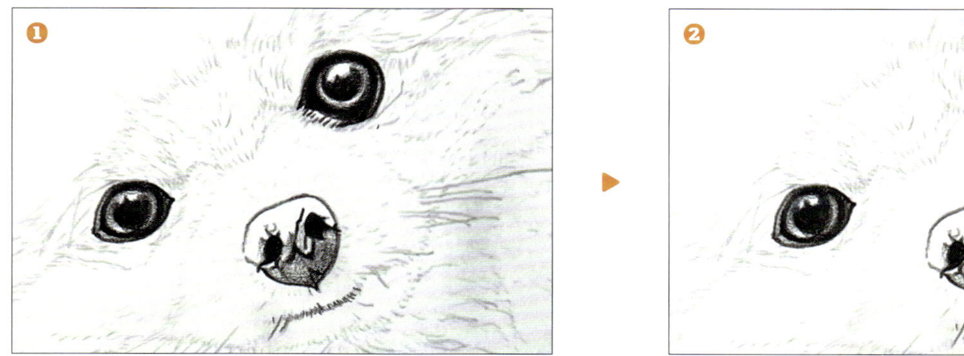

1 ❶ Color the eyes. Use black to fill in the entire eye. Observe carefully and add detail to the area around the eye and the pupil. (This step also includes drawing the outline of the nose.) ❷ The highlight in the left eye (on the right side when facing the drawing) reflects the sky, so add peacock blue in that area.

■ Black ▨ Peacock blue

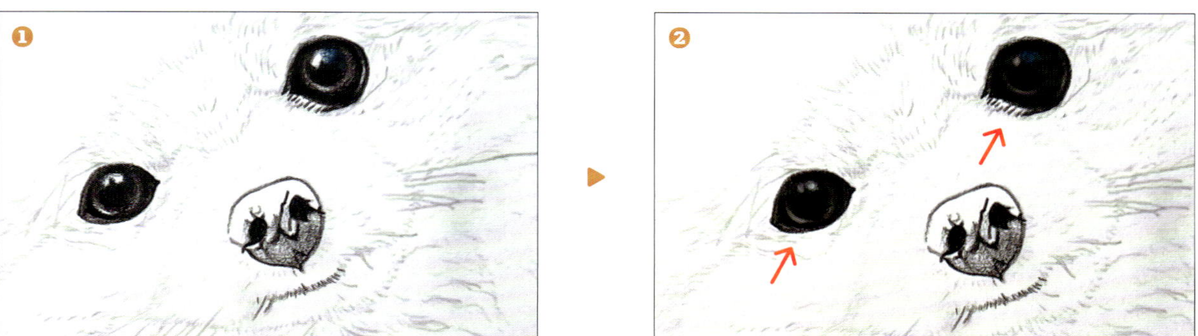

2 ❶ Color the iris using dark umber. ❷ Add reflected light coming from the lower left with warm grey 10%, then use black, peacock blue, and dark umber to burnish the area. This lowers the overall brightness of the eye.

▨ Dark umber ▢ Warm grey 10% ■ Black ▨ Peacock blue

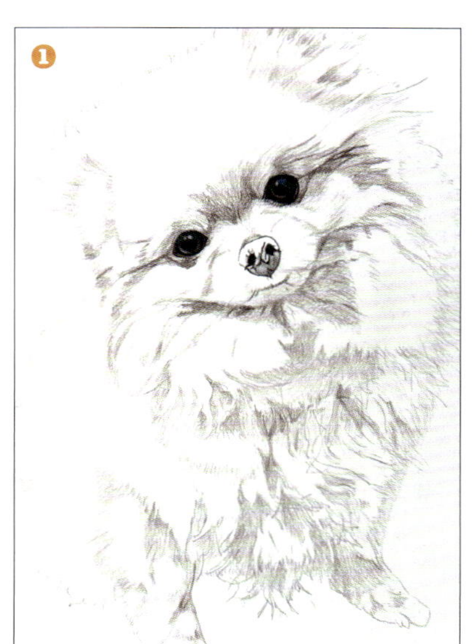

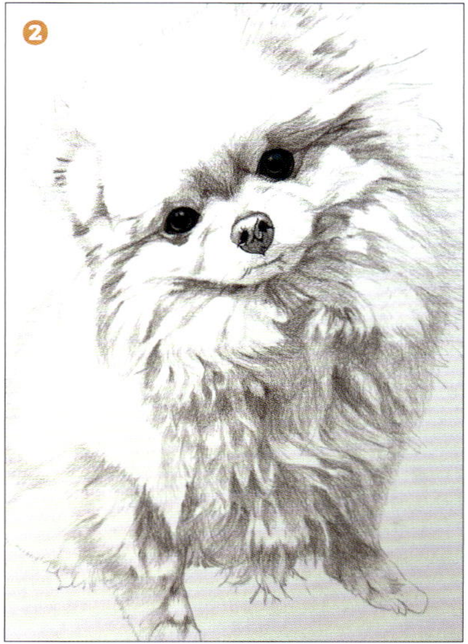

3 This is the grisaille stage. ❶ Use dark umber as an undercoat to depict the overall shading. Start by creating rough shading. ❷ Once the light and dark areas are clearly defined, start adding finer shading details. Continue shading until the general flow of the fur becomes visible. Once you've reached that point, the grisaille stage is complete.

▨ Dark umber

UNIT 15

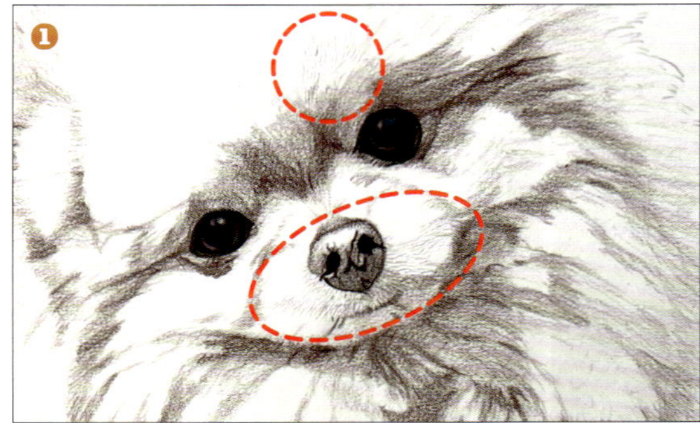
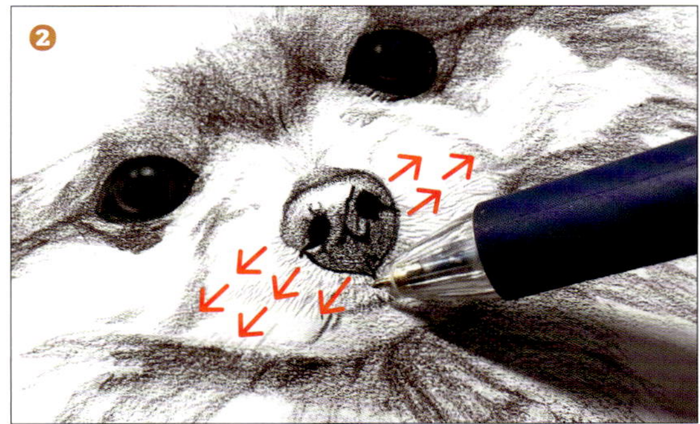

4 ❶ Depict the fur by using a stylus to make indentations on the paper. Start by selecting the areas where you want to create bright white fur. ❷ Then, using short, quick strokes, press the paper in a radiating pattern outward from the nose to recreate the fur. Since the fur in this area is short, it's best to use short, tapping motions with the stylus.

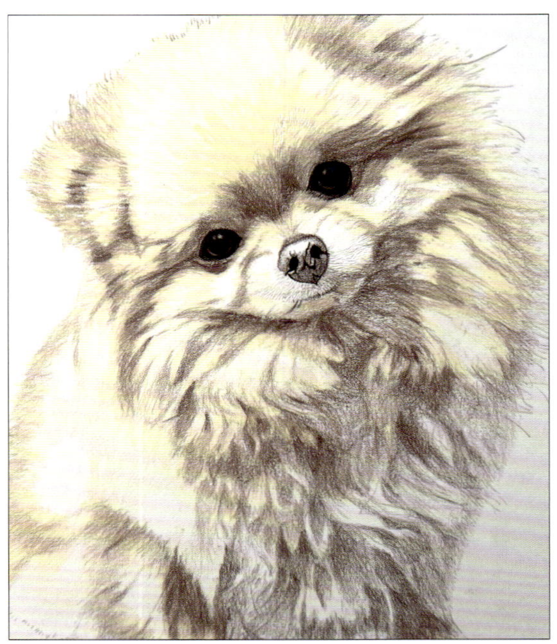

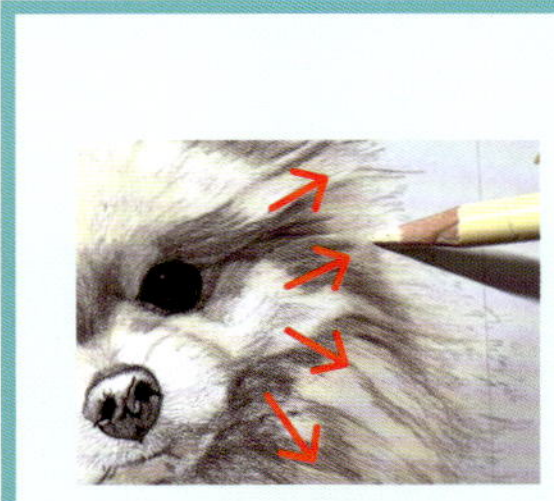

5 The fur can generally be divided into two types: "brownish fur" and "whitish fur." Use cream color to shade the lighter areas of the brownish fur.

▭ Cream

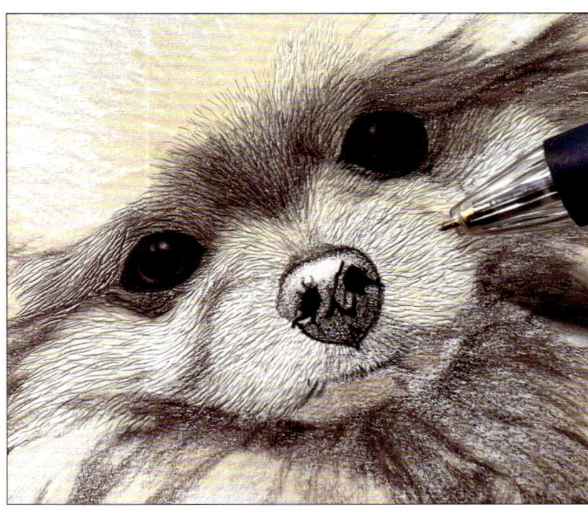

6 Indent the areas you shaded with cream using a stylus. Observe the flow and variations in the length of the fur carefully, and etch accordingly with the stylus to follow those natural patterns.

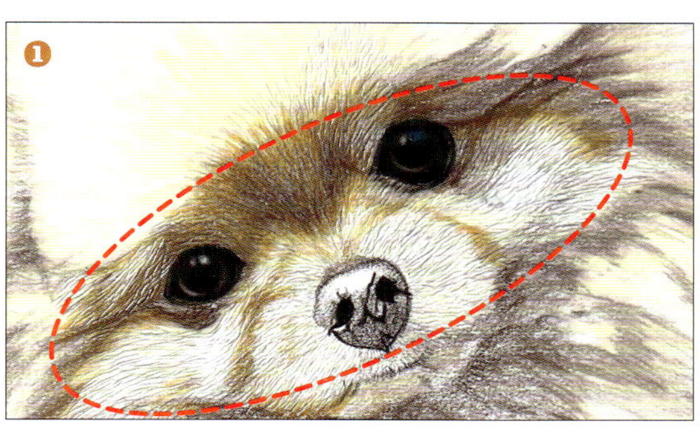 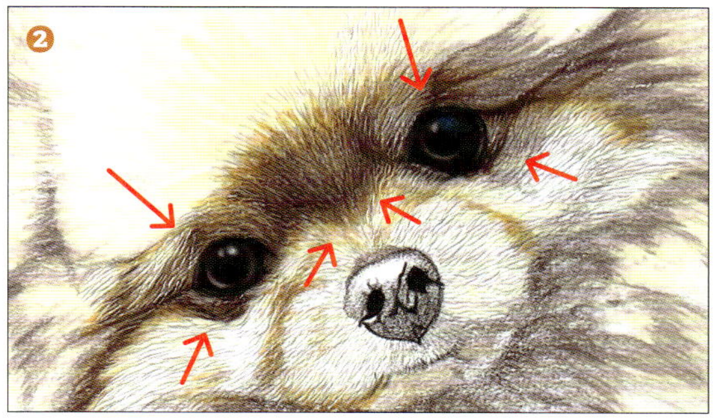

7 ❶ Shade the shadowed areas of the brownish fur with goldenrod. Be careful not to get color into the parts you etched with the stylus. ❷ Use dark umber to shade the especially dark areas within the shadows and emphasize the contrast.

▮ Goldenrod ▮ Dark umber

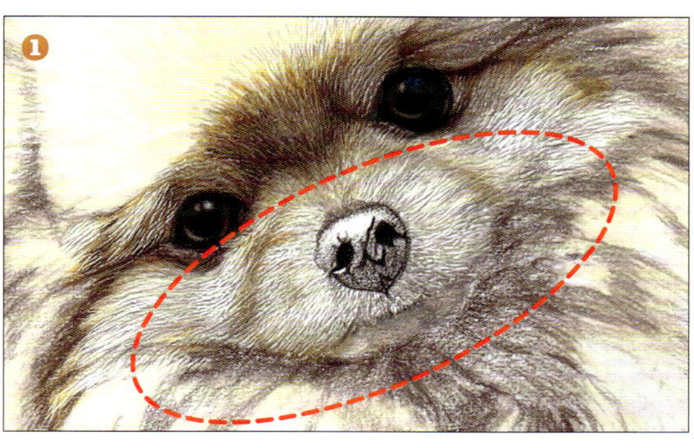 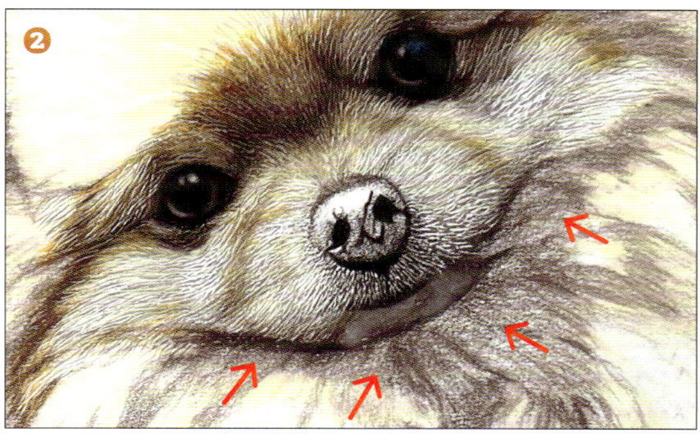

8 ❶ Shade the shadows of the whitish fur around the muzzle using warm grey 30%. ❷ Then, to further emphasize the shadows, apply warm grey 70%, and use black for the darkest areas, such as under the nose and under the chin.

▮ Warm grey 30% ▮ Warm grey 70% ▮ Black

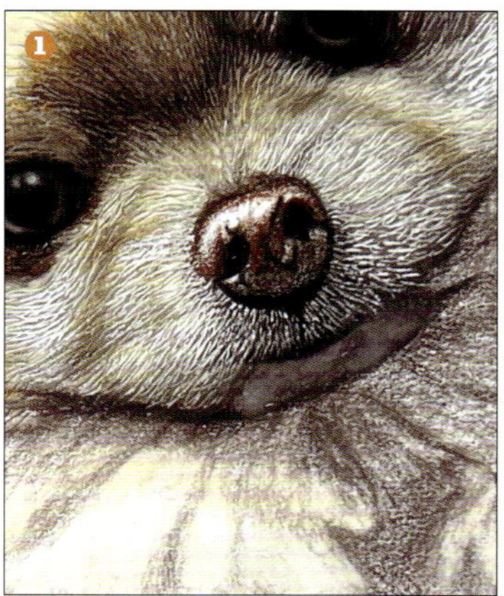 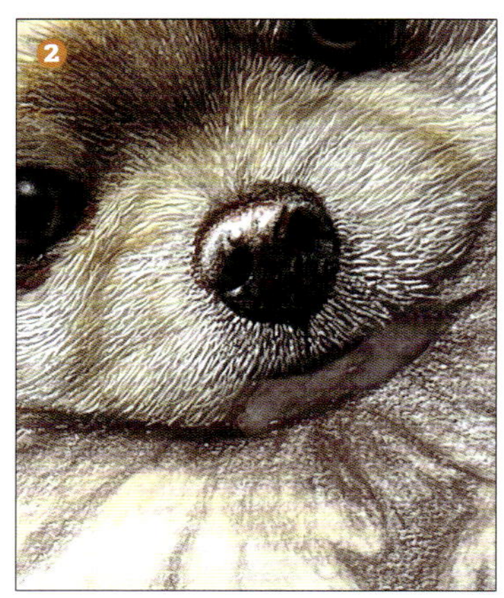 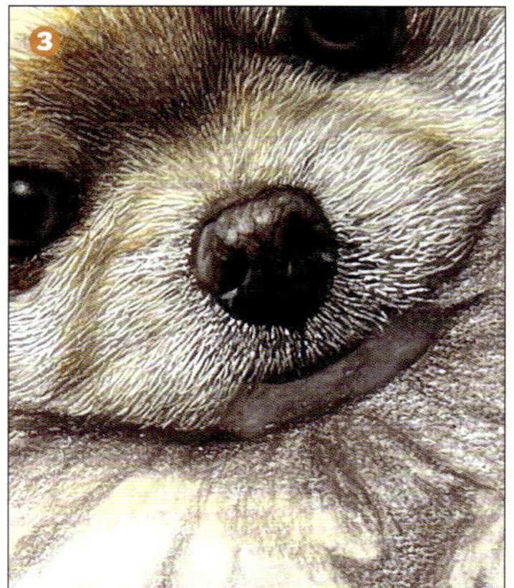

9 Color the nose. ❶ Apply pumpkin orange as a base layer for the nose. Be sure to leave the highlight area uncolored. ❷ Use black to shade the wrinkles and the darker lower half of the nose. Since the area around the nostrils is slightly brightened by the reflection of the sky, add some peacock blue there. ❸ Use warm grey 70% to soften the overall color. To keep the highlight from appearing too bright, tone it down with a warm grey 10%.

▮ Pumpkin orange ▮ Black ▮ Peacock blue ▮ Warm grey 70% ▯ Warm grey 10%

UNIT
15

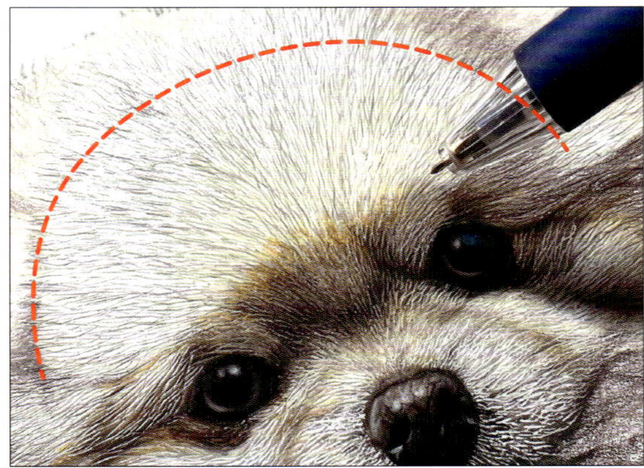

10 Carve the fur across the forehead using a stylus. The hair flows outward in a radial pattern from the center (between the eyebrows). Carve up to about the dotted line shown in the left image. For the outer area, use colored-pencil strokes to create a sense of depth by varying the focus.

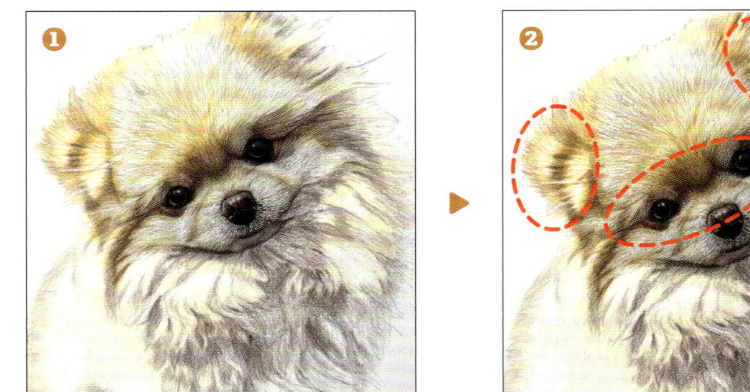

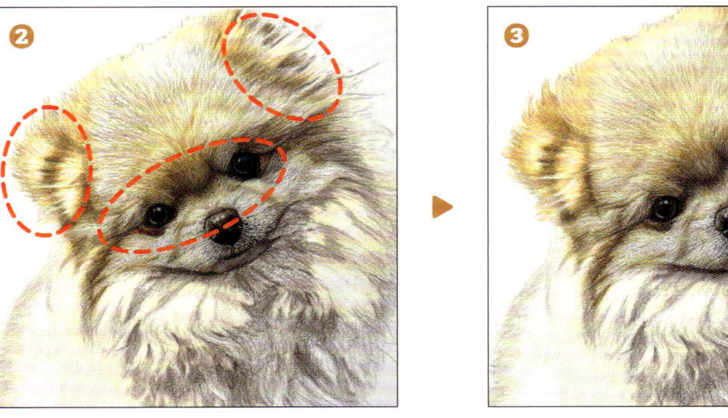

11 ❶ Add tonal variation to the entire head using goldenrod. ❷ Then use light umber and terra cotta to shade the darker areas such as the ears and eyebrows. ❸ Soften everything with beige, and apply soft white to the highlights.

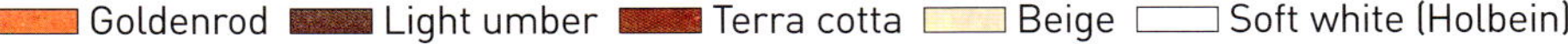

Goldenrod ▪ Light umber ▪ Terra cotta ☐ Beige ☐ Soft white (Holbein)

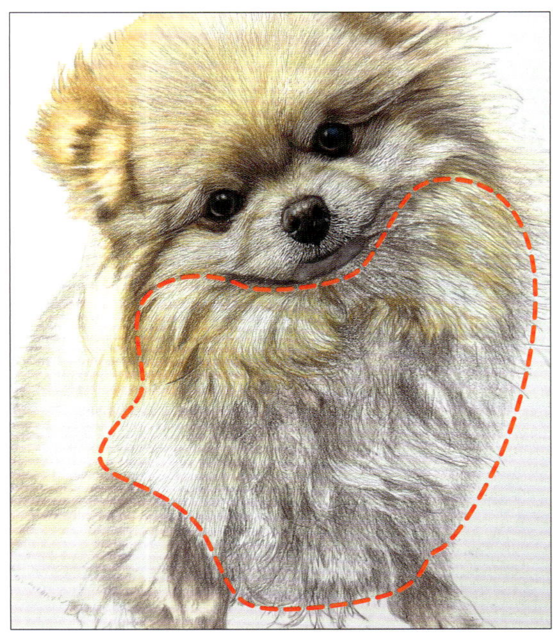

12 Engrave the area from the chest to the torso. Use a stylus to etch the hairs within the dotted area. Since the chest features the fluffy undercoat, carve it with curved strokes, while the torso's topcoat should be etched with straight strokes.

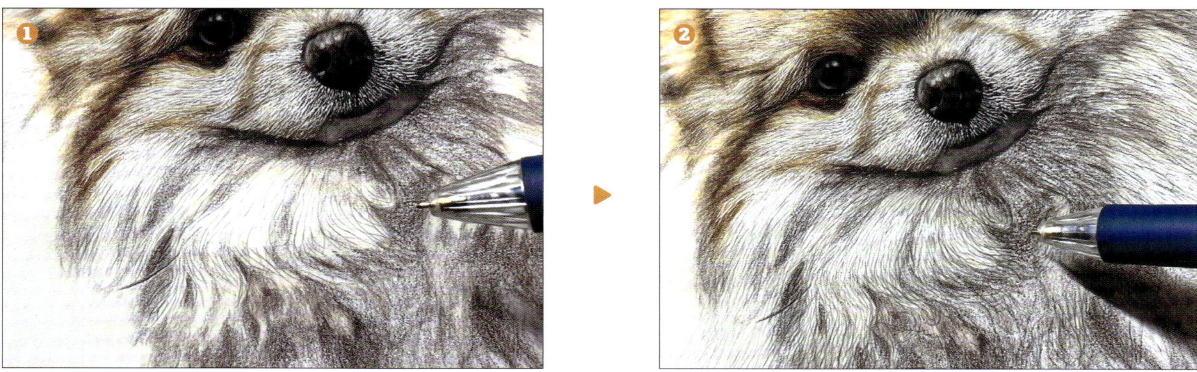

13 ❶ Since the shapes are complex, it's easier to make progress by carving in clumps of fur. Start by roughly etching along the general flow of the fur. ❷ Use those rough lines as a guide, and gradually increase the density of the stylus marks. To keep the lines from becoming monotonous, follow the overall flow but vary the direction slightly to create a more natural look.

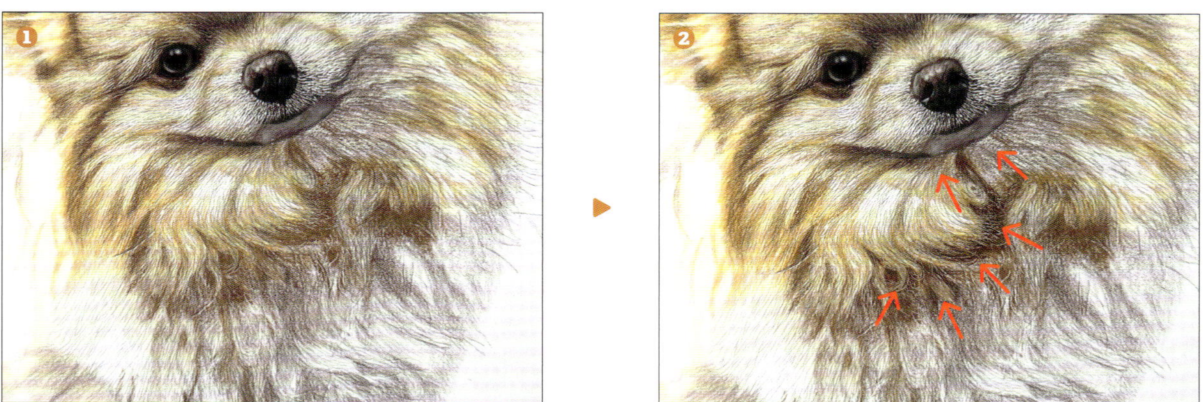

14 ❶ Shade the darker areas of the chest and torso (brown fur) using light umber, keeping the flow of the fur in mind and adding shadows to the clumps of hair. ❷ Use dark umber to further darken the roots of the fur.

■ Light umber ■ Dark umber

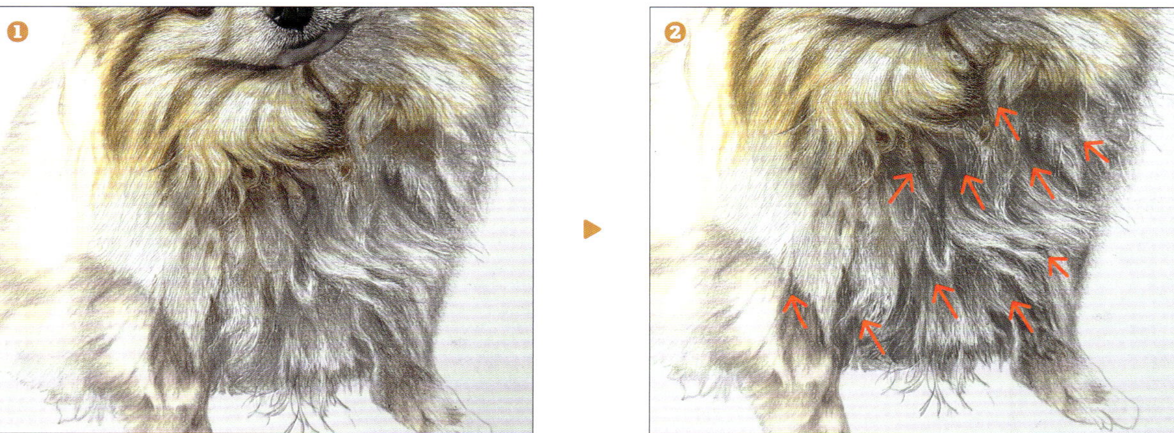

15 ❶ Shade the darker areas of the white fur on the chest and torso using warm grey 30%, just as in **Step 14**.
❷ Then darken the roots of the fur with warm grey 70%.

■ Warm grey 30% ■ Warm grey 70%

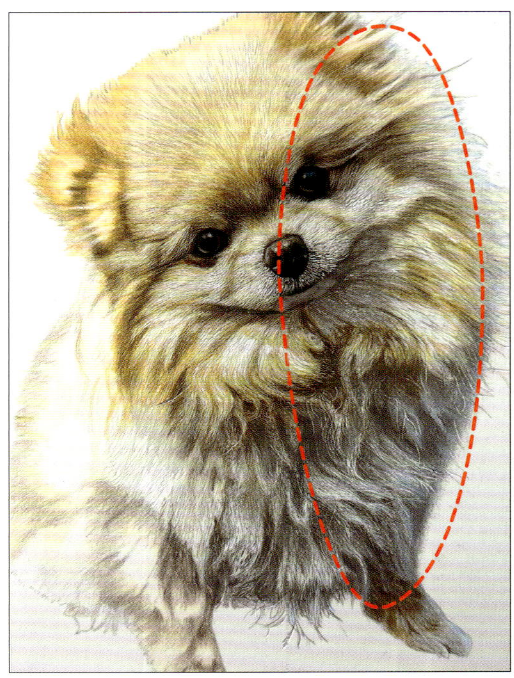

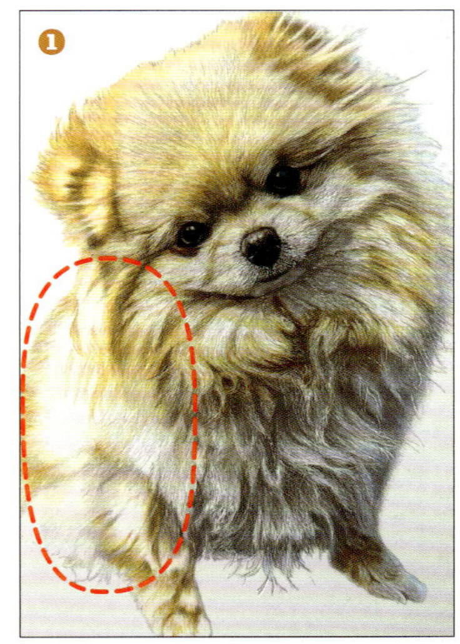

16 Depict the sunlight. In the reference photograph, the area within the red oval has a bluish tint to it from the effect of the sunlight. Use several layers of blue slate to capture that.

Blue slate

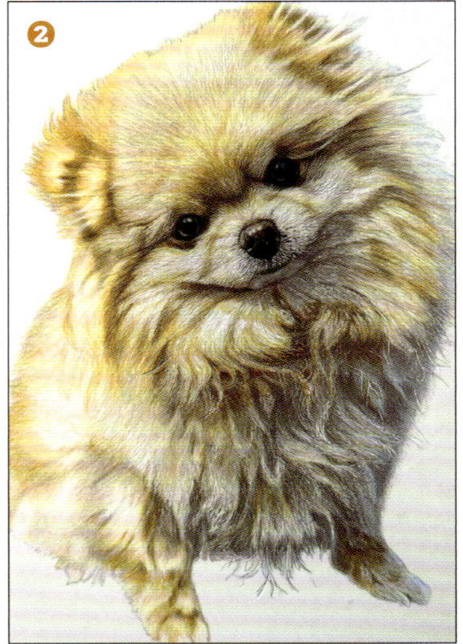

17 ❶ Color the darker areas of the brown fur on the torso with goldenrod. ❷ Color the lighter areas with beige. If you blend the beige outward from the goldenrod areas, it will result in a smoother, more polished finish.

Goldenrod
Beige

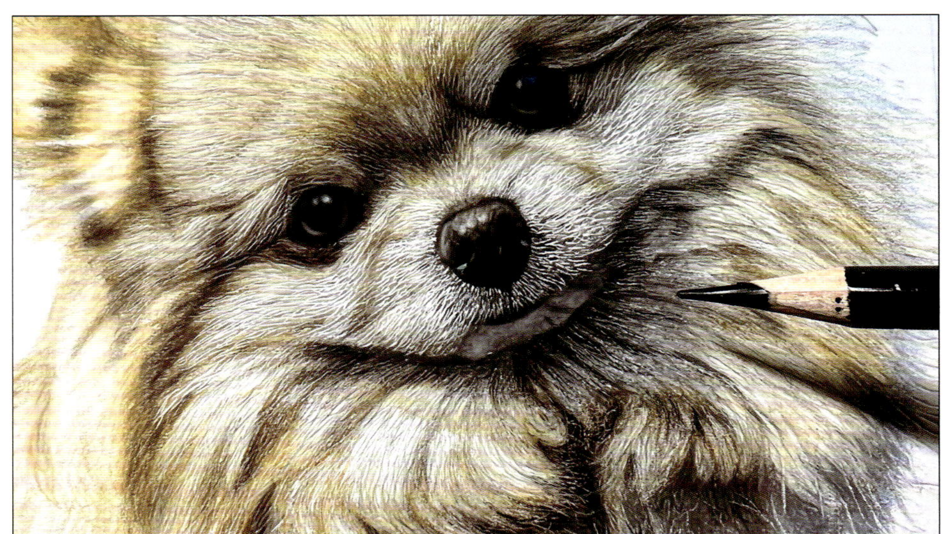

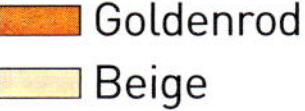

18 Emphasize the shading. Use darker colors to enhance the blurry shading. For the brown fur, use dark umber; for the white fur, use warm grey 70%. Apply black over the darkest areas in both to further deepen the contrast.

Dark umber
Warm grey 70%
Black

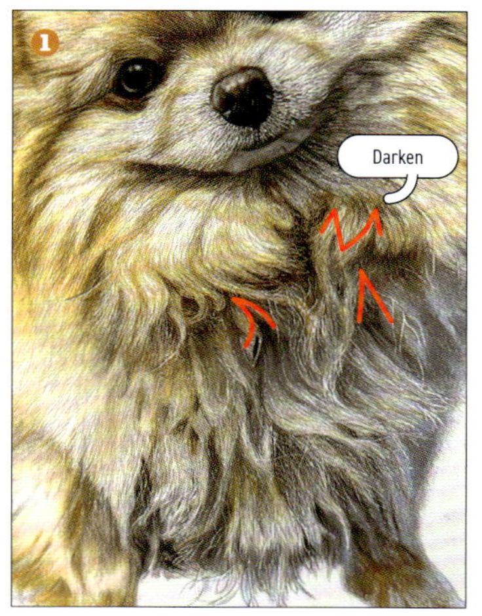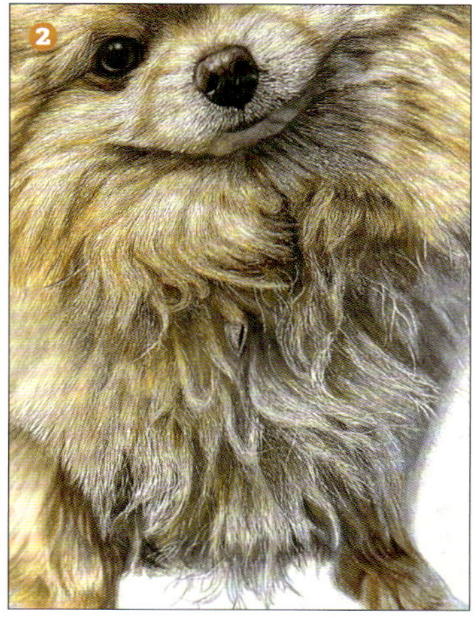

19 In particular, you can emphasize the three-dimensionality by applying wedge-shaped dark colors to the roots of the tufts of fur.

- Dark umber
- Warm grey 70%
- Black

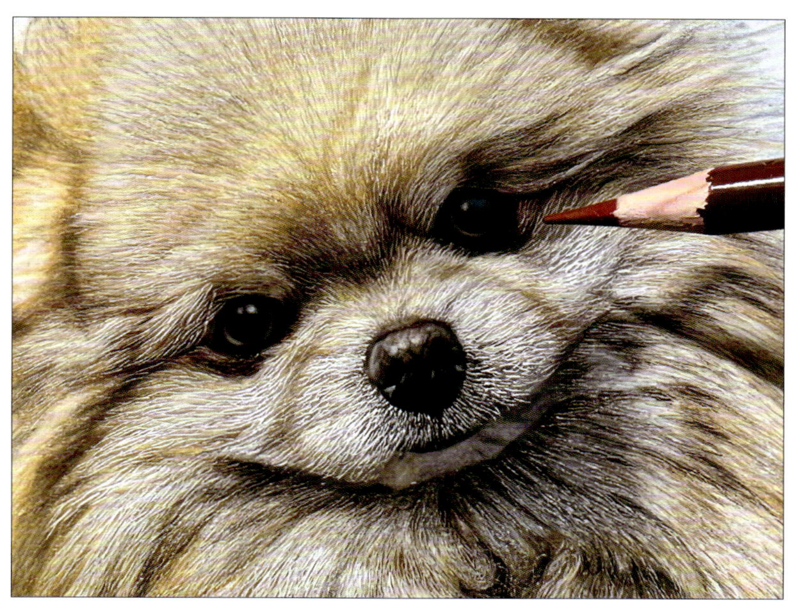

20 Enhance the color tones by adding hues closer to primary colors to increase the sense of vitality and realism in the subject.

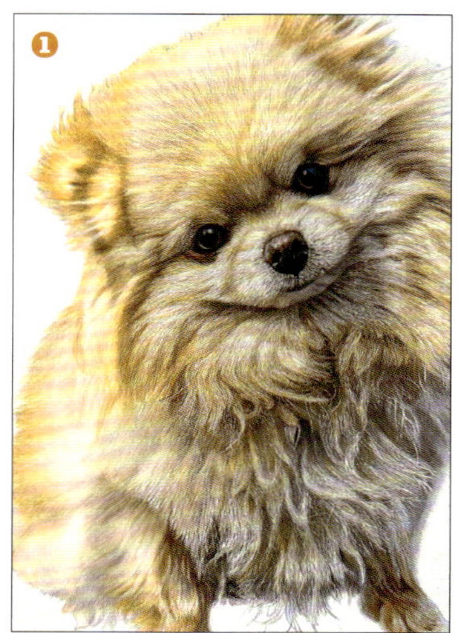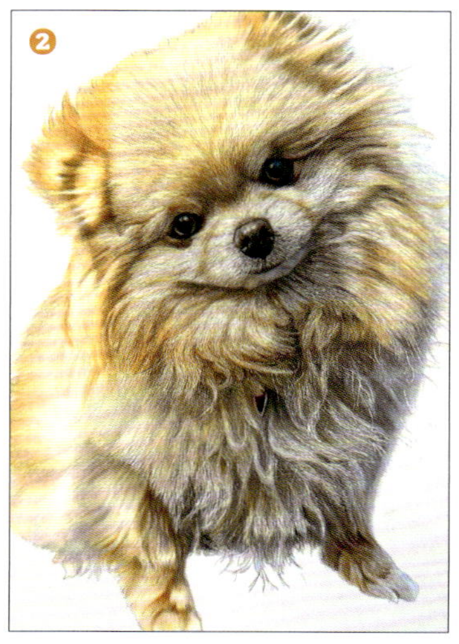

21 ❶ Add crimson lake around the eyes and layer pumpkin orange onto the darker areas of the brown fur. ❷ Color the accessory on the chest with crimson lake as well.

- Crimson lake
- Pumpkin orange

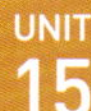

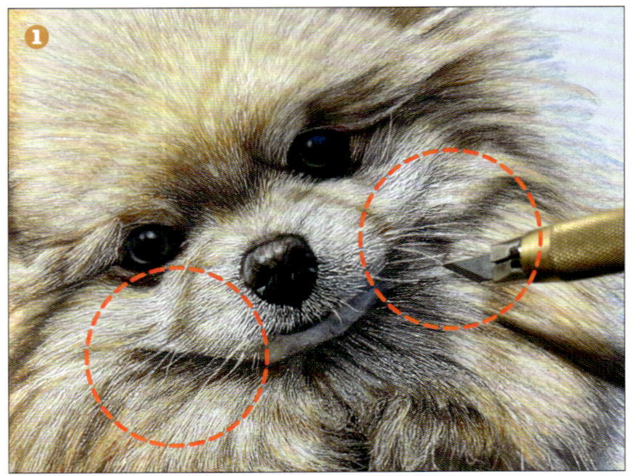

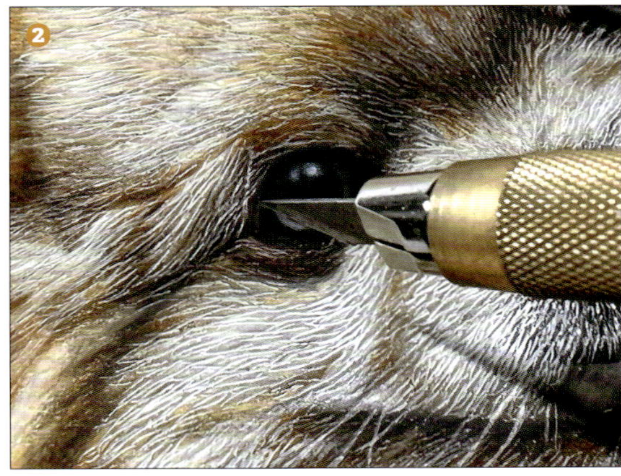

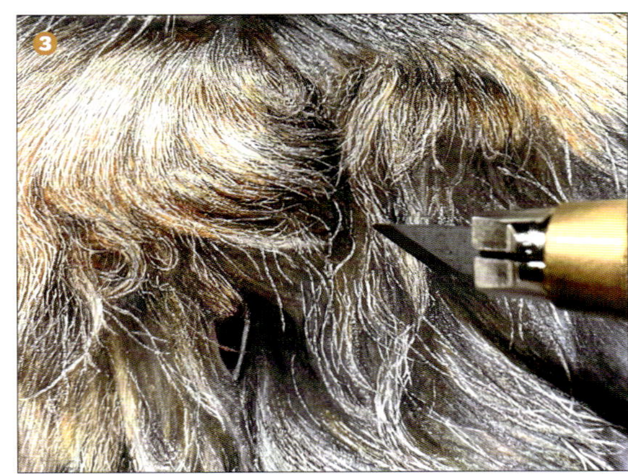

22 Scrape the colored surface to refine the finer details. ❶ Up to this point, you have depicted fur using a stylus. However, you should use a design knife for the addition of fine hairs or modification of existing hairs. For whiskers, scrape outward from the root to the tip. ❷ Use the design knife to carve out the fine hairs above the eyes and around the brow. ❸ The undercoat around the chest is fluffy and not straight, so use the design knife to carve in curved lines to reflect that texture.

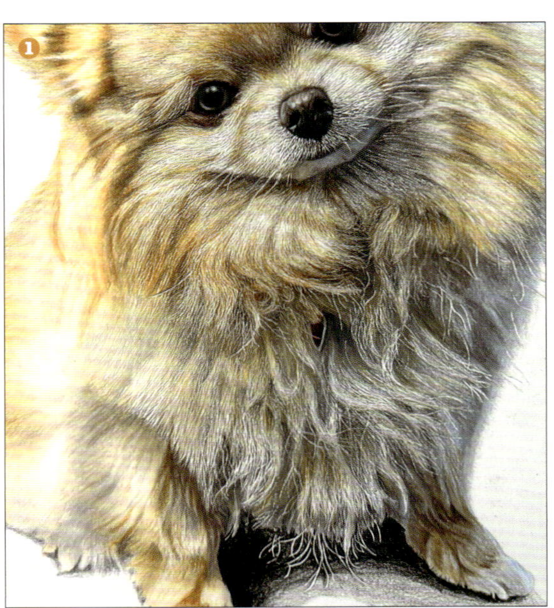

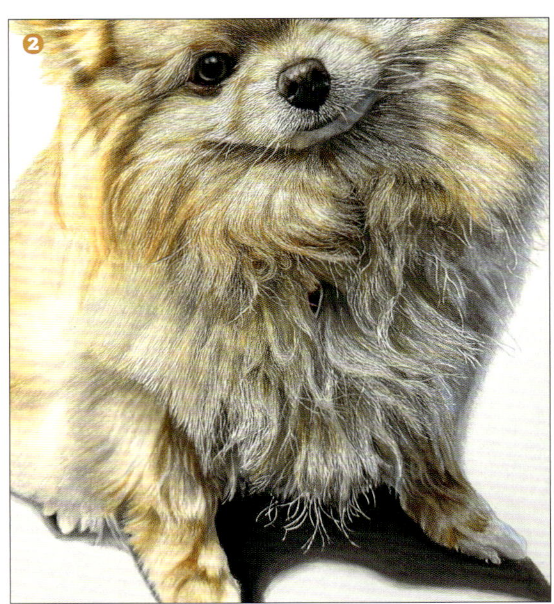

23 Color in the shadows cast on the ground. ❶ Color the darkest parts of the shadow with black, then blend it out using warm grey 70%. ❷ To finish it cleanly, soften the edges of the shadow with warm grey 10%.

■ Black　■ Warm grey 70%　□ Warm grey 10%

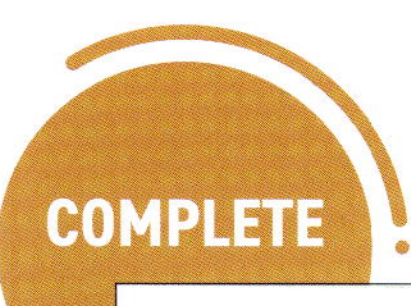
COMPLETE

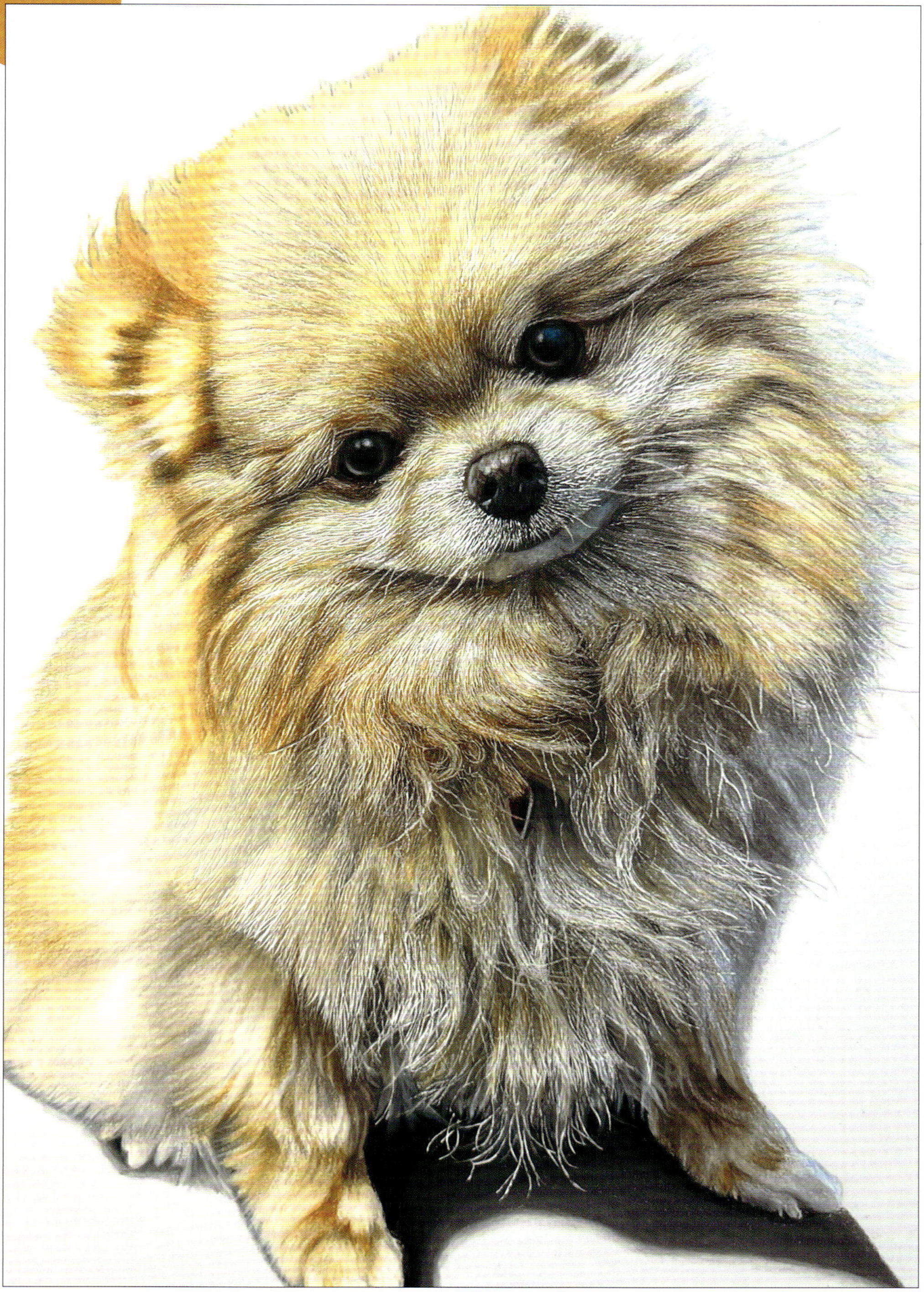

Draw an Abyssinian Cat

Colored pencils: Faber-Castell Polychromos
Paper: Daigen Thick Kent Paper
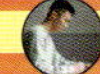 **Drawn by Haru Otomi**

Coloring Key Points

1. Pay attention to the direction, length, and density of the fur (p.15).
2. Layer colors to create a natural tone.
3. Pay attention to the amount of pressure you apply. Don't start by pressing too hard, but by lightly and smoothly laying down the color.

Colors Used

Black 199	Warm Grey VI 275
Earth Green 172	Brown Ochre 182
Earth Green Yellowish 168	Warm Grey III 272
Pine Green 267	Green Gold 268
Terracotta 186	Coral 131
Light Cobalt Turquoise 154	Beige Red 132
Walnut Brown 177	Sanguine 188
Warm Grey V 274	Burnt Ochre 187
Cream 102	White 101

Reference Photo

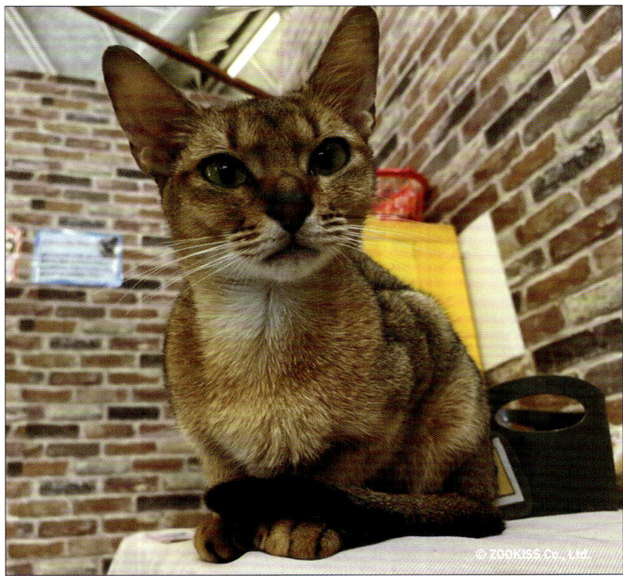

This is a brown-furred cat. To capture the texture of the fur and the sense of depth, take your time and focus on choosing appropriate colors and strokes for each area.

Preliminary Drawing

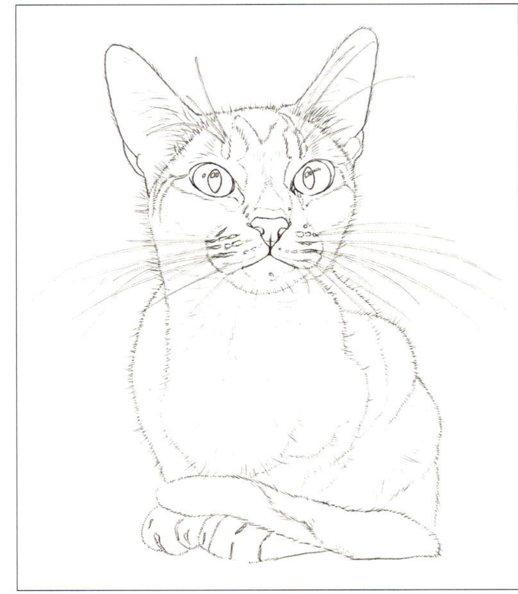

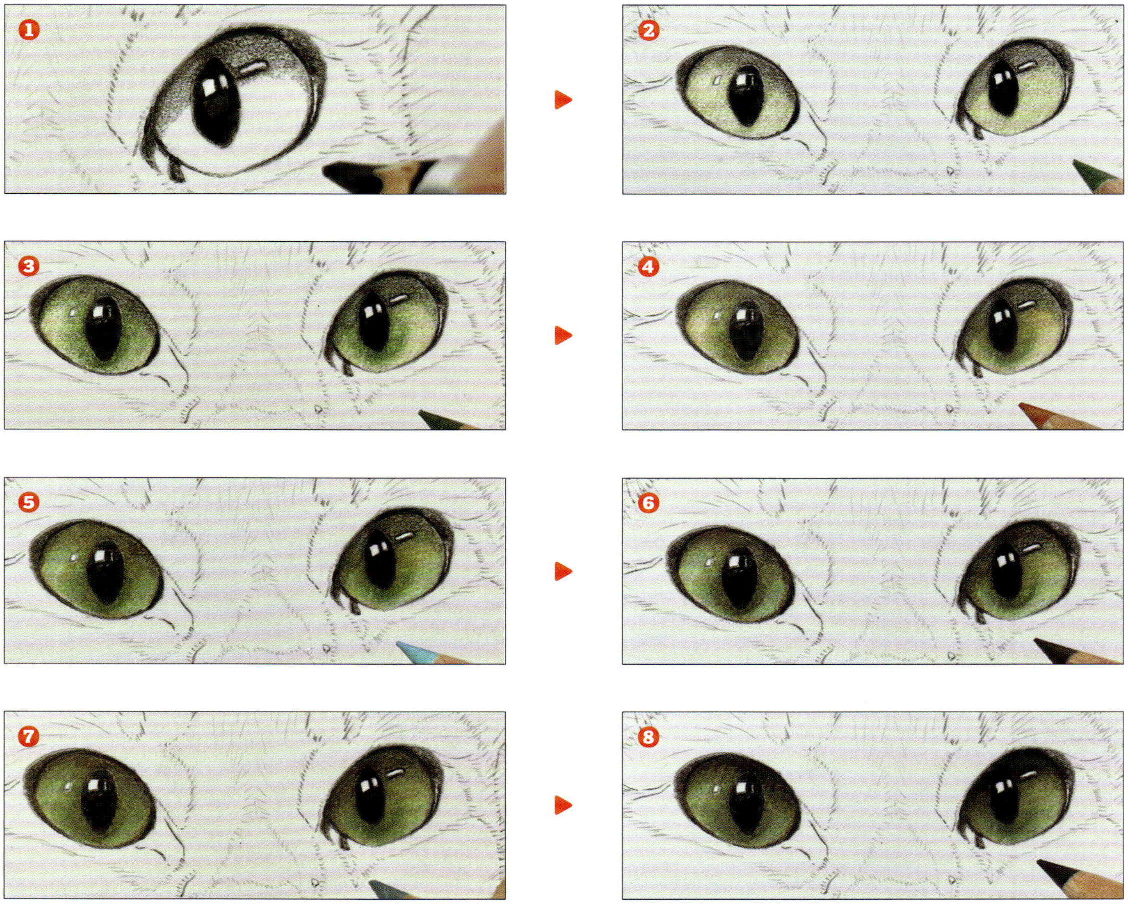

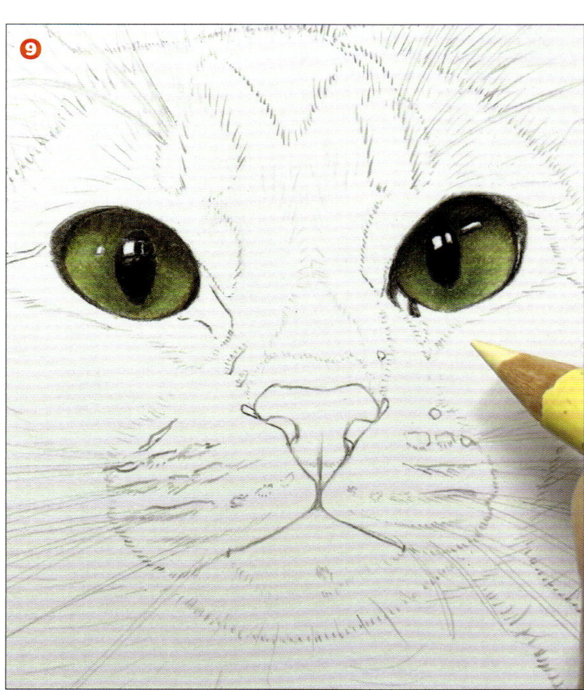

1 Start by coloring the eyes, leaving the highlights uncolored. ❶ Color the black outlines and shadows of the eyes with black; do the same for the right eye. ❷ Lightly apply earth green and earth green yellowish as the base. ❸ Use pine green to color the irises. ❹ Add terracotta to give the irises vibrancy. ❺ Then layer light cobalt turquoise over the irises to create a sense of transparency and freshness. ❻ Use walnut brown to add color to the shadows, creating more natural shading. ❼ Apply earth green over the entire area again to add depth. ❽ Reinforce the shadows that have almost disappeared under so many layers by adding warm grey V. ❾ Finally, color the whole area firmly with cream to eliminate blotchiness and enhance vividness.

- Black
- Earth green
- Earth green yellowish
- Pine green
- Terracotta
- Light cobalt turquoise
- Walnut brown
- Warm grey V
- Cream

UNIT
16

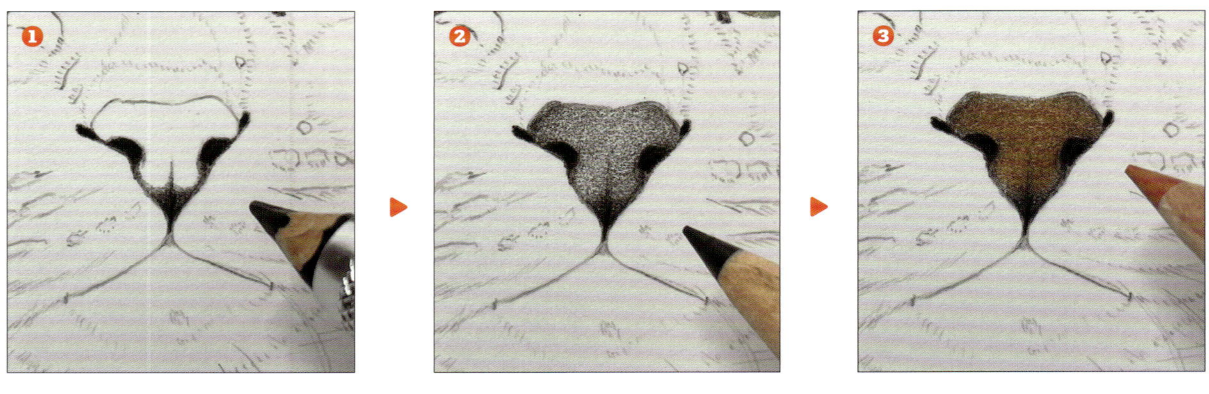

2 Color the nose. ❶ Use black to color the dark shadows on the nose. ❷ To prevent them from appearing too bright, apply warm grey VI to deepen the shadows. ❸ Then, as a base layer, apply terracotta.

▮ Black ▮ Warm grey VI ▮ Terracotta

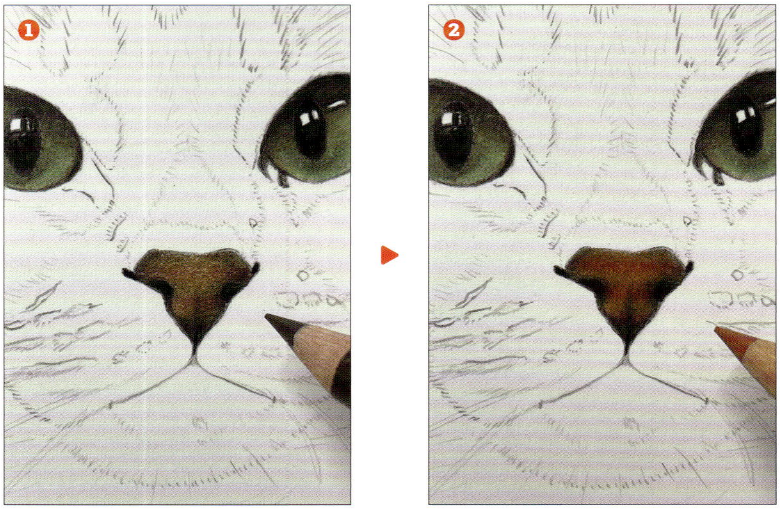

3 ❶ Use walnut brown to shade the finer shadows and create a sense of depth in the nose. ❷ Then apply a stronger layer of terracotta across the entire area.

▮ Walnut brown
▮ Terracotta

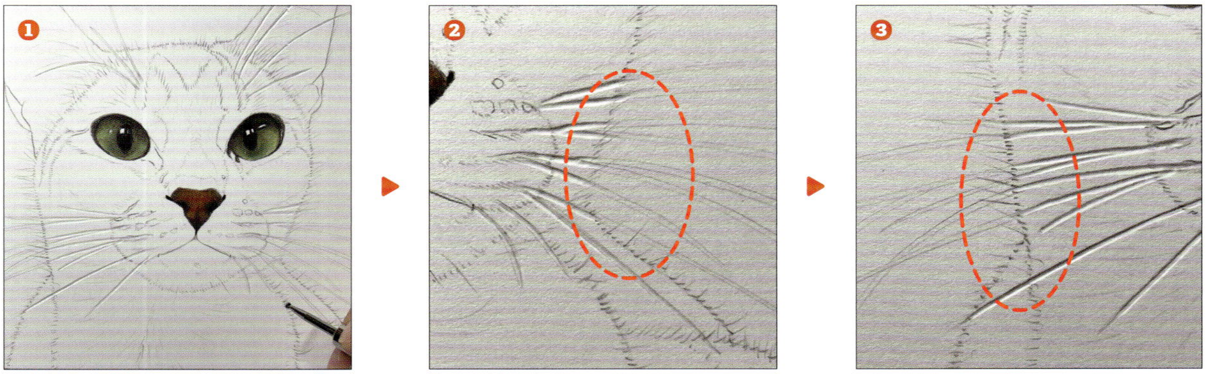

4 ❶ Before coloring the entire face, press down the areas where the whiskers will be by using a stylus. This will make the indented lines resist the colored pencil later, leaving them visible. ❷ & ❸ You could indent the whiskers all the way to their tips, but here we'll stop at the point where they extend beyond the face. That's because we want to depict the whiskers that extend into the blank background using only colored pencil (see **Step 14**).

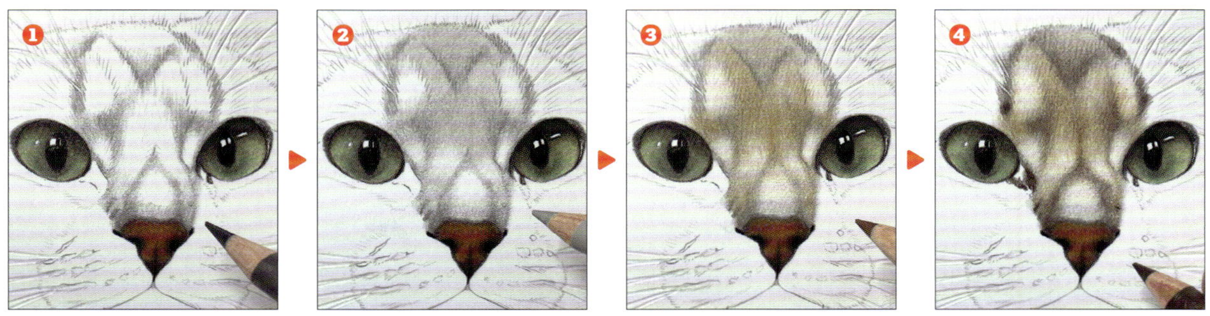

5 Now we'll start coloring the face. **❶** Use warm grey V to create a shadow from the nose up to the forehead. **❷** Use earth green to define the contours of the face through shading. **❸** Apply a brown ochre as a base layer. **❹** Use walnut brown to bring out the three-dimensionality.

▮ Warm grey V ▮ Earth green ▮ Brown ochre ▮ Walnut brown

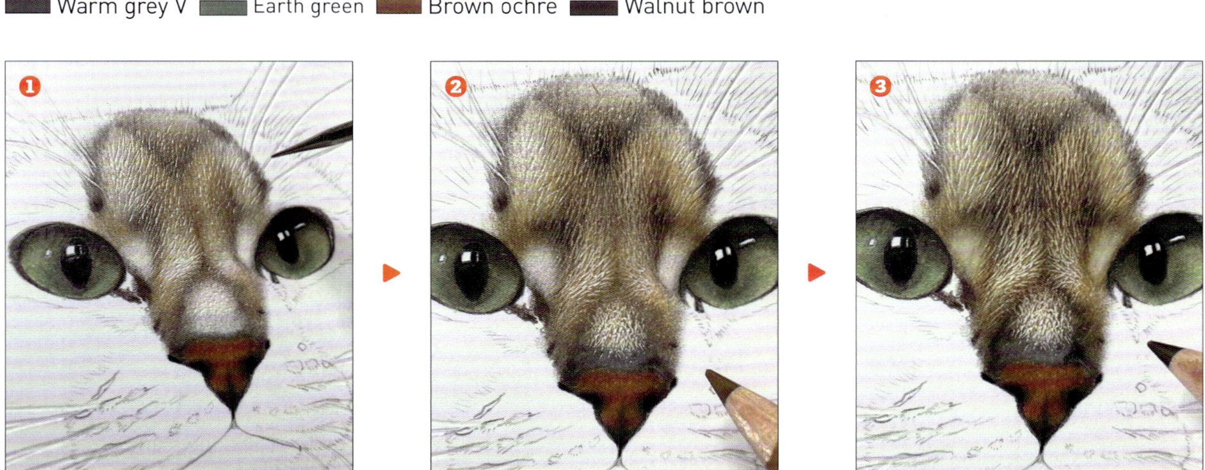

6 **❶** Use a stylus to press in fine fur lines. **❷** Tilt the brown ochre colored pencil slightly and apply it gently, being careful not to leave any color in the fur texture indentations. **❸** Then add another layer of walnut brown over it to add depth to the color.

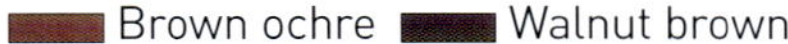 Brown ochre ▮ Walnut brown

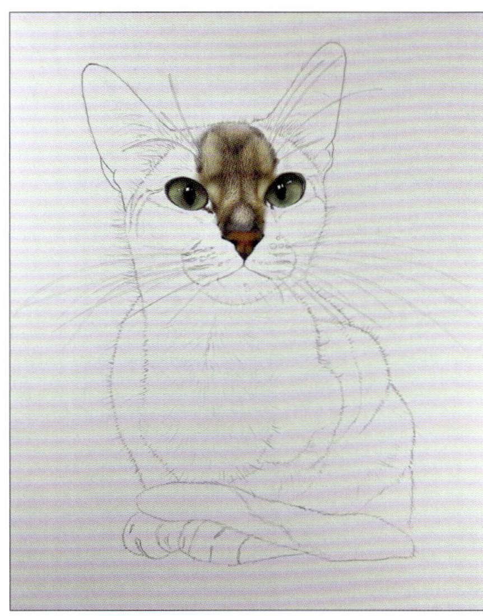

At this point, take a step back and look at the whole piece to check whether any of the areas you've colored feel off. Once you've confirmed there's no inconsistency, continue coloring.

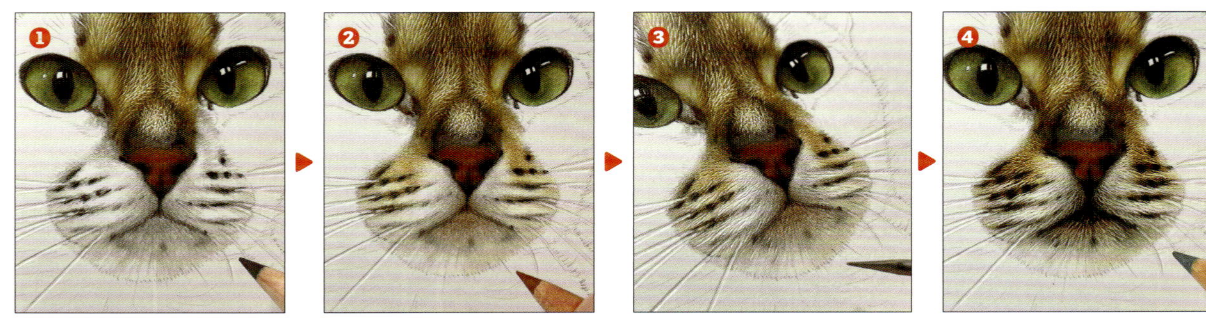

7 Color the mouth and whisker pads. ❶ First, use warm grey VI to lay down the base tone. ❷ Apply a faint underlayer with terracotta. ❸ Use a stylus to create the grooves for the fur texture. ❹ Then apply layers of terracotta and walnut brown on top. Use earth green to help create a natural-looking shadow.

■ Warm grey VI ■ Terracotta ■ Walnut brown ■ Earth green

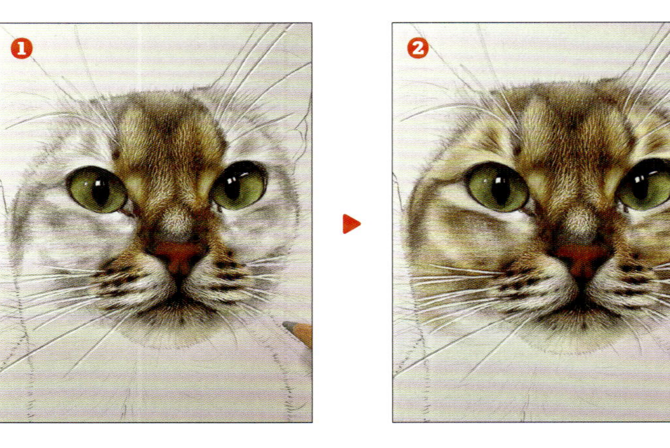

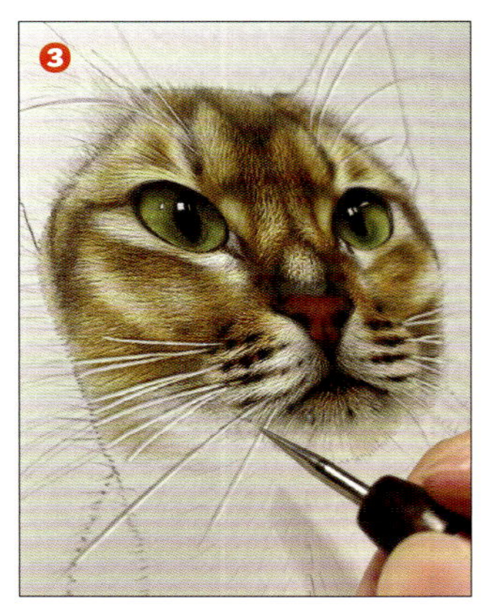

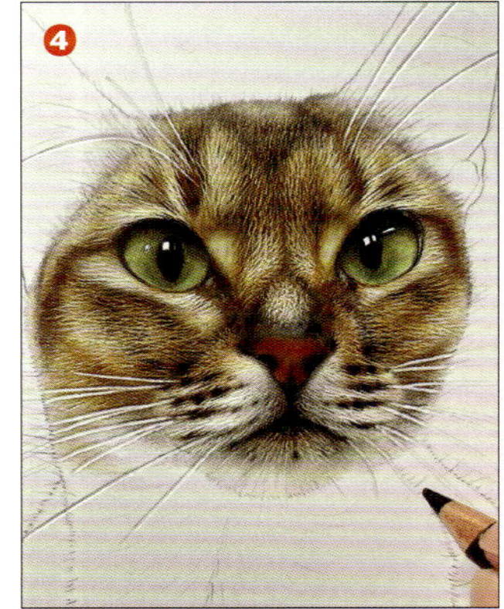

8 ❶ Color the shadows on the cheeks and sides of the face with warm grey V, then layer with warm grey III. ❷ Apply underlayers to the entire face of brown ochre, terracotta, and walnut brown while carefully observing the reference photo. ❸ Indent fur texture with a stylus. For a more natural result, use multiple stylus sizes to vary the fur thickness. ❹ Use dark colors like walnut brown and black to bring out the indent fur lines and add depth to the shading. Be careful not to hold the colored pencil too upright.

■ Warm grey V ■ Warm grey III
■ Brown ochre ■ Terracotta
■ Walnut brown ■ Black

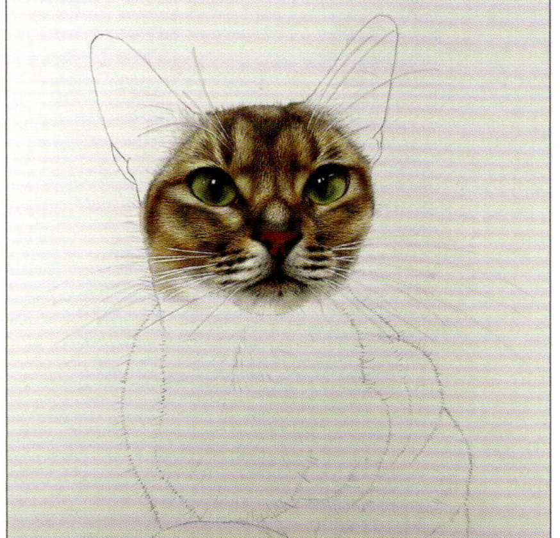

At this point, step back and look at the whole piece again to check the overall color balance.

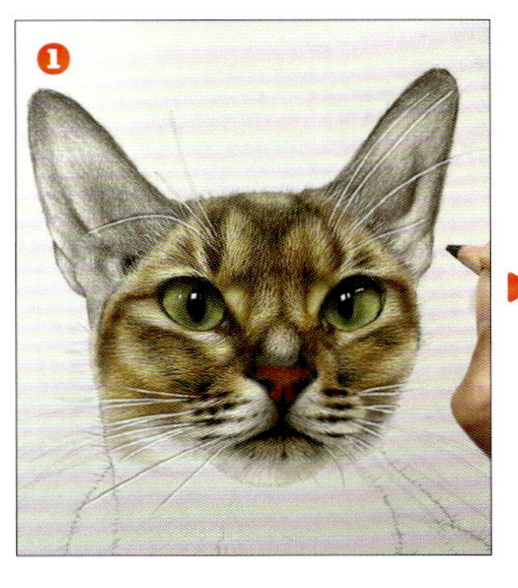 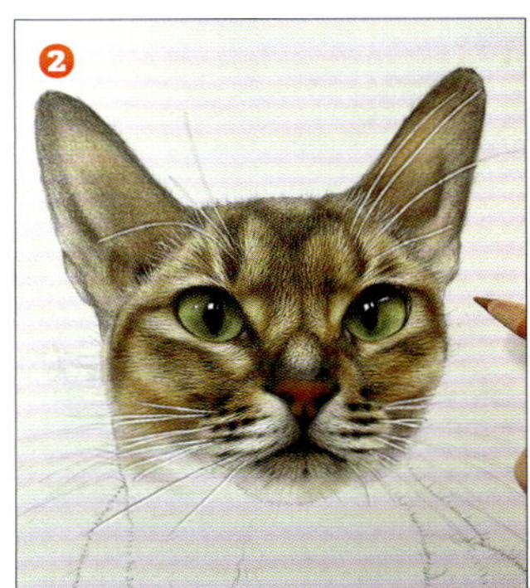

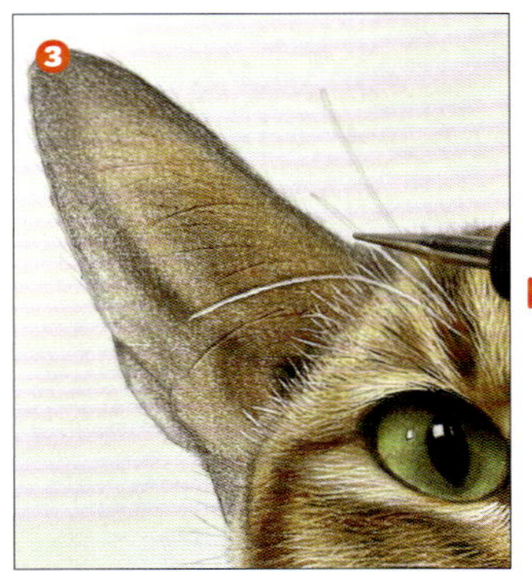 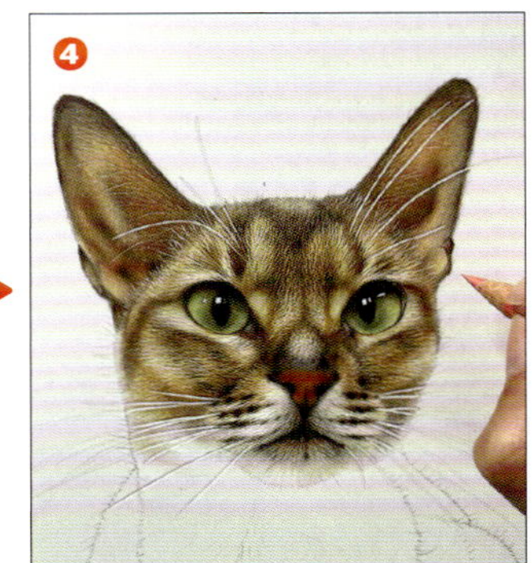

9 Color the ears. **❶** Use warm grey III, warm grey V, and warm grey VI to color the shadows on the ears. **❷** Apply underlayers of terracotta and green gold. Remembering that blood vessels run through the ears will help you create the effect of light filtering through them. **❸** Use a stylus to indent fine lines representing the thin ear hairs. **❹** Apply layers of coral, walnut brown, terracotta, and beige red using stronger pressure.

Warm grey III	Warm grey V
Warm grey VI	Terracotta
Green gold	Coral
Walnut brown	Beige red

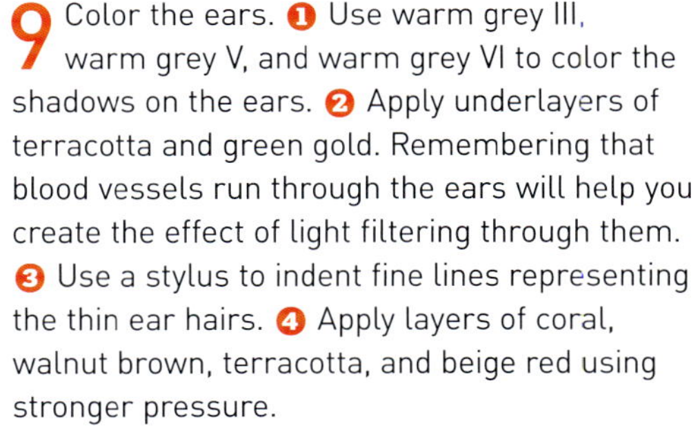

Take a look at the whole image and check that the coloring of the face and ears isn't too different.

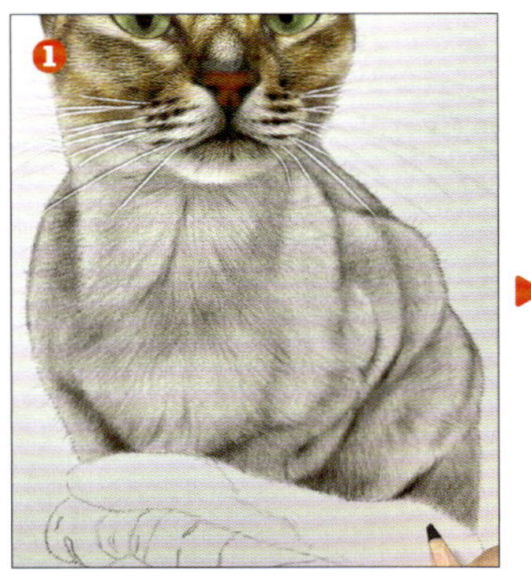 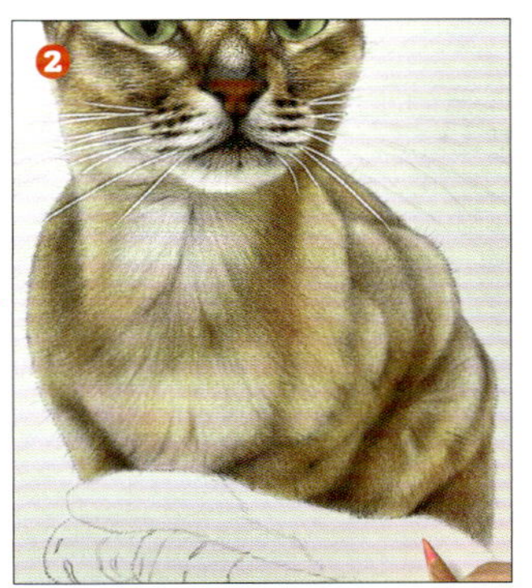

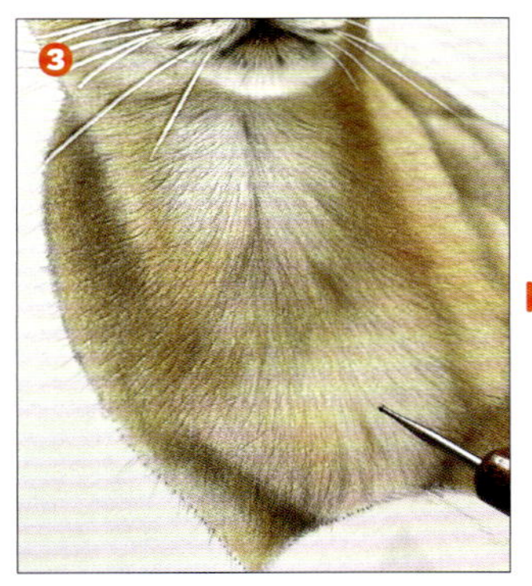 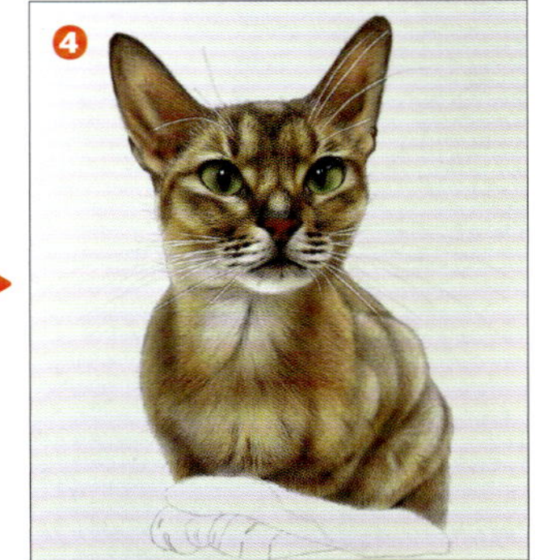

10 Color the body. **❶** Use warm grey III, warm grey V, and warm grey VI to color the shadows on the ears. **❷** Apply underlayers of coral and beige red. Keeping the direction of the fur in mind while coloring here will help later when expressing fur texture, making it easier to show the correct flow. **❸** Use a stylus to indent the fur texture. **❹** Apply layers of walnut brown, terracotta, cream, beige red, and sanguine to the whole body while carefully observing the reference photo. Start with light strokes and gradually increase pressure. This helps avoid unevenness in color.

Warm grey III	Warm grey V
Warm grey VI	Coral
Beige red	Walnut brown
Terracotta	Cream
Sanguine	

UNIT 16

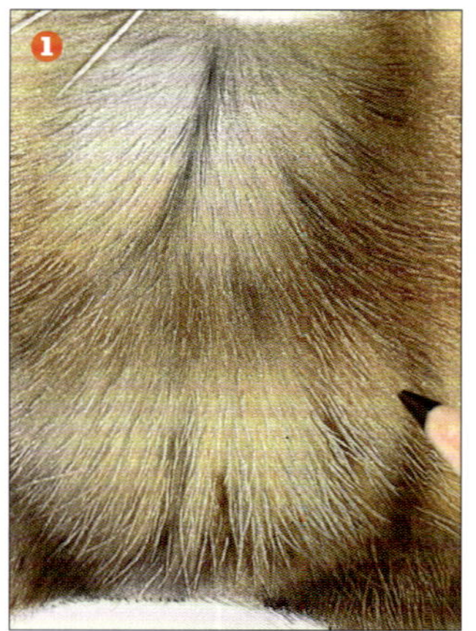 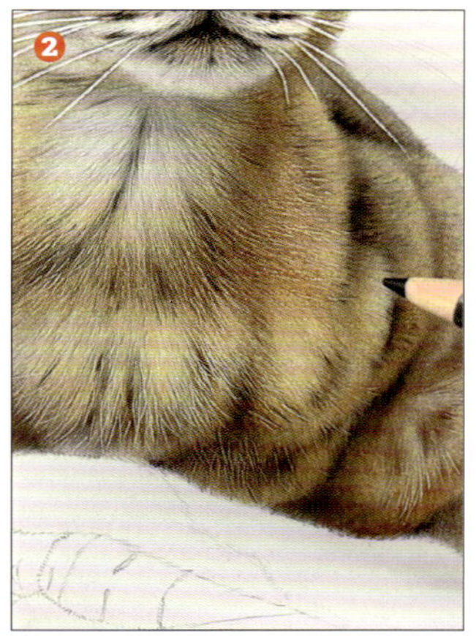

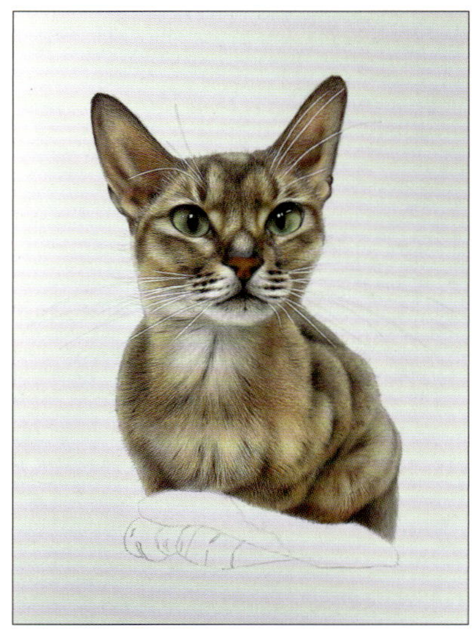

11 ❶ Use walnut brown, warm grey V, and black to add fine shadows and define the shapes of the front legs and body. ❷ Using warm grey VI, draw the darker fur that is difficult to depict with a stylus. Adjust the brightness as needed by layering with terracotta and burnt ochre as well.

▮ Walnut brown ▮ Warm grey V ▮ Black
▮ Warm grey VI ▮ Terracotta ▮ Burnt ochre

Take a step back and review the overall flow of the fur and the brightness levels once more.

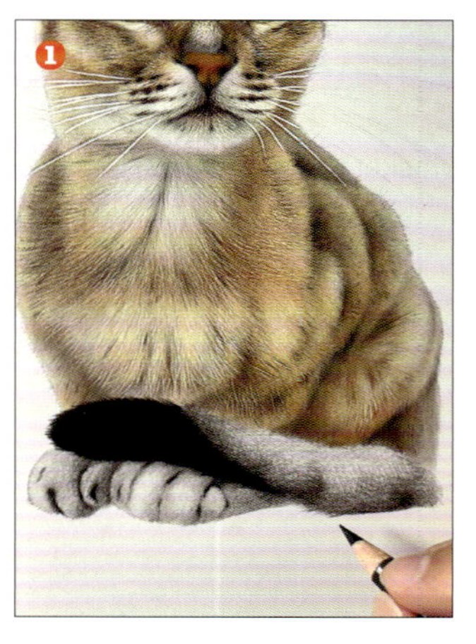 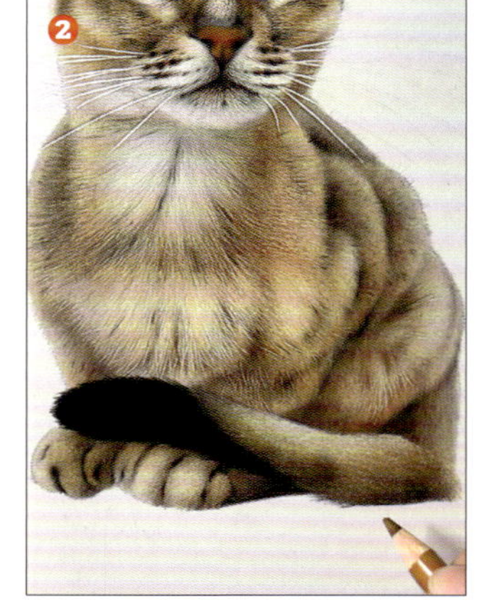

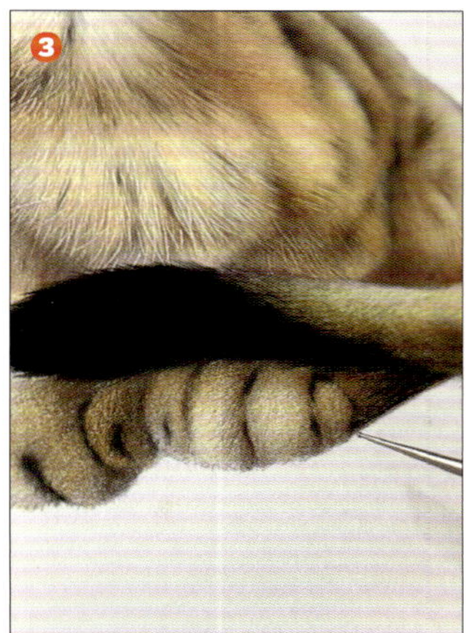 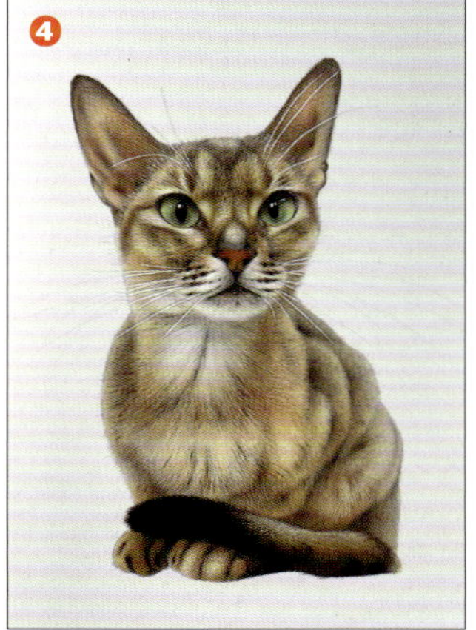

12 Color the area around the tail. ❶ Color the tail and legs with warm grey V, warm grey VI, and black, while closely observing the reference photo. ❷ Using the reference as a guide, lay down a base with green gold, brown ochre, and walnut brown. The solid black markings on the tail can be completely filled in with black from the beginning. ❸ Use a stylus tool to etch the fur texture. ❹ Then apply layers of black, warm grey VI, walnut brown, green gold, and terracotta, pressing firmly with your pencil.

▮ Warm grey V ▮ Warm grey VI
▮ Black ▮ Green gold
▮ Brown ochre ▮ Walnut brown
▮ Terracotta

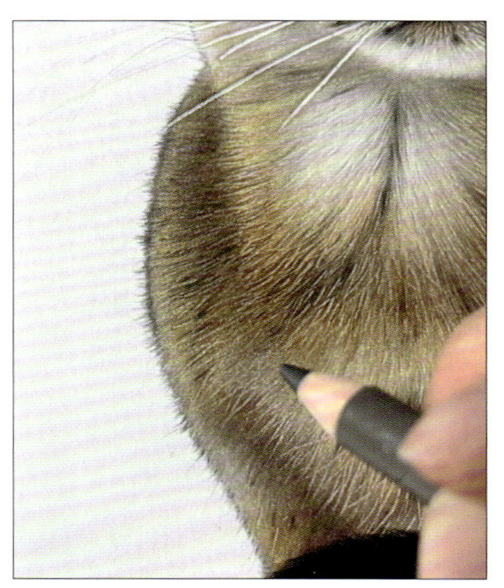

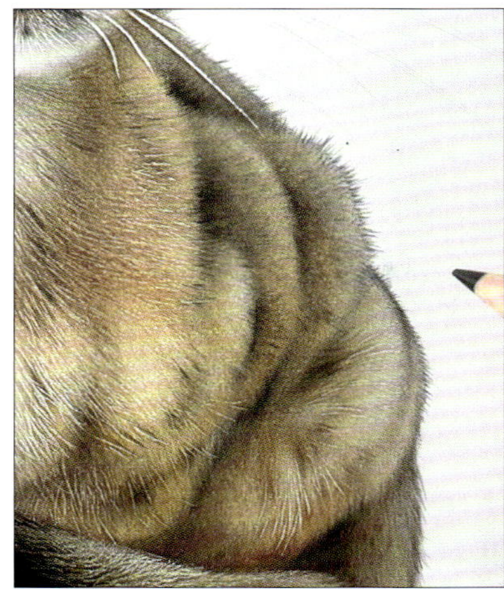

13 Now for the finishing touches. Shade the outer edges of the body with warm grey III and warm grey V, using strokes that flick outward like tufts of fur. This will help create a soft, fluffy impression.

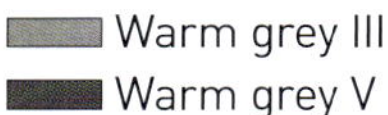

■ Warm grey III
■ Warm grey V

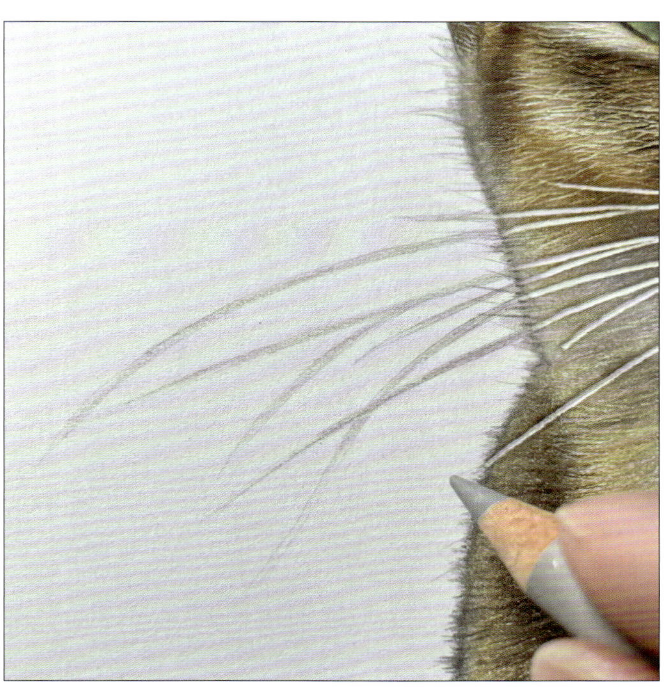

14 Extend the whiskers that were partially indented in **Step 4** using warm grey III. For the whiskers that extend into the blank background, it's best to draw each one in warm grey III rather than leaving them white like the paper, as it would be difficult to distinguish them otherwise. Be careful not to make the whiskers too dark.

■ Warm grey III

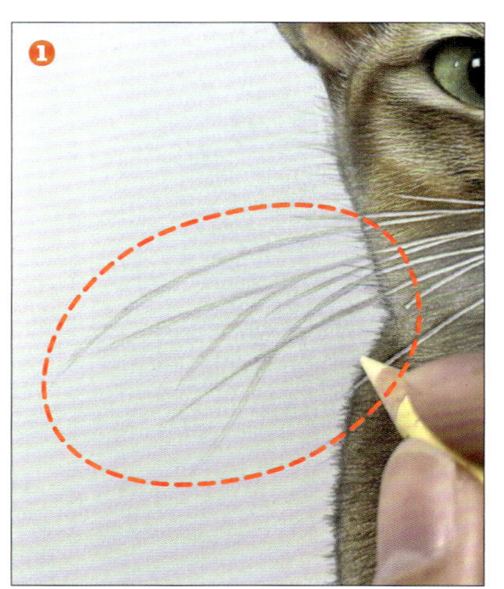

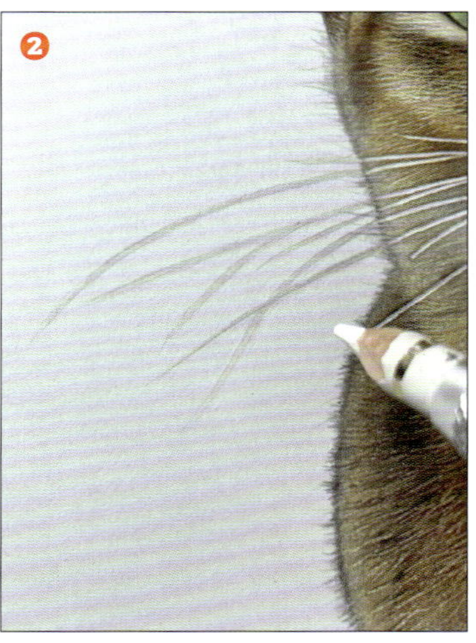

15 ❶ By applying a cream color over the area colored in **Step 14**, you can make the whiskers stand out more and also convey the effect of light hitting them. ❷ Use white to smooth out uneven areas. If the whiskers turn out too dark, you can adjust their intensity by either erasing them or coloring over them with white.

☐ Cream ☐ White

UNIT
16

COMPLETE

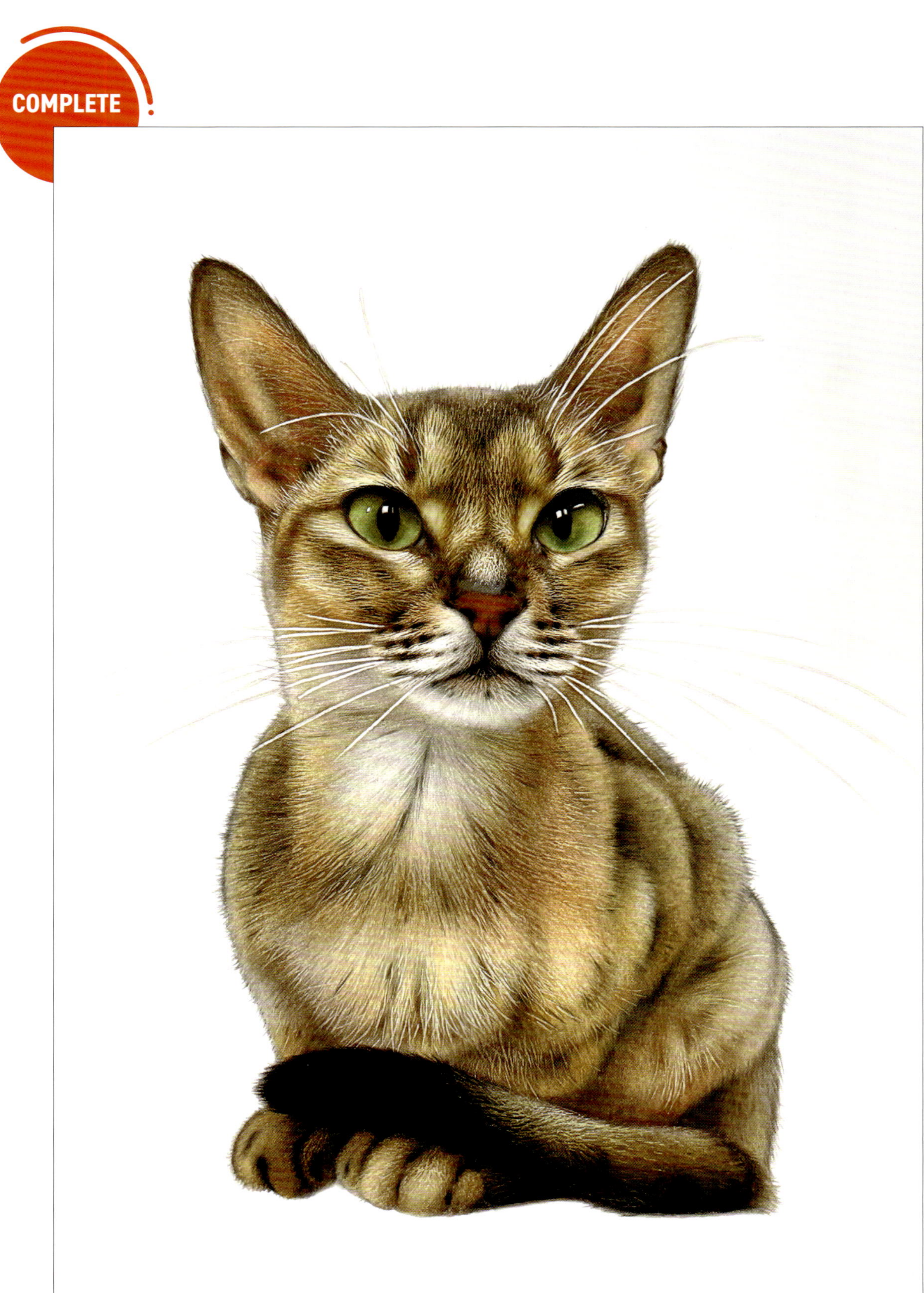

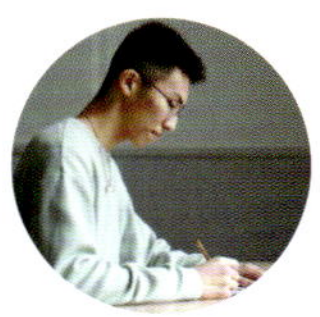

Haru Otomi
Abyssinian Cat (p.118)

Began learning colored-pencil drawing seriously in his second year of high school after being inspired by a friend. Learned the techniques independently. Began posting work on social media in 2017. Now receives requests from media and companies. Author of the book *Neko no Komeae (Cat Close-Ups)*.

X (Twitter): @huwahuwa1_25
Instagram: @haruru125_art

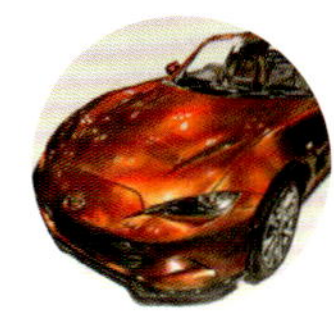

Miyakawa
Scottish Fold Cat (p.54), Dolphin (p.66), Hamster (p.94)

Began colored-pencil drawing in high school in 2014 and developed a knack for realistic tricks and trompe-l'oeil. Currently works at a company, creating illustrations on themes such as "food close-ups." Formerly involved in science museum exhibitions and web advertising design.

X (Twitter): @miya_drawing
Instagram: @miyakawadrawing

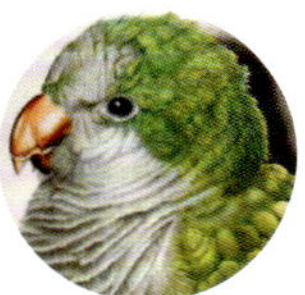

Bonbon
Peach-Faced Lovebird (p.30), Shiba Inu (p.80), Pomeranian (p.108)

Based in Osaka. Graduate of Osaka University of Arts. Works as a colored-pencil artist and instructor in the Kansai region. Won first and second place in the first and second national general colored-pencil competitions held by Kita-Boshi Pencil Co., LTD.

X (Twitter): @bonbon20170916
Instagram: @bonbon20170916

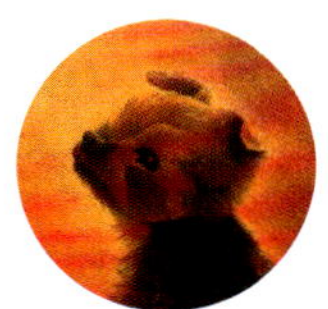

Ryosuke Mika
Tropical Fish (p.24), Penguin (p.48), Rabbit (p.72)

From Hyogo Prefecture. Graduate of Osaka University of Arts. Excels at capturing rich color nuance and soft textures. Publishes techniques and tutorials on social media. Past awards include Shimauma Print Illustration Book Contest and Osaka University of Arts Prize.

X (Twitter): @3ryocp
Instagram: @mika_coloredpencil

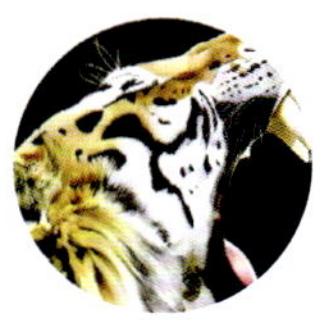

Ishikawa @ Iroenpitsu
Labrador Retriever (p.36), Red-Eyed Tree Frog (p.60), Blue Mountain Swallowtail Butterfly (p. 86)

Based in Chiba. Originally began drawing with ballpoint pens before switching to colored pencils. Began social media posts in 2018 and gained attention for lifelike animal illustrations. Winner of the New Artist Award at the 55th Toten art exhibition.

X (Twitter): @jamjamjam4649
Instagram: @ishikawa_0608

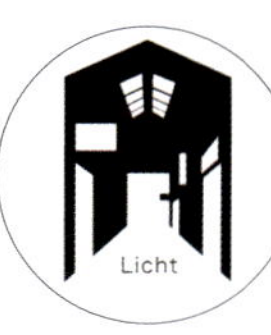

Rihito
Ladybug (p.18), Scarab Beetle (p.42), Russian Blue Cat (p.100)

Born in Tokyo. Enrolled in the Oil Painting Department of the Painting Division, Faculty of Fine Arts, Tokyo University of the Arts since 2024. After seeing the work of a certain colored pencil artist, began creating colored pencil drawings in 2019. Known for meticulous texture depiction and expression of light.

X (Twitter): @rihito1336
Instagram: @rihito1336

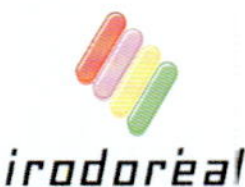

Nurieshiki Shashin rishika Mienai Iroenpitsuga Joutatsu Dril [Doubutsu hen]
© 2023 irodoreal
© 2023 GRAPHIC-SHA PUBLISHING CO,. LTD.
This book was first designed and published ni Japan ni 2023 by Graphic-sha Publishing Co., Ltd. This English edition was published in 2026 by FOX CHAPEL PUBLISHING
English translation rights arranged with GRAPHIC-SHA PUBLISHING CO., LTD. through Japan UNI Agency, Inc., Tokyo

Original Edition Creative Staff:
Design: GRiD CO., LTD. (Hiroaki Yasojima, Yuriko Kurobe)
Editorial collaboration: Kaori Odashima
Planning and Editing: Ken Imai
Co-operation: Sunshine Aquarium, ZOOKISS Co., Ltd., Westek Incorporated, MITSUBISHI PENCIL CO., LTD., Yuta Yonehara

English Edition Project Team:
Translator: Nick Bennett
Acquisitions Editor: Amelia Johanson
Editor: Madeline DeLuca
Designer: Wendy Reynolds

ISBN 978-1-4972-0676-2

How to Draw Photorealistic Animals with Colore Pencil is a revised translation of the original Japanese book. This version published by New Design Originals Corporation, an imprint of Fox Chapel Publishing Company, Inc.

COPY PERMISSION: The written instructions, photographs, designs, patterns, and projects in this publication are intended for the personal use of the reader and may be reproduced for that purpose only. Any other use, especially commercial use, is forbidden under law without the written permission of the copyright holder. Every effort has been made to ensure that all information in this book is accurate. However, due to differing conditions, tools, and individual skills, neither the author nor publisher can be responsible for any injuries, losses, or other damages which may result from the use of the information in this book.
INFORMATION: All rights reserved. All images in this book have been reproduced with the knowledge and prior consent of the artists concerned and no responsibility is accepted by producer, publisher, or printer for any infringement of copyright or otherwise, arising from the contents of this publication. Every effort has been made to ensure that credits accurately comply with information supplied.
WARNING: Due to the components used in this craft, children under 8 years of age should not have access to materials or supplies without adult supervision. Under rare circumstances components of products could cause serious or fatal injury. Please read all safety warnings for the products being used. Neither New Design Originals, the product manufacturer, or the supplier is responsible.
NOTE: The use of products and trademark names is for informational purposes only, with no intention of infringement upon those trademarks.

Library of Congress Control Number: 2025948134

To learn more about the other great books from Fox Chapel Publishing, or to find a retailer near you, call toll-free at 800-457-9112 or visit us at *www.FoxChapelPublishing.com*.

We are always looking for talented authors. To submit an idea, please send a brief inquiry to acquisitions@foxchapelpublishing.com.

Or write to:
Fox Chapel Publishing
903 Square Street
Mount Joy, PA 17552

Printed in China
First printing

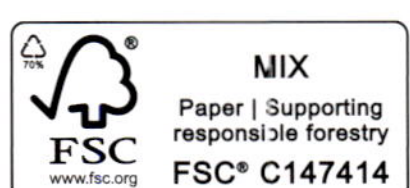

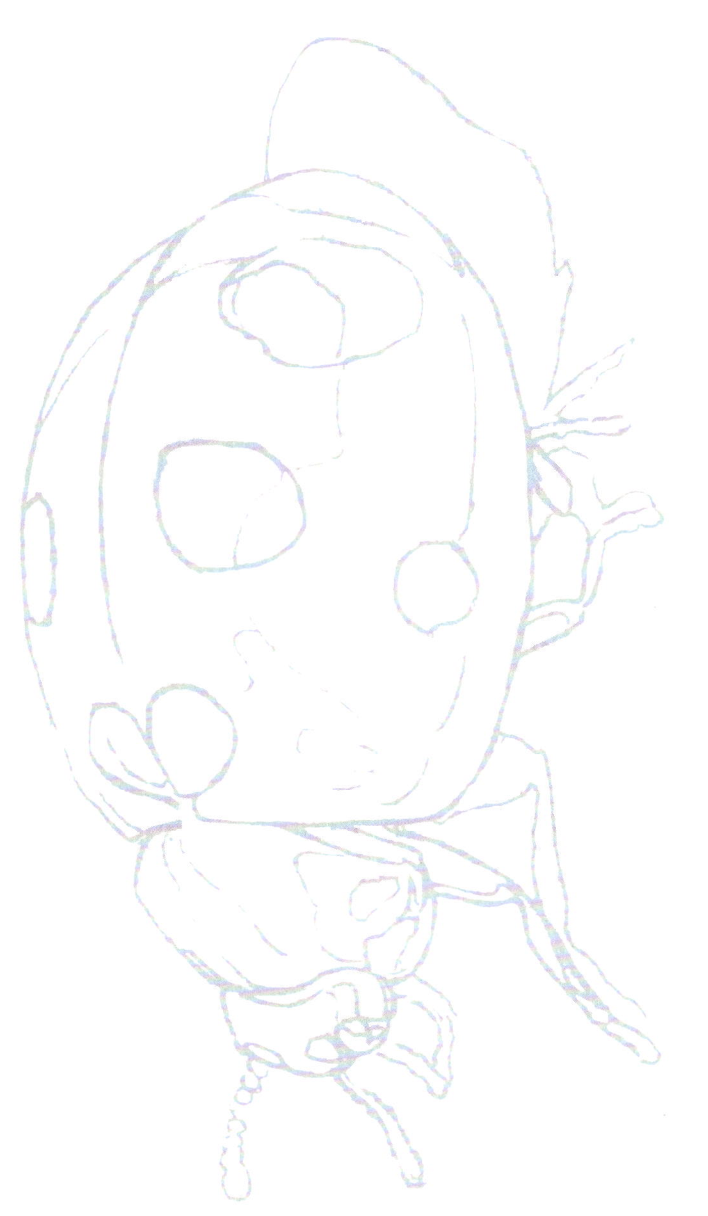

cut along these lines

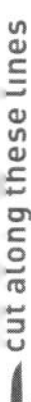
cut along these lines

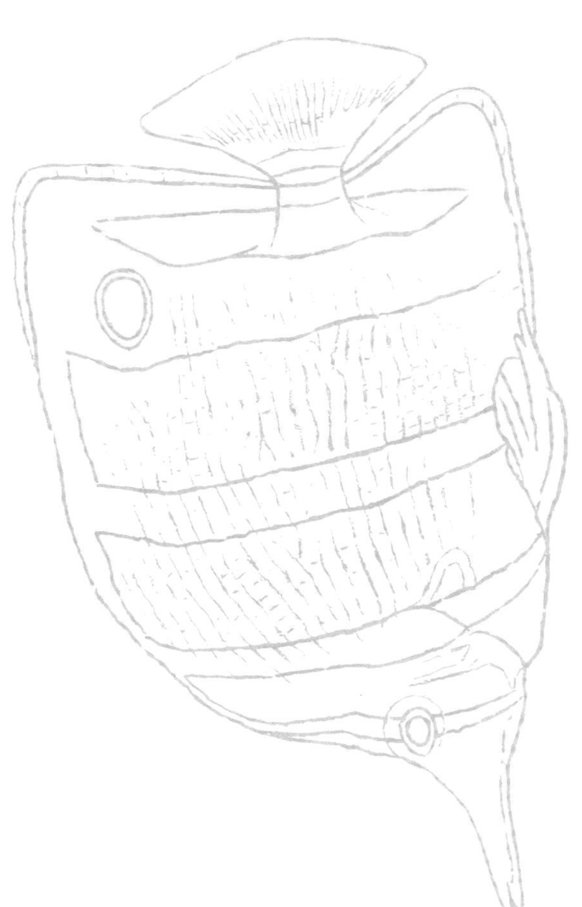

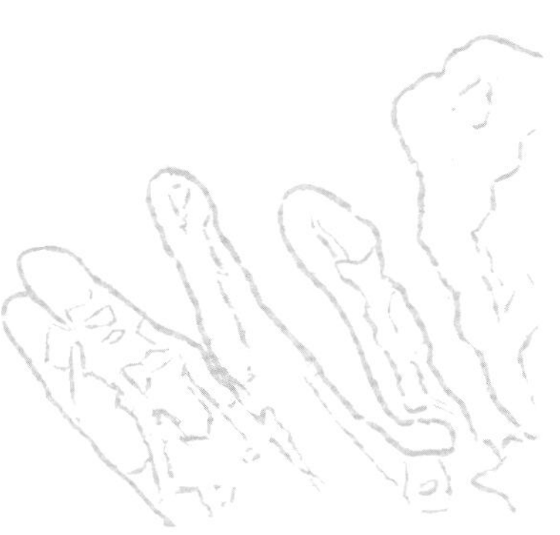

cut along these lines

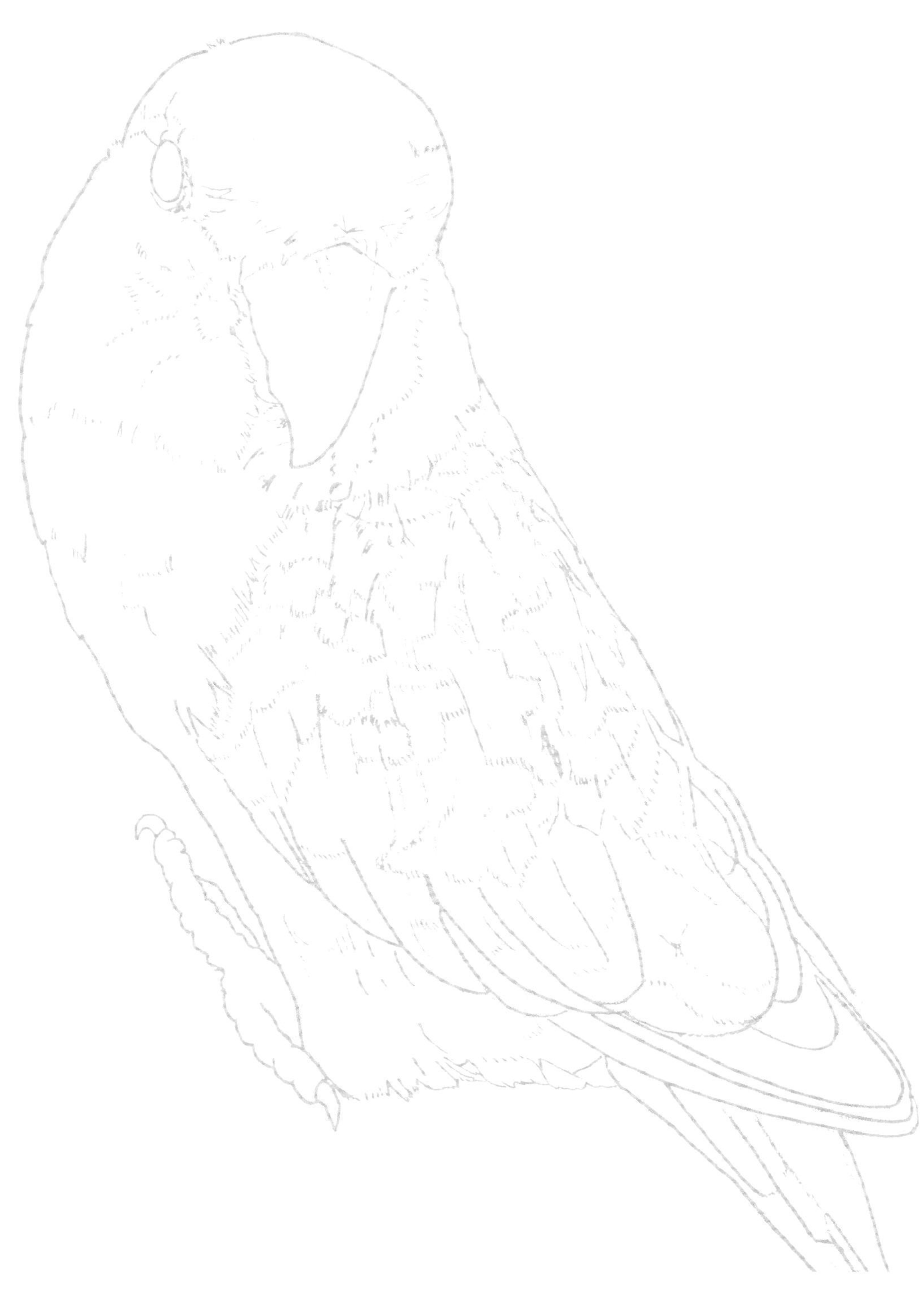

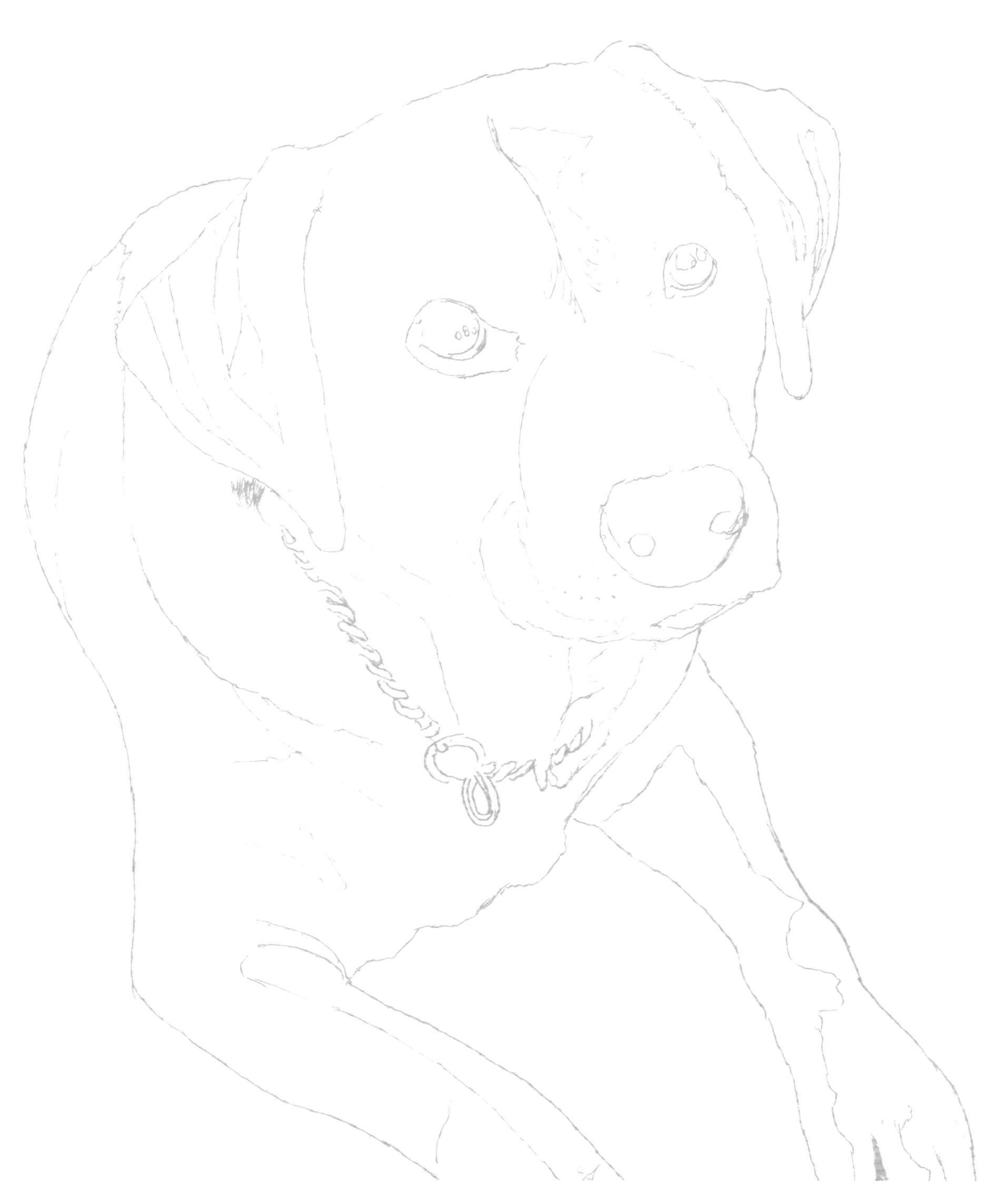

cut along these lines

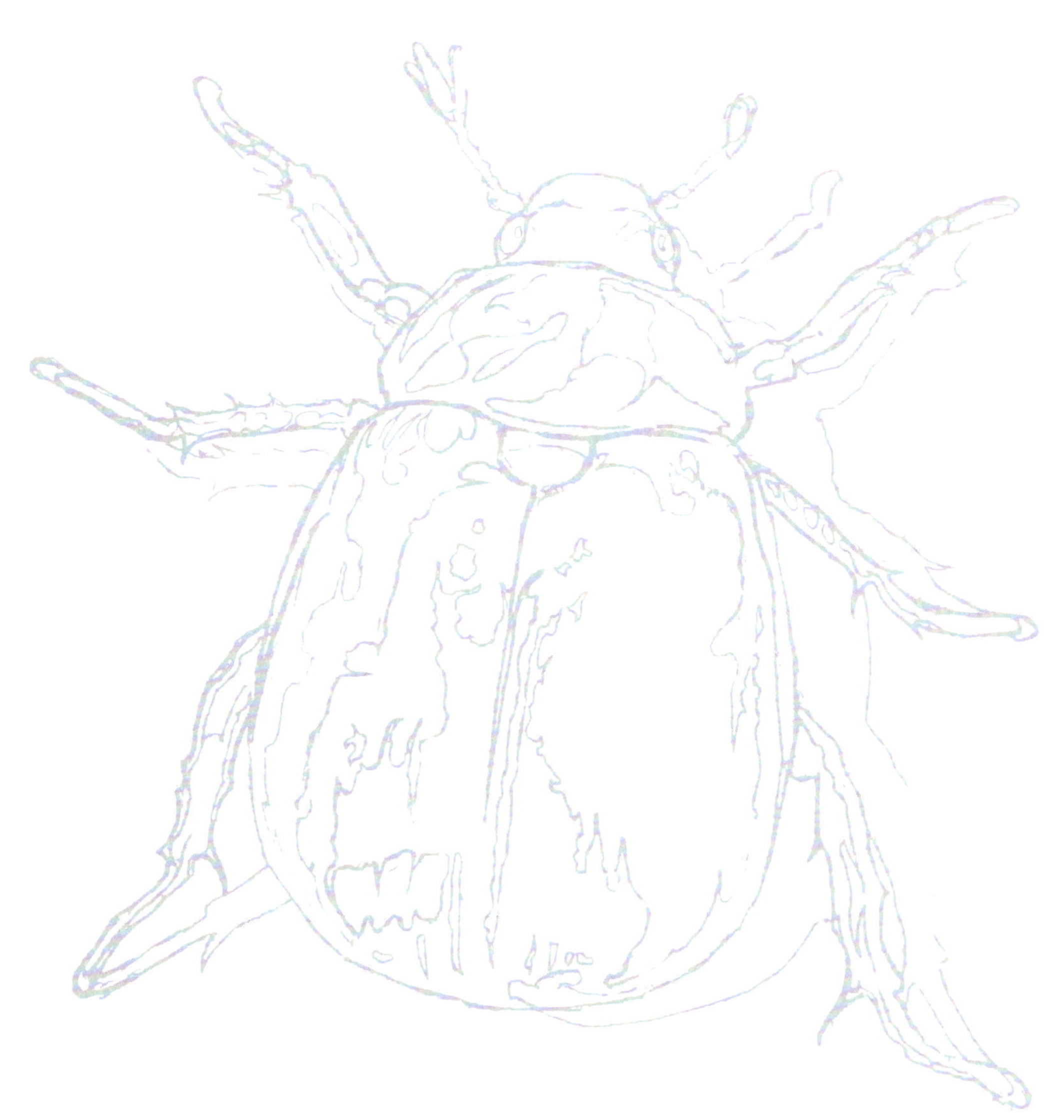

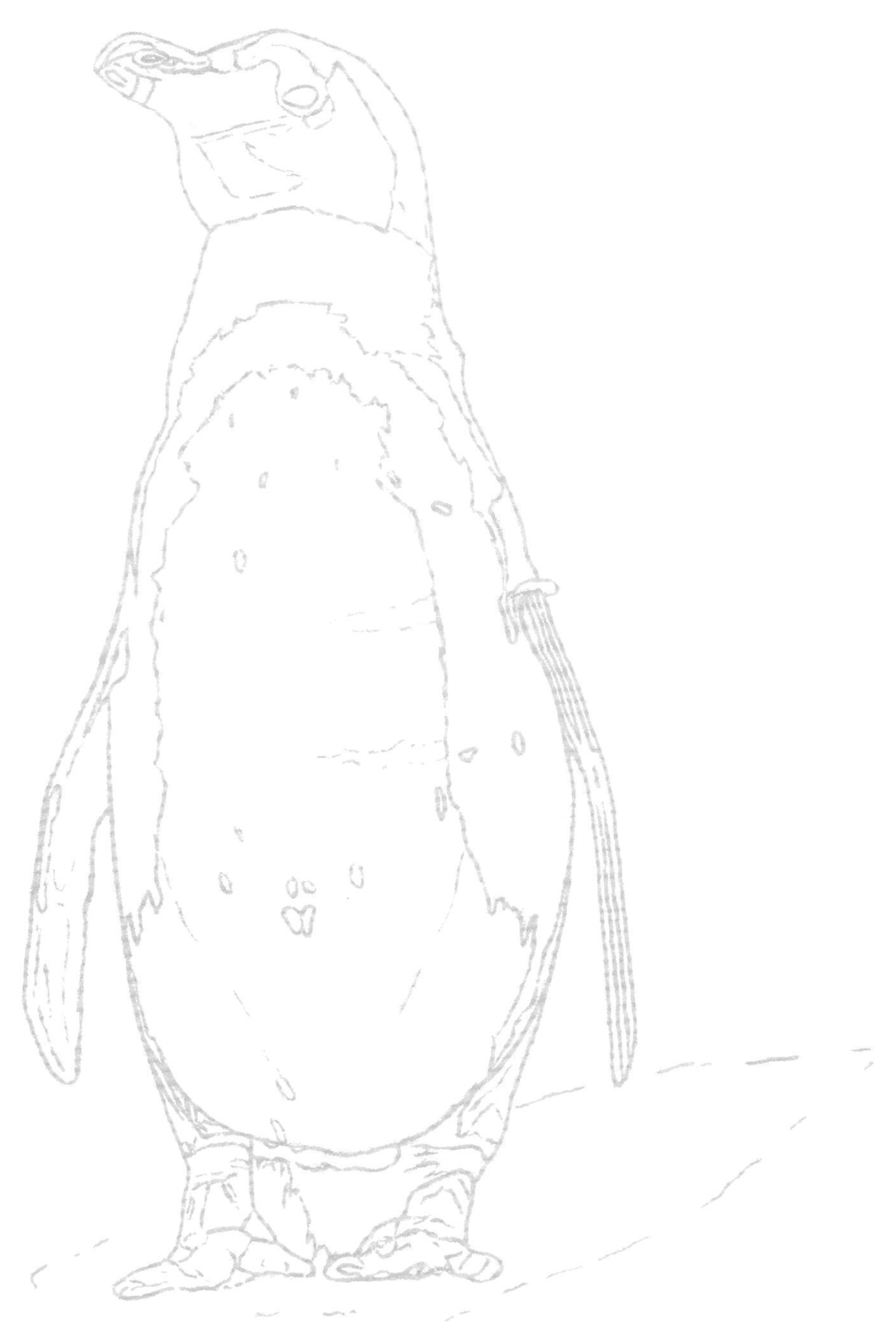

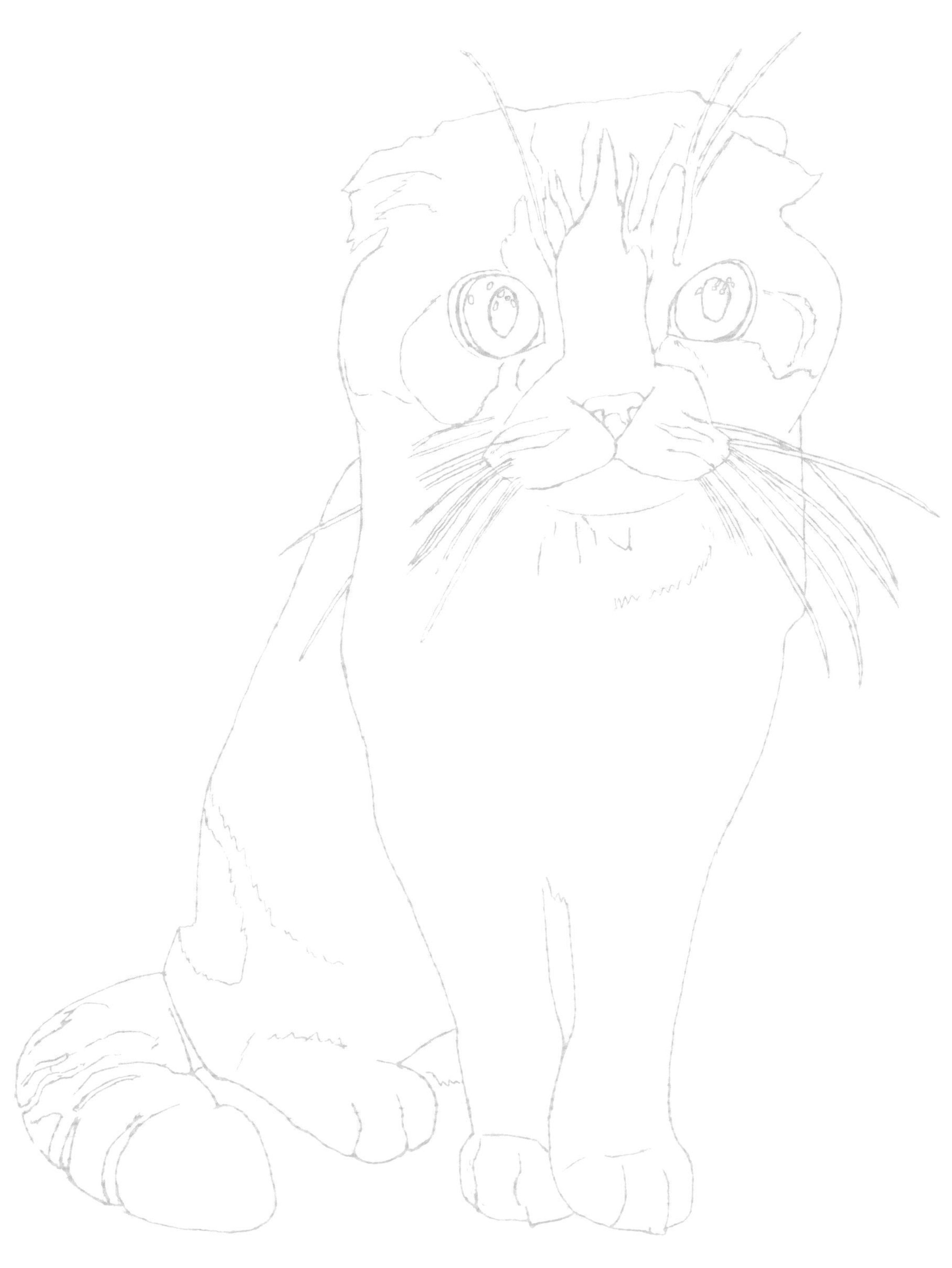
cut along these lines

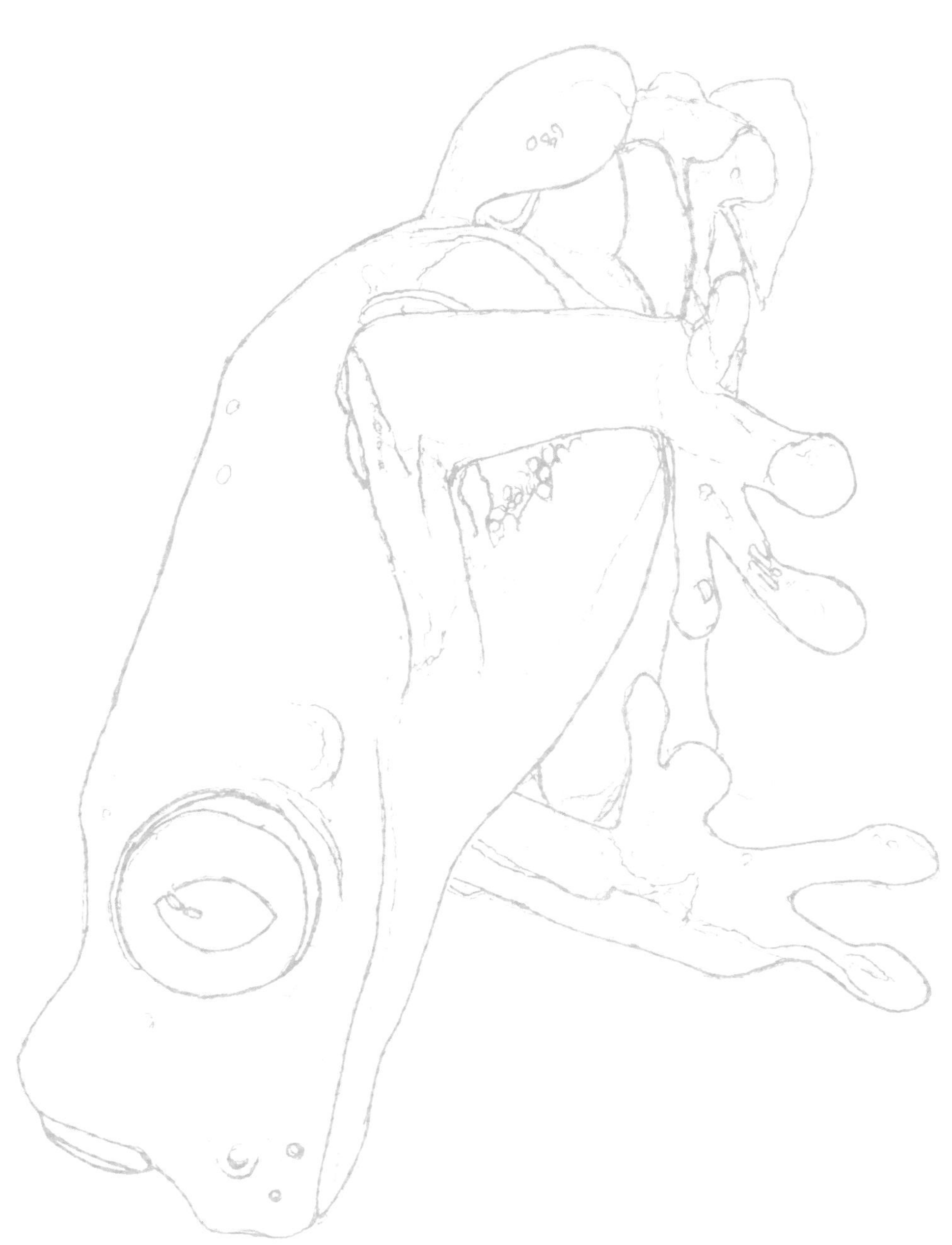

cut along these lines

cut along these lines

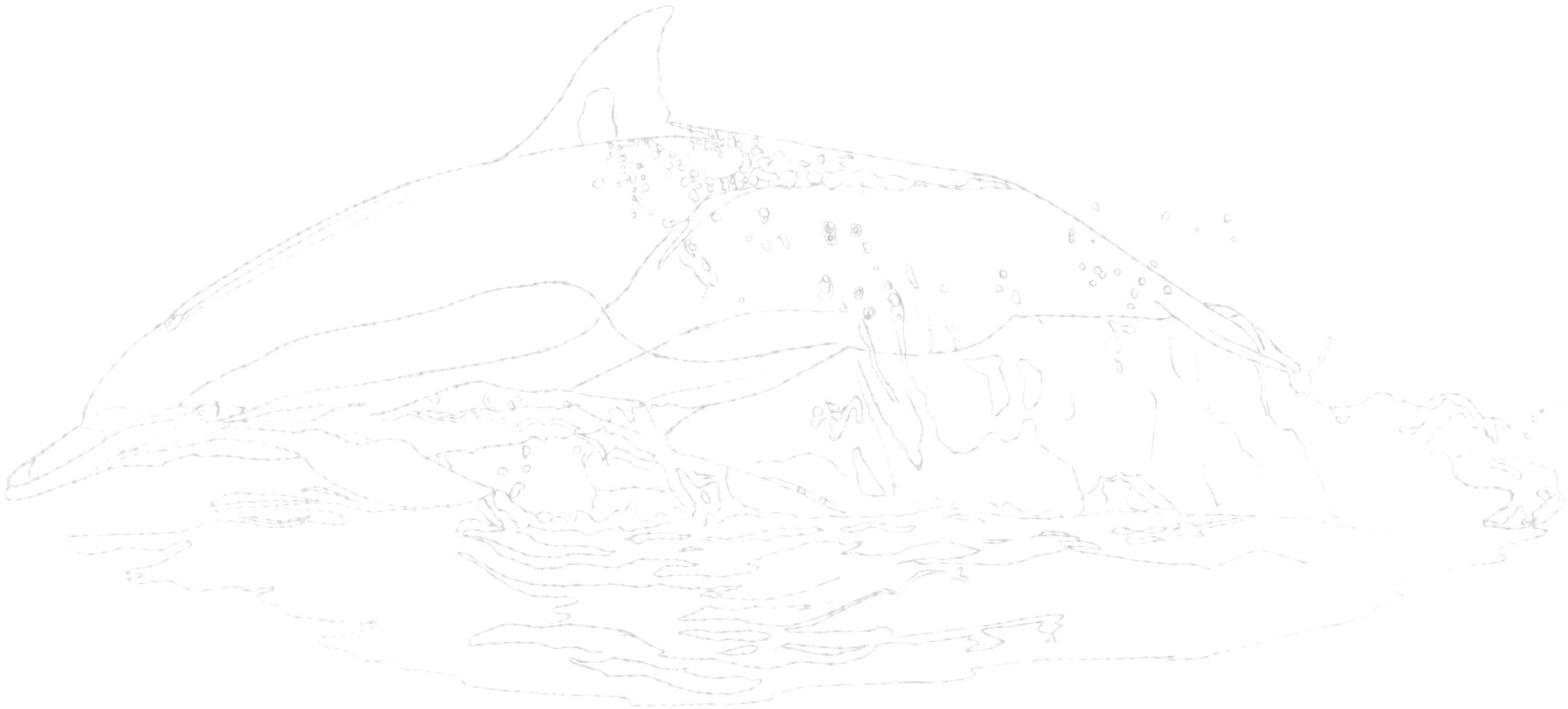

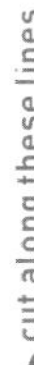

cut along these lines

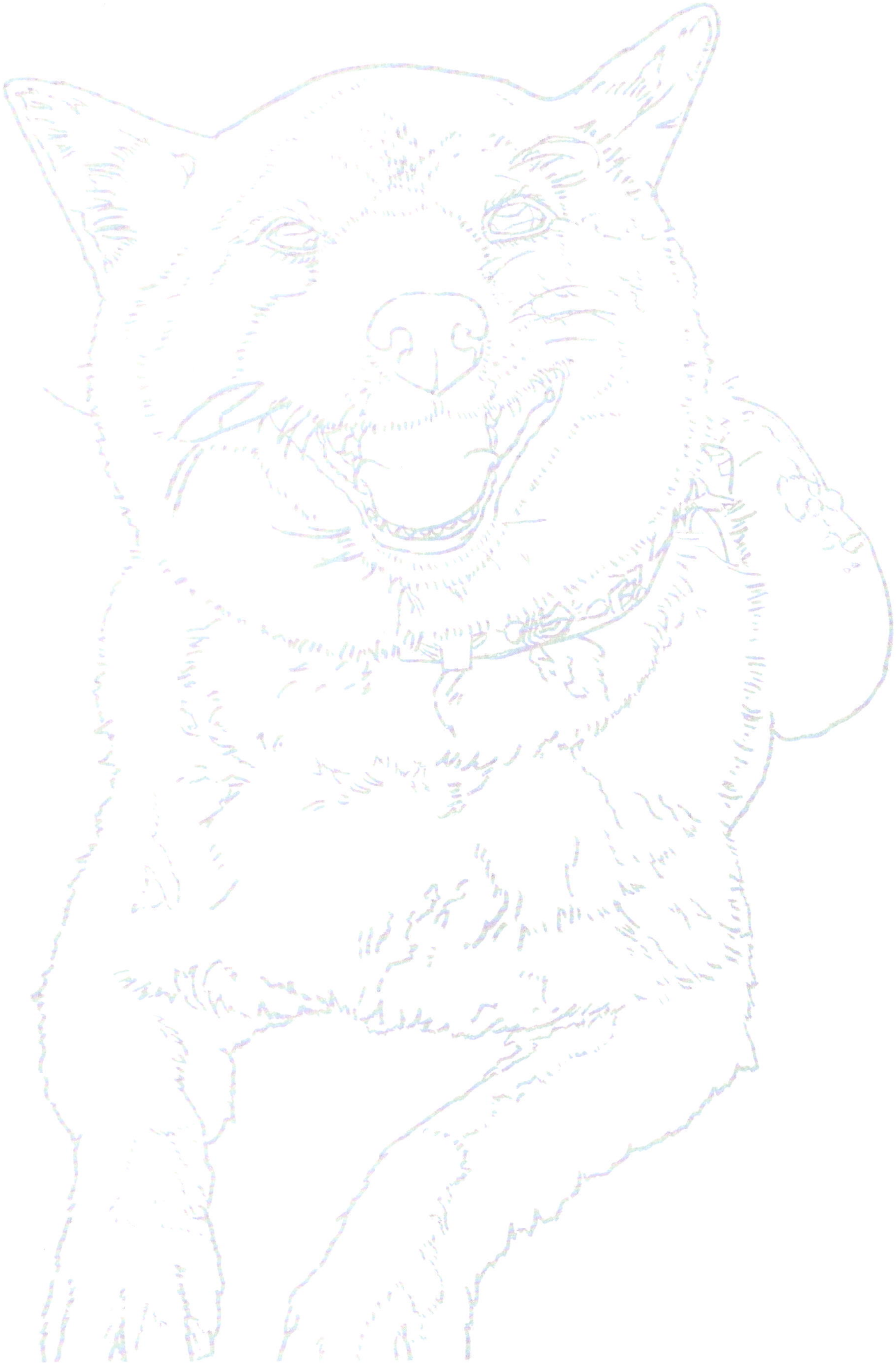

cut along these lines

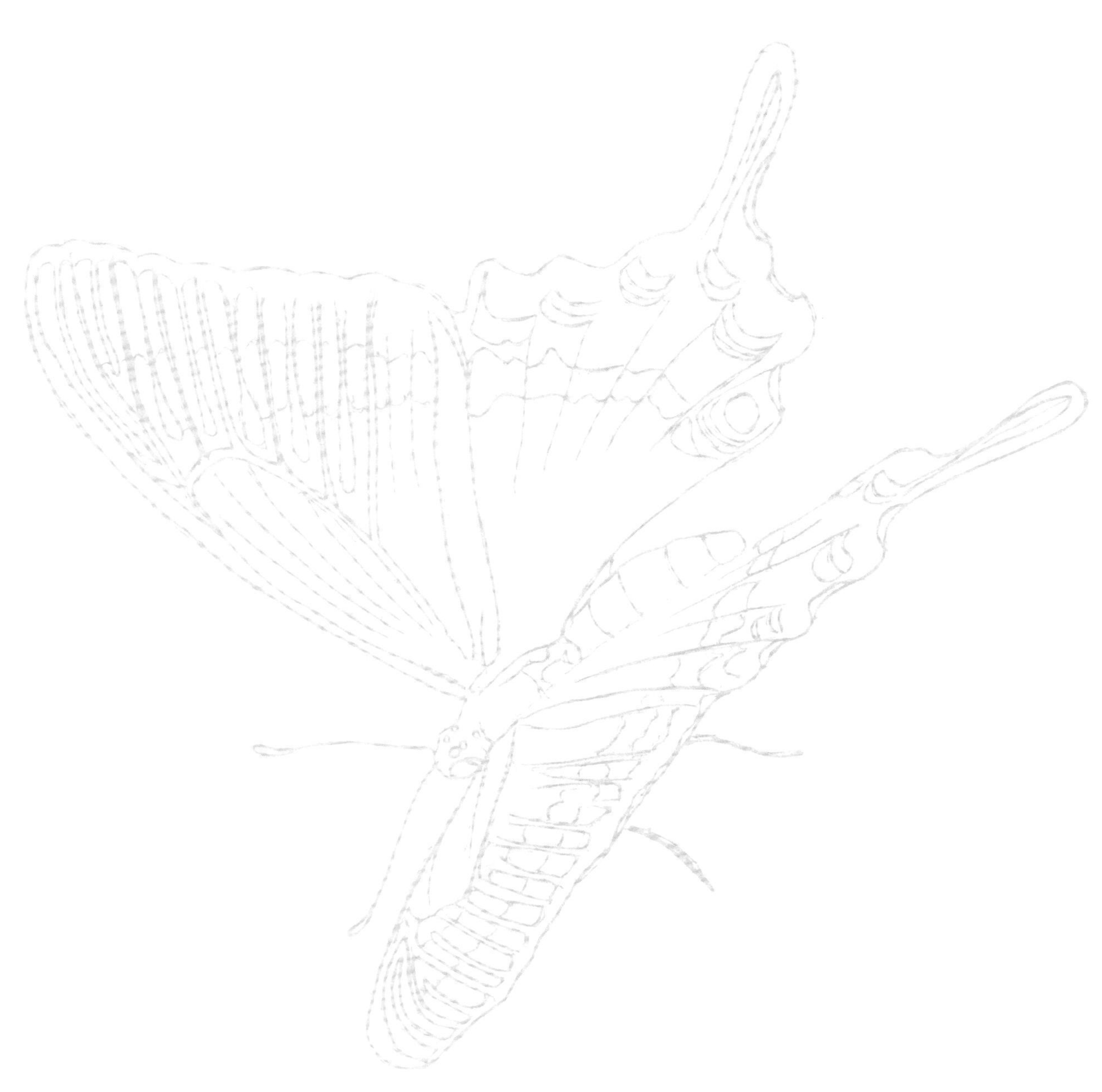

cut along these lines

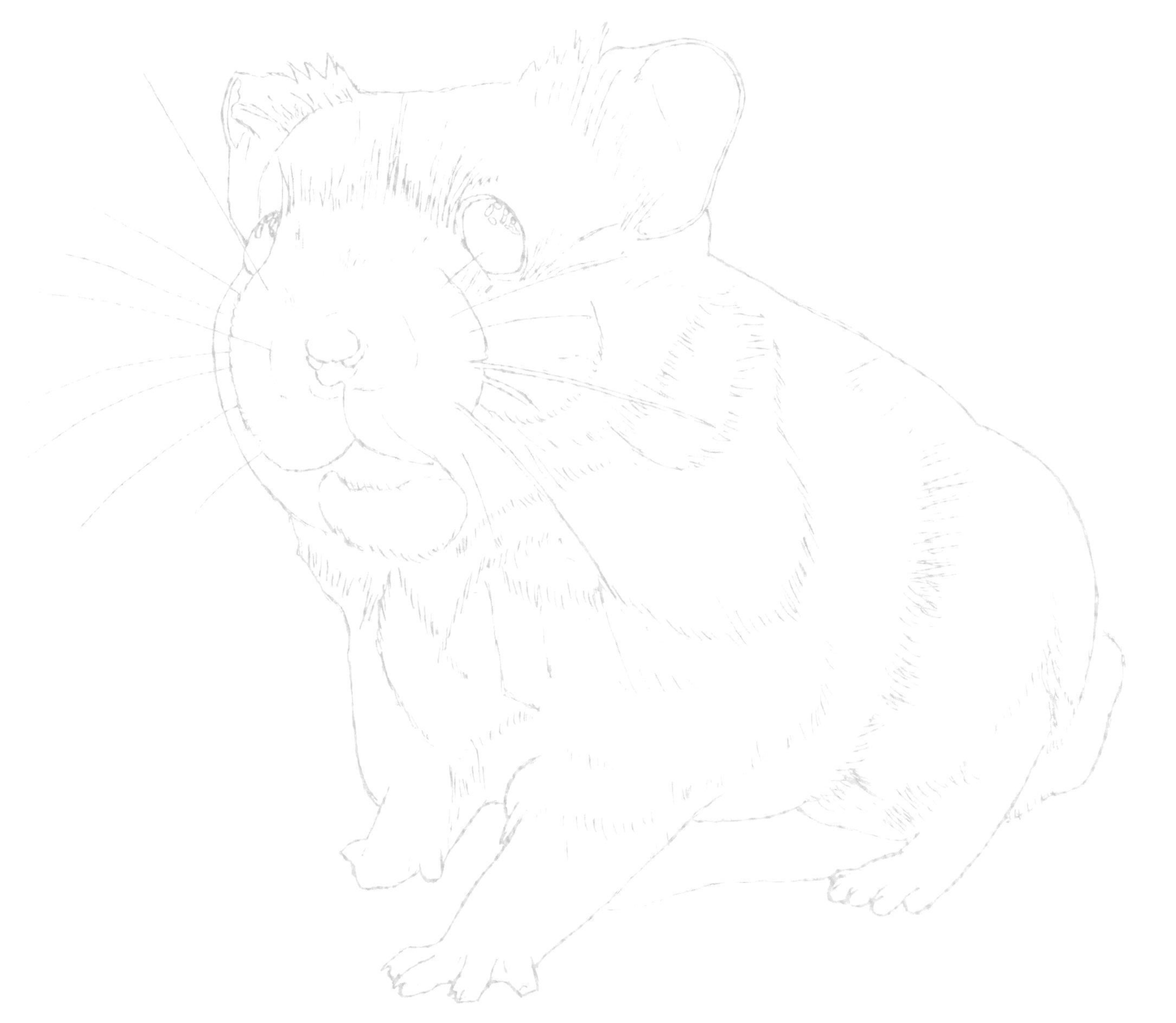

cut along these lines

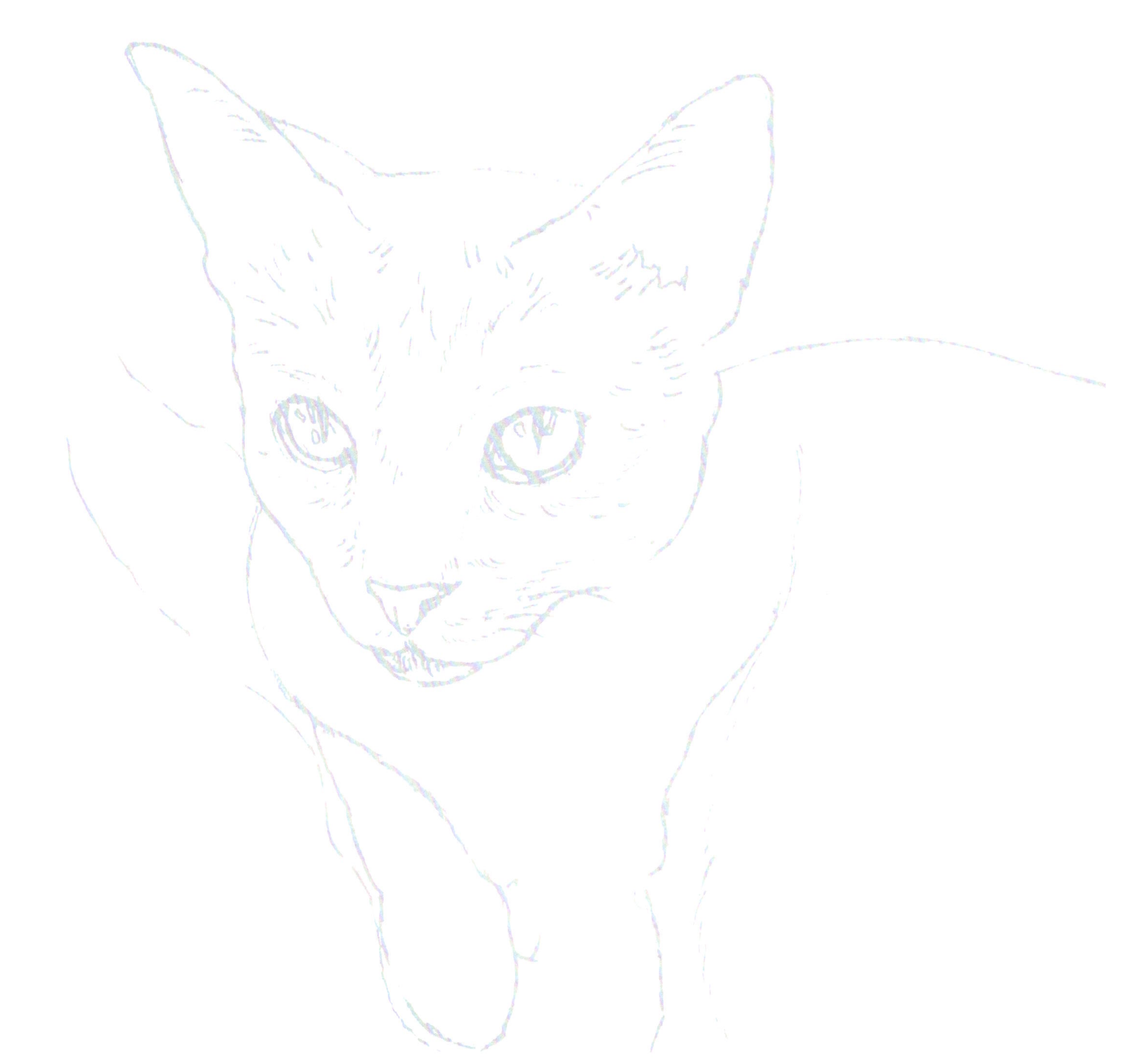

cut along these lines

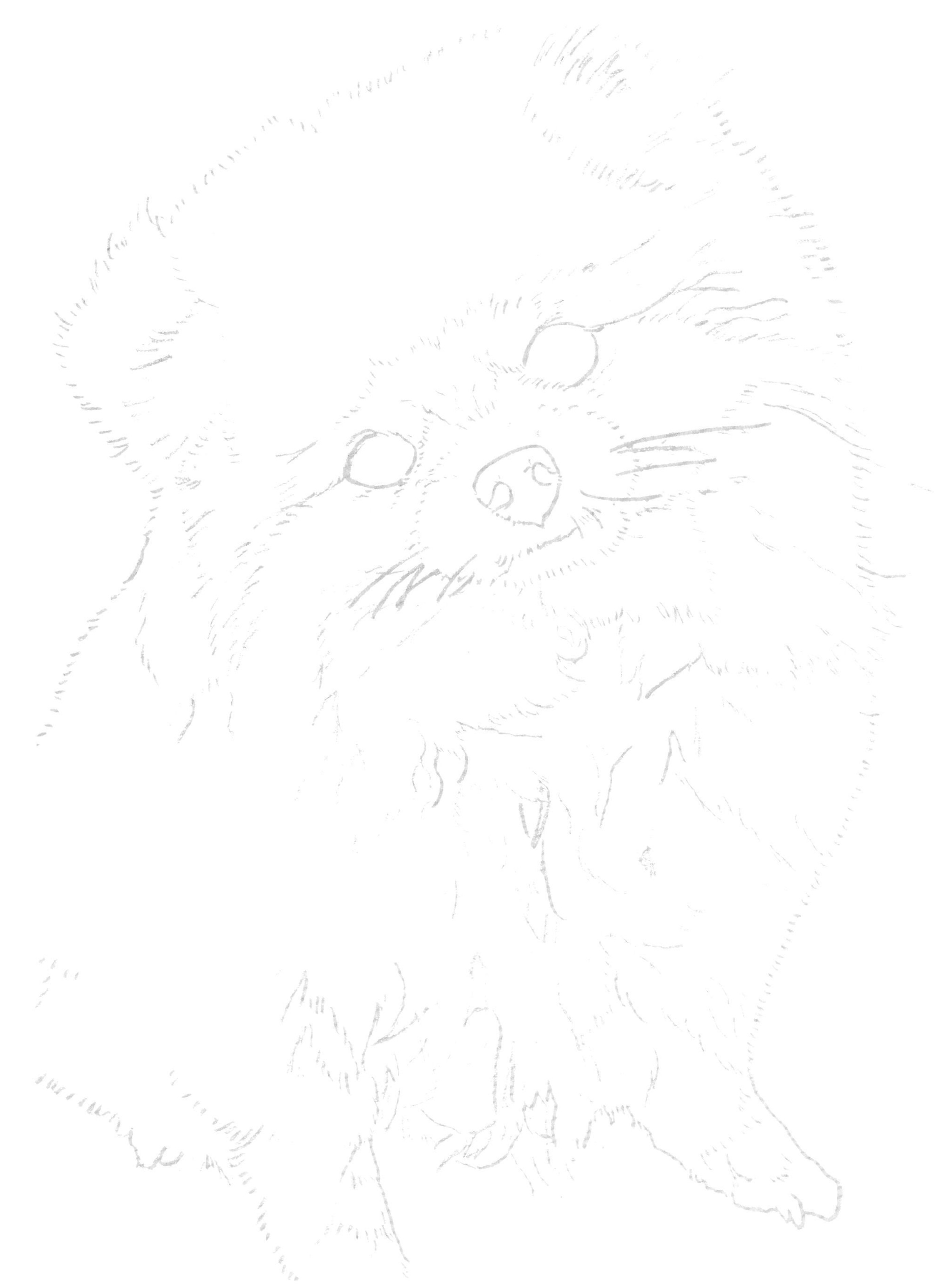

cut along these lines

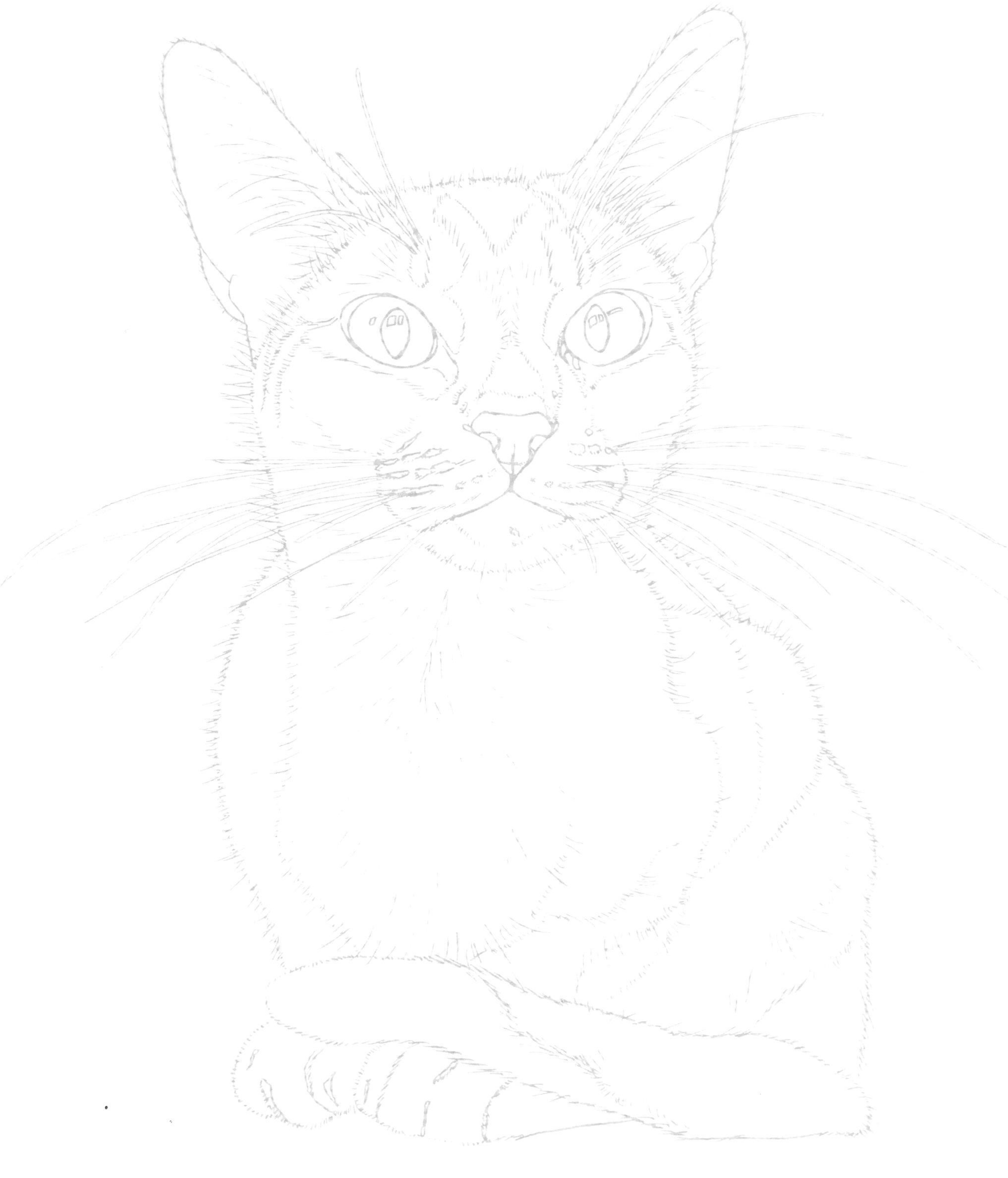

cut along these lines